D1276096

This book offers a uniquely comprehensive account of the conflict in Northern Ireland, providing a rigorous analysis of its dynamics and present structure and proposing a new approach to its resolution. It deals with historical process, communal relations, ideology, politics, economics and culture and with the wider British, Irish and international contexts. It reveals at once the enormous complexity of the conflict and shows how it is generated by a particular system of relationships which can be described precisely and clearly. The book proposes an emancipatory approach to the resolution of the conflict, conceived as the dismantling of this system of relationships. Although radical, this approach is already implicit in the converging understandings of the British and Irish governments of the causes of conflict. The authors argue that only much more determined pursuit of an emancipatory approach will allow an agreed political settlement to emerge.

The dynamics of conflict in Northern Ireland

The dynamics of conflict in Northern Ireland

Power, conflict and emancipation

Joseph Ruane and Jennifer Todd

CAMBRIDGE
UNIVERSITY PRESS

PUBLISHED BY THE PRESS SYNDICATE OF THE UNIVERSITY OF CAMBRIDGE
The Pitt Building, Trumpington Street, Cambridge, United Kingdom

CAMBRIDGE UNIVERSITY PRESS
The Edinburgh Building, Cambridge CB2 2RU, UK   http://www.cup.cam.ac.uk
40 West 20th Street, New York, NY 10011–4211, USA   http://www.cup.org
10 Stamford Road, Oakleigh, Melbourne 3166, Australia
Ruiz de Alarcón 13, 28014 Madrid, Spain

First published 1996
Reprinted 1997, 1998, 2000

Printed in the United Kingdom at the University Press, Cambridge

A catalogue record for this book is available from the British Library

Library of Congress Cataloguing in Publication data
Ruane, Joseph.
The dynamics of conflict in Northern Ireland: power, conflict,
and emancipation / by Joseph Ruane and Jennifer Todd.
    p.   cm.
ISBN 0 521 56018 7 (hc.) – ISBN 0 521 56879 X (pbk.)
1. Northern Ireland – Politics and government. 2. Social conflict –
Northern Ireland. I. Todd, Jennifer, 1952 Feb. 16–   II. Title.
DA990.U46R83 1966
941.6 – dc20 95–52013 CIP

ISBN 0 521 56018 7 hardback
ISBN 0 521 56879 X paperback

WD

For Cian and Éva
and in memory of
Sarah Linda

Contents

Figures

Tables

Preface

In retrospect, this book began as a conversation about Northern Ireland more than a decade ago. Like most first conversations on Northern Ireland it was a communication of political position rather than a serious discussion, still less a search for deeper understanding. That concern came later, but slowly. As time went on we found ourselves paying increasingly close attention to political events. First one, then the other, started reading the literature and began to write on the conflict. This led to a decision to spend a sabbatical year in Belfast in 1987–8 and while there to interview people about their perceptions of the conflict. In the summer of 1989 we responded to an invitation to write an article on Northern Ireland by offering (though that was not our original intention) a tentative analysis of the causes of the conflict.

On finishing the article, we decided that its argument merited expansion into a short book, to be written quickly and as a detour from other intellectual concerns. As the writing began, we found ourselves attempting a comprehensive analysis of the conflict. It proved a much larger and longer undertaking than we imagined, but we persevered, writing and rewriting the book in Cork, Dublin and Strasbourg during another sabbatical. Throughout this period the political situation was changing, superficially at least, with successive rounds of (failed) inter-party talks, continuing violence and death, then revelation of secret talks, the launching of a peace process and the ceasefires. We tested our interpretation against each new turn of events and modified it accordingly.

No study, still less one on Northern Ireland, is free of the politics and values of its authors. But we determined as far as possible to leave aside our personal political preferences and the instinctual responses that came from our upbringings. We worked with just two guiding principles. The first was a respect and concern for both communities in Northern Ireland and a resistance to any political outcome which represents the victory of one over the other. The second was a willingness to see the point of view of all the parties to the conflict, however reprehensible we might find their actions. Only when our interpretation had crystallised did we consider its implications for resolving the conflict; this was the first time the concept of emancipation occurred to us although, once we had thought of it, it seemed it had been in our minds all the time.

A study on Northern Ireland always requires reference to nomenclature. We have been criticised for the frequency with which we use the apparently denominational terms 'Protestants' and 'Catholics' rather than the political terms 'unionists' and 'nationalists'. Indeed, some writers prefer the terms 'Ulster British' and 'Irish' to distinguish the communities; a few speak of 'settlers' and 'natives'. We hope that the basis for our usage will become clear with the fuller presentation of our argument. The conflict is between historic communities constituted and differentiated by multiple rather than single dimensions of difference. The communities are divided not simply by religion, but also by ethnicity, notions of settler or native origin and (more recently) national identity and allegiance. In principle, therefore, any of the terms may be used to refer to the communities.

The terms, however, are not functionally equivalent. Religion more than ethnic or historical origin or politics or identity is the mark of community membership. It is religion which sorts into communities, even though the overt communal conflict is much more about economics, politics or identity than theology. That is why, when two people meet in Northern Ireland, the first priority is to establish each other's religion, and why it is important not simply to know whether a person is nationalist or unionist but whether he or she is a Catholic or a Protestant nationalist or unionist. In each case, the difference is profound.

Like the people of Northern Ireland, we use the religious labels when we are talking about communities or individuals in their communal context or membership. When the focus is on political movements, parties and their mass support, we use the terms 'nationalist' and 'unionist'. We use the terms 'British' (or 'Ulster-British') and 'Irish' to refer to identities and loyalties rather than communities. Some commentators apply these terms to communities when they wish to stress the ethnic aspect of the conflict, but the people of Northern Ireland do not do so. Unionists sometimes use the term 'the Ulster people' in reference to Protestants. Others speak of 'settlers' and 'natives'. But these are highly politicised usages.

Geographical terms also pose problems and we know that some will find certain of our terms offensive. Many Irish people object to the term the 'British Isles'; republicans object to 'Northern Ireland'; unionists dislike the term 'the North'; most 'Southerners' refer to the part of

Ireland in which they live as 'Ireland' to the discomfort of those north of the border who insist that they too live in 'Ireland', except for those who affirm that they live in 'Northern Ireland' and not in 'Ireland'. The examples could be multiplied. Unfortunately a neutral terminology is not available and choices must be made. Ours were informed by a concern to balance the sensitivities of different groups with the need for economy of expression, clarity, nuance of meaning and stylistic variation.

Finally there is the problem of how to make general statements about groups or categories and at the same time allow for individual difference. In principle every statement about a group or category requires qualification to allow for difference, but it is not practically possible constantly to make such qualifications. We know that some readers will object to the fact that we generalise about 'Protestants', 'Catholics', 'nationalists', 'unionists', 'Northerners', 'Southerners' and so on. Indeed, some see the tendency to generalise in discussions of Northern Ireland as an important source of the conflict. But general tendencies are present and have to be grasped if the conflict is to be explained; this has been our central concern. At the same time we were always conscious of variation and some parts of the book (particularly chapter 3) deal explicitly with it. For the rest, even where variation is not indicated it should always be understood.

We have accumulated many debts in the process of our research and in writing this book. We are very grateful to the numerous people in Northern Ireland, and politicians and civil servants beyond, who consented to be interviewed, in some cases over many hours, and to make further contacts for us. Those interviews were central to the understanding which we eventually developed in this book. There were many others who helped our research in innumerable ways during our sabbatical year in Belfast and since: Susan Baker, David Clow, Maurna Crozier, Maeve Doran, Hastings and Katharine Donnan, Myrtle Hill, Richard and Fionnuala Jay, Liam Kennedy, Hazel McCance, Colm Linden, Sean Loughlin, Noel and Jane McGuigan, Eithne McLaughlin, Michael Maguire, the late Patrick O'Donoghue, Liam and Geraldine O'Dowd, Berry O'Neill, Pauline Prior, David Storey, Bill Todd, Wilfred Young. Other colleagues encouraged, criticised and helped to improve our argument: the late John Whyte, James Anderson, Paul Arthur, Paul Bew, Paul Brennan, John Coakley, Bob Cormack, Colin Coulter, Brendan O'Leary and colleagues and students in the Departments of Sociology, University College Cork and Politics, University College Dublin.

We benefited from the hospitality and intellectual environment of the Institute of Irish Studies, Queens University Belfast and the help of its then Director, Professor Ronald Buchanan and its present Director, Dr Brian Walker. We benefited too from invitations from the Departments of Anthropology and Politics at Queen's University Belfast and the Universities of Paris III, Lille and Caen, to give papers there and from the use of the library of the Council of Europe in Strasbourg. We thank the Fair Employment Commission in Belfast for making its past research available to us. Jennifer Todd thanks the Arts Faculty Fund of University College Dublin for a grant, and University College Dublin for a Presidents' Research Fellowship which allowed her a year free from teaching. Joseph Ruane benefited from a sabbatical year from University College Cork in 1992–3. He wishes also to acknowledge his intellectual debt to Davydd Greenwood. Chapter 3 draws on our article published in *Irish Political Studies*, vol. 7, 1992.

In the final stages of writing the book we were fortunate to have the critical and constructive comments of those who read it in draft form. Tom Garvin, Liam Kennedy and Liam O'Dowd undertook the burdensome task of reading the entire book; John Baker, Andy Bielenberg, Paul Burgess, John Coakley, David Dickson, Mark Haugaard, Anna Murphy and Kenneth Nicholls read individual chapters. Their comments were invaluable and are much appreciated. All those who helped us may take what credit they wish for the final result; we will bear the responsibility.

1 Introduction

The IRA ceasefire of 31 August 1994 and the loyalist ceasefire six weeks later brought to an end – for a time at least – twenty-five years of violent communal conflict in Northern Ireland. During that period 3,400 people were killed and over 20,000 suffered injury; some were left permanently disabled. The people of Northern Ireland bore the greatest weight of suffering; almost half the population – over 80 per cent in some areas – knew someone killed or injured in the conflict; some experienced multiple personal tragedies. There were also deaths and injuries in the Republic of Ireland, Great Britain and on mainland Europe, sometimes of people with no conceivable relationship to the conflict.

The violence of that period damaged the whole fabric of the liberal democratic state and civic culture in Northern Ireland, the Republic and Great Britain. Normal judicial processes were suspended, there were repeated breaches of human rights, there was collusion between members of the security forces and paramilitaries, a 'war culture' emerged built around propaganda and the demonisation of the 'enemy', paramilitaries took over the functions of policing in many areas, stores of military weapons were built up in private hands. In Northern Ireland the conflict produced a generation of politicians highly skilled in conflict-related negotiation but with little or no experience in the normal business of government; in the Republic, it absorbed political and diplomatic resources out of all proportion to the capacity of a small country.

In Northern Ireland all aspects of community life became politicised, religiously homogeneous communities of defence emerged as a result of a vast process of resettlement, valued social relationships were ruptured, community trust was destroyed by government and paramilitary informants, the erection of social and physical barriers broke long established patterns of communal life, open communities were turned into closed ones. Similar tendencies emerged, although of lower intensity, in the border counties of the Republic and among sections of the Irish community in Britain.

Throughout the island of Ireland, cultural development was stunted.

Questions of cultural and national identity became the focus of intense conflict. The normal and necessary processes of culture criticism, innovation and updating were distorted by the felt need to show – or to avoid showing – solidarity with one or other of the protagonists. A dialectic of cultural oppression of the other and repression of the self was set in motion. A set of negative images and symbols of Ireland – of nationalism and unionism, Catholic and Protestant – became fixed in the mind of a whole generation.

Northern Ireland's industrial economy went into free-fall. The cost of maintaining the security forces in Northern Ireland was £1 billion in 1990–1, UK government compensation averaged over £33 million per year in the first decades of the conflict; one bomb in the City of London in 1993 cost over £1 billion in insurance payments. The cost of the Northern Ireland conflict to the Republic in the years of violence is estimated at over £100 million per year. The economic costs of the conflict are gradually being reversed; the human costs can never be.

A ceasefire is not a settlement and the conflict is not over. The two communities are still sharply divided; at the time of writing, the 'peace process' faces an impasse over the decommissioning of arms and the proposals set out by the two governments in the Frameworks Documents of February 1995. Violence continues in the form of paramilitary policing and clashes between demonstrators and police. More serious violence may recur and any settlement may have a limited time-span. Resolving the conflict remains one of the most important tasks confronting the British and Irish governments and peoples. This study offers an analysis of the causes of the conflict and proposes an emancipatory approach to resolving it.

Successive chapters present the analysis. Chapter 2 discusses the historical roots and dynamics of the conflict. Chapters 3 to 7 focus on aspects of the conflict in contemporary Northern Ireland – structures of community, ideology, the dynamics of power and inequality in the political, economic and cultural arenas. Chapters 8, 9 and 10 deal with the British, Irish and international roles in the conflict. In chapter 11 we bring the analysis of the preceding chapters to bear on the current situation and outline the possibility of an emancipatory resolution. In the remainder of chapter 1 we clarify some of the methodological principles and concepts which inform our approach.

The role of theory

Interpretations of the conflict – as of any social or cultural reality – differ in their use of theoretical models. Social scientists tend to use formal and explicit models. Thus O'Leary and McGarry distinguish their 'analytical history' from conventional history and structure their historical account in terms of the categories of nation-building.[1] Fulton uses Gramscian concepts of historic bloc and hegemony to examine the emergence of two opposed religious-political blocs on the island of Ireland.[2] Gibbon constructs his explanatory narrative of the origins of Ulster unionism around notions of modes of production and class derived from political economy.[3] Historians, in contrast, tend to work more empirically and intuitively, leaving their conceptual and analytical models implicit.

The disadvantages of the social science approach – the tendency to impose rigid or inappropriate theoretical categories on the data – are well known. The historical process in all its specificity constantly depasses the boundaries of theoretical concepts and models. But without explicit theoretical reflection, crucial issues can be elided. Theoretical models are particularly useful in identifying structures of relationships and the dynamics of change over long periods.[4] They are essential when one moves from interpretation to practical proposals, particularly emancipatory ones.

The theoretical interpretation of the conflict presented in this book is both systematic and explicit. We speak of a system of relationships with different levels which interlock and mutually reinforce each other; we postulate a dynamic for change coming in part from within, in part from without this system which has changed the balance of power underlying the system, producing in turn conflict and crisis; we use this theoretical understanding to identify the conditions for resolving the conflict. But this interpretation does not derive from the application of a general theory to the Irish case. Rather it emerged from a process of reflection on our field research and reading of primary and secondary sources.[5] Our reflection was inevitably mediated by the dominant theories and paradigms of our disciplines. But we used them in a sensitising way, as

---

[1] Brendan O'Leary and John McGarry, *The Politics of Antagonism: Understanding Northern Ireland*, London, Athlone, 1993, p. 2 and ch. 2.

[2] John Fulton, *The Tragedy of Belief: Division, Politics and Religion in Ireland*, Oxford, Clarendon, 1991, pp. 4ff.

[3] Peter Gibbon, *The Origins of Ulster Unionism: The Formation of Popular Protestant Politics and Ideology in Nineteenth Century Ireland*, Manchester, Manchester University Press, 1975, ch. 1.

[4] Cf. Alasdair MacIntyre, 'Causality and history', in Juha Manninen and Raimo Tuomela, eds., *Essays on Explanation and Understanding*, Dordrecht, D. Reidel, 1976.

[5] Our field research consisted principally of interviews and participant observation carried out while resident in Northern Ireland from October 1987 to September 1988.

heuristics and as sources of insights rather than to impose a preconceived pattern on our research findings. Our theoretical interpretation was worked out from engagement with the material.

Questions of comparison

Comparative research on Northern Ireland began early in the conflict and is now an important part of the literature. Northern Ireland has been compared, *inter alia*, with Canada, South Tyrol, Algeria, the southern US, Bohemia, Prussian Poland, ex-Yugoslavia, the Armenian–Azerbaijan frontier, and implicitly with societies such as Fiji and Burundi.[6] Our approach to comparison has been more cautious. Most comparative work takes the conflict to be an example of settler-colonial or of ethno-national conflict. There are ethno-nationalist and settler-colonial aspects to the conflict (chapter 2), but there are dangers in classifying the conflict as unambiguously ethno-national or settler-colonial and then proceeding to comparison and generalisation.

First, the comparative method itself is not without problems. One centres on cultural meaning. Meaning is constitutive of social life, not a superficial overlay; how such concepts as 'community', 'class', 'violence' or 'nation' are used partly determines their nature and their role in social life. Culturally based variations in meanings make comparison difficult even where the institutions and the words used to describe them appear much the same. Multidetermination also poses a problem for comparative analysis. If effects are determined by the *interaction* of several variables then comparison on the basis of just one variable may be seriously misleading. A further problem concerns context. All particular social realities are embedded in a wider context and this context is always simultaneously 'internal' and 'external' to them. Where contexts vary, comparison must itself be contextualised.

In the book we explore the different meanings of such terms as 'British', 'Irish', 'unionist', 'nationalist', but there are further depths, subtleties and conditionalities of meaning which became apparent to us in interviews. We stress the role of multidetermination in the conflict – the effect, for example, of the overlap between religious and other differences, and between cultural difference and structures of power –

---

6 Frank Wright, *Northern Ireland: A Comparative Analysis*, Dublin, Gill and Macmillan, 1987. John McGarry and Brendan O'Leary, eds., *The Politics of Ethnic Conflict Regulation*, London, Routledge, 1993; Christopher Hewitt, 'The roots of violence: Catholic grievances and Irish nationalism during the civil rights period', in Patrick J. Roche and Brian Barton, eds., *The Northern Ireland Question: Myth and Reality*, Aldershot, Avebury, 1991.

but here too, much remains to be said. We have tried to place Northern Ireland into its wider context, but in some respects – in particular in relation to the British context (chapter 8) – we have been opening up new ground.

In fact the Irish case poses a quite specific form of the general problem of context. At various stages in the book (chapters 2, 8 and 10) we elaborate on the wider context – British, European, international – in which Ireland has developed. Our working model is of a society shaped by the quite different – in some respects, contradictory – forces stemming from these different spheres. For example, throughout the history of the expansion and later contraction of the British world, Ireland was ambiguously located between the metropolitan and colonial spheres; some of its distinctive features derive precisely from that ambiguity. A fully contextualised understanding of Ireland's development is necessary before the possibilities and limits of comparison can be stated precisely.[7] For the present, we combine a cautious approach to comparison with further exploration of the complexities of meaning, multi-determination and context.

Structure, meaning and ideology

Many writers on Northern Ireland define the conflict as one of identity or ideology – the conflict, we are told, is one of conflicting nationalisms, a matter 'ultimately' of identities or allegiances or, for some, of the irrational expression of 'myths and fears'.[8] Others stress structural relationships, in particular the role of political and economic inequality. These perspectives on the conflict are not mutually exclusive: on the contrary, structural inequality matters so much precisely because it exists between two communities with different national identities.

In this study we present structural relations, ideas and meanings as interpenetrating in all areas of social life. Thus communal division depends upon pre-existing constructs of self and other, whether 'Protestant/Catholic', 'Irish/British' or 'settler/native'. But the origins and dynamics of such symbolic distinctions are interwoven with actual experiences rooted in social and structural relationships – position in the economy, demographic strength, access to the means of coercion – and

---

[7] Joseph Ruane, 'Colonialism and the interpretation of Irish historical development', in M. Silverman and P. Gulliver, eds., *Approaching the Past: Historical Anthropology Through Irish Case Studies*, Columbia, Columbia University Press, 1992.

[8] See Joseph Ruane and Jennifer Todd ' "Why can't you get along with each other?" Culture, structure and the Northern Ireland conflict', in Eamonn Hughes, ed., *Culture and Politics in Northern Ireland*, Milton Keynes, Open University Press, 1991.

over time such structurally based experiences have become constitutive components of communal culture and identity. Social theory tends to oscillate between an overly 'material' and an overly 'cultural' view of reality – to lose sight of culture altogether or to interpret reality as the expression of cultural symbols, ideas or language. Without attempting a theoretical synthesis of these two aspects of reality, we have sought to capture something of the interplay between them.

We also consider ideologies, conceived as elaborations of the meanings implicit in daily life into complex conceptual systems. Ideologies operate at a level removed from daily experience and seldom accurately reflect the ambiguous, mixed, often contradictory beliefs of ordinary people. Nonetheless they are centrally important, reached for in times of stress as the logical presuppositions of common sense assumptions and as a source of communal justification and certainty. They play a central role in sharpening conflict, preventing views from developing in a more plural way. Their independent significance is, however, limited; they too serve to defend or advance structurally based interests. Ideological critique without structural change has limited capacity to transform even ideology.

The locus of conflict

All interpretations of the conflict posit a geographical locus to conflict. John Whyte identified the dominant paradigm as the 'internal conflict model' – one which sees the communities in conflict and (more ambiguously) the conditions of conflict as 'internal' rather than 'external' to Northern Ireland.[9] In this understanding, the conflict is primarily between two communities in Northern Ireland; there is no essential conflict between the peoples of Great Britain and Ireland or between the British and Irish states.

This paradigm has an obvious political appeal, for example, to 'outside' political actors who wish to reassure themselves that the conflict is not of their making or to 'insiders' committed to the survival of Northern Ireland as a geo-political unit. But at first sight the paradigm also appears to have analytic merit. It is within Northern Ireland and between the two communities there that most of the overt conflict and violence has occurred during the past twenty-five years. It was mobilisation of the Northern Catholic minority in the civil rights movement, rather than pressure from outside actors or governments,

---

[9] John Whyte, *Interpreting Northern Ireland*, Oxford, Clarendon, 1990, pp. 114–15 and ch. 9.

that provoked the crisis of unionist rule.[10] Moreover the north-east of Ireland has a long history of local communal conflict. The two states and their citizens – once thought to be the main protagonists – have shown themselves to be accomodating and have cooperated with each other in trying to contain the conflict between the two Northern communities. But the conflict often seems beyond their reach, impervious to their attempts at mediation. Whatever outside actors might do, it might seem that a purely local conflict would remain.[11]

Questions of space and causality cannot, however, be resolved so simply. Societies unlike states are not bounded realms but structures of social relationships that are infinitely extensible. Moreover Northern Ireland can lay few claims even to be considered 'a society'; it is a region and, like all regions, is formed by the wider systems and cultures in which it is embedded. Overt conflict and violence may be concentrated within Northern Ireland, but the causes of conflict are not necessarily so located. Indeed one would expect the causes and conditions of any conflict to have plural and interlocking spatial loci.

Rather than working with preconceived notions of what is internal and external in the sources of this conflict, we adopted a more empirical and differentiated approach, one which started with the variables and relationships that impinged on the conflict and plotted their (changing) geographical form and boundaries. This did not preclude us from considering Northern Ireland as a distinct socio-spatial unit; on the contrary, much of the book is devoted to structures and relationships there. On the other hand, we see both the existence of Northern Ireland and the conflict as the product of a historic system of relationships that in its origins and dynamics operates at the level of the two islands. Partition restructured this system but did not dissolve it, and at the level of the system as a whole Northern Ireland is both a contingent and a fully open social world.

History

Virtually all accounts of the Northern Ireland conflict begin with an historical account as a backdrop to the present. Analysis of the conflict then proceeds synchronically by reference to present interests, ideologies, institutions or structural conditions. History as a living force enters into this analysis only in the form of the beliefs (erroneous or otherwise) of people about the past and the calculations they make on the

---

[10] *Ibid.*, p. 204.   [11] *Ibid.*, p. 196.

basis of these beliefs. This approach rigidly separates past from present, synchronic from diachronic analysis and is ill-equipped to grasp processes of change arising from evolving systems of relationships. To capture the dynamics of conflict – the central aim of our analysis – required that we identify these developing systems of relationships.

Identifying historical systems poses many problems and the search for them is currently out of fashion. 'Grand narratives' are suspect and the emphasis is on pluralities, fragmentation, discontinuities and a multiplicity of readings – and on the deconstruction of claims to anything else. Our emphasis on continuity rooted in an evolving system of relationships may suggest a prior methodological bias in favour of 'grand narrative'. This was far from the case. On the contrary, our interest in the long historical perspective and our perception of long range continuities came quite late in the analysis and we found it methodologically disconcerting rather than reassuring. However, once the extent of continuity became apparent to us it seemed more important to explain it than to deconstruct discourses about it. At the same time it was necessary to allow for change and contingency and to avoid any suggestion of an underlying determinism (see pp. 13–14 below).

Our periodisation of the development of the conflict derives from a concern to grasp its overall pattern and dynamic. Some writers locate its formative stage in the seventeenth century when the north-east of Ireland was colonised by Scots and English. Others stress the nineteenth century as the period that produced the conflicting ideologies of nationalism and unionism. Still others stress the years after partition, when Northern Ireland took on its distinctive political form and cultural ethos. We begin with the sixteenth and seventeenth centuries as the period when the system of relationships producing the conflict first emerged. But the pattern then set was not unchanging. On the contrary, the forms of conflict generated in different historical periods – the period of colonisation, the eighteenth century, the Union, partition, direct rule – were very different. We came to understand this mixture of continuity and change in terms of different orders of time, a notion that has been central to historical understanding since Braudel.[12] We have not tried to replicate Braudel's use of the concepts of *longue durée*, conjuncture and events, but we used these distinctions as guides, understanding successive short term phases of the conflict as conjunctures setting the conditions for events that then impacted back on the developing system of relationships.

---

[12] Fernand Braudel, *The Mediterranean and the Mediterranean World in the Age of Philip II*, 2 vols., London, Fontana, 1978.

The system of relationships, as we conceive it, had three interlocking levels – a set of differences, a structure of dominance, dependence and inequality and a tendency towards communal division. We discuss the emergence and formal properties of the system more fully in chapter 2. Here we relate its different aspects to current debates in the literature.

Community

The concepts of community and communal conflict are much contested in general and in their applicability to Northern Ireland. Some see community as a purely ideological concept that masks divisions of class or gender.[13] Talk of 'two communities' seems to posit two monolithic blocs whether within Northern Ireland or on the island as a whole, denying 'internal' differences and cross-cutting commonalities. Some accept that community division exists today in Northern Ireland but see the presently divided communities as in process of irretrievable fragmentation. For others, the stress on communal division obscures the facts that Northern Ireland incorporates a multiplicity of communities, each internally diverse, and is itself a community, albeit a divided one.[14] It is sometimes argued that an intellectual focus on sectarian communities emphasises, and thereby reinforces, 'unreal' communal divisions – that a focus on gender, class or ideology would help further to pluralise politics in Northern Ireland.

There is validity to many of these points: communities are social constructs and there is a danger of hypostatising them. Critically understood, however, the concept of community is necessary to any analysis of the conflict. As we use the term, communities are emergent entities, products of structurally conditioned social practices which, however, possess some general properties including a level of self-consciousness, integrating organisational networks and a capacity for boundary maintainance. Thus conceived, community is neither an essential feature of the social structure nor one which can serve as a general basis of explanation. Nonetheless, at the level of actual social organisation, relations and practices, as well as in public consciousness, communities are very real phenomena.

We use the concept of community in a non-totalising and variable way

---

[13] Desmond Bell, 'The community studies tradition and Irish social science', *International Journal of Sociology and Social Policy*, vol. 1, no. 2, 1981.

[14] See, for example, Simon Lee's submission to the Opsahl Commission, Andy Pollak, ed., *A Citizens' Inquiry: The Opsahl Report on Northern Ireland*, Dublin, Lilliput, 1993, pp. 334–5; *Alliance News*, Inter Party talks supplement, Nov.–Dec. 1992, p. 2.

that allows for overlapping membership of different communities which may have differing degrees of solidarity and boundedness. As we make clear in chapter 2, the emergence of an island-wide communal division in Ireland was a slow and complex process which was completed only in the late nineteenth century. No sooner was the forging of these two communities complete than partition created new conditions for community formation (chapter 3). But if new communities emerged in the North and the South of Ireland, they did not wholly displace those of the pre-partition period. We show in detailed empirical study the structure and conditions of communal polarisation, not in order to hypostatise sectarian communities but to explain how communal conflict is constituted. At the core of this explanation lies our analysis of the dimensions of difference and the structure of dominance, dependence and inequality.

Dimensions of difference

The literature on Northern Ireland brings out different aspects of what divides the communities. Some stress differences of ethnic origin; others religion; others colonialism – a conflict of settlers and natives and their descendants. These dimensions are sometimes combined: Akenson combines a religious and a colonial interpretation;[15] O'Leary and McGarry acknowledge all these aspects of division but see the national one as 'ultimately' most important.[16] Still others focus on more recent differences in ideology – on nationalism and unionism as conflicting politico-ideological identities and allegiances.[17] There has been no systematic attempt to clarify in a more theoretical way the relations between these structures of difference; too often they have been taken separately as the basis for contradictory (and inherently reductionist) explanations of conflict.

We stress the relative autonomy of five dimensions of difference and show how they develop, interrelate, overlap and interact with wider forces to form a basis for communal opposition. We argue that, from the sixteenth and seventeenth centuries, three socio-cultural dimensions of conflict – religion (Catholicism vs various strands of Protestantism), ethnicity (originally Gaelic-Irish, Old English, New English, Scottish)

---

[15] Donald Harman Akenson, *God's Peoples: Covenant and Land in South Africa, Israel and Ulster*, Ithaca, Cornell University Press, 1992.

[16] O'Leary and McGarry, *Politics of Antagonism*, p. 278.

[17] Richard Rose, *Governing without Consensus: An Irish Perspective*, London, Faber and Faber, 1971. B. M. Walker, *Ulster Politics: The Formative Years 1868–1886*, Belfast, Ulster Historical Foundation and Institute of Irish Studies, 1989.

and colonialism (native vs. settler) – intertwined and mutually conditioned each other. These differences had many and varied ideological
articulations. Two in particular are important. One is the distinction
between 'civility' and 'barbarism', a distinction which emerged during
the period of conquest and colonisation and evolved later into a distinction between 'progressiveness' and 'backwardness'. The second, much
more recent, distinction is that between nationalism and unionism as
conflicting bases of identity and political loyalty – British and Irish. Thus
conceived, the distinction between British and Irish is quite different
from the ethnic distinctions of the earlier period which it overlaid rather
than replaced, just as today the ethnic identity 'Ulster-Scots' is quite
distinct from the national identity 'British', and the ethnic identity
'Gaelic-Irish' distinct from the national identity 'Irish'.

These dimensions of difference represent another of the levels in our
model of a historical system of relationships. Much of their importance
derived from the fact that they overlapped – Irish Protestants were
predominantly of English or Scottish stock, came as settlers, were
imbued if not with a civilising ideology then with a self-perception as
culturally superior to the native Irish; Catholics were predominantly of
Old English or Gaelic-Irish stock, perceived themselves as displaced
natives and found themselves cast in the role of a culturally backward
people; two centuries later, Protestants became overwhelmingly unionist,
Catholics became overwhelmingly nationalist. Yet there was never total
coincidence between the dimensions. Their relative importance varied
by locality, class, individual and over time, thereby permitting a degree
of socio-cultural and ideological heterogeneity within each community.
But even where one dimension was temporarily dominant, the others
remained in existence, each reproduced and partially shaped by its
interaction with the others.

A structure of dominance, dependence and inequality

The role of relations of dominance, dependence and inequality in the
conflict is an important, though uneven, theme in the literature on
the conflict. Inequality between the communities in Northern Ireland
has received much attention, although its extent, causes and effects
are in dispute.[18] The contribution of the British state to relations of
inequality is also controversial. Today some see it as external to the
conflict, a neutral mediator, managing conflict and reforming inequality

---

[18] See David J. Smith and Gerald Chambers, *Inequality in Northern Ireland*, Oxford,
Clarendon, 1991.

within Northern Ireland; others question this.[19] We approach this issue historically, by reference to the way in which the relationships between Catholics, Protestants and the British state were forged into a structure of dominance, dependence and inequality which changed over time and which at each stage defined the interests and parameters of action of the parties to it.

This structure forms another of the levels within the system of relationships. Socio-cultural and ideological difference alone would not have produced oppositional communities or intense communal conflict. Difference became conflictual and lasting because it was the basis of access to resources and power. We locate the roots of the structure of dominance, dependence and inequality in the mode of Ireland's integration into the English/British state in the sixteenth and seventeenth centuries. This was achieved and secured by an alliance between the British state and loyal settler Protestants. A relation of mutual dependence developed between Britain, who needed Protestant support to secure its own control, and Protestants, who needed British support to maintain their position. To hold Ireland for the Crown, Protestants had to be accorded power in Ireland; thus British dominance over Ireland was further reflected in Protestant dominance within Ireland.

Subsequent political conflict in Ireland was a working out of the logic of this situation. From a British and Protestant point of view, once the structure of dominance had come into being it could not easily be altered for the alienation of Catholics from the established order was a threat to both dominant parties. The only chance of change was to remove Protestant privileges and admit Catholics to equal participation in political power, a policy bound to provoke Protestant resistance with no guarantee of gaining Catholic loyalty, and only slowly, cautiously and uncertainly embraced by the British government. Catholic pressure, Protestant resistance and British reform became the recurrent elements in political struggle.

In subsequent chapters we show how this pattern of conflict was reproduced in the newly founded Northern Ireland and still exists today. Communal inequalities are stabilised by the British state's presence even if gradually eroded by British reforming policies. These policies are a response to increasing Catholic and nationalist pressure – from the Irish state as well as Northern Catholics – and they increase Protestant insecurity and resistance to change. This structure of dominance, dependence and inequality continues to generate radically opposed interests, communal polarisation and power struggle.

---

[19] For an overview of some recent views, see Whyte, *Interpreting Northern Ireland*, pp. 141–5.

Analysis/synthesis

In the last twenty years, the literature on the Northern Ireland conflict has become increasingly specialised and there is now a wide range of sub-fields in the literature – economic and demographic analysis, studies of community relations, political analysis, comparative analysis, studies of ideology, policy-making, Anglo-Irish relations, the impact of the international context. There are also general studies but few attempts at a full synthesis, and the best of these are critical assessments of the existing literature.[20] In this study we have drawn on the literature in all of these subfields to provide as comprehensive an account as possible while still retaining an integrated interpretation. The theoretical basis of our approach is, first, an emphasis on the internal complexity of each level of the system of relationships and the relations of multidetermination which we postulate among these and, second, an emphasis on the role of the communal power balance in producing stability or change in the system.

The internal complexity of each level has already been shown; our concern here is with multidetermination and the role of power. The dimensions of difference provided the elements out of which relations of dominance, dependence and inequality could be constructed and the bases on which processes of community formation could begin. Once each level had emerged, the system as a whole became self-reinforcing. The structure of dominance generated interests of its own; defending or advancing those interests provided the basis for further communal solidarity and ever sharper communal division. Communal division intensified in turn the sense of socio-cultural and ideological difference and the interests on which the structure of dominance rested. The system has therefore had self-reproducing tendencies. However, changing power resources produced change in the system. The principal source of change was the Catholic recovery from the mid-eighteenth century. The penal laws, designed to prevent that recovery, were effective to a degree; but under conditions of incipient modernisation the logic of numbers began to assert itself. The Catholic recovery was, however, slow and uneven and three centuries later it is still going on. Today's conflict in Northern Ireland is a contemporary expression of it.

It should now be clear that our explanation of continuity does not imply a static situation or an underlying structural or cultural determinism. Our account draws attention to the contingent as well as the

---

[20] For example, Whyte, *Interpreting Northern Ireland*; John McGarry and Brendan O'Leary, *Explaining Northern Ireland: Broken Images*, Oxford, Basil Blackwell, 1995.

structural conditions which gave rise to the developing system of relationships, and stresses change as much as continuity. The role of actors and of strategic action is also made clear. The actors work under structural conditions with which they are unhappy and against which they struggle; but their actions reproduce those conditions as much as they modify them. Marx's celebrated dictum – 'Men make their own history, but they do not make it just as they please; they do not make it under circumstances chosen by themselves, but under circumstances directly encountered, given, and transmitted from the past' – seems singularly appropriate.[21]

An emancipatory approach to a solution

Three general paradigms – integrationism, regionalism and dualism – now inform the search for a solution to the conflict (chapter 11).[22] Each of these approaches posits a definite institutional form of settlement – respectively, political integration within the British or Irish states, power-sharing devolution within Northern Ireland, and joint or shared authority. Our approach differs in substantive goals and general direction and follows from our analysis of the dynamics of the conflict. If, as we argue, the conflict is the product of a system of relationships which constitutes two communities with radically conflicting interests, aspirations and identities, then the solution lies in dismantling that system. We conceive of this process in emancipatory terms.

The concept of emancipation has a long lineage in social theory, from the enlightenment through Marx to contemporary critical theory.[23] It is commonly used to describe the process whereby a particular group frees itself from political subordination by another. It also has a more general

---

[21] Karl Marx, 'The Eighteenth Brumaire of Louis Bonaparte', in David McLellan, ed., *Karl Marx: Selected Writings*, Oxford, Oxford University Press, 1977, p. 300.

[22] For representative statements of the positions, see Arthur Aughey, *Under Siege: Ulster Unionism and the Anglo-Irish Agreement*, Belfast, Blackstaff, 1989; Richard Kearney and Robin Wilson, 'Northern Ireland's future as a European region', *The Irish Review*, no. 15, 1994. Brendan O'Leary, Tom Lyne, Jim Marshall, Bob Rowthorn, *Northern Ireland: Sharing Authority*, London, Institute of Public Policy Research, 1993; for further discussion, see ch. 11.

[23] For a discussion of the concept in the early work of Jürgen Habermas, and its roots in earlier social theory, see Thomas McCarthy, *The Critical Theory of Jürgen Habermas*, Cambridge, MIT Press, 1981; for a discussion of uses of the term in the social sciences, see Jan Nederveen Pieterse, 'Emancipations, modern and postmodern', *Development and Change*, vol. 23, no. 3, 1992. For a philosophical discussion of the preconditions of emancipation, see Roy Bhaskar, *Scientific Realism and Human Emancipation*, London, Verso, 1986; for an overview, see Brian Fay, *Critical Social Science*, Cambridge, Polity, 1987.

sense: a process by which the participants in a system which determines, distorts and limits their potentialities come together actively to transform it, and in the process transform themselves. As conceived here, emancipation is general rather than particular and partial rather than total. It seeks to dismantle a system which constitutes two communities in mutually antagonistic and destructive relationships. However it is partial in the sense that the emphasis is only on dismantling this one system. It does not address the struggles of women and other groups for full inclusion, participation and social justice. In the process of restructuring that emancipation demands, however, different struggles may converge and mutually reinforce each other.

Emancipation aims to resolve conflict, not simply to manage or contain it. Its immediate aim is not a compromise political settlement but a common endeavour to dismantle the root causes of conflict. It is conceived as a process that can – indeed must – win very broad political support. It demands a commitment to engage in such a process, a conscious decision to participate in dismantling the conditions of conflict. But it is a long term process; we envisage not a revolutionary leap to a new social order, but the creation of the conditions under which political agreement becomes possible. What the final agreed constitutional settlement will be is impossible to predict; it might be some variant on the present union, a form of joint authority, or a reconstituted Ireland. But whatever the form of settlement, it can only win widespread agreement if the conditions of conflict are dismantled.

Conor Cruise O'Brien once defined Irishness as 'not primarily a question of birth or blood or language; it is the condition of being involved in the Irish situation, and usually of being mauled by it'.[24] It is time to reconstruct the Irish situation. This study is intended as an intellectual contribution to that task.

[24] Conor Cruise O'Brien, *Writers and Politics*, London, Chatto and Windus, 1965, pp. 98–9.

2 Historical formations

The conflict in Northern Ireland has its roots in developments in Europe, Britain and Ireland during the sixteenth and seventeenth centuries which set Irish society and Irish–British relations in a conflictual mould. We conceptualise this in terms of the emergence of an internally conflictual system of relationships linking the two islands. We examine the origins of this system of relationships and trace its development to the partition of Ireland in 1921. Our approach is analytical and thematic rather than purely chronological.

Origins

From the late fifteenth century a new order was emerging in Europe out of the crisis of medieval feudalism. Its economic base was a more productive and commercialised agriculture, a rising population, improved communications, expanding trade and commerce and a renewed penetration of Europe's peripheral regions.[1] Its political expression was the forging of a system of territorial states as the leading monarchs strengthened their power within their kingdoms, annexed previously autonomous political entities, and defended themselves against internal and external enemies.[2] The new order expressed itself culturally in the shattering of the single overarching church-centred world of medieval Christendom by the reformation and in the slow and uneven emergence of national cultures and nations.[3]

---

[1] Immanuel Wallerstein, *The Modern World System*, vols. 1–3, New York, Academic Press, 1974, 1980, 1988.

[2] Charles Tilly, *Coercion, Capital, and European States*, Oxford, Basil Blackwell, 1990; Stein Rokkan 'Territories, centres and peripheries: toward a geoethnic-geoeconomic–geopolitical model of differentiation within western Europe', in Jean Gottman, ed., *Centre and Periphery: Spatial variation in Politics*, Sage, London, 1980; Theodore Rabb, *The Struggle for Stability in Early Modern Europe*, New York, Oxford University Press, 1975.

[3] Benedict Anderson, *Imagined Communities: Reflections on the Origin and Spread of Nationalism*, London, Verso, rev. edn, 1991.

Simultaneously Europe was extending beyond its traditional boundaries in a process of colonisation and of empire building. The movement beyond Europe followed an earlier phase of 'internal' colonisation and was spearheaded by the Atlantic states – Portugal, Spain, France, England and Holland.[4] Merchants, adventurers, soldiers, rulers and administrators created networks of trade and government linking Europe, Africa and the colonies of the New World, turning the Atlantic ocean into a European sea.[5] The imperial dynamic came primarily from economic and political forces, but religious motives were important and the colonising process was also a vast missionary endeavour. Settler colonies emerged, in time asserting their own claims to political independence and nationhood.

These twin processes took a specific form in Britain and Ireland.[6] From the eleventh century onwards the English Crown had been sufficiently powerful to prevent rival political centres emerging in England, to maintain colonial beachheads in Wales and Ireland, to exercise a sway over Scotland, and – most impressively – to defend, and for a time expand, its interests in France. However French consolidation from the fourteenth century brought English possessions in France finally to an end in 1540. English expansion thereafter concentrated on Wales, Scotland and Ireland and on the world beyond Europe. Out of this would emerge a complex and territorially extensive British world (chapter 8).

The economic, political and cultural shape of this world owed much to the successful resolution of a number of issues which were at the heart of English and European politics during the sixteenth and seventeenth centuries: the religious and constitutional form of the state, the economic and political exigencies of an emergent capitalist economy, the problem of national defence in an increasingly conflictual European system of states, and the challenges presented by imperialism and colonialism. On balance England managed those problems very well: it emerged from this period economically and politically unified, ruled by a constitutional monarchy sensitive to the concerns of market orientated landowners and merchants, self-consciously and aggressively Protestant, in control of the whole of the British Isles, strong enough to influence the balance of power on the continent and to mount a challenge to the other colonising

[4] Robert Bartlett, *The Making of Europe: Conquest, Colonization and Cultural Change 950–1350*, London, Penguin, 1994.
[5] G. V. Scammell, *The World Encompassed: The First European Maritime Empires c. 800–1650*, London, Methuen, 1981; Wallerstein, *Modern World System*.
[6] For an overview, see Hugh Kearney, *The British Isles: A History of Four Nations*, Cambridge, Cambridge University Press, 1989.

powers.[7] However success was uneven and the integration of Ireland in particular stored up problems for the future.

Integrating Wales had posed few problems. It was small and close to hand, a combination of marcher and autonomous lordships, more a geographical expression than a coherent entity. The fifteenth-century Welsh were becoming a cultural nation, but any hope of political autonomy died with the defeat of Glyndwyr in 1406. Thereafter Wales became progressively part of the wider English world; the Acts of Union (passed between 1536 and 1542) were perceived as opening up new possibilities for Welsh people in a new 'Britain'; the reformation met with limited opposition and would sink deep roots.[8]

Scotland was a different proposition. It was already a state whose independence was internationally recognised despite English claims to hegemony. It was geographically farther from the centre of English power and had traditionally allied itself with France. Simple annexation was not possible. Scotland's reorientation towards England came with the reformation and the succession, through an accident of inheritance, of the King of Scotland to the throne of England in 1603. The process of integration was long drawn out. Differences within the reformed faith in Scotland became entangled with religious and political conflicts in England, at times bringing the complex process of negotiated integration to the point of collapse.[9] Eventually a settlement emerged based on legislative and economic union but with Presbyterianism as the established religion in Scotland and an independent Scottish legal system.

Ireland was different again. It had been extensively if unevenly colonised by Anglo-Normans and their English tenants in the twelfth and thirteenth centuries and a central administration had been established; however the colony was in decline from the early fourteenth century and Ireland, like Wales, had become a frontier region of semi-autonomous Anglo-Irish marcher lordships and autonomous Gaelic ones. The Crown remained the sole overarching political authority but outside the Pale its power was weak or non-existent and settler and native lordships were left largely to their own devices. Nevertheless the most powerful Anglo-Irish magnates remained loyal and through alliances and submissions were

---

[7] Christopher Hill, *Reformation to Industrial Revolution*, Harmondsworth, Penguin, 1969.

[8] Kearney, *British Isles*, pp. 116–18; Gwyn Williams, *When Was Wales? A History of the Welsh*, Harmondsworth, Penguin, 1985, ch. 6.

[9] Kearney, *British Isles*, pp. 119–22; Arthur H. Williamson, *Scottish National Consciousness in the Age of James VI: The Apocalypse, the Union and the shaping of Scotland's Public Culture*, Edinburgh, John Donald, 1979.

able to exert some order and control over the complex, shifting, conflictual social whole.[10]

The reassertion of English control over Ireland was motivated partly by a desire to secure its own western flank, partly by a concern to bring a Crown possession long perceived as lawless, costly, unproductive and culturally backward into line with its own developing notions of religion, statehood, economy and culture. The policies changed over time but there were continuities – securing conformity to the established religion, undermining the power bases of the independent lords, renewing and extending the institutions of government, opening up the economy, making the administration of Ireland self-financing and if possible a source of revenue for the Crown, spreading civility and the English language.[11] The problem was to decide what combination of conciliation and coercion, political pressure and moral persuasion, would achieve this, and whether success would be more rapid or more certain by working with the existing population or by sponsoring and encouraging new settlement.

Initially the stress was on conciliation and on bringing the existing lords into the new framework of law and government. However the policy of conciliation broke down and by the end of the sixteenth century a policy of coercion and displacement was in place. The shift from conciliation to coercion was not inevitable, but a number of factors made it likely. Ireland's social structure was unstable and the arrival of powerful and ambitious newcomers – officials, soldiers, administrators, clergy and their retinues – posed a challenge to the existing power-holders;[12] the gap between Gaelic-Irish and English notions of economy and politics was very wide; should difficulties arise, there was an obvious temptation to follow the medieval precedent of colonisation and the contemporary example of European expansion in the New World; there were strong – albeit fluctuating – economic and demographic pressures in Scotland and England for settlement in Ireland. Finally, the arrival

---

[10] Ciaran Brady, 'The decline of the Irish kingdom', in Mark Greengrass, ed., *Conquest and Coalescence: The Shaping of the State in Early Modern Europe*, London, Edward Arnold, 1991.

[11] Ciaran Brady and Raymond Gillespie, eds., *Natives and Newcomers: The Making of Irish Colonial Society 1534–1641*, Dublin, Irish Academic Press, 1986; Colm Lennon, *Sixteenth-Century Ireland: The Incomplete Conquest*, Dublin, Gill and Macmillan, 1994; Brendan Fitzpatrick, *Seventeenth-Century Ireland: The Wars of Religions*, Dublin, Gill and Macmillan, 1988.

[12] Brady, 'Decline of the Irish kingdom'; Brady and Gillespie, eds., *Natives and Newcomers*; Lennon, *Sixteenth Century Ireland*; Nicholas Canny, *The Elizabethan Conquest of Ireland: A Pattern Established, 1565–76*, Hassocks, Sussex, Harvester Press, 1976; Nicholas Canny, *From Reformation to Restoration: Ireland 1534–1660*, Dublin, Helicon, 1987.

and success of the counter-reformation in Ireland set limits to the peaceful accommodation of newcomers and natives.

The progress of the newcomers was rapid. They profited from privileged access to official positions, Crown leases and concealed Crown titles and from direct grants of land. The Ulster plantation brought a decisive advance and by 1641 Protestants owned 41 per cent of the land and held a majority of the seats in both houses of the Irish parliament.[13] Not all immigrants to Ireland came as part of the official plantation process. Many came on their own account or in response to landowners seeking skilled tenants to develop underpopulated lands; the settlement of east Ulster was largely of this form.[14] However the ability of immigrants to establish themselves was enhanced by the opening up of the economy by formal colonisation and by the political dominance of the settler and Protestant interest. They too became part of the colonising process and – as the events of 1641–2 in non-planted counties such as Clare revealed – were perceived as such by the native population.[15]

Despite their success, the settlers were very vulnerable during the first half of the seventeenth century. They were a small proportion of the total population and the shifting sands of political influence in London could leave them politically exposed. Their military weakness was evident in the 1640s when the Old English joined the Gaelic-Irish in rebellion; only divisions in the Catholic camp and Scottish intervention in Ulster saved them from annihilation. However the 1640s proved a watershed. The Cromwellian victory was followed by the wholesale confiscation of Catholic lands, the expulsion of Catholics from the major towns and the banning of their priests and bishops. By 1688 Catholic ownership of land had fallen to 22 per cent of the total; further confiscation followed the defeat of the supporters of James II and by 1703 the proportion had fallen to 14 per cent.[16] Meanwhile Protestant numbers had recovered from the crisis years of the 1640s with further extensive immigration particularly from Scotland to Ulster. The demographic and cultural impact of these developments was profound. According to one estimate, no less than

13 Fitzpatrick, *Seventeenth Century Ireland*, p. 46; Ruth Dudley Edwards, *An Atlas of Irish History*, London, Methuen, 1973, pp. 165–6.
14 Nicholas Canny, 'Conquest and colonisation: the implications of these processes for modern Irish history', in O. MacDonagh and W. F. Mandle, eds., *Irish-Australian Studies: Papers Delivered at the Fifth Irish–Australian Conference*, Canberra, Australian National University, 1989; Raymond Gillespie, *Colonial Ulster: The Settlement of East Ulster 1600–1641*, Cork, Cork University Press, 1985.
15 See Ciarán Ó Murchadha, *Land and Society in Seventeenth-Century Clare*, Ph.D. Thesis, Department of History, University College Galway, 1982.
16 Edwards, *Atlas of Irish History*, pp. 165–6.

27 per cent of the population was of recent immigrant stock at the end of the seventeenth century, by which time they were also in firm control of the country's economy and political institutions.[17] The regional and local effect was uneven. In some regions native displacement had occurred only at the higher echelons; in others, above all in Ulster, it took place at all levels.

The English policy embarked upon in the 1530s – that of securing Ireland and bringing it into line with contemporary English practices – was in many ways a success. By the end of the seventeenth century the authority of the state was uncontested throughout the country and the loyalty of the dominant landowning class was not in question; the economy had been opened up to market forces and brought much more into line with prevailing patterns in western Europe;[18] Anglicanism was the established religion and the faith of almost the whole of the landed class and of the richest and most influential merchants in the major towns; English was the language of a greatly extended public sphere; the Catholic church was on the defensive and the political and economic base of a self-confident Gaelic culture had been destroyed.

In other respects – and certainly by comparison with Wales and Scotland – the outcome was unsatisfactory and far from the original goal. The new order had been established primarily by coercion and rested on a narrow and insecure base – on the control of a settler minority whose economic and political power depended on the legal and social exclusion of the majority and continued British support. The majority Old English and Gaelic-Irish population was staunchly Catholic, whether counter-reformation or traditional, and viewed the settlers and their descendants as intruders, usurpers and heretics. Their loyalty to the Crown was not wholly at an end (see below) but they were embittered and alienated from the new regime.

Structurally and institutionally the new society had many of the characteristics of the European *ancien régime*; but the path which Ireland had traversed in its journey from late medieval to early modern society also gave it a colonial cast.[19] It led to the emergence of a distinctive

---

[17] Louis Cullen, *The Emergence of Modern Ireland 1600–1900*, London, Batsford, 1981, p. 15.

[18] This is a central theme in Cullen, *ibid.*

[19] On the distinctive nature of the outcome, see Nicholas Canny, 'Early modern Ireland, c. 1500–1700', in R. F. Foster, ed., *The Oxford Illustrated History of Ireland*, Oxford, Oxford University Press, 1989, p. 160, and Brady and Gillespie, *Natives and New-comers*, p. 17; for a view of Ireland as *ancien régime*, see S. J. Connolly, *Religion, Law and Power: The Making of Protestant Ireland 1660–1760*, Oxford, Clarendon Press, 1992, and C. D. A. Leighton, *Catholicism in a Protestant Kingdom: A Study of the Irish* Ancien Régime, Dublin, Gill and Macmillan, 1994.

system of relationships with three interlocking and mutually reinforcing levels: a set of socio-cultural and ideological differences; a structure of dominance, dependence and inequality; and a tendency towards communal polarisation. We look at each in turn.

Dimensions of difference

Ireland's mode of integration into the emerging British world introduced into its culture and social relationships four overlapping socio-cultural and ideological differences which would prove enduring – based on religion, ethnicity, settler–native status and concepts of progress and backwardness. To these would be added in the nineteenth century a further difference based on national identity and allegiance.

Religion

Religion was the single most important difference both for its doctrinal and its social and political significance. The divide between Protestantism and Catholicism was the critical one, but each was internally differentiated. Protestants comprised mainly members of the Church of Ireland and Presbyterians, with other smaller denominations. Presbyterians (based primarily in Ulster) were subject to further internal doctrinal and organisational divisions. There were also differences within Catholicism. The orthodox counter-reformation Catholicism of the educated middle and upper classes was very different from the traditional folk Catholicism of the rural masses. The differences began to disappear only with the destruction of the cottier and labouring classes in the mid-nineteenth century, the strengthening of church organisation and the rapid growth in the proportion of clergy to people.[20]

Conflict between Catholics and Protestants or between the different strands of Protestantism centred on questions of doctrine and religious organisation. The intensity of conflict varied over time, but there was continuity in the issues, real or imagined, which separated the different religions. Protestants saw Catholics as steeped in superstition and kept ignorant of the word of God by a despotic and intolerant clergy and papacy; the more radical Calvinist strands denied that Catholicism was a Christian religion at all, saw its elaborate rituals as idolatrous and declared the pope to be the anti-Christ. For Catholics, all strands of Protestantism were heresies from the One True Church; eternal

[20] K. Theodore Hoppen, *Ireland since 1800: Conflict and Conformity*, London, Longman, 1989, pp. 60–71.

damnation was to be the Protestant fate. Conflicts between Anglicanism and Presbyterianism centred on specific aspects of reformation theology and of practical organisation.

Doctrinal difference as a source of conflict moderated somewhat in the later eighteenth century but intensified again during the nineteenth century. A Protestant evangelical movement stressed forcefully its objections to Catholicism and the proselytising crusade of the 1820s and after greatly exacerbated religious tension.[21] Tension was further heightened by developments on the Catholic side – the growing ascendance of ultramontanism, the declaration of papal infallibility and the immaculate conception and in 1908 the *Ne Temere* decree. Meanwhile Protestant fundamentalism took firmer root after the Great Revival of 1859 and the forging of bonds across the different Protestant denominations.

The conflict of Protestant and Catholic in Ireland had a clear theological base; but it derived further intensity from its relationship to social structural and political differences. Anglicans covered the entire social range from aristocracy and gentry to day labourers, but had an upwardly biased class profile compared to Catholics, while Presbyterians were particularly prominent in the intermediate classes.[22] Class differences among Catholics were also considerable but the distinctive feature of Catholicism was its predominance among the poorest social groups. The Catholic social profile improved during the nineteenth century but due as much to the destruction of the poorer classes as to increased mobility.

The denominations also differed markedly in their relative access to political power. The Williamite settlement gave a monopoly of political power to Anglicans in the eighteenth century. Catholics were excluded by law from the entire state apparatus, national and local, for virtually the whole of the eighteenth century; the removal of the last legal restrictions came only with Catholic emancipation in 1829. Dissenters were likewise restricted in their access to public positions although to a lesser degree and for a shorter period; the last of the restrictions were removed in 1780. Even with the removal of legal restrictions the stronger Anglican class base ensured their continued preeminence until the extension of the franchise and institutional reform in the later nineteenth century.

---

[21] *Ibid.*, pp. 71–6; Desmond Bowen, *The Protestant Crusade in Ireland, 1800–70: A Study of Protestant–Catholic Relations between the Act of Union and Disestablishment*, Dublin, Gill and Macmillan, 1978.

[22] For Belfast, see A. C. Hepburn, 'Work, class and religion in Belfast, 1871–1911', *Irish Economic and Social History*, vol. 10, 1983.

Ethnicity

At the beginning of the sixteenth century Ireland consisted of two distinct (if in some degree overlapping) ethnic groups – those of Gaelic-Irish stock and the English speaking descendants of late medieval Norman settlers. The sixteenth and seventeenth century brought two further groups to Ireland – lowland Scots and English. Once in Ireland they took on the cultural colouring of their local area and of the island as a whole. However they remained conscious of their distinctive origins, thought of themselves as different from the rest on the island (and from each other) and remained open to continuing influence from their country of origin. There was a distinct regional pattern to this; the Scots element had primacy in Ulster (despite the mixture of English and Scottish settlers); elsewhere the identification was exclusively English.

The development of Catholics into a single cultural group was a complex and long drawn out process. The Old English and Gaelic-Irish elites were merging in the seventeenth century and by the eighteenth century there existed a distinct 'Catholic Irish' community, English speaking but in many cases bilingual. Monoglot Irish speakers, concentrated at the lower class levels, were a culture apart but one which exerted an influence on all cultural strands in Ireland. Much later, under the influence of Gaelic revivalism, Catholics would define themselves uniquely in terms of their Gaelic ancestry but their culture was a hybrid one, whose roots lay in the Old English legacy, Gaelic-Irish traditions and the Protestant and British ethos of the public sphere.

The importance of ethnicity as a dimension of difference is difficult to determine because of its close links to religion. One view denies it virtually any significance and attributes its persistence solely to religion; thus the argument that ethnic differences would have quickly disappeared but for religion.[23] A more nuanced view is necessary. There is no doubt that of the two variables religion was the stronger and that when religion and ethnicity clashed, religion won. Patronymics often contradicted prevailing assumptions of the historical relationship between ethnicity and religion, but they were no predictor of cultural or political attitude. This is true even of those of noble Gaelic stock who had conformed to the established religion; they remained conscious of their Gaelic origins but this had little cultural or political significance.

---

[23] For example, R. H. Buchanan, 'The Planter and the Gael', in F. W. Boal and J. N. H. Douglas, eds., *Integration and Division: Geographical Perspectives on the Northern Ireland Problem*, London, Academic Press, 1982.

Religion was sufficiently important to bind the Old English to the Gaelic-Irish rather than to the New English with whom ethnically they had more in common. At the same time the conflicts associated with Ireland's integration into the British state were not simply religious; the cultural gap was wide and events were mediated by hostile ethnic perceptions of long standing (see below pp. 43–5). The loyalty of the Old English was considered suspect primarily because of their religion; but their disloyalty was attributed also to cultural 'degeneration' stemming from their long contact with the Gaelic-Irish. Similarly, the Catholicism of the Gaelic-Irish was perceived as just one strand in their culture which predisposed them to disloyalty.[24] Again the Old English and Gaelic-Irish response to reformation Protestantism owes something to the fact that it came to Ireland dressed in English and Scottish cultural garb.

Settler and native

The conquest and colonisations of the sixteenth and seventeenth centuries left as their legacy an enduring distinction between 'settlers' and 'natives'. The settler–native distinction was interwoven with the religious and ethnic one but is not reducible to it. A wholly indigenous but incomplete reformation would have left – as in many European countries – a legacy of religious conflict but without the assumption that Protestants were essentially 'foreigners'. Immigration of a more conventional kind might have left a legacy of ethnic difference and conflict, but it would not have generated the psychology of dispossession and reciprocal fear of expulsion which animated conflict in Ireland.[25]

In practice many of those who made up the 'settler' population were descended from people who came simply as immigrants, just as many eighteenth- and nineteenth-century Protestants were of native stock. But they were part of a society defined in terms of 'settlers' and 'natives' and took their appointed place within it. Similarly, the vast majority of those who considered themselves the descendants of the dispossessed 'had not technically been deprived of anything' – only the ruling families lost their lands and of these most were killed or left the country.[26] However

---

[24] See, for example, the excerpt from the writings of Barnaby Rich in Andrew Hadfield and John McVeagh, eds., *Strangers to that Land: British Perceptions of Ireland from the Reformation to the Famine*, Gerrards Cross, Colin Smythe, 1994, pp. 45–7.

[25] Despite the difference in scale and timing, the experience of the Jewish community in Ireland offers a useful point of comparison in this respect.

[26] Nicholas Canny, 'Early modern Ireland, *c.* 1500–1700', in Foster, ed., *Oxford Illustrated History of Ireland*, pp. 159–60.

they had been dispossessed in other ways – they had been deprived of cultural and religious affinity with the ruling class, access (for the more upwardly mobile) to the public sphere and a sense of continuity with the past.

The division of the society around the settler–native issue was to prove remarkably resilient. The descendants of the settlers soon identified with Ireland and regarded themselves as 'Irish' but they did not forget their origins or their difference from those they saw as the native Irish – nor were they permitted to. They could not easily identify with the history of a country whose traditions they saw as barbarous and wished to destroy and which, even two centuries later, they believed they held in trust for Britain.[27] If in time some, like the poet Samuel Ferguson, sought to immerse themselves in the Irish past and to locate themselves within a single unfolding tradition, the majority kept a careful distance from it.

The other side of the coin was the sense of loss of those who saw themselves as the true and native Irish, deprived of their property and position, on whom an alien culture and language had been imposed. The narrative of defeat and dispossession in the eighteenth century owed much to the displaced poets of the old order. O'Connell gave it mass political form in the early nineteenth century. Gaelic cultural nationalism gave it its greatest and most potent elaboration at the end of the century and intensified the sense of loss with a tantalising image of what might have been – a distinctive Gaelic nation with an unbroken cultural tradition.[28]

Civility and barbarism; progress and backwardness

The reimposition of English rule on Ireland in the sixteenth and seventeenth centuries was legitimated in multiple ways, including the renewal of rightful ancient claims and the advance of the true religion. But it was also justified – particularly in its coercive aspects – by the argument that it brought civility and progress to a barbarous and backward people.[29] The wellspring of Irish barbarism and backwardness was thought to lie in the primitiveness of Gaelic-Irish culture, with the Old English

---

[27] See, for example, T. Sinclair, 'The position of Ulster', in S. Rosenbaum, ed., *Against Home Rule: The Case for the Union*, London, Frederick Warne, 1912, p. 171.

[28] For an overview, see Tom Garvin, *The Evolution of Irish Nationalist Politics*, Dublin, Gill and Macmillan, 1981.

[29] D. B. Quinn, *The Elizabethans and the Irish*, Ithaca, Cornell University Press, 1966; Hadfield and McVeagh, eds., *Strangers to that Land*; Brendan Bradshaw, Andrew Hadfield and Willy Maley, eds., *Representing Ireland: Literature and the Origins of Conflict, 1534–1660*, Cambridge, Cambridge University Press, 1993.

becoming degenerate as a result of prolonged exposure to it. The Old English were hotly to contest that view of themselves and of the Gaelic-Irish in the seventeenth century but the equating of British and Protestant with civility and progress and of Irish and Catholic with barbarism and backwardness would prove enduring.[30]

All settler groups use such discourses to rationalise their power, not least when their actions towards the native population breach the norms they observe in respect of one another. But more is involved than simply settler ideology. We noted above that sixteenth-century Ireland was, by contemporary European standards, economically underdeveloped and politically fragmented. Colonisation brought the economy much more into line with conditions elsewhere and created effective central rule, and in the process established a historical correlation between colonisation and 'modernisation'.[31]

Subsequently the descendants of the settlers controlled the commanding heights of the economy and the country's political and cultural institutions and remained in close contact with Britain. They were therefore more exposed to British developments in technology, institutions and ideas and, in transmitting them, remained the face of modernity in Ireland. The most dramatic examples were in the economic domain. The Protestants of east Ulster, in close contact with their Scottish and English counterparts, showed a striking capacity for innovation in the domestic linen industry in the eighteenth century and in its reconstitution on capitalist lines in the nineteenth. Later in the century local initiative combined with an influx of English and Scottish entrepreneurs and skilled workers to make Belfast one of the success stories of the industrial revolution.

Protestants had therefore some claim to be considered the modernising element in Irish society. However this too has to be qualified. There was a long tradition of Catholic modernisation which included the embracing of the counter-reformation in the sixteenth and seventeenth centuries, the innovations of Catholic entrepreneurs in the eighteenth century, the mass political mobilisation of the early nineteenth century, the formation of a disciplined political party and land reform movement and the (re)inventing of Irish field sports in the later nineteenth century, the pioneering of the techniques of political

---

[30] See L. Perry Curtis Jr, *Apes and Angels, The Irishman in Victorian Caricature*, Newton Abbot, David and Charles, 1971; for examples of discourses of modernity and progress among late nineteenth-century unionists, see Henry Patterson, *Class Conflict and Sectarianism: The Protestant Working Class and the Belfast Labour Movement 1868–1920*, Belfast, Blackstaff Press, 1980.

[31] Cullen, *Emergence of Modern Ireland*.

separatism and guerilla warfare in the twentieth century.[32] Not surprisingly perhaps, such examples of innovation or modernisation made little impact on Protestant perceptions; on the contrary, they saw them – if not the innovations themselves, then the goals they served – as further expressions of Catholic backwardness.

Nationalism and unionism

Ireland was ethnically divided on recognisably modern lines from the sixteenth and seventeenth centuries, but the emergence of a society divided by reference to national identity and allegiance – into nationalists and unionists – dates only from the nineteenth century. Its late emergence reflects in part the constitutional change effected by the Act of Union, but more importantly the fact that the nationalist presuppositions on which both ideologies are based themselves emerged only in the nineteenth century. National identities existed prior to the nineteenth century although primarily among elites; they also tended to be separate from questions of political allegiance which were determined more by tradition, self-interest or by religious or dynastic loyalty.[33]

Nineteenth-century nationalism advanced the concept of the nation as a self-determining community with its own unique history and culture, offering and demanding from all its members a strong identification, commitment and loyalty, and claiming the right to pursue its destiny by means of a state of its own, the political embodiment of its national life. Throughout Europe the claims of nationality provoked crises of political allegiance wherever the culture of the rulers and that of the masses did not coincide. It also provoked crises for societies with cultural minorities unwilling or unable to identify fully with the nation as conceived by the majority. The rise of nationalism raised fundamental questions for Ireland – not simply how to define the nation but what political consequences should follow from that definition – and nineteenth-century Ireland divided into an Irish-identifying separatist Catholic community and a British-identifying Protestant one committed to the union.

There is a widespread tendency to attribute that division wholly to the

---

[32] See John Bossy, 'The counter-reformation and the people of Catholic Ireland, 1596–1641', in T. D. Williams, ed., *Historical Studies VIII*, Dublin, Gill and Macmillan, 1971; David Dickson, 'Catholics and trade in eighteenth-century Ireland: an old debate revisited', in T. P. Power and K. Whelan, eds., *Endurance and Emergence: Catholics in Ireland in the Eighteenth Century*, Dublin, Irish Academic Press, 1990, p. 97; Garvin, *The Evolution of Irish Nationalist Politics*; W. F. Mandle, 'The Gaelic Athletic Association and popular culture, 1884–1924', in O. MacDonagh, W. F. Mandle and P. Travers, eds., *Irish Culture and Nationalism, 1750–1950*, London, Macmillan, 1983.

[33] See Ernest Gellner, *Nations and Nationalism*, Oxford, Basil Blackwell, 1983.

cultural and religious exclusivism of Gaelic-Catholic nationalism – its assumption that only Irish Catholics belonged to the Irish nation, that Protestants were alien interlopers who could become truly Irish only by assimilating to the majority community.[34] This argument ignores the role which individual Protestants played in the Irish nationalist movement. It also ignores the emergence at the same time of the concept of a 'British nation' – attractive to many Irish Protestants – as a family of peoples, racially Anglo-Saxon, Protestant in religion, whose origins lay in Great Britain but who might now be scattered throughout the empire.[35] For Protestants this British identity coexisted easily with an Irish identity; that option was not open to Catholics. But there is a more fundamental problem with arguments which attribute later divisions to competing concepts of nationhood: the difficulty of arriving at a shared concept of national identity and allegiance in the face of a pre-existing, deeply rooted communal division. Later conflicts of identity and allegiance were the effect of that communal division, not its cause.

On the other hand, the new concepts of national identity and allegiance exacerbated division by adding a new dimension of difference to the existing ones and doing so in a totalising way. Nationalism described an Ireland economically laid waste by centuries of British rule, whose rightful owners had been dispossessed, their religion persecuted, their culture all but destroyed – but which once free would use its talents and resources to rebuild itself. Unionism described a backward Ireland to which Britain had brought political order, cultural advance and religious liberty, and whose resources Irish Protestants of British stock had developed using their talents, education and enterprise; outside of the British context Ireland and Irish Protestants would undergo irreversible decline.[36]

The overlapping of the dimensions of difference

As totalising ideologies nationalism and unionism gave expression to a tendency that was marked from the outset – for the differences in religion, ethnicity, settler–native status and attributions of progress and

---

[34] For example, Conor Cruise O'Brien, *Ancestral Voices: Religion and Nationalism in Ireland*, Dublin, Poolbeg Press, 1994.

[35] Keith Robbins, *Nineteenth Century Britain: England, Scotland, and Wales: The Making of a Nation*, Oxford, Oxford University Press, 1989; Thomas Hennessey 'Ulster unionist territorial and national identities 1886–1893: province, island, kingdom and empire', *Irish Political Studies*, vol. 8, 1993.

[36] For the contrast in ideologies, see Dennis Pringle, *One Ireland, Two Nations: A Political Geographical Analysis of the National Conflict in Ireland*, Letchworth, Research Studies Press, 1985, chs. 6 and 7.

backwardness to overlap. The Protestant English and Scottish settlers of the sixteenth and seventeenth centuries and their descendants saw themselves as part of a process that was bringing at once the true religion, civility and material progress to Ireland; Catholics then and later saw themselves as the dispossessed native population of the island, more fully Irish than the settlers could ever be, and as members of the church founded by Christ.

The tendency of the different dimensions of conflict to overlap had two important consequences. First, it meant that developments along any one dimension were conditioned by what was happening on others. For example, the developing religious ethos of Irish Protestants, including their theology, was shaped by their English and Scottish identities, their self-image as the progressive force in Irish life and their sense of political insecurity.[37] Similarly, the religious ethos of Irish Catholics was influenced by the fact that their church – even in its later anglicised and strongly ultramontane form – claimed to speak for the native population of the island and offered to its congregation an alternative version of the European 'civilising process'.[38]

Second, overlap enabled individual freedom and variation to coexist with communal polarisation. The fact that the communities were divided on multiple dimensions did not mean that each individual drew on all the dimensions in constructing his or her opposition to the members of the other community. For some, religion was the central issue; for others, political allegiance. But overlap meant that even if an individual stressed only one dimension of difference, he or she could still identify fully with his or her community in opposition to the other.

Dominance, dependence and inequality

The coercive nature and at best partial success of English policies in Ireland during the sixteenth and seventeenth centuries left in their wake a legacy of conflict within Ireland and in Irish-British relations. Irish Protestants now controlled Ireland and its resources. But they were a minority and were themselves divided on religious and ethnic lines; Anglicans and Presbyterians were united in their loyalty to the British Crown as the guarantor of the Protestant constitution, but they

---

[37] Alan Ford, 'The Protestant reformation in Ireland', in Brady and Gillespie, eds., *Natives and Newcomers*; Phil Kilroy, 'Protestantism in Ulster, 1610–1641', in Brian MacCuarta SJ, ed., *Ulster 1641: Aspects of the Rising*, Belfast, Institute of Irish Studies, 1993.

[38] Tom Inglis, *Moral Monopoly: The Catholic Church in Modern Irish Society*, Dublin, Gill and Macmillan, 1987.

mistrusted each other. Presbyterians resented Anglican dominance. Anglicans feared Presbyterians as a 'nation within a nation' who might possibly challenge their status as the established church.[39] Catholics however were the common enemy. Protestants had secured their land and positions by displacing Catholics, often if not always in a coercive way. Catholics had already made two attempts to dislodge them, in the 1640s and in 1689–91, and in both cases Protestant victory had been a close run thing. Catholics were now quiescent, but they did not accept the legitimacy of the new order.

For Protestants there was a security in the British connection but they were unwilling to depend completely on it. The form of English involvement in Irish affairs over the past 150 years was less than reassuring. With the exception of the Cromwellian period there had been no systematic programme of conquest relentlessly followed through; nor had the government unambiguously supported the New English interest. Instead it had intervened spasmodically, had shown itself open to appeals from all sides and had played one off against the other.[40] The New English had emerged victorious but this was not inevitable; the Old English might have succeeded in reaching an accomodation with the English state, or the pre-1650 settlers might have lost out to the Cromwellians.[41] On the other hand, given that they had won out the British government had an interest in supporting them – they were Protestant, identified culturally with England and were unambiguous in their assertions of loyalty. Dependence on a vulnerable minority was not ideal, but after a century and more of conflict and instability they were the best hope of a stable, loyal and politically compliant Ireland.

Despite the mutual dependence of the British government and Irish Protestants, relations between them were far from easy. The British government insisted on maintaining considerable control over Irish affairs. The requirement dating from 1494 that Irish bills be approved by the British privy council before being enacted in Ireland remained in place; in 1720 the British parliament declared its right to legislate directly for Ireland; the Irish executive was British appointed and Ireland was subjected to the standard colonial restrictions in respect of trade. For Irish Protestants, believing themselves to be in possession of a country that was a kingdom in its own right and entitled to full English liberties,

---

[39] See Thomas Bartlett 'The origins and progress of the Catholic question in Ireland', in Power and Whelan, eds., *Endurance and Emergence*, p. 3.
[40] Canny 'Conquest and colonisation'.
[41] Toby Barnard, 'Planters and policies in Cromwellian Ireland', *Past and Present*, vol. 61, 1973.

this was demeaning. From early in the eighteenth century they were pressing for more control over their political affairs and the removal of mercantilist restrictions.

In their relations with one another, the British government and Irish Protestants (whatever their denomination) had to take account of a potential Catholic threat. Initially the threat seemed minimal. The Williamite wars broke the morale and the military capacity of Catholics; confiscation had already eroded their economic and social base. The status quo was then reinforced by putting in place a comprehensive set of legal restrictions on Catholic economic, political and educational activity. Not all of these laws were rigorously applied but their effect was far from negligible.[42] At the same time the Catholic threat did not disappear. Jacobite rebellions in Britain met no support in Ireland, but Jacobite feeling remained strong in some regions, particularly Munster, and hope of a restoration remained. The death of James III in 1766 finally brought Jacobitism to an end, but already a different source of pressure had emerged with the formation in 1760 of a Catholic Committee to lobby for the removal of the penal laws.

Pressure for reform was in many ways as threatening as Jacobitism. Stability had been achieved by placing a settler Protestant minority in control in Ireland and by marginalising and subordinating the Catholic majority. Even limited reform could act as the thin edge of a Catholic wedge – strengthening Catholics and heightening their ability to extract further reforms, weakening and sowing further discord among Protestants, and sooner or later putting the whole structure of Protestant – and perhaps British – control at risk. Faced with such an outcome most Protestants were determined to hold the line and resist changes that threatened their position.

The British government was more open.[43] Having cast its lot in favour of the Protestant interest, it could not now reverse its position without provoking a Protestant revolt. Yet it was conscious of the weak legitimacy of the new order and if possible wished to strengthen it; it could also contemplate, with greater equanimity than Protestants, measures to improve the position of Catholics in return for their loyalty. The difficulty was that the reforms necessary to satisfy Catholics were certain to alarm Protestants and possibly threaten the British position in Ireland.

---

[42] Foster stresses that the effects of the penal laws have been exaggerated, but also comments that 'in the early years of the eighteenth century the laws provided a key mechanism for the reinforcement of Ascendancy', R. F. Foster, *Modern Ireland 1600–1972*, Allen Lane, Penguin Press, 1988, p. 206.

[43] For an analysis of British government concerns and strategies in the eighteenth century, see Bartlett 'Origins and progress'.

At the same time there was little likelihood that Catholics would accept the status quo. They had suffered a traumatic defeat and had few options. They could assimiliate to the new order; but this was a culturally self-annihilating process open to relatively few and even then at a considerable cost to the first generation. They could accept their defeat as individuals and concentrate on doing as well as possible in the areas still open to them; however this meant acquiescing in their subordination. The only realistic option was some form of resistance.

An internally conflictual set of relationships had emerged which simultaneously generated and blocked pressure for change. Catholics were motivated to challenge the existing order by their sense of subordination and marginalisation. Protestants felt impelled to resist this challenge out of fear for their own position and future on the island. The British government had a strategic interest in conciliating Catholics to secure their loyalty, but within the limits set by its own interests in securing Ireland and maintaining Protestant loyalty.

Despite its internal tensions this conflictual political order could have survived – perhaps indefinitely – under *ancien régime* conditions. External and minority rule and privilege can easily be sustained under conditions of an underdeveloped economy, a rural population living in localised communities, a caste-like stratification system, non-literacy, an acceptance of oligarchical rule and of coercion. Moreover the climate of opinion in eighteenth-century Europe permitted quite drastic methods to protect governments against religious dissidents which could also be used against a religious majority.[44] Catholics might be a large demographic majority but their political class was much smaller and it had little interest in mobilising the masses even if it were capable of it. In the event, these conditions began to change in the second part of the eighteenth century in ways that simultaneously increased the ability of Catholics to press for reform and the willingness of the British government to conciliate them. But this reflected a change in the balance of power within the structure of dominance, dependence and inequality, not a fundamental departure from it.

The tendency toward communal polarisation

The polarisation of Ireland at national level into two separate and solidaristic Protestant and Catholic communities dates only from the later nineteenth century. Eighteenth-century Catholics were not a single

---

[44] Jeremy Black, *Eighteenth Century Europe 1700–1789*, London, Macmillan, 1990, pp. 169–80.

national community in any significant meaning of the term; Presbyterians were a cohesive community but were concentrated in Ulster; only Anglicans were well organised at national level. Anglicans and Presbyterians shared a common political interest – the defence of the Protestant constitution – but their religious and political differences were deep and they were two communities rather than one.[45]

The eighteenth-century Anglican community found its symbolic centre in the established church and in the state whose political, judicial and coercive institutions it controlled. The community was highly stratified, and it was the upper class that exercised political control and owned the bulk of the land and property. But the different layers of the community were joined to it and to each other by multiple ties – kinship, economic, political, religious. The middle strata were often distant relatives of the leading families, their privileged tenants, their supports at election time, their pastors and the educators of their children. The less well off depended on those above them for work or patronage; in many cases they were live-in servants. Rich and poor worshipped together and participated in the annual celebrations of the success and survival of the community in the face of adversity. All were conscious of a common interest in the established order.[46]

Eighteenth-century Presbyterians also achieved an impressive level of communal solidarity, though for different reasons than Anglicans. It came from their geographical cohesiveness, their concentration in a relatively small area even of Ulster, their identification and continuing links with Scotland, their relative homogeneity in class terms, the communal nature of their church organisation, their self-perception as a group disadvantaged by the theological and political opposition of the Anglican establishment, their status as a middle group politically (though not religiously) between Anglican and Catholic.[47]

The nineteenth century saw a gradual convergence between Anglicans and Presbyterians. Radical Presbyterians allied with Catholics in the revolutionary United Irishmen in the 1790s, but the alliance was short-lived. The rising in the north was suppressed and that in Wexford degenerated into sectarian strife that alarmed all Protestants. The ensuing Act of Union abolished the Anglican controlled, apparently

---

[45] It is important not to overstress the boundedness of the separate religious-political communities in the eighteenth century or even later; in local communities there was both integration and separation; see Connolly, *Religion, Law and Power*, pp. 124–43.

[46] See J. C. Beckett, *The Anglo-Irish Tradition*, London, Faber and Faber, 1976.

[47] Peter Brooke, *Ulster Presbyterianism: The Historical Perspective 1610–1970*, Dublin, Gill and Macmillan, 1987; Ian McBride 'Presbyterians in the Penal Era', *Bullán*, vol. 1, no. 2, 1994.

unreformable, Dublin parliament which Presbyterians had so much resented. Anglicans remained dominant in electoral politics until the end of the century, but the centre of power was now at Westminster. Successful Catholic agitation against tithes, against the established status of the Church of Ireland and for land reform removed residual Presbyterian grievances. Both groups found common political cause in defending the union against Catholic pressure for repeal; from the 1820s the evangelical movement was forging links across the Protestant denominations; later in the century industrialisation and urbanisation (particularly in Belfast) brought closer and more intimate contact.

The development of Catholics into a coherent community followed a different route. Eighteenth-century Catholics were much less a single community than either Anglicans or Presbyterians. The higher strata were interlinked at a national level and formed in some cases cohesive regional blocs, but the vast majority were locality-centred in their concerns and consciousness.[48] Many were poorly integrated into commercial networks, excluded from the political system, with low levels of education and little if any access to the print media. The elite was English speaking; the masses were monoglot Irish speakers. The Catholic church had reemerged organisationally by the 1730s but for political reasons its emphasis was local and even there its resources were inadequate to the large and growing Catholic population. Catholic solidarity was strengthened by a shared sense of displacement and subordination, but the practical meaning of this varied widely from one subgroup to another and it did not have the integrative power that anti-Catholicism had for Protestants.

The nineteenth century brought change. The expansion of the commercial economy integrated all Catholics directly into the national economy and expanded its middle and lower-middle-class component. Improvements in communications opened up previously inaccessible areas to outside influence. The political mobilisation of the Catholic masses under middle-class control – to achieve Catholic emancipation and repeal in the 1820s and 1840s – gave Catholics for the first time a single political identity. The changing rural economy, the Famine and emigration simplified the class structure and moderated division. The Catholic church reorganised itself locally and achieved much greater cohesion nationally; the Devotional Revolution and near universal

---

[48] For a description of one very influential regional group, see Kevin Whelan, 'Catholic mobilisation, 1750–1850', in Centre de Recherches Historiques, ed., *Culture et Pratiques Politiques en France et en Irlande, XVIe–XVIIIe Siècle*, Paris, Centre de Recherches Historiques, 1991.

Sunday mass attendance from the 1860s gave Catholics a new religious unity and discipline. The national school system and spread of the English language forged a new cultural and linguistic unity. The Catholic middle class was expanding, producers and consumers of a burgeoning Catholic and/or nationalist literature in newspapers, periodicals and books.[49]

By the late nineteenth century the structural preconditions existed for the emergence of just two communities, one Protestant, one Catholic. All that was needed was a catalyst. It came from the convergence of interests and opinions on both sides into radically conflicting views of the union – Catholics in opposition to it, Protestants in support. The small minorities of Catholic unionists and Protestant nationalists dwindled to insignificance. The struggle for and against the union completed the process of welding Catholics and Protestants into two separate and opposing communal blocs. Intra-community differences of a religious, political or class nature did not disappear. Unionism was divided between north and south and Protestants were divided theologically along denominational and liberal-fundamentalist lines. Catholics were united religiously but politically more divided. Class was a potent source of division within both blocs. Local and regional identities, organisations and rivalries also persisted. But overall the level of intracommunal solidarity and intercommunal division was very high.

The roots of this tendency toward communal polarisation do not reside simply in the presence of difference in the society, or even in the fact that these differences overlapped. The tendency comes rather from the system of relationships as a whole. The existence of overlapping socio-cultural and ideological differences provided the distinctions on which a structure of dominance, dependence and inequality was built. This structure in turn generated the interests and alliances which – when wider social and cultural conditions permitted – made for an ever sharper communal division. The process was self-reinforcing. Communal division further intensified the sense of socio-cultural and ideological difference and the interests on which the structure of dominance rested, generating further tendencies toward communal division.

The three levels of the system of relationships interlocked and it had

---

[49] Garvin, *Evolution of Irish Nationalist Politics*; Tom Garvin, *Nationalist Revolutionaries in Ireland 1858–1928*, Oxford, Clarendon Press, 1987; Samuel Clark, *Social Origins of the Land War*, Princeton, Princeton University Press, 1979; Desmond Keenan, *The Catholic Church in Nineteenth-Century Ireland: A Sociological Survey*, Dublin, Gill and Macmillan, 1983; Barbara Hayley, 'A reading and a thinking nation: periodicals as the voice of nineteenth-century Ireland', in B. Hayley and E. McKay, eds., *Three Hundred Years of Irish Periodicals*, Mullingar, Lilliput Press, 1987.

strong self-reproducing tendencies. But there was also pressure for change. A system resting on power – on dominance, dependence and inequality – must needs adjust when the balance of power changes. The United Irish movement of the 1790s sought to harness the growing strength of the middle and lower classes across the denominations to mount a direct challenge to that system. The rebellion failed and it left as its legacy an intensified sectarianism and the Act of Union. Subsequent challenges came predominantly from one community – Catholics – and were made possible by a Catholic recovery of power.

The Catholic recovery

The Catholic recovery was simultaneously economic, political and cultural. The conditions for economic recovery lay in the range of new middle level positions which began to emerge as the economy developed. Catholics in the early eighteenth century were in the main poor either because of the displacements and dislocations of the seventeenth century or because they were from strata that had always been so. But not all were impoverished. Some Catholic gentry retained their lands; others survived as a lease-holding subgentry class often on the lands they had originally owned. More important for the long term, Catholics were prominent in the class of strong farmers emerging in the eighteenth century out of the previously undifferentiated peasantry.[50] This class would survive the fragmentation and immiseration that took place among fellow Catholics at the lower levels of the rural class structure in the early nineteenth century; indeed the destruction of the cottier and labouring class by famine and emigration in the nineteenth century would enable them further to consolidate.

The Catholic recovery in other sectors of the economy was less impressive. According to Dickson, 'The *relative* importance of catholic merchants probably increased during the decades of rapid economic growth after 1747, but even by 1775 less than a third of Dublin's whole-sale merchants were catholic, less than a quarter of Cork's.'[51] Banking in eighteenth-century Ireland was largely a Protestant affair, and despite Catholic inroads remained so in the nineteenth century.[52] Catholic involvement in the retailing sector increased rapidly in the nineteenth century, although again much more at the lower than higher levels.

[50] L. Cullen, 'Catholic social classes under the penal laws', in Power and Whelan, eds., *Endurance and Emergence*.
[51] David Dickson, *New Foundations: Ireland 1660–1800*, Dublin, Helicon, 1987, p. 121, emphasis in original.
[52] Dickson, 'Catholics and trade'.

Catholics had some success in the proto-industrial sectors in the eighteenth century although they were almost completely absent from the most dynamic sector of all, the Ulster linen industry. They also appear to have fared relatively badly in the restructuring (and by northern standards, decline) of the south's industrial economy in the nineteenth century. At the end of the century Catholics in the two major cities – Dublin and Belfast – were underrepresented in the skilled working class, massively overrepresented in the unskilled.[53] Similarly, while Catholics were present in the major professions they were still seriously underrepresented there, as they were in the clerical grades.[54]

Catholics began the eighteenth century from a position of almost complete political powerlessness; their economic base had been gravely weakened, their military capacity had been destroyed, they were totally excluded from the apparatus of state and the alliance between Protestants and the British state was secure. But from mid-eighteenth century the winds of political fortune were shifting. From the 1760s the British government adopted a more conciliatory line. Catholics had been politically quiescent for more than half a century and the Jacobite threat had now disappeared. Catholics were needed as recruits for the army and navy and a reconciled Catholic population would reduce the dangers of French invasion and provide greater political stability. An openness to the Catholic interest would also remind Protestants of their vulnerability and curb their assertiveness.[55] By the end of the century, Catholic influence was such that the union could not have been considered without their tacit consent.[56]

This period of active British concern with conciliating Catholics ended with the Act of Union; subsequent progress came from the growth in autonomous Catholic political resources and a new assertiveness. Three factors contributed to it. One was the development of a more democratic political culture which gave Catholics a new political status and influence as the majority community in Ireland. The change here was gradual. The franchise was extremely limited to begin with and was further restricted after the granting of Catholic emancipation in 1829. It was widened in 1850 and again in 1868 but did not reach a significant mass of the

[53] Hepburn, 'Work, class and religion in Belfast'; Martin Maguire, 'A socio-economic analysis of the Dublin Protestant working class, 1870–1926', *Irish Economic and Social History*, vol. 20, 1993.
[54] John Hutchinson, *The Dynamics of Cultural Nationalism: The Gaelic Revival and the Creation of the Irish Nation State*, London, Allen and Unwin, 1987, ch. 8.
[55] Bartlett, 'Origins and progress', p. 4.
[56] Thomas Bartlett, 'From Irish state to British empire: reflections on state-building in Ireland, 1690–1830', *Études Irlandaises*, vol. 20, no. 1, 1995, p. 33.

people (all householders) until 1884. Moreover popular sovereignty in the British constitutional tradition was expressed through the Crown in parliament. Irish Catholic representatives formed only a small minority in the House of Commons and had little support in the House of Lords.

The second factor was the success of Catholics in organising and exploiting the new possibilities their numbers and growing wealth gave them. The 1820s saw the first general Catholic political mobilisation in the form of the Catholic Association conceived as a mass organisation under middle class (lay and clerical) control to bring extra-parliamentary pressure to bear on the British parliament to legislate for Catholic emancipation. The tactic proved highly effective – although the issue was one on which the government had already conceded the need for change. A decade later the attempt to use the same tactic to secure something to which the British government was actively opposed – repeal of the union – was easily faced down. But later in the century this general approach – adapted to the conditions of a changed economy and society, an extended franchise and a House of Commons dominated by party politics – would be used successfully to push for home rule.[57]

The third factor was the increased Catholic involvement in the apparatus of the state. This began in the later eighteenth century. Catholics were inducted into British regiments from the 1760s for service outside Ireland, later in Ireland itself; from the 1790s they entered in large numbers into the newly formed Irish Militia, a predominantly Catholic force though with exclusively Protestant officers. Catholics became a major presence in the police from the formation of the centralised Irish Constabulary which replaced the Protestant dominated County Constabularies in 1836. They were 51 per cent of the force in 1841 and the proportion continued to rise, although they remained seriously underrepresented at the higher levels of the force.[58] Catholic participation in the judiciary and administration system was also increasing through the nineteenth century but was low until the end of the century.[59]

The third aspect of the Catholic recovery was cultural. Catholics were

---

[57] Garvin, *Evolution of Irish Nationalist Politics*.

[58] Brian Griffin, 'Religion and opportunity in the Irish police forces, 1836–1914', in R. V. Comerford, Mary Cullen, Jacqueline Hill and Colm Lennon, eds., *Religion, Conflict and Coexistence in Ireland*, Dublin, Gill and Macmillan, 1990.

[59] Lawrence McBride, *The Greening of Dublin Castle: The Transformation of Bureaucratic and Judicial Personnel in Ireland 1892–1922*, Washington, Catholic University of America Press, 1991; Colum Kenny 'The exclusion of Catholics from the legal profession in Ireland, 1537–1829', *Irish Historical Studies*, vol. 25, no. 100, 1987.

culturally divided during the eighteenth century – between the emerging new hybrid English-speaking culture and the monoglot Gaelic culture of the rural lower classes. The famine of 1846–9 dealt the latter its final death blow, but already the former was becoming the dominant culture of the Catholic population. It was a complex, multilayered and adaptable culture, but it also lacked historical depth, continuity and self-confidence. Greater self-confidence came from increased wealth, education and a sense of growing political power. Developments in Catholicism internationally also contributed. The church had survived the trauma of the French Revolution and the Napoleonic era and was now elaborating a new, more assertive and imperial vision with which Irish Catholics enthusiastically identified. Cultural nationalism reinforced this, giving Catholics a new pride in themselves as a people with an ancient and venerable civilisation. But this was a two-edged sword. By giving those of Gaelic stock a heroic image of what they had once 'been', it heightened their sense of inadequacy at what they had become.

The Catholic recovery from the mid eighteenth century was unmistakable. But it was from a very low base and its progress was slow and socially and spatially uneven. The Anglican aristocracy and gentry remained a powerful force until the very end of the nineteenth century. Their eclipse then was very rapid but the erosion of Protestant power was less apparent at other social levels. Proportionate to their numbers in the total population Protestants were still overrepresented in the higher economic, social and educational strata and controlled key positions in government, finance, industry, the army and Royal Irish Constabulary. East Ulster, particularly the Belfast region, was also developing as a centre of concentrated Protestant power. From the eighteenth century it had been by far the most dynamic region of Ireland. In the nineteenth century large-scale industrialisation in the north-east and the extraordinary growth of Belfast – eclipsing Dublin in population size in 1901 – widened the economic gap still more between east Ulster and the rest of Ireland. Ulster Protestants were growing in wealth and self-confidence and in political influence in London. They had a solid demographic base from which to elect MPs to parliament and on which later to build a military capacity; their economic achievement provided further evidence for their claim to be the dynamic and progressive community on the island.[60]

From the time the Catholic recovery became apparent the question facing the British government and Protestants was how and to what

---

[60] D. George Boyce, *Ireland 1828–1923: From Ascendancy to Democracy*, Oxford, Blackwell, 1992, p. 75.

purpose they would use their growing power. The British government was concerned to secure a stable, peaceful and loyal Ireland and it was increasingly clear that Catholic consent and loyalty were necessary for that – this meant reform and integrating Catholics into the political system. Protestants, concerned primarily about their own security, privileges and civil and religious liberties, reacted with alarm. The dilemma both faced was that integrating Catholics into the prevailing order might also give them the power to overturn it.[61] The dilemma was made all the greater by the complex dynamics of loyalty in Ireland and the conditional nature of the loyalty of both communities.

Loyalty, disloyalty and loyalism

The British government's support for the Protestant interest in Ireland in the seventeenth century and later was based on the presumption of Irish Protestant loyalty and Irish Catholic disloyalty. The presumption was justified by events, but the dynamics of Irish loyalty and disloyalty were more complex than this suggests. Loyalty may be defined as allegiance to a ruling political authority and acceptance of its legitimacy. But there is also loyal*ism* – the proffering of loyalty subject to certain conditions being met. Loyalism is typically associated with Protestants, but Catholics also were loyalist.[62]

The first Irish loyalists were the descendants of the Anglo-Normans of the twelfth century. Most were by culture and tradition loyal to the English Crown but loyalty was also a means of defending their position against the Gaelic-Irish. The established Old English (and increasingly the Gaelic-Irish) families of the sixteenth and early seventeenth centuries were also loyal. Bartlett points out that in the sixteenth century 'The idea that Ireland could exist on her own – both *independent of* and *separate from* England – seems to have been largely unthinkable,' and Canny has noted 'the surprising extent to which the Irish population generally had by 1641 come to see themselves as loyal subjects of the English monarch'.[63] But

---

[61] For an overview, see Boyce, *ibid.*

[62] The classic discussion of Protestant loyalism is David Miller, *Queen's Rebels: Ulster Loyalism in Historical Perspective*, Dublin, Gill and Macmillan, 1978.

[63] Thomas Bartlett 'The burden of the present: Theobald Wolfe Tone, republican and separatist', in Dickson, Keogh and Whelan, eds., *The United Irishmen*, p. 8; Nicholas Canny 'In defence of the constitution? The nature of Irish revolt in the seventeenth century', in Centre de Recherches Historiques, ed., *Culture et Pratiques Politiques*, p. 29; see also Breandán Ó Buachalla, 'James our true king: the ideology of Irish royalism in the seventeenth century', in D. George Boyce, Robert Eccleshall and Vincent Geoghegan, eds., *Political Thought in Ireland since the Seventeenth Century*, London, Routledge, 1993.

there was a strategic element here as well – loyalty was offered to secure their position against family collaterals and to defend themselves against Protestant New English claims to be the only truly loyal section of the population.

The Catholic rebellion of 1641 and its sequel illustrate Catholics' complex blend of loyalty and loyalism. They rebelled, but in support of the Crown against parliament and out of fear of the latter's intentions towards them.[64] Defeat and displacement did not end Catholic loyalty or loyalism. In the aftermath of the Williamite victory, they remained loyal to the Stuart succession both because they believed the Stuarts to be their legitimate sovereigns and saw in their restoration their last remaining hope of recovering their estates. The final collapse of Jacobitism opened the way to an acceptance of the legitimacy of the Hanoverian succession, and it became possible to accompany pressures for political reform with genuine declarations of loyalty.

Such declarations were commonplace during the nineteenth century particularly when reforms were being sought. O'Connell combined them with pressure for repeal in the 1840s; the Irish Parliamentary Party combined pressure for home rule with affirmations of its compatibility with loyalty to the Crown and empire. The last great expression of Catholic Irish loyalty – Redmond's encouragement of the Irish Volunteers to join the British army in 1914 – was given in the context of the imminent granting of home rule. However within five years the majority of Catholics had committed themselves unambiguously and irrevocably to full separation.

The breakdown of Catholic loyalty at a time when British policies toward Ireland – more particularly towards Irish Catholics – were becoming more benign is sometimes attributed to an ideological development – the rise of nationalism which relocated political identity and allegiance in the nation and demanded for it a separate state. But the United Kingdom was (in theory at least) a multinational state and commitment to the Irish nation did not of necessity rule out membership of it. Other, more specific, factors were at work. One was the incompatibility of Catholic and Protestant loyalism – the fact that each offered loyalty but on conditions that were mutually exclusive. Protestants sought to ensure their security and (in their view, well deserved) privileges by retaining control in Ireland; Catholics sought the rights they believed they possessed as the native and majority community. From a British point of view, tradition and strategy dictated that the Protestant

---

[64] Canny, 'In defence of the constitution'.

interest be protected while cautiously making concessions to Catholics. Concessions were made but slowly and only after concerted Catholic pressure; the result, far from nurturing Catholic loyalty, was to undermine it.

The second factor eroding Catholic loyalty was the fate of the Irish economy under the union. Union was widely expected to bring an inflow of capital and enterprise to develop the economy. In the event only the north-east benefited significantly and industrialised along metropolitan British lines. Elsewhere there were acute crises of adjustment, including three years of devastating famine at mid-century to which the British government had responded with at best a half-hearted relief effort. Industrialisation was limited, there was large scale emigration and the population of the island as a whole declined steadily from the 1840s onwards. The reasons for this spatial unevenness are complex and appear to have roots in the longer term evolution of social and economic structures in Ireland. The union may not have been the cause of Ireland's economic problems, but outside the north-east it had brought few of the economic benefits promised.[65] There were *prima facie* grounds for believing that a native government could do better.

The third factor making Irish Catholics separatist was cultural – the existence of a British Isles-wide ethno-cultural hierarchy which placed the Catholic Irish on the lowest rung. We consider the contribution of this to Catholic separatism in the next section.

Cultural representations and power

There is a long history of hostile English discourse about Ireland and the Irish. It has its roots in the medieval period but it was renewed in the sixteenth and seventeenth centuries at a time when recognisably modern notions of England and Englishness were crystallising. Its point of departure is Irish 'difference' – not simply from the English but from other European peoples – and Ireland as a place where the normal conventions and rules do not apply. The images have not always been hostile – the Irish were often described as friendly, hospitable, good humoured, brave soldiers, talented in the arts, good musicians; but harsher images have been more frequent – the Irish are a savage people, emotionally volatile, troublesome, obsessed with the past and with ancient quarrels, violent, disloyal and treacherous, culturally backward, dirty, in thrall to despotic leaders whether secular or religious, irrational,

---

[65] See Cormac Ó Gráda, *A New Economic History of Ireland*, Oxford, Clarendon Press, 1994, pp. 306–13.

stupid, comical.[66] Implicit, at times explicit, in such judgements is the English self-image as intelligent, moderate, practical, rational, a progressive and industrious people, law makers and forgers of empire.[67]

English images of the Irish referred initially and most of all to the Gaelic-Irish and later to the Catholic Irish. Attitudes to the descendants of English settlers in Ireland, whether late medieval or early modern, were more ambiguous. If they remained true to their cultural roots little separated them from the English themselves; on the other hand it was assumed that the settlers would assimilate to the native culture to some degree making the stereotype of the native applicable also to them. Thus the Old English came to be viewed as having undergone a process of 'degeneration' as a result of contact with the Gaelic-Irish; and Irish Protestants, once in Ireland, were thought to have abandoned the moderation, fairmindedness and industriousness of their English heritage to become extreme in their political and religious views, excessively harsh in their dealings with the native population and – in the case of the landlord class – indifferent to the material progress of Ireland.[68]

Like their medieval antecedents, Irish Protestants deeply resented such views which they attributed either to ignorance or – more worrying – to rationalisations for policies that would serve English interests at their expense. In their minds they had retained the qualities of their ancestors – they were religiously enlightened, rational, law-abiding, hardworking, loyal, true to their word, valuing cleanliness, sobriety, virtue, progress – in short the civilised and civilising strand within the Irish mosaic. Their view of the Gaelic-Irish, and later Irish Catholics, tended towards the darker English view: as savage, seditious, superstitious, backward, resistant to progress and the rule of law, lacking in principle and untrustworthy.[69]

---

[66] For the medieval period, see F. X. Martin, 'The image of the Irish – medieval and modern – continuity and change', in Richard Wall, ed., *Medieval and Modern Ireland*, Totowa, Barnes and Noble, 1988; on later English images of the Irish, see Hadfield and McVeagh, *Strangers to that Land*; Bradshaw, Hadfield and Maley, *Representing Ireland*; Joseph Th. Leersen, *Mere Irish and Fior-Ghael: Studies in the Idea of Irish Nationality, its Development and Literary Expression prior to the Nineteenth Century*, Amsterdam, John Benjamins, 1986; D. Hayton 'From barbarian to burlesque: English images of the Irish c. 1660–1750', *Irish Economic and Social History*, vol. 15, 1988.

[67] On the origins of English identity, see Liah Greenwood, *Nationalism: Five Roads to Modernity*, Cambridge, Mass. Harvard University Press, 1992, ch. 1.

[68] On English attitudes to different strands within Irish Protestantism in the nineteenth century, see Ned Lebow, 'British images of poverty in pre-Famine Ireland', in Daniel J. Casey and Robert E. Rhodes, eds., *Views of the Irish Peasantry 1800–1916*, Connecticut, Archon Books, 1977.

[69] See, for example, eighteenth-century Protestant sermons as discussed in Robert Eccleshall, 'Anglican political thought in the century after the Revolution of 1688', in Boyce, Eccleshall and Geoghegan, eds., *Political Thought in Ireland*.

Catholics had their own tradition of hostile representation. For the Gaelic-Irish, the descendants of the Anglo-Normans remained foreigners despite the passing of generations and there is a recurring perception of them as arrogant, domineering, deceitful and treacherous;[70] similar attitudes greeted the New English. Old English attitudes to the New English were determined primarily by religion and became increasingly hostile as the counter-reformation gained pace. Both strands – ethnic and religious – coalesced in the early seventeenth century to produce an assertive Catholic proto-nationalism first among the elites, then among the wider population, developing in time into a 'diffuse, anti-Protestant and anti-English popular nationalism'.[71] By the end of the nineteenth century anti-Englishness and anti-Britishness had become intense.[72]

Communal cultural representations on all sides therefore were pervaded by mutual hostility. But there was one major difference. Historically it was the Protestants, not the Catholics, who had won and who with British support now occupied the positions of wealth and power in the society; it was their norms, and those of the British state, which defined the terms of discourse and interaction in the public domain. Catholics might resent this but they could not easily challenge it. Their weaker economic and political position placed them at a disadvantage, and their own (internalised) hybrid culture was based in part on those norms.

Catholic powerlessness in the face of denigratory Protestant and English discourses played a potent role in reproducing internal division in Ireland and in contributing to the rise of popular cultural nationalism in the nineteenth century. Significantly it coincided with a new set of English cultural discourses about Ireland; some were positive, most were negative.[73] Cultural nationalists, Catholic and Protestant, responded by rejecting English culture and its civilising claims and elaborated their alternative vision of Ireland, its glorious past and unlimited future potential. But such claims could make little impact on an ethno-cultural

---

[70] James Lydon, 'The middle nation', in James Lydon, ed., *The English in Medieval Ireland*, Dublin, Royal Irish Academy, 1984.

[71] Garvin, *Evolution of Irish Nationalist Politics*, p. 16. For the early seventeenth century, see Bernadette Cunningham, 'Seventeenth century interpretations of the past: the case of Geoffrey Keating', *Irish Historical Studies*, vol. 25, no. 98, 1986, and 'The culture and ideology of Irish Franciscan historians at Louvain, 1607–1650', in Ciaran Brady, ed., *Ideology and the Historians*, Dublin, Lilliput Press, 1991.

[72] Garvin, *Nationalist Revolutionaries*.

[73] See Lebow, 'British images of poverty in pre-Famine Ireland'; Patrick Sims-Williams, 'The visionary Celt: the construction of an ethnic preconception', *Cambridge Medieval Celtic Studies*, vol. 2, 1986; Curtis, *Apes and Angels*.

hierarchy rooted in relations of economic and political power, which divided Catholic and Protestant in Ireland. For Catholic nationalists – more than Protestant nationalists – the answer was to be found in separation.

The balance of coercive power

The balance of coercive power between the British state and Irish Protestants on the one hand and Irish Catholics on the other played a crucial role in determining the social and political order that emerged out of the seventeenth century. The two great military contests between Irish Catholics and Protestants in the seventeenth century – during the 1640s and 1689–91 – ended in the total defeat of the Catholics; the victors were able unilaterally to determine the shape of the new order. The destruction of the Catholic military capacity was permanent and they were never again to mount a military challenge on such a scale.

The quiesence of eighteenth-century Catholics reflected their political and military weakness rather than any deep acceptance of the legitimacy of the new order. At the end of the century radical Catholic political and religious discontent found an outlet in the revolutionary United Irishmen and the agrarian, sectarian and proto-nationalist Defender movement. The rebellion of 1798 gave birth in turn to a largely Catholic tradition of conspiratorial insurrectionism that continued down to 1916. Insurrection was more an idea than a practice and was condemned by the church and moderate opinion; but it played an important symbolic role in reinforcing Catholic belief in the illegitimacy of the existing order and the possibility of an alternative.

The insurrectionary tradition also overlapped in personnel if not in ideology with a quite different form of Catholic violence – one which sought to achieve its largely agrarian and/or sectarian goals by quite different methods – threats, intimidation, destruction of property, assassination. Constitutional politicians concerned with wider issues typically condemned such practices, but also used them to conjure up the violence that might be unleashed if their political demands were not met. O'Connell strengthened his campaign for Catholic emancipation in this way; Parnell did the same to place land reform and home rule on the political agenda.[74] Eventually threat became action when in 1919–21

---

[74] L. Perry Curtis, 'Moral and physical force: the language of violence in Irish nationalism', *Journal of British Studies*, vol. 27, no. 2, 1988; Garvin, *Evolution of Irish Nationalist Politics*.

nationalists used or endorsed these methods in the struggle to achieve independence.

Reliance on this form of violence reflected continuing Catholic weakness in conventional military warfare; indeed even their capacity for guerrilla violence was limited. The targets of the Irish Republican Army (IRA) in 1919–21 were 'soft' – the RIC, off-duty army officers, civilians – and in the months before the truce Michael Collins's estimation of its ability to continue was pessimistic. Its achievements are also open to question. It is striking that the partition settlement secured for the Irish Free State only those parts of the country in which Catholics were overwhelmingly the dominant community. The highest percentage of Protestants in any county included in the Irish Free State was Monaghan with 24.7 per cent; Tyrone with 56 per cent of Catholics was included in Northern Ireland. By implication the effectiveness of Catholic coercive power depended ultimately on the strength of their position in civil society. Alternatively viewed, violence simply gave a 'final push' to bring political institutions into line with an existing dominance in the civil sphere. At the same time, the acquisition by Catholics of the means of guerrilla violence was an important development which further strengthened their political position.

The military capacity of Ulster Protestants was, however, more impressive. Ulster Protestants had their own traditions of threat, intimidation, destruction of property, assassination developed in the course of agrarian and sectarian struggle. But when they mobilised to resist home rule in 1912 they formed a conventional military force – the Ulster Volunteers – to fight a territorial war. Catholics responded with the Irish Volunteers, but there was a marked difference in the military effectiveness of the two forces. The superior Protestant capacity was due to several factors: their long tradition of communal self-defence, their closer identification with the state and with the techniques, modes of organisation and ethos of British militarism, the strength of the social bonds and institutions (in particular the Orange Order) linking the different strata of Protestant society, their determination to defend their Ulster homeland against the nationalist threat.

Crisis and partition

The conflict of nationalism and unionism in the late nineteenth and early twentieth centuries and its outcome – partition – is one of the great crises of Irish development. A variety of explanations of the crisis – many of them single factor – have been advanced, ranging from the uneven development of capitalism in nineteenth century Ireland to supremacist tendencies within Catholic nationalism or Ulster unionism. A more comprehensive explanation is necessary; we relate it to the unfolding dynamic of the historic system of relationships we have described.

Ireland's mode of integration into the English/British state in the sixteenth and seventeenth centuries produced a system of relationships which ensured British control over Ireland, privileged Protestants and subordinated and marginalised Catholics. As soon as wider structural transformations permitted a Catholic recovery, Catholics demanded change. Threatened by the immediate and long-term implications of this, Protestants resisted. The British government sought to conciliate Catholics as a means of securing their loyalty, but it was mindful of the concerns of Protestants and uncertain about long term Catholic intentions. Change would be slow and only in response to persistent Catholic pressure. The slow pace of political reform, the uneven development of the economy and persistent feeling of cultural oppression among Catholics undermined an (at best) ambivalent Catholic loyalty and increased the appeal of separatist nationalism.

The resulting conflict between Catholic separatist nationalism and Protestant unionism was no mere clash of short-term political or cultural ideologies. The Catholic demand for home rule was in essence a challenge to the system of relationships which had been laid down in the seventeenth century, more particularly to the structure of dominance, dependence and inequality. Home rule would have reversed the historic relationship between Protestants and Catholics, making Catholics the dominant community in Ireland and, inevitably, privileging their relationship to the British state over that of Protestants. To what degree Catholics would have sought to subordinate Protestants in a home rule Ireland cannot be known, but they would have had the capacity to do so. Over most of Ireland, Protestants had no choice but to accept the logic of Catholic numbers, but the strong and well-resourced Protestants of east Ulster were able to resist; they also had the sympathy and support of important elements of the British ruling class. Faced with the prospect of civil war, the British government, unionists and the majority of southern nationalists adopted what appeared to be the simplest and least costly solution – partition.

In this sense partition was an attempt to accommodate, rather than to transcend or resolve, the historic conflicts on the island. In the chapters that follow we trace the consequences of this politics of accommodation.

3   The reconstruction of communal division

The nineteenth century saw the emergence of two culturally and politically polarised communities in Ireland. Partition created new conditions for community formation, identity and solidarity, but deep communal polarisation has persisted. In this chapter we look at the dynamics of community formation in the post-partition period, describe community structure in Northern Ireland today and explore some of the ways in which that structure contributes to continuing communal polarisation.

The reconstruction of community, 1920s–1960s

Protestants

Protestants formed an island-wide community at the start of the twentieth century, sharing wider political goals and loyalties and bound by religious, cultural and social ties. The community was internally differentiated religiously and in class and regional terms. Ulster Protestants saw themselves and were recognised as different from Protestants in the other three provinces because of the strength of the Scottish and Presbyterian influence, their demographic majority, their participation in the industrial revolution and the presence of a stronger religious fundamentalism. From 1905, with the formation of the Ulster Unionist Council, their political strategy, organisation and proximate aims diverged from those of the Irish Unionists.[1] Within Ulster itself, internal Protestant religious and class divisions were strong and Protestant settlement had a marked core–periphery form. East Ulster, with Belfast as its centre, had long been the core of Ulster Protestant economic and political life and culture, the area of densest Protestant population and closest links to Scotland and England. The farther one

---

[1] Alvin Jackson, *The Ulster Party: Irish Unionists in the House of Commons 1884–1911*, Oxford, Clarendon, 1989, pp. 5ff. and ch. 7.

moved from the eastern core, the weaker and more fragmented Ulster Protestants became. At the periphery, Protestant Ulster extended into the wider Irish Protestant community centred on Dublin.

The formation of Northern Ireland based on six of the nine counties of historic Ulster cut off the outer periphery of Ulster Protestants from the core and, to an even greater degree, weakened the links between Northern Irish Protestants and Protestants outside Ulster. An institutionally and imaginatively cohesive Northern Protestant community crystallised. The Northern Ireland state became the main focus of communal identification and its policies helped sustain Northern Protestant communal solidarity (chapters 5, 6, 7). Their identity was given a stronger British focus by the experience of the Second World War, when Northern Ireland's participation in the British war effort contrasted with the South's neutrality, and by the post-war integration of Northern Ireland into the British welfare state. Meanwhile, Protestants in the rest of Ireland struggled to maintain their cultural distinctiveness and communal solidarity in a state whose cultural and political ideals were at marked variance with their own (chapter 9).

Northern Protestant guilt or regret at the sundering of the Ulster or island-wide Protestant community was tempered by awareness that only thus could their economic and religious interests be protected. Their greatest concern was with Protestants in the three excluded Ulster counties, many of whom subsequently migrated or married across the border. They were less concerned about Protestants in the other three provinces. Unionist legitimations of partition had emphasised the deep historical and cultural divisions between North and South, implicitly denying the island-wide context of past Protestant identification. Identification weakened further as the British identity of Northern Protestants strengthened and that of Southern Protestants faded; the harsh cultural and class stereotypes which Northern and Southern Protestants already held of the other became more prominent. At the same time religious, educational and kin contacts continued to link all Protestants on the island. On both sides of the border there was a sense of separation and loss. But Northern Protestants nostalgic for a past unity thought in terms of an Ireland within the United Kingdom, not reunification – or even close contact – with the new Catholic, nationalist and re-Gaelicising state emerging in the South.

The uneven nature of the change was reflected at the level of culture and politics. Northern Protestants became more determinedly British in identity and unionist in politics. Protestants in the three counties of Ulster incorporated into the South identified culturally with Northern Protestants and to a considerable degree with their politics.[2] Protestants elsewhere remained conscious of their difference from the majority Catholic community but slowly abandoned their British identity and unionist politics (chapter 9).[3] The Irish Protestant community, whose unity had always been fragile, had now clearly fragmented into three parts: a strong and cohesive Northern Protestant community orientated towards Britain, a fragment Ulster Protestant community located in the three excluded Ulster counties orientated at once towards North and South, and a small and widely dispersed Southern Protestant community in the other three provinces committed to working within an Irish context.

Catholics

Irish Catholics before partition were, at the level of the island as whole, a much more cohesive community than were Irish Protestants. The Irish Catholic church in the late nineteenth century had centralised its organisation, standardised its rites and asserted a strong ideological control over its members. Cultural and political nationalism integrated virtually all Catholics into a single national community. Ulster had a distinct regional identity for Catholics – it was the most Gaelic of the provinces at the time of the conquest and had suffered most from plantation. But it shared a common religious, political and cultural heritage with the rest of the island. Regional differences continued, as much within the North as between North and South, but they were of degree and situation not of kind.[4] The trauma of partition for Northern Catholics lay in the fracturing of this perceived unity and their exclusion from the wider Irish community.

The Catholics incorporated into Northern Ireland lacked even the coherence of the historic regional province. They were simply the Catholics resident in the territory which Northern Protestants had marked out as their own – a geographical category rather than a community, produced by the Ulster Protestant drive for self-determination rather than by any will or intention of their own. They were politically divided – Belfast and border Catholics differed in political strategies and proximate aims – but each of the strands of Northern Catholic politics

---

[2] Kurt Bowen, *Protestants in a Catholic State: Ireland's Privileged Minority*, Dublin, Gill and Macmillan, 1983, p. 68; E. E. Davis and Richard Sinnott, *Attitudes in the Republic of Ireland Relevant to the Northern Ireland Problem*, Dublin, Economic and Social Research Institute, 1979, p. 49, table 12.

[3] Bowen, *Protestants in a Catholic State*, pp. 66–70.

[4] Eamon Phoenix, *Northern Nationalism: Nationalist Politics, Partition and the Catholic Minority in Northern Ireland 1890–1940*, Belfast, Ulster Historical Foundation, 1994.

situated itself within the island-wide Irish nationalist tradition.[5] Northern Catholics would become a community, but slowly, painfully and ambivalently, with their communal organisation and identity always reaching out to the island as a whole.

At partition, Northern Catholics were internally divided by class, political ideology and region. They lacked any geographical centre of identity: Belfast was on all counts a Protestant city; Catholics were a demographic majority in Derry but economically and politically marginal. Northern Catholics had limited experience of independent political or ideological action; their participation in national politics and in the Gaelic revival had been as part of a wider island movement the initiative for which had come from elsewhere. To take independent action now was to accept and extend the separateness which they sought to counter. They responded to their new situation in different ways. Those with particular interests – Belfast businessmen with economic concerns and religious leaders concerned to safeguard their educational interests – sought to reach some kind of accomodation with the state, however uneasy. Political leaders had more difficulty in developing an agreed strategy; only by 1926 did they try to create a unified political organisation, and then with limited success.[6] Viewed as a whole, the Catholic population kept a resentful distance from the state and became 'a society within a society'.

The development of a cohesive Northern Catholic community was a slow process, in part because of internal divisions, in part because of an unwillingness to acknowledge the division of the island. However the conditions for communal development improved as economic and social linkages within Northern Ireland became more dense and the experience of Northern and Southern Catholics diverged.[7] At the same time, an island-wide identity was not abandoned and the final phase in the formation of a cohesive community – the political and cultural mobilisation of the late 1960s and early 1970s – was accompanied by a reaffirmation of the unity of the island-wide nationalist community. The crisis that followed forced Southerners to confront the island-wide context of nationalist politics and to rebuild – with difficulty (chapter 9) – their relationship with Northern Catholics.

---

[5] *Ibid.*, chs. 1–4, 7.
[6] *Ibid.*, ch. 9.
[7] For discussions of the Northern Catholic community in the Stormont years, see Bob Purdie, *Politics in the Streets: The Origins of the Civil Rights Movement in Northern Ireland*, Belfast, Blackstaff, 1990, chs. 1 and 2; Desmond Fennell, *The Northern Catholic: An Inquiry*, an extended version of a series of articles published in the *Irish Times*, 5–10 May 1958, Dublin, Mount Salus Press, n.d.

Partition was not the trauma for Southern Catholics that it was for their Northern counterparts, but it was far from inconsequential.[8] Partition violated the nationalist belief in the fundamental unity of Ireland; De Valera's dictum that 'Ireland can be Ireland without the North' was one side of the coin, of which the other was a sense of a divided and diminished national community. Northern Catholic reproaches and pressures to take action on their behalf were resisted, but their ill-treatment at the hands of Northern Protestants was for Southerners a painful reminder of their own past and their current powerlessness. But partition also brought some benefits, giving Southern nationalists the possibility of building a new state and nation as they saw fit, unencumbered by the objections and opposition of a sizeable Protestant and unionist minority.

From early on, two distinct tendencies coexisted in the South. One was towards the emergence of a distinct Southern community (predominantly although in later years not exclusively Catholic) developing around the new institutions of state, the new economic, social and educational networks and the new media whose concerns centred primarily on the affairs of the South. The other was towards the preservation of the historic island-wide national community together with a commitment to restore the unity of the island. The island-wide community lacked a state, but it was institutionally and symbolically embodied in a variety of non-state organisations – in particular, the Catholic church and Gaelic-Irish cultural and sporting organisations – and in such political provisions as Articles 2 and 3 of the 1937 Constitution and the automatic extension of Irish citizenship rights to Northerners.

The sense of the historic island-wide community became more abstract over time, the difficulties of mutual understanding increased, and there was at times resentment on both sides of the border at the obligations it entailed. But the community did not fragment to the degree that the Irish Protestant community had, still less disappear. The more nationalist denied that partition had had any effect; those who recognised that differences had emerged insisted that an underlying unity remained. For Northern Catholics in particular, the building of a separate community was always ambivalent, conditional and strategic.

---

[8] For some it appeared to be; see Clare O'Halloran, *Partition and the Limits of Irish Nationalism: An Ideology Under Stress*, Dublin, Gill and Macmillan, 1987, pp. 20–9 and ch. 3.

Community structure in Northern Ireland today

The two communities in Northern Ireland have changed considerably in recent decades in response to economic and political restructuring (chapters 5–7). Each community is internally differentiated in respect of religion, politics and culture; class divisions have become more overt; there is a desire for looser communal bonds typical of the late twentieth century and greater resistance to pressures to conform to communal norms. Nonetheless intracommunal solidarity and intercommunal division remain strong. In the next sections we explore the differences within the communities and show how, despite difference, solidarity is maintained.

The Northern Protestant community

Divisions within the Protestant community were deep even in the Stormont period: they have intensified in the recent period and are now politically more focused. The Protestant community, however, continues to construct its unity out of division and remains a central point of identification for those who otherwise differ radically in their political views and cultural attitudes.

Religious differences. Religious diversity is part of the tradition of the Protestant community.[9] In 1991, Presbyterians formed 42 per cent of the Protestant population, Church of Ireland 35 per cent, Methodists 7.5 per cent – in each case a slight decrease since 1971 – with smaller sects proliferating and gaining more adherents.[10] Each of the main denominations is itself internally divided between fundamentalists, liberals and an intermediate group of 'liberal-conservatives'.[11] Fundamentalists form a relatively cohesive sub-body within Protestantism, integrated by a variety of practices from summer evangelical witnesses to weekly prayer and bible meetings. The other Protestant groups are less cohesive. Many are not regular church goers; less than half attend weekly services and a steadily increasing 15 per cent never go to church.[12]

---

[9] Fred Boal, John A. Campbell and David Livingstone, 'The Protestant mosaic: a majority of minorities', in Patrick J. Roche and Brian Barton, eds., *The Northern Ireland Question: Myth and Reality*, Aldershot, Avebury, 1991; Terence Brown, *The Whole Protestant Community*, Field Day pamphlet no. 7, Derry, Field Day, 1985.

[10] 1991 Census; John Whyte, *Interpreting Northern Ireland*, Oxford, Clarendon, 1990, pp. 28–9.

[11] Boal, Campbell and Livingstone, 'The Protestant mosaic', pp. 106–9.

[12] John Curtice and Anthony Gallagher, 'The Northern Ireland dimension', in R. Jowell, S. Witherspoon, L. Brook with B. Taylor, eds., *British Social Attitudes: The 7th Report*, Aldershot, Gower, 1990, p. 187.

Theologically, little is common to all Protestants except some shared reference points in reformation theology, history and dogma. This gives at most a bare and partial common language which – outside of conflict with Catholics – does not overcome organisationally based divisions.

Political differences. Politically, Protestants remain united in their broad aims – to retain the union and prevent its erosion – although differing in reasons, motives, strategies and means adopted. In one recent survey, 71 per cent of Protestants identified themselves as unionists, and most of the rest support the union.[13] The proportion supporting a united Ireland is tiny; it has stayed between 1–3 per cent in most surveys since the outbreak of the troubles.[14] A larger, and recently increasing, proportion favours an independent Ulster.[15] There appears to be relatively little gender differentiation in political attitudes or preferences.[16]

Protestants differ in their reasons for valuing the union. Some do so because they feel a deep sense of loyalty and affinity with the British world or fellow British subjects, others because of a commitment to what Arthur Aughey has called the 'idea of the Union'.[17] Others value particular British institutions or traditions – the respect for individual rights, the welfare state, the labourist tradition – or the British economic subvention. For still others the union serves a purely defensive function – it is a defence of Protestant interests against Roman Catholicism and a united Ireland.[18] For many, there is a strong conditional quality to their support; if the benefits ceased, loyalty would no longer be assured. Some unionists see themselves forced into a conditional stance by British

---

[13] *Ibid.*, pp. 193–4, 204; *Irish Political Studies*, 9, 1994, data section, pp. 225, 228.

[14] Curtice and Gallagher, 'Northern Ireland dimension', p. 204; Brendan O'Leary, 'Public opinion and Northern Irish futures', *The Political Quarterly*, vol. 63, no. 2, 1992, p. 152; *Irish Political Studies*, vol. 9, 1994, data section, pp. 225, 228; David J. Smith and Gerald Chambers, *Inequality in Northern Ireland*, Oxford, Clarendon, 1991, p. 96, record a figure of 5 per cent.

[15] Coopers and Lybrand, *Poll for Ulster Television/Fortnight Magazine March 1988*, Belfast, Coopers and Lybrand, 1988, table 3a; O'Leary, 'Public opinion', p. 152; *Irish Political Studies*, vol. 9, 1994, data section, p. 228.

[16] Valerie Morgan, 'Bridging the divide: women and political and community issues', in Peter Stringer and Gillian Robinson, eds., *Social Attitudes in Northern Ireland: The Second Report*, Belfast, Blackstaff, 1992, p. 137.

[17] Arthur Aughey, *Under Siege: Ulster Unionism and the Anglo-Irish Agreement*, Belfast, Blackstaff, 1989, ch. 1.

[18] Cf. Edward Moxon-Browne, *Nation, Class and Creed in Northern Ireland*, Aldershot, Gower, 1983, p. 13.

policies: members of the Unionist Task Force of 1987, for example, favoured negotiated independence for Northern Ireland if the alternative was to be a weaker union.[19]

Protestant reasons for rejecting a united Ireland also vary. Those strongly and positively committed to the union reject it on principle because it would mean the end of the valued link with Britain. For some, however, opposition derives from the economic weakness of the Republic, its dominant Catholic ethos, its stress on Ireland's Gaelic past, its record on issues of liberal principle, individual rights and women's equality, and concern about being a minority within such a state.[20] By implication a different situation and choice would obtain if the Republic were a different sort of country. Such attitudes are usually expressed privately, but they also occur from time to time in the public statements of some unionist politicians.[21] However, feeling against unification in present circumstances (and for many in all circumstances) is intense. Veiled threats and occluded statements of intent are common. In one survey most Protestants projected violent conflict in the event of unity – there would be increased political violence, Protestants would take up arms, there would be civil war, Protestants would emigrate.[22]

Security policy is another area of Protestant political agreement, not least because of its implications for the stability of the state. The vast majority of Protestants, 85 per cent, are satisfied with the police; 80 per cent oppose the disbandment of the Ulster Defence Regiment (UDR) and its replacement, the Royal Irish Regiment (RIR); 86 per cent support the use of plastic bullets in riots; 74 per cent favour capital punishment for murder by terrorists; 60 per cent disagree that the police and army get away with offences they commit.[23] Perceptions of employment opportunities are also an area of relative Protestant

---

[19] The Task Force Report, *An End to Drift*, abridged version, 1987, p. 8.

[20] Moxon-Browne, *Nation, Class and Creed*, p. 38; Boal, Campbell and Livingstone, 'Protestant mosaic', p. 125; James H. Allister, *Irish Unification: Anathema. The Reasons why Northern Ireland Rejects Unification with the Republic of Ireland*, Belfast, Crown Publications, n.d., pp. 10–23.

[21] R. L. McCartney, *Liberty and Authority in Ireland*, Field Day Pamphlet no. 7, Derry, Field Day, 1985, pp. 25–7; Ken Maginnis, L & H debate, University College Dublin, broadcast BBC radio 4, 18 February 1990.

[22] Smith and Chambers, *Inequality in Northern Ireland*, p. 96.

[23] John D. Brewer, 'The public and the police', in Stringer and Robinson, eds., *Social Attitudes: The Second Report*, p. 61; A. M. Gallagher, 'Civil liberties and the state', in *ibid.*, p. 85; A. M. Gallagher, 'Community relations', in Peter Stringer and Gillian Robinson, eds., *Social Attitudes in Northern Ireland: The Third Report*, Belfast, Blackstaff, 1993, p. 43; Edward Moxon-Browne, 'Alienation: the case of Catholics in Northern Ireland', *Journal of Political Science*, vol. 14, nos. 1–2, 1986, p. 82.

unanimity: no more than 10 per cent think the system biased against Catholics.[24]

In other political matters, divergence is the norm. Unionists divide in party support between the Ulster Unionist Party (UUP) and the Democratic Unionist Party (DUP); in the 1993 local elections the proportion was 5:3. Six per cent of Protestants voice support in opinion polls for the Alliance Party of Northern Ireland (APNI), a proportion which, like the overall Alliance vote, has dropped significantly since the 1970s. Five percent of Protestants voice support for the Conservatives; if we assume that most Conservative voters are Protestant, about 3 per cent vote for them.[25] The most popular institutional preference within the union is integration with Britain followed by power sharing and majority rule devolution. The relative popularity has varied dramatically over the last twenty years. The lack of any clear trend suggests that variation here is strategic and situational. Finally Protestants differ in their attitudes to political violence. In Rose's 1968 study, over half of Protestants (52 per cent) were willing to endorse the use of violence to keep Northern Ireland 'Protestant', while 45 per cent were not.[26] In Moxon-Browne's 1978 study, 43.9 per cent of Protestant respondents agreed that the 'actions of Loyalist paramilitaries are a justified reaction' to events, and Moxon-Browne notes that this proportion is likely to vary with the events in question.[27]

Cultural differences. Cultural differences among Protestants are more marked than political. There is no agreement on their construction of ethnic or national identity. In the Stormont period, divisions here, rather than in political views, formed the basis of internal Protestant differentiation.[28] At least four wider cultural identities, each associated with a distinct imagined community, sense of history and family of values, exist in the Northern Protestant tradition. These identities are not mutually exclusive and nesting is common: Northern Irish identifiers

---

[24] Whyte, *Interpreting Northern Ireland*, p. 66; see R. D. Osborne, 'Discrimination and fair employment', in Peter Stringer and Gillian Robinson, eds., *Social Attitudes in Northern Ireland*, Belfast, Blackstaff, 1991, p. 33; Gallagher, 'Community relations', p. 39.

[25] Whyte, *Interpreting Northern Ireland*, p. 76; for figures of party support and voting in 1993 local elections, *Irish Political Studies*, vol. 9, 1994, pp. 199, 226.

[26] Richard Rose, *Governing without Consensus: An Irish Perspective*, London, Faber and Faber, 1971, pp. 192–3.

[27] Moxon-Browne, *Nation, Class and Creed*, p. 87.

[28] See Jennifer Todd, 'Two traditions in unionist political culture', *Irish Political Studies*, vol. 2, 1987, and Jennifer Todd, 'Unionist political thought 1920–1970', in D. G. Boyce, R. Eccleshall and V. Geoghegan, eds., *Political Thought in Ireland since the Seventeenth Century*, London, Routledge, 1993.

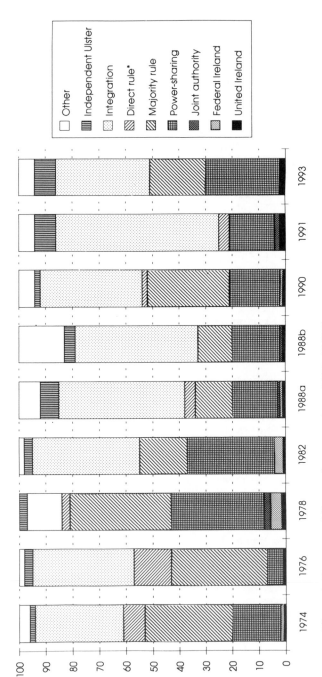

Figure 1. Protestants' first preference options, 1974–1993[29]

Table 1. *Cultural identity among Protestants*

Identity	Imagined community
I British	The British realm, British subjects or citizens
II Ulster	The Ulster Protestant people
III Northern Irish	Northern Ireland (including both its Protestant and Catholic inhabitants), understood as a region of cultural overlap between Britain and Ireland, with the Northern Irish identity opening out to Irish, British and possibly European dimensions.
IV Irish	All on the island, Protestant and Catholic

may see themselves as also British, Ulster, and/or Irish Protestant, in any permutation or combination; Ulster identifiers may see themselves as members of the 'British nation' living in Northern Ireland, and also as Irish Protestants as well as Northern Irish Protestants.[30] A British identity is usually seen as an addition to rather than a replacement of more specific Northern Irish, Ulster or Irish Protestant identities. In the recent period, however, a British identity has emerged as an alternative, rather than an addition, to the more specific identities, and even as a primary ethnic identity in its own right.[31] This remains, however, a minority position; interviews and speeches suggest that – for the most part – a British identity is seen as an enhancement of a more specific communal identity. For the vast majority of Northern Protestants, the core community is the Protestants of Ulster or Northern Ireland;[32] British is the dominant overarching identity with Irish as a possible intervening level.

It is difficult to be precise about the relative importance of each identity or to map changes over time. In surveys, two-thirds of

[29] Figure 1 shows responses in surveys and opinion polls to questions which ask respondents for their most favoured solutions. In not all of the surveys were exactly the same range of options given: for this reason, the pre-1974 surveys which typically did not distinguish between a preference for majority rule and power sharing devolution were not used. Still there are some anomalies in the post-1974 data: for example, in 1974 joint authority and in 1991 majority rule were not listed as options for respondents; after 1985, a preference for direct rule was normally interpreted to involve a continuation of the Irish input through the Anglo-Irish conference; in some surveys (1988b), respondents were asked their preferences 'over the next five years'; in most surveys there was no such explicit time-specification; see Appendix A for sources.

[30] Examples of people with such nesting identities include John Hewitt, Ian Paisley, Martin Smyth and Chris McGimpsey.

[31] Cf. Colin Coulter, 'The character of unionism', *Irish Political Studies*, vol. 9, 1994, p. 18.

[32] Only within the dissenting tradition is the boundedness of the Ulster or Northern Protestant community seriously challenged.

Protestants now identify themselves as British, a quarter as either Ulster or Northern Irish, and a small minority (3 per cent) as Irish.[33] This appears to mark a radical change from Rose's 1968 pre-Troubles survey where 39 per cent identified as British, 20 per cent as Irish and 32 per cent as Ulster.[34] However the strong British and weak (10 per cent) Ulster identifications in recent surveys do not cohere with other evidence of cultural identity. DUP rhetoric suggests that their supporters tend towards an 'Ulster' identification, as do young working class Protestants and sections of the UUP.[35] The responses may reflect practical political realities rather than a deep sense of cultural identity. For example, Rose's survey, carried out when the political motivation for a British identity was much less pressing than today, shows that half of the 39 per cent of British identifiers gave as the reason for their choice the simple fact of living 'under British rule'.[36] The difficulties of drawing firm conclusions on identity may be seen from the response of one of our interviewees to a question when asked how she perceived herself: 'I would say "Ulster" but that sounds too extreme; I won't say "Irish" for that would only please them [i.e. Catholics]; I will say "British" for that sounds neutral.'

Ideological clusters and subgroups. The internal diversity of the Protestant community is a matter of communal pride and at the level of individuals, every combination of religious, political and cultural views exists. Nonetheless, there is a certain amount of clustering of views and the clusters provide alternative bases for identity and ideology (chapter 4). There are two major clusters – 'loyalists' and 'unionists' – and two minor ones – 'bridge-builders' and 'dissenters'.

'Loyalists' tend toward fundamentalist Protestantism, conditional unionism, and an Ulster identity. They form the core of Democratic Unionist Party (DUP) voters. There is also a secular loyalist strand, numerically large but, at least until the very recent period, ideologically and politically subordinate. Measured by the core DUP vote, loyalists constitute about a quarter of the Protestant population. 'Unionists' tend towards mainstream Protestantism, a more principled unionism, and a

---

[33] Edward Moxon-Browne, 'National identity in Northern Ireland', in Stringer and Robinson, eds., *Social Attitudes in Northern Ireland*, 1991, p. 25.

[34] Rose, *Governing without Consensus*, p. 208.

[35] Jim Allister, Ivan Foster, William McCrea, Peter Robinson, *Northern Ireland: 'A war to be won'*, Belfast, DUP, 1984, p. 42; Desmond Bell, *Acts of Union: Youth Culture and Sectarianism in Northern Ireland*, London, Macmillan, 1990, p. 160; Steve Bruce, *The Edge of the Union: The Ulster Loyalist Political Vision*, Oxford, Clarendon, 1994, p. 30 suggests that increasing numbers are turning to an Ulster loyalist identity.

[36] Rose, *Governing without Consensus*, pp. 208–9.

'British' identity. They are at the core of the Ulster Unionist Party, although the UUP as a broad and diverse party is not a secure guide to the number in this cluster. 'Bridge-builders' are ecumenist on religious issues, pro-union on pragmatic grounds and also pro-power-sharing, and have a Northern Irish identity. They form the core of (Protestant) Alliance, Workers Party (WP) and Democratic Left (DL) support, and form considerably less than 10 per cent of the Protestant population. 'Dissenters' tend to identify with radical and anti-fundamentalist currents in Protestant theology, to have an Irish identity and to be open to a pluralist united Ireland established by consent. As a group they are very small and are not directly represented at the level of party politics – one outlet is the New Ireland Group.

There is a class basis to these intra-communal differences.[37] Bitter and periodically intense class conflict has long been endemic in the Protestant community; in the decades after partition, it was only partially mediated by the Unionist state.[38] Class divisions have widened in the recent period. Industrial decline has hit many working-class Protestant communities; unemployment and a sense of pressure from neighbouring Catholic areas have led many young males to turn to a street culture of loyalism.[39] Meanwhile, middle-class unionists have sought to secure their position in the changing economy and politics of direct rule and are attempting more systematically to assimilate to wider British norms.

Class divisions are also reflected at the level of party politics, although the community is not politically fractured on class lines. As Table 2 shows, the Official Unionist Party (OUP) – now the UUP – gathers support across all social classes. Support for the other major parties – DUP and Alliance – is more skewed, but support for the DUP is weak only in the professional and managerial class. The sharpest class difference appears in support for the Alliance party whose support falls off

---

[37] Ed Cairns, 'Political violence, social values and the generation gap', in Stringer and Robinson, eds., *Social Attitudes: The Second Report*, p. 153; Steve Bruce and Fiona Alderdice, 'Religious belief and behaviour', in Stringer and Robinson, eds., *Social Attitudes: The Third Report*, pp. 18–19; Smith and Chambers, *Inequality in Northern Ireland*, p. 72; Bruce, *Edge of the Union*, p. 5; Moxon-Browne, 'National identity', p. 26.

[38] Henry Patterson, *Class Conflict and Sectarianism: The Protestant Working Class and the Belfast Labour Movement 1868–1920*, Belfast, Blackstaff, 1980; Maurice Goldring, *Belfast: From Loyalty to Rebellion*, London, Lawrence and Wishart, 1991; Paul Bew, Peter Gibbon and Henry Patterson, *Northern Ireland 1921–1994: Political Forces and Social Classes*, London, Serif, 1995, chs. 1–4.

[39] Desmond Bell, *Acts of Union*; Andrew Hamilton, Clem McCartney, Tony Anderson, Ann Finn, *Violence in the Communities: The Impact of Political Violence in Northern Ireland on Intra-community, Inter-community and Community-state Relationships*, Coleraine, Centre for the Study of Conflict, 1990, ch. 3; James W. McAuley, *The Politics of Identity: A Loyalist Community in Belfast*, Aldershot, Avebury, 1994.

rapidly as one descends the social scale; Protestants in the professional and managerial categories are seven times more likely to support Alliance than are semi or unskilled Protestant manual workers.[40] Despite the cross-class nature of UUP support, there is a class edge to competition between it and the DUP, with the DUP decidedly more activist, egalitarian and populist in style than the UUP.[41] There is also a youth and unemployed bias among DUP supporters. The left-wing parties (WP, DL and Labour/Socialist) have almost no support. The support base of the recently formed Conservative party is also very small, being limited to the stable Protestant middle-class areas, for example North Down, with easy access to British networks.

There is also a spatial basis to Protestant divisions. Fundamentalist Protestantism and DUP support are strong in rural areas, while Alliance – the party most open on the union and on power-sharing – finds its core strength in Belfast, secondarily in other urban areas, least of all in rural areas.[42] Core–periphery, cultural and class divisions intersect to produce, in the greater Belfast and east coast area, a cohesive, high status group of upper-middle-class British (and to a lesser extent Northern Irish) identifiers from which Ulster identifiers tend to be excluded. The socio-political tensions between the clusters – always deep – are exacerbated by increasing class division and status bitterness.

Community integration and boundary maintenance. In the face of socially and spatially patterned difference and division, the Protestant community is held together by a multiplicity of integrative practices and networks: traditional practices with unintended cohesive effects, more consciously strategic modes of action, and an ideological emphasis on common cultural reference points.

Older traditions of intra-Protestant cooperation remain important. Mutual attendance at other Protestant churches for joint services and for social events is common, perhaps even more so for women than for men – mother-and-child groups and Womens' Institute meetings are often held in church premises.[43] Intermarriage across denominational boundaries is generally accepted and encourages extensive social contact

40 David J. Smith, *Equality and Inequality in Northern Ireland. Part 3: Perceptions and Views*, London, Policy Studies Institute, 1987, table 120; Moxon-Browne, *Nation, Class and Creed*, p. 67.
41 Michael Diskin, 'Official or Democratic? The battle for Unionist votes in Northern Ireland', Ph.D. thesis, Centre for the Study of Public Policy, University of Strathclyde, 1985.
42 Moxon-Browne, *Nation, Class and Creed*, pp. 67, 96.
43 Duncan Morrow, *The Churches and Inter-community Relationships*, Coleraine, Centre for the Study of Conflict 1991, pp. 19, 38.

Table 2. *Party identification among Protestants by socio-economic group*

	Professional/ managerial %	Other non-manual %	Skilled manual %	Semi-skilled manual %	Unskilled manual %	Not classified %
DUP	9	22	28	32	34	10
OUP	51	42	46	49	40	58
Other unionist	6	4	2	1	3	7
Alliance	21	17	6	3	3	7
Workers Party		1	1	1		1
Labour/Socialist	1	3	2	2	3	2
SDLP			1			
None/not stated	11	12	13	12	16	17

Source: Smith, *Equality and Inequality*, Table 120.

with in-laws of different denominations.[44] Fundamentalist and non-fundamentalist Protestants of all denominations attend state schools (typically mixed-sex) where they share religious education and develop social networks of importance in later life.

Religious division as such has no divisive political effects.[45] All the churches implicitly promote a common acceptance of the state: they often display British flags, welcome the security forces, and promote a generalised acceptance that the state is legitimate and its representatives benign. Class divisions are underplayed by unionists and loyalists in favour of the notion of a single Protestant community – the 'unionist family' – defending itself from its enemies and owing allegiance to Britain. Traditional institutions and practices – the Orange Order, ritual marches, service in the armed and security forces of the state – serve at once to integrate different groups of Protestants and to fuse their religious, cultural and political views: for many Protestants, Britishness is synonymous with Protestantism and unionism, or difficult fully to distinguish from it.[46]

Tendencies toward political diversity are held in check by more conscious means. The main political parties – DUP and UUP – although expressing deep differences within the community, mediate the tensions

---

[44] Whyte, *Interpreting Northern Ireland*, pp. 41–2; Rosemary Harris, *Prejudice and Tolerance in Ulster: A Study of Neighbours and 'Strangers' in a Border Community*, Manchester, Manchester, University Press, 1972, pp. 143–6.

[45] Moxon-Browne, *Nation, Class and Creed*, pp. 91–94.

[46] Interviews; see also M. W. Dewar, *Why Orangeism*, Belfast, Grand Orange Lodge of Ireland, 1959, p. 22.

between the dominant clusters. Conflicting views are expressed, at times intensely, but they have not been allowed to fracture the community. The parties draw on common symbols, appeal to shared understandings, and each seeks to reach all in the community, not just a part of it. They are careful to show solidarity on the core issues – the limits to reform, the union, resistance to Dublin involvement – especially when under pressure to compromise on them. Joint UUP and DUP opposition to the Anglo-Irish agreement was solid, politically and ideologically, with considerable moderation of organisational competition in election pacts; joint opposition to the Frameworks Documents seems likely to be equally so. Those who threaten the security or solidarity of the community are dealt with harshly. The most feared and detested is the 'Lundy', the active betrayer of the community, who must be expelled from it. Those who compromise with nationalists are also seen as betrayers; they too must be rejected. Thus the prime minister Terence O'Neill was forced out by his own party and the power-sharing executive of 1973–4 was brought down by an unparalleled assertion of Protestant solidarity.

At the cultural level, integration is enhanced by the sharing of symbols, meanings and reference points even where interpretations and beliefs about them differ radically. Reformation Protestantism is a common reference point for atheist, liberal and fundamentalist alike, each of whom defines their religious position as a rejection, revision or continuation of this theology. The symbolism of monarchy and state may vary in its meaning for different groups of Protestants, but retains a positive value for almost all.[47] Acceptance of state authority, law and order, and support for the security forces are shared by almost all Protestants. Where they disagree or conflict, they do so for the most part in terms of concepts which are mutually understood and ideals and identities which are shared. Conflict within the Protestant and unionist population does not typically involve denial of each other's identity, but recognition of it.

Communal solidarity and the boundary between the communities are also maintained by structural and institutional mechanisms. Territorial segregation – most common among the working class and the product both of security concerns and of a desire to 'live with one's own' – makes communal boundaries automatic in the normal course of life.[48] It also

[47] Finlay Holmes, *Our Irish Presbyterian Heritage*, Belfast, Publications Committee of the Presbyterian Church in Ireland, 1985, p. 169.

[48] Whyte, *Interpreting Northern Ireland*, pp. 34–5; Hastings Donnan and Graham MacFarlane, 'Informal social organisation', in John Darby, ed., *Northern Ireland: The Background to the Conflict*, Belfast, Appletree, 1983; Hamilton et al., *Violence and the Communities*, ch. 3.

increases the likelihood of marital endogamy and segregation in the school and workplace, in part by making it easier to enforce. Endogamy in Northern Ireland is very high; in a recent survey only 3 per cent of Protestants were in mixed marriages although intermarriage is increasing and the situation appears to vary from locality to locality.[49]

The separate educational systems for Protestant and Catholic have a similar effect. Gallagher and Dunn, writing in 1991, noted that only 1 per cent of pupils were enrolled in fully integrated primary and secondary schools although this is increasing gradually with additional state support.[50] Institutional segregation in the school is reinforced by practices of segregation in sports and youth clubs, typically formally or informally associated with one or other religion. Where contact does take place between Protestant and Catholic, widely accepted cultural norms function to make it as superficial as possible: refusing to engage in contentious political and religious topics in conversation with Catholics; bantering and joking which at once denies and highlights the divisions; or stereotyping.[51]

The boundaries between the communities are also highlighted and reinforced in explicitly oppositional ways. Protestant fundamentalists define the Catholic church as idolatrous, blasphemous and even Satanic, and theological hostility of a milder kind is found among many non-fundamentalist and secular Protestants.[52] In politics, the organisation, ethos and symbolism of the unionist parties is clearly 'Protestant', from the role of the Orange Order and the Protestant clergy to the symbolism, frequently displayed, which Catholics associate with Protestant ascendancy – the Union Jack, the British national anthem, red white and blue colours, the name 'Ulster'. Politico-religious institutions (the Orange Order, the Apprentice Boys, marching bands) dramatise ritually – not least through public marches – the irreconcilability of Catholic and Protestant (chapter 4). At the cultural level, Protestants mark the boundary between Catholic and Protestant by ridiculing and down-grading Gaelic-Irish and Catholic culture (chapters 4 and 7).

[49] A. M. Gallagher and S. Dunn, 'Community relations in Northern Ireland: Attitudes to contact and integration', in Stringer and Robinson, eds., Social Attitudes, 1991, p. 11; Whyte, Interpreting Northern Ireland, pp. 40–1.

[50] Gallagher and Dunn, 'Community relations in Northern Ireland', p. 15.

[51] Graham McFarlane, '"It's not as simple as that." The expression of the Catholic and Protestant boundary in Northern Irish rural communities', in Anthony P. Cohen, ed., Symbolising Boundaries: Identity and Diversity in British Cultures, Manchester, Manchester University Press, 1986, pp. 92–3, 95–6.

[52] Morrow, Churches and Inter-community Relationships, pp. 114–15.

The Northern Catholic community

The cohesion of the Northern Catholic community is likewise achieved despite internal divisions, some of which have increased since direct rule (chapter 7).

Religious differences. At first sight Northern Catholics appear homogenous in religious matters in that theological disputation is rare and the vast majority – 86 per cent – are weekly churchgoers.[53] However Catholics vary in the extent of their piety, obedience to church teaching and respect for the church hierarchy. Some are deeply attached to the church as an institution and support it almost unconditionally; others are scathing in their criticism of it. Some find deep spiritual meaning in Catholic devotional practices that others view as irrelevant or even distasteful. Some adhere rigorously to church teaching even if they do not accept its rationale; the approach of others is self-consciously *à la carte*.

Political differences. Catholics differ widely in their political attitudes and goals. It is frequently assumed that all Catholics aspire to a united Ireland. The reality is more complex. While about 80 per cent of Catholics say they would like to see a united Ireland in the long term, only a fifth want it immediately and unconditionally and about a sixth do not want it at all.[54] Some surveys offer respondents a direct choice between a united Ireland and the United Kingdom.[55] In a recent survey, when asked to make such a definitive choice, half of Catholics opted for a united Ireland – more men than women, who are more likely to be undecided – while over a quarter wished to remain in the United Kingdom (Figure 2).[56]

Catholic responses to opinion poll questions regarding their first preference solution show a wide variation, as Figure 3 below shows.[57] Only a third of Catholics give a united Ireland as their first preference solution; a proportion varying from 8 to 12 per cent favours an

[53] Curtice and Gallagher, 'The Northern Irish dimension', p. 187.
[54] Whyte, *Interpreting Northern Ireland*, p. 80; Smith and Chambers, *Inequality in Northern Ireland*, p. 96. *Belfast Telegraph*, 5 Oct. 1988; Coopers and Lybrand, *Poll*, table 3a.
[55] The form of the question varies; one example is 'If a referendum was held today, would you vote for Northern Ireland to stay in the United Kingdom or to become part of a united Ireland?' In 1967, half of Catholics rejected both options, preferring a united Ireland within the United Kingdom; in 1993, 20 per cent of Catholics stated no preference. See Appendix A for sources.
[56] *Irish Political Studies*, vol. 9, 1994, data section, p. 225.
[57] See footnote 29.

independent Ulster; up to 14 per cent prefer joint authority.[58] There has been a slight increase in each of these preferences since the 1970s. Devolution with power-sharing remains the most favoured first preference option within the context of the union, but it has declined significantly in popularity since the 1970s in favour of a stronger Irish dimension, whether in the form of constitutional change or provision for a continued Irish input into administration through the Anglo-Irish Agreement.

The differences within the Catholic population are reflected in party divisions. The largest party with around two-thirds of the Catholic vote – the Social Democratic and Labour Party (SDLP) – favours unity in the long term; between a half and two-thirds of SDLP supporters favour a united Ireland as a middle-term policy option while a third would vote to stay in the United Kingdom if a referendum were to be held today.[59] The second largest party with around one-third of the Catholic vote – Sinn Féin (SF) – supports rapid progress to a united Ireland; the vast majority of its supporters want a united Ireland, some on nationalist principle, others because they do not believe change is possible within Northern Ireland.

Alliance Party policy on Irish unity is open; it is willing to support it if a majority of the people of Northern Ireland supports it. About 7 per cent of Catholics support Alliance (a significant drop from the declared support of 21 per cent in 1978 or 14 per cent in 1986); 61 per cent of Alliance supporters (Protestant and Catholic) would vote to remain in the United Kingdom if a referendum were held today; in the middle term, between a third and a fifth of Alliance Catholics favour Irish unity as a policy option, about half take a pragmatic line or voice no opinion and a quarter oppose it.[60] The bulk of Alliance supporters (67 per cent, Catholic and Protestant) favour power sharing devolution as a first or second preference, while the figures for SDLP and SF are 46 per cent and 20 per cent respectively.[61] There is some gender basis to party support and political attitudes: Catholic women have consistently been

---

[58] O'Leary, 'Public opinion', p. 152, table 2. *Irish Political Studies*, vol. 9, 1994, data section, p. 228.

[59] Smith and Chambers, *Inequality in Northern Ireland*, p. 96; Smith, *Equality and Inequality*, table 47; Curtice and Gallagher, 'The Northern Irish dimension', p. 196; *Irish Political Studies*, vol. 9, 1994, data section, p. 225.

[60] Curtice and Gallagher, 'The Northern Irish dimension', p. 194; *Irish Political Studies*, 9, 1994, data section, p. 225. Moxon-Browne in 1978 found that a third of Catholic (and a fifth of Protestant) Alliance supporters favoured some form of all-Ireland solution, *Nation, Class and Creed*, p. 108; Smith in 1986 found that almost a fifth of Alliance Catholics (and a fifth of Alliance Protestants) favoured a united Ireland, while just over a quarter of Alliance Catholics (and half of Alliance Protestants) opposed it, *Equality and Inequality*, table 47.

[61] O'Leary, 'Public opinion', pp. 154–5, tables 3, 4.

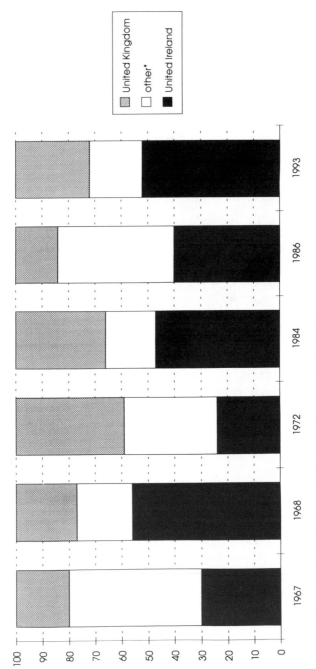

Figure 2 Catholics' constitutional preferences, 1967–1993

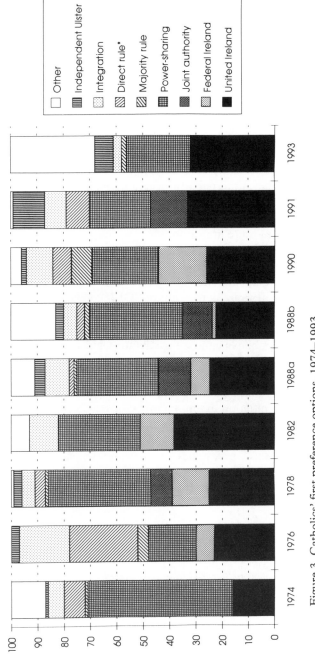

Figure 3 Catholics' first preference options, 1974–1993

less likely to voice support for SF and – in most but not all surveys – more likely to support Alliance.[62]

Qualitative research reveals further nuances.[63] Many Catholics have difficulty envisaging what a united Ireland would be like or how it might be achieved. Some who hold the aspiration do not really care whether it is ever achieved; some aspire to unity, but are not sure they would like it; others do not think a united Ireland particularly desirable in itself, but prefer it to present conditions in Northern Ireland.[64] Some who oppose it do so on particular issues – the position of women, social legislation, the economy – rather than on principle. Some do not want it under present circumstances but would abstain rather than vote against it. Policy preferences for unity are not related to any particular liking for or fellow feeling with Southerners.[65] Surveys show that significant numbers of Catholics put such constitutional questions relatively low in their priorities; in one recent survey a third of Catholics saw social and economic issues as more important.[66]

Catholics differ in their attitudes to political violence. In 1984, four out of five SDLP supporters rejected it, while 70 per cent of SF supporters supported it.[67] There was more tolerance of IRA motives than of their actions: in the same poll, 39 per cent of SDLP voters, and 77 per cent of SF voters, agreed that the 'IRA are basically patriots and idealists'.[68] Before the IRA ceasefire there was disagreement both on the moral justification of republican violence and its strategic necessity, and support for violence appeared to be decreasing even among SF supporters. The ceasefire was welcomed in all sections of the community.

There is more Catholic unity in opposition to perceived abuses of state power and discrimination in employment – over 85 per cent oppose the use of plastic bullets, three quarters think the UDR/RIR should be abolished, 70 per cent agree that the police and army get away with offences they commit, over a half believe employment opportunities are biased against Catholics. Recent surveys suggest greater diversity than before in Catholic attitudes to the police and the legal system.[69]

---

[62] *Irish Political Studies*, vol. 9, 1994, data section, p. 226; Morgan, 'Bridging the divide', p. 137.
[63] Interviews; Fionnuala O'Connor, *In Search of a State: Catholics in Northern Ireland*, Belfast, Blackstaff, 1993.
[64] Interviews; O'Connor, *In Search of a State*, pp. 61, 89ff., 270.
[65] *Ibid.*, ch. 7.
[66] Smith and Chambers, *Inequality in Northern Ireland*, pp. 73–9.
[67] Moxon-Browne, 'Alienation: the case of Catholics', p. 84.
[68] *Ibid.*
[69] Gallagher 'Community relations', pp. 39–40, 43–4; Moxon-Browne, 'Alienation: the case of Catholics', p. 82; Brewer, 'The public and the police'.

Table 3. *Cultural identity among Catholics*

Identity	Imagined community
I Irish	The island and/or people of Ireland. This may include a strong sense of regional identity as 'Ulster', or 'northern' within the category 'Irish'
II Northern Irish	Northern Ireland and its people, Protestant and Catholic. This often opens up to a wider Irish and/or British and European identity
III British	The United Kingdom and its citizens

Cultural differences. There is greater cultural than political unity among Catholics. Three basic cultural identities exist within the Northern Catholic community: Irish, Northern Irish and British.

This structure of identities allows for some nesting, though less so than among Protestants. A Northern Irish identity often combines with an Irish and less often with a British identity; an Irish identity very rarely combines with a British one. Recent survey figures show 60 per cent identifying as Irish; a quarter, and almost half of Catholics in the highest social class, identify as Northern Irish, 8 per cent as British and 2 per cent as Ulster.[70] Survey data, however, are not always an accurate guide to identity. The high rate of Northern Irish identification may be an example of 'moderate' views being overestimated in surveys.[71] Moreover, while few Catholics identify as British, our interviews suggested that a larger number recognise a British dimension to their culture. However, by all accounts, an Irish identity remains strong, even among those whose political preferences are no longer nationalist.[72] Thus far at least, most Northern Catholics appear to resist redefinition in ways that radically separate them from an island-wide national community.

Ideological clusters and subgroups. Individual Catholics show remarkable variety in their views with no necessary connection between political preference, religious faith or national identity. As with Protestants, however, there is clustering. There are two major clusters – 'republicans' and 'nationalists' – and two minor ones – 'bridge-builders' and 'Catholic unionists'. 'Republicans' tend to be anti-clerical, to be committed to Irish unity as soon as possible by the most effective means

---

[70] Moxon-Browne, 'National identity', pp. 25–6.
[71] Whyte, *Interpreting Northern Ireland*, pp. 4–5.
[72] Interviews; O'Connor, *In Search of a State*, ch. 9.

available, and to assert a strongly Irish identity; they form the core of SF support. There is, however, also a tendency in republicanism, now mostly among older, rural republicans, towards traditional Catholicism. 'Nationalists' (when the term is used in contradistinction to 'republicans') tend to be orthodox Catholics, to seek power-sharing and an 'Irish dimension' in the short-to-medium term while aspiring to Irish unity in the long term, and to have a less assertive (though no less deep) Irish identity; they form the core of SDLP support.

There are also two minor clusters. 'Bridge-builders' comprise people who are ecumenist or secular on religious issues, pragmatic or 'agnostic' on constitutional matters, and with a Northern Irish identity; they form the core of Catholic Alliance, WP and DL support. Finally there is also a 'Catholic unionist' cluster composed of people who are agnostic or ecumenist on religious issues, with a Northern Irish and British identity, who – though not identifying with traditional Protestant unionism – support the union. Most support the Alliance party or movements such as the Campaign for Equal Citizenship, the Campaign for Labour Representation, or the Conservatives, though a few vote for the Protestant Unionist parties.

Relations between the subgroups constituted by these clusters are often tense. Catholics with a British identity who are unionist in politics are already a group apart and are seen as such by other Catholics. Nationalists and republicans are more closely linked, but often in antagonistic ways. For Ciarán de Baróid, writing of the republican, working-class Ballymurphy area of Belfast in 1972, 'Not alone were the people totally alienated from the British state and its paraphernalia, but they were also becoming increasingly disgusted by the behaviour of the nationalist middle class, the Catholic hierarchy and the Dublin government.'[73] The disgust was mutual.[74] Republicans were even more alienated from the 'bridge-builders' – the 'nice people' who in their view lacked understanding or sympathy for the conditions under which republicans lived; bridge-builders in turn found republican violence and intimidation the most serious cause of ordinary people's problems. Relations between 'nationalists' and 'bridge-builders' have been at best guarded, at worst covertly vicious with mutual accusations of 'sectarianism' or of being 'Castle Catholics'. Many of these tensions eased with the end of IRA violence.

These differences must be seen in the context of growing class

---

[73] Ciarán de Baróid, *Ballymurphy and the Irish War*, Dublin, Aisling, 1989, p. 197.
[74] Cf. John Darby, *Intimidation and the Control of Conflict*, Dublin, Gill and Macmillan, 1986, p. 156.

divergence over the past twenty years. Traditionally class differences among Catholics were less pronounced structurally and ideologically than among Protestants. However the expansion of the state service sector together with state-sponsored policies of fair employment have created new opportunities for upward mobility. There has been a growth in the traditional Catholic middle and lower-middle class – the lawyers, doctors, teachers, social workers and nurses who service the Catholic community. There has also been an expansion of the 'universal' middle class in both the state and private sectors. Some of the new middle-class positions have been filled from within that class but many have been filled by Catholics of working-class origins. Meanwhile, in working-class areas, recession has still further lessened chances of Catholic employment. The class divide has widened and is now to a greater degree social, political and cultural as well as economic. However Catholic class divisions still lack the depth and intensity of Protestant ones and many of the new Catholic middle class are just one generation from the working class.

Table 4 shows patterns of party identification among Catholics by socio-economic group. As in the Protestant community, there is a single large cross-class party – the SDLP – with support for two others – SF and Alliance – more skewed; support for SF falls off as one ascends the social scale, support for Alliance rises (although unevenly). Core SDLP voters, those who have never had any support for SF, are more likely to be middle class; Alliance support is even more markedly middle class; core SF voters, those whose support for SF never wavered, are more likely to be young working class and unemployed.[75] In addition, it is the young male working class who are most likely to want Irish unity immediately.[76] Table 4 also shows the Catholic community to be politically more fragmented and uncertain than the Protestant one, with the major party commanding less overall support, a much stronger left-wing vote, and higher proportions reporting no identification with the existing parties.

Though class is increasingly important, the community has not fractured politically on class lines. More unemployed Catholics voice support for the SDLP than for SF, and about 10 per cent of SF supporters (compared to almost 20 per cent of SDLP) are in the upper middle and middle classes.[77] Just over a quarter of middle-class Catholics, and almost the same proportion of working-class Catholics report that their

[75] Coopers and Lybrand, table 19d; Smith, *Equality and Inequality*, tables 120, 121.
[76] Coopers and Lybrand, *Poll*, table 3a.
[77] Smith, *Equality and Inequality*, table 121; Edward Moxon-Browne and Cynthia Irvine, 'Not many floating voters here', *Fortnight*, no. 273, 1989, p. 9.

views on SF waver with events.[78] The class effect among Catholics appears to be moderated by such factors as the dependence of Catholic professionals on the wider Catholic community for their clients, and the recent nature of Catholic upward mobility.[79] The upwardly mobile in particular cross the class divide – themselves successful professionals, they are linked by family memory and kin contacts (and sometimes residential proximity) to the increasingly disadvantaged working class.

There is also a gender, generational and territorial basis to Catholic differences. In addition to being working class, republicans are likely to be young, male and concentrated in West Belfast and in some rural and border areas. Bridge-builders are likely to be middle class and concentrated in Belfast and its suburbs. The nationalist cluster has a less clear social basis, although its core is middle aged and employed. The survey evidence suggests less strong support among women than among men either for Irish unity or for SF.

Integration and boundary maintenance. The unity of the Catholic community is challenged by internal religious, political and cultural differences and by the tendency toward internal clustering. But tendencies for the community to divide or dissolve are held in check by traditional religious and cultural institutions and practices and by strategic political choices.

Despite the partial erosion of its position, the Catholic church remains the single most important integrating social force; its multifunctional character – at once religious, social and educational – extends its influence to all areas of communal life.[80] Organisations concerned to foster Gaelic-Irish culture – the language, music, dance, games – also create cross-cutting linkages which help integrate the community. Most of these organisations are island-wide but account is usually taken, at least informally, of the specificity of the Northern Irish situation within the wider Irish one. The effect is simultaneously to open Northern Catholics to a wider Irish (primarily Catholic) community and to give them a heightened sense of their distinctiveness and shared interests within that.

Common political and cultural reference points also perform an integrative function – identification with the Irish flag and national anthem, the choice of an Irish over a British passport, support for the existence of a separate Irish state if not necessarily the one that now

---

[78] Coopers and Lybrand, *Poll*, table 19d.
[79] Cf. O'Connor, *In Search of a State*, p. 19.
[80] Morrow, *Churches and Inter-community Relationships*', pp. 50–5.

Table 4. *Party identification among Catholics by socio-economic group*

	Professional/ managerial	Other non-manual	Skilled manual	Semi-skilled manual	Unskilled manual	Not classified
	%	%	%	%	%	%
Sinn Féin	4	9	12	12	18	6
SDLP	49	42	39	38	38	42
Alliance	19	23	11	9	12	11
Irish Independence Party	1		2	1	3	
Workers Party	5	1	5	4	5	4
Labour/Socialist	4	2	2	7	5	4
OUP, DUP		2	1	1		3
None/not stated	16	22	28	26	18	31

Source: Smith, Equality and Inequality, Table 120.

exists, an interest in Irish history, the Irish language and Gaelic culture. Here too the effect is often simultaneously to integrate Northern Catholics into a wider Irish community and to heighten their sense of distinctiveness within it. The core symbols of Irish identity are island-wide but their meanings often differ north and south of the border. For example, Southerners have no choice of what passport to hold and while their Irish passport has some meaning at the level of identity, it is much less than for Northerners for whom holding an Irish passport is a conscious choice often involving some inconvenience. Other shared political reference points relate to the Northern state – the belief in its illegitimacy, a distrust of the security forces, belief in past or present discrimination and 'second class citizenship' – and doubts about the concern and/or goodwill of the British and Irish governments.

The two Catholic political parties – SDLP and SF – have been conscious of the need to maintain the integration and solidarity of the community. Competition between them has at times been bitter, and was particularly so during the early 1980s when, for a time, it seemed that SF might supplant the SDLP as the sole representative of the Catholic community.[81] Since the late 1980s neither party believes this will happen, and while local contests are still intensely fought and sometimes violent, the two party leaders temper considerations of party advantage with concern to maintain the political strength of the Catholic com-

[81] For example, see Henry Patterson, *The Politics of Illusion: Republicanism and Socialism in Modern Ireland*, London, Hutchinson, 1989, p. 176.

munity. Both are careful to speak in the name of the whole community, not just a part of it; thus Gerry Adams's claim in 1988 that 'What constitutional nationalists and republicans really have in common at this time is a shared constituency – the nationalist people.'[82] In the more recent period there has been an increasing convergence in terminology and to some degree in analysis (chapter 4).

Social and geographical segregation perform an integrative and boundary-maintaining function for Catholics as much as for Protestants. However there are subtle differences in the way in which this operates. In general Catholics have more experience of, and are more in favour of, cross-community mixing than are Protestants.[83] In the Stormont period, where Protestants often refused Catholics entrance to their leisure, sports or youth clubs or political parties, Catholics often welcomed those few Protestants who chose to attend (with the exception of Protestants in the security forces). Catholics have traditionally welcomed the interest of Protestants in the different expressions of Gaelic culture – Irish music, Gaelic games, the Irish language, Irish or bi-lingual street signs. The nationalist and republican political parties welcome Protestant members. The Catholic community has seen this 'openness' and 'tolerance' as part of its communal tradition in which it can take pride. On the other hand, while Protestants are welcomed it is very much on Catholic terms and frequently seen as a first step in a political conversion – an attitude which deters most Protestants.

Moreover the Catholic church adheres to policies which, whatever their intent, are segregationist in effect. Catholic religious attitudes have become much more liberal in recent years with clergy and laity supporting ecumenical contacts. However Catholic ecumenism is more principled than practised; in such strategic areas as marriage, education and even religious services, progress towards interdenominationalism is slow.[84]

Northern Ireland: two communities or one?

There is little doubt about the depth of communal division in Northern Ireland. Apart from religious differences, over 80 per cent of the

---

[82] Gerry Adams, *A Pathway to Peace*, Cork, Mercier, 1988, pp. 60–1.

[83] Smith and Chambers, *Inequality in Northern Ireland*, pp. 101–4; Gallagher and Dunn, 'Community relations in Northern Ireland'.

[84] The Irish hierarchy has been much more restrictive, for example in its policy on mixed marriages, than the hierarchy in France or many other parts of continental Europe; Gerald McElroy, *The Catholic Church and the Northern Ireland Crisis 1968–86*, Dublin, Gill and Macmillan, 1991, pp. 180–7.

population vote for parties which appeal to one community only.[85] The communities take sharply opposed views on such issues as the future of the union, security, fair employment and national identity.[86] Even where there is movement there is little sign of convergence. For example, while Protestants in recent years have come to accept power-sharing, Catholics have shifted their preferences to a strong Irish dimension. On attitudes to the border, the 'difference index', a measure of the degree of difference of views between the communities, had reached a high of 75 in 1974, in 1986 it was 64 and remained at 62 in 1993.[87]

Despite such polarisation it is often said that Protestants and Catholics in Northern Ireland today have more in common with each other than either community has with the wider British or Irish societies with which they identify[88] – that the people of Northern Ireland should be seen, not as two separate communities, but as a single divided community. Certainly Northern Protestants and Catholics have much in common. The political entity which circumscribes their lives has been in existence now for seventy-five years and it has its own distinctive institutions, ethos and culture. Protestants and Catholics participate in many of the same institutions and networks, have common traditions, attitudes and values, and distinguish sharply between those born and brought up in Northern Ireland and outsiders.[89] There is a regional cultural style readily distinguishable from other parts of the two islands. It is sufficiently common to Protestants and Catholics to make it difficult at times even for people in Northern Ireland to 'tell' a person's religion. The concentration of the violence of the past twenty-five years largely within Northern Ireland also differentiates Northern Catholics and Protestants from outsiders. Northern Ireland's politicians appear at ease when travelling together on trade trips to the United States and in cooperating

---

[85] Whyte, *Interpreting Northern Ireland*, p. 73.

[86] See above, and Ulster Marketing Surveys for ITN 17/18 December 1993, *Irish Political Studies*, vol. 9, 1994, p. 225; Gallagher, 'Civil liberties', p. 83; Smith, *Equality and Inequality*, table 74; Moxon-Browne, 'National identity', p. 25.

[87] Richard Rose, Ian McAllister and Peter Mair, *Is there a Concurring Majority about Northern Ireland?*, Glasgow, Centre for the Study of Public Policy, University of Strathclyde, paper no. 22, 1978, pp. 12–13; Smith, *Equality and Inequality*, table 44; *Irish Political Studies*, vol. 9, 1994, data section p. 225, own calculation.

[88] Alliance party submission to the Brooke/Mayhew talks; *Alliance News Inter-Party Talks Supplement*, Nov./Dec. 1992, pp. 1–2; cf. Feargal Cochrane, 'Any takers? The isolation of Northern Ireland', *Political Studies*, vol. 42, no. 3, 1994.

[89] Anthony D. Buckley, 'Collecting Ulster's culture: Are there *really* two traditions?', in Alan Gailey, ed., *The Use of Tradition: Essays Presented to G. B. Thompson*, Cultra, Ulster Folk and Transport Museum, 1988; Maurna Crozier, 'Good leaders and "decent" men: an Ulster contradiction', in Myrtle Hill and Sarah Barber, eds., *Aspects of Irish Studies*, Belfast, Institute of Irish Studies, 1990.

together in the European Union on matters of general benefit to Northern Ireland.

Opinion surveys show a wide measure of agreement between Protestant and Catholic on issues unrelated to the political conflict.[90] They also show significant support in each community for closer contact with the other. On the sensitive issue of mixed marriage, a majority of Catholics and a significant minority of Protestants favour more mixing.[91] Consistently in polls since 1974, a large majority of Catholics and a (bare) majority of Protestants have stated their willingness to accept power-sharing devolution, at least in principle.[92] Only a minority of Catholics seek a united Ireland in the immediate future. Even if only a fifth of the population chooses a 'Northern Irish' identity, all are conscious of being from Northern Ireland.

Despite these common features, it is inappropriate to view Northern Ireland as a single community for two interrelated reasons. First, there is no shared commitment to the survival of Northern Ireland as a distinct entity. The majority of Catholics do not accept its legitimacy and aspire one day to see it dissolved in a united Ireland. Indeed they actively resist the notion that there is a single Northern Ireland community, in considerable part because it weakens the potential for the island-wide community to which they aspire. Second, neither community has a developed concept of a general interest which transcends its own particular interests. Both communities remain conscious that Northern Ireland was established to defend the interests of the Protestant community and that it remains in existence at Protestant insistence. Moreover, since its foundation, most Protestants have conceived of Northern Ireland in exclusionary terms, differing only in whether they exclude all Catholics, just nationalists or simply republicans.[93] Catholic opposition to the existence of Northern Ireland is similarly underpinned by particularist concerns.

For Northern Ireland to exist as a community in its own right, there would have to be a majority in both communities wholeheartedly committed to the establishment of an overarching and inclusive community embracing all its people. There are some who are so committed, but they are a small minority.

[90] Curtice and Gallagher, 'The Northern Irish dimension', pp. 200–2. Rose, *Governing without Consensus*, pp. 315–16.

[91] Gallagher and Dunn, 'Community relations in Northern Ireland', pp. 11–12.

[92] Whyte, *Interpreting Northern Ireland*, p. 82; see also Sidney Elliott, 'Unpopular opinions', *Fortnight*, no. 282, 1990, pp. 6–7.

[93] Todd, 'Unionist political thought', p. 197; John Doyle, 'Workers and outlaws: Unionism and fair employment in Northern Ireland', *Irish Political Studies*, vol. 9, 1994, pp. 48–52, 57; see also ch. 4 below.

Communal structure and the persistence of division

Appeals are frequently made to the communities to put aside their differences and to concentrate on what they have in common – the needs of their local area, the interests of the people of Northern Ireland as a whole, of the working class, or of women. Examples of common action on cross-community lines are frequently referred to and celebrated[94] and there have been attempts by voluntary and state-sponsored organisations to reduce the division between the communities (chapter 7). Such efforts have had some success in moderating division at local level and in particular organisations; they have been much less successful at the level of Northern Ireland as a whole. There are many reasons why division persists; here we focus on two aspects of community structure. One relates to the complex pattern of division and integration *within* each community; the other to the way in which each community links itself to the wider community with which it identifies. Both frustrate the efforts of bridge-builders to moderate and transcend division.

Intracommunal division and the limits to bridge-building

The internal structure of both communities – the existence of distinct ideological clusters and subgroups and the relationship of alliance and/or antagonism between them – contributes to the persistence of conflict. We can best see this by looking at the difficulties bridge-builders in both communities have faced in trying to gain support for their vision of a middle ground and an inclusive Northern Irish community. They have four potential sources of increased support – the three other clusters in their community and those who resist identification with any cluster – the 'marginals'.

At first sight the 'marginals', as the least politically committed, appear to offer the most promising source of support. The difficulty is that most marginals have distanced themselves not simply from the dominant culture and politics of their community but from any politics specific to Northern Ireland or any attempt to reform a particularly 'Northern Irish' political culture. If they are politically active at all they are most likely to be concerned with non-constitutional single issues – the environment, abortion, homosexual law reform, feminist causes. They might offer

[94] Paddy Devlin, *Yes We Have No Bananas: Outdoor Relief in Belfast 1920–1939*, Belfast, Blackstaff, 1981; Ronnie Munck and Bill Rolston, *Belfast in the Thirties: An Oral History*, Belfast, Blackstaff, 1987; Frank Curran, *Derry: Countdown to Disaster*, Dublin, Gill and Macmillan, 1986; Ciaran McKeown, *The Passion of Peace*, Belfast, Blackstaff, 1984.

support on specific issues, but would resist committing themselves to the practical political task of building 'middle ground' cultural or political institutions.

The prospects of gaining increased support among the minor clusters of Protestant dissenters and Catholic unionists are also poor. Bridge-builders attempt to mediate between two opposed communities and aspirations; most remain socially within their own community while becoming culturally and politically more open to contact and dialogue with those in the other community; they neither 'go over' to the other side nor reject their own but emphasise and develop what is common between the two. The distinguishing feature of both Protestant dissenters and Catholic unionists is their dissatisfaction with the existence of two communal blocs based on religion, politics and culture. They do not want to mediate between these divided communities; they want to undercut the oppositions on which they are based.

This leaves the major clusters as a source of increased support. Here the most likely constituency are the moderates within the larger clusters – moderate unionists and moderate nationalists. The numbers involved are hard to assess, but if one takes those UUP and SDLP party supporters whose first preference solution is power-sharing devolution, the size of this group amounts to almost 15 per cent of the population.[95] The size of this group makes it potentially important. Moderate nationalists and unionists are integrated into the major cluster in their communities, share many of its values and may command a certain trust and respect; if they could be recruited for bridge-building politics, in time more might follow.

The positions articulated verbally by moderates are, however, often abandoned when attitudes must be translated into practical action.[96] Particularly at times of crisis for their community, moderates, whatever their own personal views, tend to side with the majority in their community. They may do this from the most honourable of motives – not just fear of losing status or fear of intimidation, but a desire to provide leadership within their community and to restrain 'their own' extremists. This is the 'troublemaker veto' to which Frank Wright has referred, which binds together moderates and extremists within each community.[97] Moderates are vulnerable to it precisely because they are still so deeply involved in the networks, relationships and symbols

---

[95] Own calculation from O'Leary, 'Public opinion', p. 154, table 3.
[96] Cf. Elliott, 'Unpopular opinions'.
[97] Frank Wright, *Northern Ireland: A Comparative Analysis*. Dublin: Gill and Macmillan, 1987, pp. 123ff.

of their communities. Without the moderates, however, bridge-builders have little change of expanding their numbers.

The fact that each community possesses two major clusters, one more 'extreme' than the other, increases the importance of the troublemaker veto. In the Stormont period, unionism and loyalism were mobilised under a single 'unionist' banner that, despite tensions, was sufficiently strong to contain the more radical loyalist pressures.[98] The separate political mobilisation of loyalism makes it more difficult for moderates within unionism to press their case; the fate of the Faulknerite unionists of 1973–4 was an example to all unionists (chapter 5). A similar development has occurred within the Catholic community. Until the 1960s, nationalism was dominant and republicans were politically marginalised, most of their energy concentrated on intermittent military activity. The recent political mobilisation of republicans now sets clear limits to nationalist room for manoeuvre.

Intracommunal political and ideological differentiation has therefore stimulated centrifugal party competition with the more moderate party restrained from compromise because of competition with the more extreme. It has had the further effect of allowing bridge-builders to be represented as 'deviants' within their communities. The political consequences have been serious since bridge-builders' electoral support is integrated into the mainstream of their communities: most Alliance party supporters are divided in their attitudes on Protestant/Catholic lines and remain more closely linked to other groups in their own community than to middle ground supporters within the other community.[99]

Differences in wider communal identities and allegiances

Communal structure also contributes to communal division in the different ways in which – not simply the fact that – each community forms part of a wider community. Protestants identify with a British community, Catholics with an Irish one. The ways in which they construct these relationships are not, however, identical. The primary ethnic community for most Protestants is Ulster (or Northern Irish) Protestants. Their identification with Britishness is (for the most part) secondary in nature and for many has a strong conditional quality. This conditional quality derives in part from the fact that many people in

[98] Paul Bew, Peter Gibbon and Henry Patterson, *The State in Northern Ireland 1921–71: Political Forces and Social Classes*, Manchester, Manchester University Press, 1979, chs. 3–5; Todd, 'Unionist political thought', pp. 195–208.

[99] Moxon-Browne, *Nation, Class and Creed*, pp. 72–8.

Great Britain see Northern Protestants in a purely Ulster or Irish context, not as part of a wider British 'family' or 'nation' (chapter 8). In these circumstances it is inappropriate to treat all or even most Northern Protestants as 'members of the British nation' or to assume that their relationship with the wider British community is analogous to Northern Catholics' relationship with the Irish nation.[100]

We have stressed the effects of partition on the solidarity of the island-wide national Irish community. A distance has grown up between Northern and Southern Catholics in the years since partition, and today the relationship between them is often fraught. Indeed some sections of the middle class both North and South appear open to a permanent sundering of the two parts of the island and of the single 'Irish nation' of the past (chapter 9). But this remains a minority position on both sides of the border; an island-wide (predominantly Catholic) nationalist imagined community still exists. Like all human relationships, it has a conditional component, but it is much less than is the case with Protestants and the wider British community.

The difference has important implications for achieving accomodation between the two communities in Northern Ireland. On the Protestant side the tenuous nature of their relationship with the wider British community heightens their cultural and political vulnerability. They know that the British public is largely indifferent to their fate, and that if the British state departs from Northern Ireland the British political elite will quickly forget about them. The sense of belonging to a wider British community would have great difficulty surviving separation; the experience of Southern Protestants makes this clear. There is no parallel in the case of Northern Catholics. Historically and geographically, North and South are inextricably bound together; there is no process of Southern withdrawal analogous to a British one. This is why Northern Catholics have been able to maintain their identification with an island-wide nation and to force the South to honour the obligations that entails despite partition. Such an option would not be open to Protestants in the event of a British withdrawal.

At the same time, and for related reasons, Northern Protestants are culturally and emotionally less dependent on the people of Great Britain than Northern Catholics are on the people of the rest of Ireland. Northern Protestants form a primary community and, for most, 'British' is a second level identity and community: the Protestant community can survive political changes which threaten to destroy its British national

---

[100] For discussion, see Michael Gallagher, 'How many nations are there in Ireland?', *Ethnic and Racial Studies*, vol. 18, no. 4, Oct. 1995.

identity; indeed it becomes the more politically assertive and independent when rejected by the people of Great Britain. Northern Catholics are a fragment of a primary community existing at the level of the island as a whole; this makes their need for recognition of their 'Irishness' culturally and emotionally acute.

The asymmetry in the relationship between the two communities and the larger societies with which they identify, and the non-equivalence of the needs and interests on both sides, make it difficult to secure a solution based on compromise and parity of esteem for both identities. For Protestants, the fragile political base of their British identity leads them to resist any compromise – including parity of esteem for nationalists – that would dilute this identity. For Catholics, the primary nature of their Irish identity leads them to reject anything less than full parity of esteem for it.

Conclusion

Partition created new bases for community formation, identity and solidarity and the structure of community on the island is now much more complex than it was seventy years ago; identities are more diverse, contested, contradictory and ambiguous than they were in the past. New structures of community have emerged; however the old is still visible in the new and the historic tendency towards communal division has persisted. It is at its most intense in Northern Ireland where internal communal structures exacerbate division. Moreover, communal division in Northern Ireland opens out to continuing communal division at the level of the island as a whole (chapters 9 and 11).

4   Ideology and conflict

The conflict in Ireland has been mediated by ideologies which at once express and constitute social relationships and communal interests (chapter 2). Each ideology is distinctive in its conceptual structure, embodies a specific family of concepts and is embedded in specific communal organisations and political projects;[1] at the same time each ideology interacts with and influences others. Partition institutionalised the dominant ideologies of the pre-partition period in the new state structures. Since the 1950s there have been flows and counterflows – moderation, reaction, innovation, reconstruction – but ideological opposition and conflict have persisted. In this chapter we trace the changes and continuities and show how ideological opposition is reproduced. We begin by sketching the pre-partition origins and developing forms of these ideologies.

Ideological traditions

Loyalism

Loyalism is the oldest of the Protestant ideologies. Its origins lie in the seventeenth-century experience of colonisation and religious conflict and it posits an irreconcilable conflict between Protestant and Catholic, settler and native, loyal and disloyal. A Protestant communal identity lies at the core of the ideology, together with an insistence on the need for metropolitan support to ensure Protestant survival in Ireland. This is expressed in contractarian political terms: loyalty to the Crown is conditional on the Crown's support for Protestant rights and the Protestant community against its enemies; if support is not forthcoming

---

[1] For a more detailed discussion, see Jennifer Todd, 'Two traditions in unionist political culture', *Irish Political Studies*, vol. 2, 1987, and Jennifer Todd, 'Northern Irish nationalist political culture', *Irish Political Studies*, vol. 5, 1990.

the community will look to its own defence.[2] The conflictual and unstable nature of the seventeenth-century settlement continually generated conflicts with the Catholic population which confirmed the loyalist vision.

Initially an ideology of all Irish Protestants, loyalism was particularly strong and enduring among Ulster Protestants.[3] In Ulster, loyalist beliefs in the irreconcilability of settler and native, Protestant and Catholic were given sharper focus by the Calvinist dichotomy of Good and Evil, elect and damned.[4] The Scottish tradition of covenanting provided a language of conditional political allegiance, and the traditions of 'public banding' affirmed the primacy of the local community and the imperative of communal self-defence.[5] Among Ulster Protestants, loyalism was strongest in the 'frontier' conditions west of the Bann where settlement, displacement and resistance had been most intense.

The formation of the Orange Order in 1795 gave loyalism greater ideological focus, a specific political project – the defence of the Protestant Constitution – and an organisational form adaptable to the emerging urban-industrial economy and to the politics of mass mobilisation. In the nineteenth century the ideology was strengthened by the new evangelism, which eroded religious divisions among Protestants, and it incorporated imperial themes. It was renewed as a mass movement in the home rule crisis. Loyalists stressed the threat which home rule posed to Protestants' religious and civil liberties; the powerfully symbolic Ulster Covenant of 1912 consciously referred back to the formative seventeenth century; the Orange Order provided recruits for the Ulster Volunteer Force which gave unionism its military backing.[6]

The crucial role which loyalism played in the Ulster unionist victory ensured it a prominent place in the new state. Loyalists infused the state and its public culture with their stance of combativeness and confidence born out of past victories, defensiveness and fearfulness from the ever-present possibility of defeat, and incapacity to conceive of compromise.

---

[2] D. W. Miller, *Queen's Rebels: Ulster Loyalism in Historical Perspective*, Dublin, Gill and Macmillan, 1978.

[3] Stewart notes that the planters brought with them 'all the mental luggage of sixteenth- and seventeenth-century colonizers', A. T. Q. Stewart, *The Narrow Ground: Aspects of Ulster 1609–1969*, London, Faber and Faber, 1977, pp. 46–7.

[4] Finlay Holmes, *Our Irish Presbyterian Heritage*, Belfast, Publications Committee of the Presbyterian Church in Ireland, 1985, ch. 2; Donald Harman Akenson, *God's Peoples: Covenant and Land in South Africa, Israel and Ulster*, Ithaca, Cornell University Press, 1992, p. 112; Miller, *Queen's Rebels*, ch. 1.

[5] Miller, *Queen's Rebels*, pp. 21ff., 37.

[6] *Ibid.*, pp. 96ff.; Philip Orr, *The Road to the Somme: Men of the Ulster Division Tell Their Story*, Belfast, Blackstaff, 1987, ch. 1.

Dissent

Dissent's historical and cultural roots lie in the eighteenth century, in the enlightened Presbyterian tradition and in contemporary notions of civic republicanism. It emphasises and seeks to embody the individualistic, democratic and egalitarian aspects of Protestantism. Dissent was shaped politically by the tensions experienced by Presbyterians in the eighteenth century. They were part of the minority settler community but, as dissenters from the established church, they were subject to economic, political and religious disabilities. They were also strongly represented among the merchant and professional classes and shared their resentment of aristocratic dominance. At the end of the century, dissent took a radical political form under the influence of the American and French revolutions. Sections of the newly emergent Ulster Presbyterian middle class and independent artisanate sought to counter aristocratic and British control with a new political ideal – that of an independent democratic political community in Ireland in which Protestant, Catholic and Dissenter would be reconciled in relations of fairness and equality.

Dissent lost its radical edge and declined in importance in the nineteenth century. The sectarianism that accompanied the 1798 rebellion in Wexford challenged some of its assumptions about the potential for reconciling religious differences; the Act of Union abolished the aristocratically controlled Dublin parliament and brought economic benefits;[7] industrialisation and urbanisation eroded the independent artisanate which had been an important part of dissent's support base. At the same time many of dissent's ideals – the opposition to Protestant communal power and privilege, the search for reconciliation with Catholics – survived, informing Protestant liberalism and land agitation and strengthening Presbyterian resistance to remaining Anglican privileges. During the home rule crisis, J. B. Armour – the most prominent of the Protestant home rulers – voiced classic dissenting values: the independence of the Protestant (more precisely, Presbyterian) tradition; the damaging effects of a unionism that encouraged deference and intimidation, that discouraged radical individualism and silenced the voice of conscience; the spiritual and ethical corruption involved in defending privilege out of fear of the unfairly treated majority.[8]

---

[7] Donald Harman Akenson, *Between Two Revolutions: Islandmagee, Co. Antrim 1798–1920*, Dublin, Academy Press, 1979.

[8] J. R. B. McMinn, ed., *Against the Tide: J. B. Armour, Irish Presbyterian Minister and Home Ruler 1869–1914*, Belfast, PRONI, 1985.

Nationalism and republicanism

The roots of Irish nationalism have been variously located in the sixteenth and seventeenth-century defeat of the Catholic Old English and Gaelic-Irish and in the 'colonial nationalism' of eighteenth century Protestant patriots. However it took its modern form in the nineteenth century under the influence of European nationalisms. Much of the intellectual impetus came from Protestants seeking to reconcile Catholic and Protestant, settler and native; their most important legacy was the concept of a single, inclusive Irish nation.[9] But the depth and intensity of feeling came from Catholics – from their historic defeat and subordination as a community and from their sense of being the main victims of the economic peripheralisation of much of the Irish economy during the nineteenth century (chapter 2).

At the centre of this nationalism was a narrative construction of the history of the Irish nation. This narrative posited a golden age, a fall and a process of rebirth. Ireland was the home of an ancient and independent people with its own distinctive language and culture. In this period of freedom the Irish lived in peace and harmony, the arts and industries flourished. The unique potential of this civilisation was cut short first by Viking attacks, later by the Anglo-Norman invasion which prepared the way for centuries of English rule. With foreign domination came division, decline and decay. The English reconquest in the sixteenth and seventeenth centuries combined religious oppression, political domination and economic exploitation, and a sustained effort was made to destroy Ireland's distinctive culture and language. Following the challenge to English rule by the Irish parliament and United Irishmen at the end of the eighteenth century, the British government forced through the Act of Union by bribery and threats. With union came the destruction of Irish industry, the decline of the Irish language and a devastating famine. But the will to resist remained, growing stronger in the knowledge that only freedom would bring national recovery, the rebuilding of the economy, the halting of the decline in the native language and culture. The 1916 rebellion and the war of independence were the culmination of this long struggle.

The Irish nation thus imagined includes the Gaelic-Irish and those descendants of the settlers – late medieval or early modern – who resisted English rule in Ireland. The Catholic Old English and their descendants are automatically included; so too are those of more recent settler stock

---

[9] Cf. John Hutchinson, *The Dynamics of Cultural Nationalism: The Gaelic Revival and the Creation of the Irish Nation State*, London, Allen and Unwin, 1987, chs. 3, 4, 5.

who accept this narrative understanding and support nationalist cultural and political ideals; others are excluded. The narrative carries the implicit goal of freedom and fulfilment for the Irish people so defined. This goal has been understood in diverse ways and embodied in very different political programmes – from the constitutionalist gradualism of the Irish parliamentary party to the insurrectionary radicalism of the Fenians, from the universalistic ideals of Patrick Pearse to the more pointedly Gaelic-Catholic nationalism of writers such as D. P. Moran, from the desire for limited self-government within the empire to the republican separatist insistence on an independent state for the Irish nation.[10]

Unionism

Unionist ideology emerged in reaction to nationalist claims and aspirations and used the contemporary language of British political identity, economic progress and liberal political rights to counter nationalist arguments. From the outset it had two strands – an explicit defence of Protestant interests and an argument that the union brought benefits not just to Protestants but to the whole of Ireland, the British Isles and the empire.

For unionists, the economic achievements of east Ulster showed the potential of the union for the whole of Ireland. Indeed all of Ireland had already benefited: one writer contrasted the fate of victims of the famine of 1846–9 with the even worse fate of those of 1740–1.[11] If much of Ireland had economic problems, the causes lay in Ireland rather than in the union and they would be better dealt with by a powerful and wealthy imperial government than by an impoverished home rule government which could only make matters worse.[12] Ulster in particular would suffer – contemporary Ulster unionist postcards showed Portadown and Belfast, bustling and prosperous under the Union, decaying under home rule.[13]

[10] Maurice Goldring, *Faith of our Fathers: The Formation of Irish Nationalist Ideology*, Dublin, Repsol, 1982; Tom Garvin, *Nationalist Revolutionaries in Ireland 1858–1928*, Oxford, Clarendon, 1987; D. G. Boyce, *Nationalism in Ireland*, London, Croom Helm, 1982.

[11] Patrick Buckland, *Irish Unionism 1885–1923: A Documentary History*, Belfast, HMSO, 1973, p. 5.

[12] *Ibid.*, pp. 18ff.; cf. Sir Edward Carson, 'Introduction' to S. Rosenbaum, ed., *Against Home Rule: The Case for the Union*, London, Frederick Warner, 1912, p. 25; see also chs. 7 and 16.

[13] John Killen, *John Bull's Famous Circus: Ulster history through the postcard*, Dublin, O'Brien, 1985, pp. 50, 53; Buckland, *Irish Unionism*, pp. 15–17; see Jennifer Todd, 'Unionist political thought 1920–1972', in D. G. Boyce, R. Eccleshall and

Unionists also pointed to the political and cultural benefits of the union. Whatever about the past, Catholics and Protestants now enjoyed full and equal freedom under the union, and the imperial parliament had shown constant concern to redress the historic grievances of Catholics.[14] Only a section of the Catholic population, hostile to Protestants, property and to England, wanted change. Unionists also contrasted the progressive, vibrant metropolitan and imperial culture of Britain with (Catholic) Ireland's rural, backward looking peasant culture; Britain's 'civilising' role – preventing Irish tendencies towards backwardness from becoming dominant – was a recurring theme.[15]

While all of Ireland would suffer under home rule, Protestants in particular would suffer since their political and religious rights, guaranteed under the union, would be overridden by the weight of Catholic dogma in a home rule parliament.[16] The British identity and loyalties of Protestants were also emphasised. Sometimes unionists posited two races, two nations, two civilisations in Ireland, with the British government obliged to defend the British.[17] To defend the Protestant interest in Ireland was – so it seemed to unionists – no mere particularism but itself a defence of British values. Britishness in this context had a strong imperial component. Unionists, especially when they were addressing a British audience, emphasised the threat of a home rule or independent Ireland to the empire.[18] The threat was not simply from independence or even from a Catholic parliament but from the fact that the kind of Catholics who would control it were the sworn enemies of England and of the empire.

Labourism and socialist republicanism

Increasing industrialisation in Ireland, as elsewhere, led to the development of socialist ideologies which articulated working-class interests. All

V. Geoghegan, eds., *Political Thought in Ireland since the Seventeenth Century*, London, Routledge, 1993, p. 193.

[14] Buckland, *Irish Unionism*, p. 12; P. Kerr-Smiley, *The Peril of Home Rule*, London, Cassell and Co. Ltd, 1911, pp. 32, 129; Rosenbaum, ed., *Against Home Rule*, pp. 204, 213–14, 218.

[15] Buckland, *Irish Unionism*, p. 21; T. MacKnight, *Ulster as it is, or Twenty-eight Years Experience as an Irish Editor*, London, Macmillan, 2 vols., 1896, vol. 2, p. 334; The Marquis of Londonderry, 'The Ulster Question', in Rosenbaum, ed., *Against Home Rule*, pp. 165–6; cf. Todd, 'Unionist political thought', p. 193.

[16] Kerr-Smiley, *Peril of Home Rule*, ch. 6 and pp. 131–2; Rosenbaum, ed., *Against Home Rule*, Introduction and chs. 8 and 12.

[17] MacKnight, *Ulster as it is*, vol. 1, p. 299, vol. 2, pp. 185, 380.

[18] Rosenbaum, ed., *Against Home Rule*, Introduction, ch. 3. Kerr-Smiley, *Perils of Home Rule*, ch. 4.

strands of socialism, however, had to address the deep political and religious division within the working class. Two main tendencies emerged.

Labourism was largely a Belfast phenomenon. Reformist and trade unionist rather than revolutionary, it drew on emerging British socialist ideas; its institutional base was the trade union movement, particularly in the large high-skill industries. There was a determined effort to side-line the divisive constitutional issue and to remain non-sectarian.[19] However the predominantly Protestant nature of the workforce, the strength of loyalism and Orangeism within it, and the dependence of Ulster industry on British markets made such questions impossible to avoid. In addition there was a belief in the increasing potential of the British labour and trade union movement to effect positive change on behalf of workers throughout the United Kingdom. Thus a labourist consciousness was quite compatible – and frequently coexisted – with an unquestioned unionism, a belief in the progressiveness of the British empire and the regressive character of Irish nationalism.[20]

The much weaker revolutionary socialist tradition was largely Dublin-based, Catholic and republican.[21] James Connolly and Jim Larkin saw the organisation of the working class as a step to radical social and political change, not simply as a means of improving working conditions. Connolly came to believe that there could be a dove-tailing of socialist and advanced nationalist revolution, that republican socialists could play a leading role in the national struggle, and thereby shape the newly independent state along socialist lines.[22] The major problem lay in the fact that the largest section of the Irish working class – the Belfast Protestant working class – was resolutely anti-nationalist. Working-class unity fell apart when the constitutional question was foregrounded or the stability of the state came into question.[23] For socialist republicans this showed the Protestant working class to be mere dupes of British capitalism and imperialism.[24]

---

[19] See Henry Patterson, *Class Conflict and Sectarianism: The Protestant Working Class and the Belfast Labour Movement 1868–1920*, Belfast, Blackstaff, 1980.

[20] Patterson, *Class Conflict*, ch. 3 and p. 86.

[21] See Boyce, *Nationalism in Ireland*, ch. 10.

[22] For a selection of writings on these issues, see James Connolly, *Collected Works*, vol. 1, Dublin, New Books Publications, 1987, pp. 304–464; for conflicting interpretations, see John Newsinger, 'Connolly and his biographers', *Irish Political Studies*, vol. 5, 1990.

[23] John Gray, *City in Revolt: James Larkin and the Belfast Dock Strike of 1907*, Belfast, Blackstaff, 1985.

[24] Patterson, *Class Conflict*, pp. 83–5.

Ideology and ideological change since partition

Unionism/loyalism and nationalism/republicanism were – though in different ways and in different degrees – ideologies of communal assertion and defence in late nineteenth and early twentieth-century Ireland. They were institutionalised as state ideologies after partition, but without ceasing to be communal ones. Conditions in both states – one suffering from chronic division, the other from a frustrated sense of national destiny – strengthened the particularist tendencies inherent in both ideological families. By the 1950s some rethinking was occurring on both sides of the border; the crisis of the 1960s produced further movement.

Institutionalisation and consolidation

There had always been a tendency within unionism to identify the general with the Protestant interest. In the state-building process, this intensified. The new state was self-evidently a Northern Protestant creation, a product of their will to self-determination, of their desire to build a state 'of their own', formed in accordance with their British and Protestant ethos.[25] Republican attacks on the state in its early years and the continued refusal of nationalists to accord it legitimacy strengthened unionism's particularist tendencies and undermined its liberal claims. Liberal unionists were discomforted by some of the measures adopted to defend the state – repressive security, internment, economic and political discrimination (chapters 5, 6) – but went along with them.[26] No unionist saw good reason to integrate nationalists into the institutions of state. Liberal and pluralist principles were articulated by some unionist leaders during the 1920s but were not embodied in policy; by the 1930s, even the rhetoric was abandoned.[27] Some universalistic themes survived – for example, the general economic, political and cultural benefits of the union and the vast superiority of the conditions in the North to those in the Free State[28] – but as arguments to justify and defend the state rather than to broaden its communal base.

[25] For example, see Brian Barton, *Brookeborough: The Making of a Prime Minister*, Belfast, Institute of Irish Studies, 1988, p. 127.
[26] *Ibid*, pp. 78–85.
[27] For the early ideals, see H. M. Hyde, *Carson: A Biography*, London, Heinemann, 1953, p. 449; James Craig, *Belfast Newsletter* 8 Feb. 1921, quoted in D. Kennedy, *The Widening Gulf: Northern Attitudes to the Independent Irish State 1919–1949*, Belfast, Blackstaff, 1988, p. 59.
[28] Kennedy, *The Widening Gulf*, chs. 8–11.

Unionism was the official ideology of the state, informing its self-presentation in Britain and abroad and the beliefs of a section of the political elite. But loyalism was also integrated into the state at all levels, including government. It had institutionalised weight in the Orange Order's links with the Unionist Party and in the state's dependence on popular loyalist support in local and regional politics and in the security forces; its importance was symbolised and reinforced in the annual Orange marches which became the occasion of public holiday (see pp. 108–10 below and chapter 5). There was a class basis to the ideological distinction, with loyalism providing a vehicle for Protestant working-class assertion. Loyalism also provided the cutting edge of Protestant particularism and exercised a restraint on any tendencies within unionism to a more inclusivist or pluralist polity. But Protestant particularism was common to unionism and loyalism and the distinction between them was more blurred in this period than before or since. Significantly, unionist politicians did not challenge the assumptions behind loyalist demands that the state should favour the Protestant interest: they simply showed that it did.[29]

The vast majority of Catholics interpreted their situation in traditional nationalist terms. The new state was as much an alien imposition as British rule in Ireland had been in the past. There was now the injustice of partition – 'the mutilation of a nation', 'the dismemberment of our fatherland', the breaking of the 'ancient stem' of Ireland, an 'abortion wrenched from the parent womb'.[30] The only possible response was resistance – internal if not external – and the hope of redemption.[31]

Moderation

The 1950s saw signs of moderation in some sections of unionism and nationalism. Unionists were now more self-confident. Their contribution in the war and continued role in Western defence seemed to assure their place within the United Kingdom and confirmed their self-conception as part of the progressive free world. The British welfare state was bringing

[29] Jonathan Bardon, *History of Ulster*, Belfast, Whiterow, 1992, p. 498.
[30] The quotations come respectively from Cahir Healy, *The Mutilation of a Nation*, Derry, Derry Journal, 1945; T. J. Campbell, *Fifty Years of Ulster: 1890–1940*, Belfast, *The Irish News*, 1941, p. 104; Bishop Mageean commenting on Ultach, 'The real case against partition', *Capuchin Annual*, 1943, pp. 315–16; Paddy Doherty, 'A Catholic looks at the Northern State', in John Fairleigh et al., eds., *Sectarianism: Roads to Reconciliation*, Dublin, Three Candles, 1975, p. 36.
[31] The concept of redemption is used and quoted widely in Eamon Phoenix, *Northern Nationalism: Nationalist Politics, Partition and the Catholic Minority in Northern Ireland 1890–1940*, Belfast, Ulster Historical Foundation, 1994, e.g. pp. 109, 310, 340.

economic benefits at a time when the Republic was economically stagnant and internationally marginal. Unionist rhetoric became more modernising and technocratic, and also more universalist than it had been in the pre-war period, emphasising the benefits the union brought to all in Northern Ireland, not simply Protestants. Liberal unionists also began more self-consciously to distance themselves from loyalism, a tendency which increased in the 1960s and was further accentuated by the accession of Terence O'Neill to the premiership.

The conceptual structure of unionist ideology had not, however, changed. The choice, in unionist eyes, was more than ever one between an affluent, progressive, modernising North and a poor, backward, reactionary, superstitious South. Moderation owed much to the expectation that the merits of the union would now be evident to Catholics, who might – preferably quietly and gradually – be included in the state.[32] It was common at this time for unionists to see institutional biases against Catholics as minor anachronisms which would be eased gradually; few, even the most liberal, saw any essential contradiction between their liberal ideals and political institutions or practices in Northern Ireland.[33] Moreover unionism's modernising turn came in part from an attempt to meet the strong challenge of the Northern Ireland Labour Party's (NILP) programme for social, economic and political reform within the union.[34]

Moderate currents were also emerging within the Catholic community. There were explicit statements of what had always been a minority position within the community – an acceptance of (or at least an unwillingness to challenge) the legitimacy of the state and the sincerity of unionist reformers' motives, and a 'readiness to serve' in public office.[35] A less accomodating but nonetheless moderate and modernising nationalism also appeared, making explicit its commitment to unity only by consent and stressing economic and social issues.[36] Finally,

---

[32] Todd, 'Unionist political thought', pp. 205–7; report on Northern Ireland cabinet papers by Eamon Phoenix, Anne Flaherty, and Mark Brennock, *Irish Times* 1–2 Jan. 1991, p. 6.

[33] John A. Oliver, 'The Stormont administration', in Patrick J. Roche and Brian Barton, eds., *The Northern Ireland Question: Myth and Reality*, Aldershot, Avebury, 1991, pp. 80–6, 92–7. Tom Wilson, *Ulster: Conflict and Consent*, Oxford, Basil Blackwell, 1989, chs. 8, 11, 12, 13; The Cadogan Group, *Northern Limits: Boundaries of the Attainable in Northern Ireland Politics*, Belfast, Cadogan Group, 1992, pp. 4–8; Robin Boyd, 'Northern Protestants – By themselves', *Irish Times*, 20 Mar. 1986.

[34] Paul Bew, Peter Gibbon and Henry Patterson, *Northern Ireland 1921–1994: Political Forces and Social Classes*, London, Serif, 1995, ch. 4.

[35] G. B. Newe, 'The Catholic in the Northern Ireland community', *Christus Rex*, vol. 18, no. 1, 1964, p. 31.

[36] Michael McKeown, *The Greening of a Nationalist*, Lucan, Co. Dublin, Murlough Press, 1986, ch. 3.

republicans, after the collapse of the border campaign of the late 1950s, abandoned violence and embraced a new form of socialist republicanism that sought to democratise the Northern state as a first stage in winning working-class unity for the demand of a united Ireland.[37] In the late 1960s these strands coalesced around the issue of civil rights within Northern Ireland.[38]

Reaction

Loyalism. Unionist moderation in the 1960s may have been limited in extent, but it coincided with a new phase of economic and political restructuring and of religious ecumenism that deeply worried loyalists (chapter 5). Ian Paisley articulated loyalist unease, re-emphasising the distinction between loyalism and unionism which had become blurred in the Stormont period. His emergence marked a radical challenge to loyalism's integration into the unionist state, a regeneration of loyalism as protest and an insistence that the state be brought back to its contractual obligations to the Protestant people. His language and conceptual oppositions were traditional, with a strong fundamentalist and evangelical religious emphasis – the Pope as the whore of Rome whose overarching political ambitions threatened the Protestant people of Ulster, Irish nationalism as identical to Catholicism and both aiming at the destruction of Northern Protestants, loyalty to the Protestant Crown (not the British state or nation) conditional on its protection of the Protestant people.[39]

For much of the 1960s Paisley was viewed as a fringe figure, a throw-back to earlier periods of Ulster's history. But already by 1966 the climate of opinion he had helped generate had led to a small-scale revival of Protestant paramilitarism (chapter 5). The situation changed radically with the birth of the civil rights movement and its adoption of street protests. Loyalists saw the civil rights movement as a direct attack on the state and set out to disrupt it at every turn. The re-emergence of armed republicanism in 1969–70 convinced them that they had been right all along and that the Protestants of Ulster faced a challenge to their very

---

[37] Henry Patterson, *The Politics of Illusion: Republicanism and Socialism in Modern Ireland,* London, Hutchinson, 1989, ch. 4.

[38] See Bob Purdie, *Politics in the Streets: The Origins of the Civil Rights Movement in Northern Ireland,* Belfast, Blackstaff, 1990.

[39] Steve Bruce, *God Save Ulster: The Religion and Politics of Paisleyism,* Oxford, Clarendon, 1986; Clifford Smyth, *Ian Paisley: Voice of Protestant Ulster,* Edinburgh, Scottish Academic Press Ltd, 1987, ch. 4; Ed Moloney and Andy Pollak, *Paisley,* Swords, Co. Dublin, Poolbeg Press, 1986.

existence. Sarah Nelson reports being asked on the Shankill Road in the early 1970s 'Will you Scots take us in when they drive us out.'[40] Loyalist paramilitarism now emerged on a large scale.

The conceptual structure of loyalism was powerfully reinforced by the experience of communal conflict. Classic religio-political certainties were expressed by the fundamentalist leadership of the DUP and in the literature of the Orange Order. Contemporary events were seen in terms of images of the past: Protestants were being pushed out of their traditional areas and workplaces, they were under siege, subject to genocidal attack, forced to retaliate.[41] Only loyalist organisation, vigilance and militancy could defend the Protestant population.

Republicanism. The crisis of 1969 also renewed traditional republicanism. State resistance to reform, loyalist and security force attacks on Catholic homes, British backing of unionist security policy seemed to many Catholics to offer palpable confirmation of traditional nationalist assumptions. The republican movement split. The Provisional wing discarded the social republican and socialist assumptions characteristic of republicanism in the 1960s and returned to the militant nationalism characteristic of Belfast republicanism in the 1930s and 1940s.[42]

The demands of the civil rights movement for limited internal reforms gave way to traditional republican demands (complete British withdrawal), aims (an independent, united, Irish state), and principles (national self-determination). Republican violence was justified in the name of the Irish people who, when last permitted an undivided response in 1918, voted clearly for the independence of the whole of the island; it was not sectarian violence but the violence of a suppressed people that had risen again in rebellion. As in the past, independence was conceived in cultural as well as political terms and there was an intensified interest in the Irish language and Gaelic-Irish culture.[43]

Republicans saw their struggle directed against the British state presence, not against Protestants who were part of the Irish nation. However Protestants who actively supported the British state were

40 Sarah Nelson, *Ulster's Uncertain Defenders: Loyalists and the Northern Ireland Conflict*, Belfast, Appletree, 1984, p. 30.
41 James W. McAuley, *The Politics of Identity: A Loyalist Community in Belfast*, Aldershot, Avebury, 1994, pp. 129–36.
42 Ronnie Munck and Bill Rolston, *Belfast in the Thirties: An Oral History*, Belfast, Blackstaff, 1987, ch. 5.
43 For the earlier period, see Garvin, *Nationalist Revolutionaries*, ch. 5; for the contemporary period see Felim Hamill, 'Belfast: The Irish language', *Éire-Ireland*, vol. 21, no. 4, 1986.

deemed legitimate IRA targets; those who refused to accept Irish unity had the option of political marginalisation or repatriation to Britain. Despite its universalist claims, republicanism made little effort to disguise its own Catholic roots, particularly at moments of communal crisis. Thus the hunger strikers were portrayed in literature and murals as Christ-like figures; Marian themes were important; the saying of the rosary was a common feature of political meetings during the hunger strikes.

Innovation

The crisis of the late 1960s led to the articulation of at least two new ideologies, bridge-building and Catholic unionism.

Bridge-building. Bridge-building ideology – motivated by a desire to break from past patterns of communal conflict – has precursors in nineteenth-century liberalism, twentieth-century labourism and ecumenical movements. Only with the crisis of the late 1960s, however, was it articulated as a distinct ideology by a succession of middle-ground, cross-community groups.[44] In bridge-building ideology, effective history – the history that creates the conditions for conflict and defines the arena for reconciliation – dates from the foundation of Northern Ireland in 1920. The more distant historical origins of the conflict are no longer relevant. In the past, it may have been an island-wide conflict, but now Northern Ireland is a real working region, not a mere failed political entity, and the people of Northern Ireland are a distinctive community quite separate from the South and from Britain.[45] The problem is one of communal division within Northern Ireland.

The intensity of division emanates from the conflicting goals of nationalism and unionism. Both ideologies are now outdated: the question in Northern Ireland should be, as it is elsewhere in contemporary Europe, one of ensuring fair treatment for minorities within existing state boundaries. While in principle the majority's right to its constitutional preference is accepted, there is an attempt to set aside the constitutional question. 'Provocative debate' about constitutional change was seen, in an early Alliance party statement of basic principle, as 'the primary cause

---

[44] The most important of these was the New Ulster Movement. For example, New Ulster Movement, *The Reform of Stormont*, Belfast, New Ulster Movement, 1971, *Two Irelands or One?*, Belfast, New Ulster Movement, 1972, *Tribalism or Christianity in Ireland?*, Belfast, New Ulster Movement, 1973.

[45] Cf. Robin Glendinning's submission to New Ireland Forum, *Proceedings*, no. 4, p. 13; *Alliance News*, Inter-Party talks supplement, Nov.–Dec. 1992, p. 2.

of our most fundamental troubles'. In fact, a majority of bridge-builders prefer the union but they distinguish this preference from the British nationalism of unionists and the Protestant supremacism of loyalists.

Modernity and modernisation are core values for bridge-builders. They urge a break with the outdated allegiances and loyalties of the past as well as a willingness to devise new imaginative solutions to overcome division – consociational democracy, bills of rights, protection for all religious, sexual and racial minorities. There is a commitment to the pluralist values of the contemporary liberal tradition, to regionalism and to contemporary moves towards post-nationalism in a European context.[46] The various notions of modernity are united in opposition to 'hidebound nationalisms'.[47] Violence – republican and loyalist – is seen as destructive and disruptive of gradual progress in advancing these concerns.

While accepting the legitimacy of the state, bridge-builders are willing to change its structures and institutions to give all groups a fair deal within it and and to change its cultural character so that all citizens can identify with it. Some bridge-builders urge very far-reaching reform to address inequality within Northern Ireland.[48] Others imply that the main aspects of Catholic inequality are now resolved: the main enemy is the communal structure itself and communal belief systems and myths.[49] Bridge-building ideology leaves open a very wide range of possible judgements.

Catholic unionism. Since 1969 a radically new form of unionism has emerged among Catholics. It finds support among those who are young, middle class or upwardly mobile, unconcerned with questions of cultural identity, critical of the treatment of Catholics under Stormont but conscious of the material benefits offered by the British state. This ideology criticises equally the 'backwardness' of the South of Ireland and of the nationalist tradition and the 'sectarianism' of the main unionist parties. It rejects the unionist tradition as it has developed in Northern Ireland but in principle favours the British link.[50] Partition is seen

---

[46] The current affairs magazine, *Fortnight*, has embodied this perspective in many articles and editorials over the last decade.

[47] Cf. letter by Philip J. McGarry, *Alliance News*, Mar. 1988, p. 4.

[48] Robin Wilson, as editor of *Fortnight*, consistently took this view.

[49] The view that inequality is now largely a thing of the past is usually implicit rather than explicit – reflected in the absence of reference to inequality as an important factor in the conflict. It is most marked in approaches which focus on communal myths, fears or prejudices and see the conflict as one between differing 'cultural traditions'.

[50] For examples, see Joe Keenan, *An Argument on Behalf of the Catholics of Northern Ireland*, Belfast, Athol, 1987.

as permanent; the goal is a reformed Northern Ireland within the framework of a new non-sectarian concept of the union and of 'Britishness'.

The ideological origins and motivating ideals of this form of unionism lie in the civil rights movement. For Brendan Clifford, 'The implication of the Civil Rights slogans of 1968–9 was a programme of normalising Ulster as a region of the UK.'[51] British development is seen as progressive and modernising, able to give the full citizenship demanded by civil rights activists. Irish nationalist and Northern Irish communal politics are seen as backward and sectarian. The insulation of Northern Ireland from mainstream British politics has encouraged Protestant sectarianism and Catholic nationalism.[52] Full integration of Northern Ireland into the United Kingdom would sweep away entrenched institutions and attitudes, the organisation of British parties in Northern Ireland would destroy the peculiarities of the Northern Ireland political system with the effect of ending the inequalities from which Catholics have traditionally suffered.

This ideology seeks to articulate a concept of the union and of Britishness as essentially progressive and to separate it from the cultural trappings, emotional patriotism and binary opposition to Irishness characteristic of the dominant form of unionism. The emphasis is on the citizenship features of the British state, its laws, particularly those guaranteeing individual liberties, the liberal attitude to sexual and reproductive politics, the welfare and educational resources which allow opportunities for upward social mobility, the intellectual opportunities, the multinational and multiethnic character of the United Kingdom, the political division on left-right ideological grounds. Catholic unionism exhibits therefore much of the 'pure' political allegiance to the British state which Arthur Aughey attributes to the entire unionist tradition.[53]

Reconstruction

The most important ideological developments during the past twenty-five years have been the attempts to reconstruct the major ideologies – nationalism, unionism, republicanism and loyalism. The reconstructed ideologies use a more pluralist language and are more principledly

---

[51] Brendan Clifford, *Parliamentary Despotism*, Belfast, Athol, 1986, p. 17, quoted in Arthur Aughey, *Under Siege: Ulster Unionism and the Anglo-Irish Agreement*, Belfast, Blackstaff, 1989, p. 147.
[52] Keenan, *Argument on Behalf of Catholics*, pp. 5–6, 20–1.
[53] Cf. Aughey, *Under Siege*, ch. 1.

universalistic. They have not, however, definitively broken with the older conceptual structures and combine a universalist thrust with many of the traditional categories.

Nationalism. In 1973 Eddie MacAteer, last leader of the Nationalist party, described the conflict in Northern Ireland as 'a rerun of a very, very old film . . . colonists from England came as conquerors, stole our land, and endeavored to replace the Irish with their own people. This was called the Plantation of Ulster. That contest between the colonials and the natives is, strange to say, still actively in force.'[54] However even while he spoke his language was no longer that of the new generation of nationalists in Northern Ireland. A reconstruction and modernisation of nationalism was underway. Its articulators have been politicians (above all John Hume), clergy and journalists.[55]

The reconstruction of nationalism is closely bound up with the crystallisation of a Northern Catholic community with a sense of its own separate identity and interests within the wider Irish national community (chapter 3). Significantly, the nature of that identity and those interests is left open – one of the distinctive features of this new reconstructed nationalism is its pragmatism and openness to the future. The axioms of the old nationalism – Britain's role in Ireland is a colonial one, only a united Ireland can have real political legitimacy, Catholics can never get a fair deal in Northern Ireland – have now consciously been put in the balance. It is accepted that the role of the British state in Ireland has changed and that Northern Ireland may be reformable. If that is the case, nationalists might accept to work within a Northern Ireland context for the foreseeable future.

A reformed Northern Ireland would, however, have to be of a distinct kind, sometimes expressed in the formula 'absolute equality of the two traditions in Northern Ireland and an open agenda'. Equality is variously interpreted but the implicit concept is one of substantive economic, political and cultural equality between the communities which would, in turn, require a substantive Irish dimension (chapter 5). The 'open agenda' means that Irish unity cannot be ruled out as an ultimate goal and nationalists must be free to work to achieve it by peaceful means if they so choose. There is a recognition that they may not so choose. Irish unity remains the ideal in this reconstructed nationalism but not a very

---

[54] Eddie McAteer in W. H. Van Voris, *Violence in Ulster: An Oral Documentary*, Amherst, University of Massachusetts Press, 1975, p. 12.

[55] For example, John Hume's speeches to SDLP annual conferences; Archbishop Cahal B. Daly, *The Price of Peace*, Belfast, Blackstaff, 1991; also see editorials in the *Irish News*.

pressing one. There is a keen awareness of the economic weakness of the Southern state and disquiet at the way the South has responded to the Northern crisis over the past twenty-five years (chapter 9); there is also the sense that unity may not mean much in the context of European integration. The current demand is for a new Northern Ireland; a new Ireland is for the future.

If Northern Ireland might ultimately win the allegiance of nationalists, it does not yet do so. The structural and institutional legacy of the past – for example in the economy and the security forces – is still too great. More important, legitimacy can only exist when Catholics have willingly consented to the structures under which they are governed and they have not yet been offered an acceptable framework. The responsibility for this is thought to lie with the unionists and loyalists who refuse to accept the legitimacy of nationalist demands and many of whom (it is believed) still retain a hankering for the old order. But the British government is not entirely trusted either.

The weakening in the desire for Irish unity comes not from an abandonment of Irish identity but from the view that in a new Northern Ireland it would be possible to 'be Irish'. This would require increased contact between North and South as a tangible expression of such an identity. A strengthened Southern link is also strategically important. The new nationalism is a great deal more self-confident than in the past, but it retains a strong sense of its own vulnerability. It is conscious of the need to balance unionists' demographic and economic strength by securing Southern and international support. At the same time, there is a desire to get beyond the communal power struggle by working out some form of agreement among the people of Northern Ireland and of the island as a whole.

The need to get beyond the past is a recurring theme. There is a reluctance to harp on the experiences of the Stormont years; too much concentration on old grievances – whether before or after partition – is seen as unnecessary 'whingeing'.[56] Yet any denial of the injustices of the past meets a swift response. The colonial nature of British rule in the past, its role in underwriting unionist domination during the Stormont years and its continuing legacy in unionist attitudes frame the understanding of the present. The point is to get beyond the past, but to do this requires a dismantling of the legacy of the past; the desired accommodation and respect for differences requires full equality of the traditions and cannot be achieved if one community has power over the other.

---

[56] John Hume, Address to 16th conference of the SDLP, 21–3 November 1986, p. 9 (published in booklet form by SDLP).

The new nationalism self-consciously espouses liberal and pluralist principles, sees itself as working within a multi-stranded context – internal Northern Irish, North–South, British–Irish, European – and is anxious to avoid appearing nationalist in the traditional sense. Thus, the SDLP redefines the Irish nation in explicitly pluralist terms which include unionists.[57] While it has recently (re)embraced the concept of 'the self-determination of the Irish people', it immediately qualifies this with the recognition that the people of Ireland are divided as to how to exercise that right and that the first priority must be agreement on how to exercise it. Similarly, while Irish unity is still an ideal, the emphasis is on uniting the people of Ireland rather than the territory.[58]

The extent of conceptual revision, however, remains ambiguous. The notion of the Irish nation may be reformulated in pluralist terms, but a more traditional notion of Irish identity, which implicitly refers to the traditional nationalist construction of identity, remains central to most discussion of the 'nationalist tradition' and its rights.[59] There is certainly a greater willingness to accept and accomodate the Britishness of the 'roughly one million' unionists who are *'the* "British presence" in Ireland'.[60] Yet what this involves is less clear – certainly not an acceptance of the unionist view of Britishness as requiring full member-ship of the United Kingdom.[61] The territorial and constitutional implications that might follow from uniting the Irish people are left unexplored; the implication is that a united state could – and some believe would – follow. This vagueness and ambiguity allows the new nationalism to encompass genuinely reconciliatory and pluralist tendencies together with more traditional nationalist understandings.[62] Both strands exist within it, in many cases within the same people.

Republicanism. With the split in the republican movement in 1969 traditional militant republican ideology became dominant among provisional republicans. Soon, however, some provisional republicans –

---

[57] John Hume, Commencement Address at the University of Massachusetts, *Congressional Record*, vol. 131, no. 67, 21 May 1985.

[58] See John Hume's letter to Gerry Adams, *Sinn Féin/SDLP Talks*, Belfast, Sinn Féin, 1988, pp. 10–11. John Hume, 'A new Ireland – the acceptance of diversity', *Irish Times* 13 Sept. 1986.

[59] Daly, *Price of Peace*, p. 5l; *Irish News*, editorial, 6 July 1990, reprinted *Irish Times* 7 July 1990.

[60] Daly, *Price of Peace*, p. 4.

[61] New Ireland Forum, *Report*, Dublin, Stationery Office, 1984 at once asserts the rights of unionists to effective expression of their identity, ethos and way of life (para. 4.15) and has as its preferred solution a united Ireland by agreement (paras 5.4, 5.5).

[62] Conor Cruise O'Brien emphasises the traditional nationalist understandings in *Ancestral Voices: Religion and Nationalism in Ireland*, Dublin, Poolbeg Press, 1994.

particularly those who were interned or in jail – began to re-evaluate traditional ideology. By the mid-1970s, the tone of discussions in republican journals became questioning, irreverent and increasingly open to socialist republican ideology.[63] The development of the political wing of the movement in the 1980s after the hunger strikes enabled those once involved in violence to devote their energies to political activity and brought in individuals, many of them women, without previous links to republicanism. By the late 1980s, the ethos was more pluralist, encompassing secular, feminist, socialist and liberation theology strands as well as more traditional Catholic nationalist ones. In the 1980s, as well, republicans were beginning to realise that their traditional goals could not be achieved. Some rethinking was necessary.

There was little change in the analysis of the problem. The British presence in Ireland continued to be defined as colonial.[64] The structure of the Northern state and society was irredeemably coloured by colonial relations: Northern Ireland was the embodiment of colonial violence and lacked legitimacy; it was a 'corrupt state' with 'courts which dispense injustice, parliaments which work for the advantage of only a section of the people, police who attack rather than defend, churches which contribute not to human dignity but to human pain'.[65] In opposing this, republicanism saw itself as 'almost by definition, an ideology of the dispossessed seeking equality'.[66] The colonial nature of the British presence in Ireland justified violence to remove it. For Gerry Adams writing in 1986 'The IRA is ordinary people facing up against the monster of imperial power.'[67] The effects of partition were deep and destructive. It had created Catholic dominance, narrow communal priorities, a deep social conservatism and economic dependence in the twenty-six counties and repression, injustice and conflict in the six counties. Its removal was a condition of real progress in Ireland. The problems of the island arose from the denial of the right of the Irish people to self-determination.

There was, however, increasing recognition – it would seem principled as well as strategic – that republicans could not simply impose their views on everyone else. Republicans had a vision of what they thought a future

---

[63] See, for example, the letters from prison in *Republican News*, 1975–1977; cf. Patterson, *Politics of Illusion*, ch. 6.

[64] Gerry Adams, *Politics of Irish Freedom*, Dingle, Brandon, 1986, pp. 88ff. Sinn Féin, *Scenario for Peace*, 1987, reprinted in Gerry Adams, *A Pathway to Peace*, Cork, Mercier, 1988, pp. 85, 87.

[65] Des Wilson, *An End to Silence*, Cork, Royal Carbery, 1985, p. 7.

[66] Adams, *Politics of Irish Freedom*, p. 113.

[67] *Ibid.*, p. 69.

Ireland should be, but they recognised that the majority on the island did not agree with it. The concept of self-determination became more formal – a context whereby the different groups on the island of Ireland would freely decide on its constitutional and institutional future and in which minority rights would be fully protected.[68] But no group had the right to opt out of this process and no section of the Irish people had the right to partition Ireland and to maintain it under the British Crown. In practice, a strategic flexibility would emerge in this area as well.

The shift in republican thinking has some of the same causes as the reconstruction of nationalism – the changing nature of the Catholic community in the North and its difficult relations with the South – and follows a similar direction; the origins of the shift coincide with the first talks between Gerry Adams and John Hume in 1988. Qualitative differences between republicanism and nationalism remain, however. Republicans continue to deny the legitimacy of the British presence and emphasise its negative effects rather than its neutrality: they actively aspire to Irish reunification; they defend the *right* to use violence if the (now redefined) process of Irish self-determination is indefinitely blocked; they remain very sceptical of the possibilities of reform in Northern Ireland.

Unionism. The process of ideological reconstruction within unionism has been less cohesive than within nationalism. Political priorities and cultural affinities differ more sharply among Protestants than among Catholics, and their political situation has presented strategic dilemmas for which there are no clear answers. The result has been disagreement on the most basic directions of the unionist project: whether the union can best be secured by relying on their own resources or seeking the protection of the British government, seeking full integration with Britain or devolved institutions over which they might exercise some control, defending the union on cultural or on political or economic grounds, defining themselves as a ethno-national community or in individual/post-national terms, differentiating themselves radically from Northern Catholics or emphasising the commonalities of culture or class, maximising support for the union within the Protestant community or seeking the support of Catholics, engaging with the South or refusing to have anything to do with it, seeking allies within Britain or in the wider international arena.

Thus far no single redefinition of unionism has achieved dominance.

---

[68] See the John Hume/Gerry Adams joint statement of September 1993 (reprinted, for example, in *Irish Times*, 31 Jan. 1994); cf. also Gerry Adams, *Irish Times* 14 Jan. 1994.

The claimants span a very wide range. Some make consequentialist arguments based on the superior benefits – economic or political – offered in the United Kingdom. Thus it is commonplace to point to the deep economic dependence of the Northern Ireland economy on the British exchequer and the inability (and unwillingness) of the Irish state to bankroll Northern Ireland's present living standards.[69] Robert McCartney – on classic liberal individualist principles – argues for the union in terms of the fuller civil liberties and individual rights offered in the United Kingdom than in Ireland.[70] A less conditional form of unionism focuses on unionists' British identity and sees the conflict as an ethno-national one.[71] Christopher and Michael McGimpsey describe a distinctive, multilevelled unionist national identity, at once British and Irish, and see it as providing a rationale for the union: their British identity is dependent on their involvement in British institutions and, if it is to be respected, so too must be the union.[72] Arthur Aughey combines liberal values and traditional commitment in an argument which rules out nationalist counter-claims.[73] He bases unionist allegiance on the 'idea of the union' – the ideal of a modern state committed to treating all of its citizens, whatever their culture or ethnicity, equally. For Aughey, the commitment to the union has been forged in peace and war, and has a weight deserving of respect; moreover unlike Irish citizenship and nationality which are ethnically based, the union damages no one's rights since it allows full expression of all cultural and national identities.

These reconstructions stress the changed nature of the British state – post-imperial, post-Protestant, post-'ethnic' – and of unionism within it. They nevertheless exhibit many of the features of traditional unionism, including the binary opposition of the British and Irish spheres with the British taken as self-evidently more progressive than the Irish. The United Kingdom is taken as paradigmatically modern, non-unionist Ireland as paradigmatically backward. The unionist image of the South remains that of a society that is parochially minded, economically backward, politically illiberal, culturally rural, religiously superstitious, nationalist in a retrograde way, ambivalent or hostile to modernity.[74] By

---

[69] The Cadogan Group, *Northern Limits*, pp. 22–3 and Appendix.
[70] R. L. McCartney, *Liberty and Authority in Ireland*, Field Day Pamphlet no. 7, Derry, Field Day, 1985.
[71] Ulster Society, *Ulster, an Ethnic Nation?*, Lurgan, Ulster Society, 1986; Anthony Alcock, *Understanding Ulster*, Lurgan, Co. Armagh, Ulster Society (Publications) Ltd., 1994, pp. 144–5.
[72] Christopher and Michael McGimpsey in public session of New Ireland Forum, 19 Jan. 1984; *Proceedings*, pp. 21ff.
[73] Aughey, *Under Siege*.
[74] See e.g., *ibid.*, pp. 45, 48, 205.

contrast unionists see themselves sharing in the wider culture of the United Kingdom: outward-looking, industrial, urban, religiously and politically liberal, culturally pluralist, modernising. Each of the positions uses different arguments to arrive at a traditional unionist conclusion: that the unionist constitutional preference has priority over that of the nationalist, thus ruling out the new nationalist claim for full 'parity of esteem' on the constitutional issue.[75]

Like the new nationalism, these reconstructions of unionism encompass a range of views – at once genuine attempts to offer a union which will be of benefit to all in Northern Ireland and more sophisticated versions of the old unionism, determined to limit Catholic and nationalist equality to ensure Protestant dominance and the continuance of the union.

Loyalism. There have been attempts also to articulate new forms of loyalism. Ulster nationalist writings identified the origins of the Ulster Protestant people (and more ambiguously also Ulster Catholics) in an aboriginal Ulster inhabited by the Cruithin who were cast out to Scotland by the invading Celts/Gaels, thus making the arrival of Scottish settlers in the seventeenth century no dispossession but an act of repossession by the true natives of the region.[76] Side by side with this tentative experiment in ethnogenesis, some paramilitary leaders explored new possibilities of political compromise in an independent Ulster, or, later, in a power-sharing devolved government.[77] Within the paramilitary organisations, however, there was little enthusiasm either for the cultural or the political innovations.[78]

The post-ceasefire period has seen the emergence of a new loyalist politics. The 'new loyalists' stress the shared and equal deprivation of all working-class people under the Stormont regime and the need for a realignment of politics on class lines; they also endorse power-sharing within Northern Ireland. However they are uncompromisingly majoritarian in their opposition to any dilution of the union. As with the newer strands of republicanism, there is a question of how far the new loyalism has moved from traditional loyalism. It is best seen as a clear and independent articulation of the secular, working-class strand of loyalism

---

[75] *Ibid.*, p. 39.
[76] Ian Adamson, *The Identity of Ulster*, Belfast, Pretani, 1982.
[77] New Ulster Political Research Group, *Beyond the Religious Divide*, Belfast, New Ulster Political Research Group, 1979; Ulster Political Research Group, *Common Sense*, Belfast, 1987.
[78] Steve Bruce, 'The politics of the loyalist paramilitaries', in Brian Barton and Patrick J. Roche, eds., *The Northern Ireland Question: Perspectives and Policies*, Aldershot, Avebury, 1994, pp. 109–10, 116–17.

which had for long been ideologically subordinated to evangelical loyalism. The implications of this move are as yet unclear. The new loyalism presents itself as a genuine attempt at reconciliation which breaks with the view of irreconcilable communal conflict. But opposition to nationalism and republicanism remains intense and the conciliatory and egalitarian image fractures easily under pressure.

Other ideologies. In recent decades, the distinctive concepts and themes of labourism have, for the most part, been incorporated within bridge-building, new loyalist and Catholic unionist ideologies. There remain labourist groupings, but they are small and marginal. Similarly, socialist republicanism, while still expressed by a range of small leftist groups, has largely been incorporated within the new republicanism. Dissent has experienced a minor but perhaps significant re-birth with Terence McCaughey's use of contemporary theology and narrative theory to give a full restatement of dissenting ideals in his *Memory and Redemption*, and already in the peace process other dissenting voices have emerged.[79]

Ideology, structure and change

The limits to ideological change

The persistence of ideological opposition in Northern Ireland requires explanation. Many commentators see the communities as trapped in the past, adhering to old ideologies which the rest of the world is progressively abandoning.[80] They have subjected the ideologies to 'debunking' intellectual critique, showing that the assumptions about history are based on myth, that the beliefs and expectations are irrational, that the political claims are indefensible, that the core concepts are anachronistic. The expectation is that once the outdated nature of the ideologies is made evident, support for them will fade away. This assumes, however, a static and conformist quality to political reflection in Northern Ireland that is far from the case. There is a high level of

---

[79] Terence McCaughey, *Memory and Redemption: Church, Politics and Prophetic Theology in Ireland*, Dublin, Gill and Macmillan, 1993; also see John Dunlop, *A Precarious Belonging: Presbyterians and the Conflict in Ireland*, Belfast, Blackstaff, 1995.

[80] For discussions, see Joseph Ruane and Jennifer Todd, ' "Why can't you get along with each other?" Structure and culture in Northern Ireland', in Eamonn Hughes, ed., *Culture and Politics in Northern Ireland*, Milton Keynes, Open University Press, 1991, and Colin Coulter, 'Class, ethnicity and political identity in Northern Ireland', *Irish Journal of Sociology*, vol. 4, 1994.

reflectiveness in both communities and, as we have seen, there is both ideological innovation and reconstruction. Moreover, wider European ideological developments have provided core concepts – pluralism, post-nationalism, citizenship – for these new ideologies.

Ideological continuity derives not from the refusal of people, or their leaders, to contemplate new ideas, but from continuity in the structure of the conflict itself (see chapter 11). We saw in chapter 2 that the conflict is the product of overlapping and mutually reinforcing cultural dimensions of difference, a structure of dominance, dependence and inequality and a tendency towards communal polarisation. Each of these sets limits to ideological change.

The overlapping and mutually reinforcing nature of the dimensions of conflict makes difficult ideological reconstruction on less conflictual lines. For example, the new nationalism consciously avoids talking about 'settlers' or 'natives'; a new strand of unionism argues that the conflict is not about religion, ethnicity or even nationality but about the form of the state. However downplaying or avoiding some dimensions does not do away with them; the interlinkage of the dimensions in language and tradition means that they remain latent in the hearer's preunderstandings. Thus the concept of 'Irish identity' central to reconstructed nationalism evokes a narrative understanding of Irish history in which all the dimensions are involved. Similarly, unionists who argue for a religiously neutral, culture free, progressive notion of Britishness work with an interrelated set of religious, colonial and ethnic assumptions which echo older arguments about the civilising nature of the British link.

The conflict of interests – economic, political, cultural – generated by the structure of dominance, dependence and inequality (chapters 5, 6, 7) also limits the scope for ideological change. Each community is aware that its view of the world is founded in part on myth and prejudice; but it does not feel inclined, still less compelled, to revise it on that account. Both communities are aware of the relationship between their ideologies and their interests and act accordingly. Catholics seek reassurance that any reconstruction of nationalism or republicanism will not leave them more vulnerable than before, and respond warily and strategically to new currents within unionism. Protestants apply equally pragmatic and strategic principles in relation to their own and nationalist ideologies. The centrality of interests also rules out solutions conceived solely at the level of ideology. Neither community feels free to engage in open-minded, open-ended self-critical ideological exploration, because there are some interests they cannot afford to endanger, some positions they cannot afford to put in question.

Finally, the tendency toward communal division (chapter 3) sets limits to change by placing all the ideologies in a context of communal opposition and struggle. The universalistic principles of the reconstructed ideologies – parity of esteem, equal citizenship – are open to interpretation as strategies in the communal struggle, designed to outflank the ideological weapons of the other community. Within each community, the trouble-maker veto operates as much in the ideological as the political domain. Even the most universalistic and altruistic ideology presupposes – or is slow to criticise – unsaid communal understandings and oppositions, which may in turn be the condition of the influence or support it enjoys. For example, in contrast to republicans, nationalists now avoid references to colonialism but they work with a concept of Irish history and nationality which does not preclude a colonial understanding. Unionists distinguish their liberal and progressive concept of Britishness from (in their view) the cruder, dominatory one of loyalists, but both assume the superiority of British/Protestant over Irish/Catholic culture and the need for Protestants to maintain control in Northern Ireland.

Ideology and social practice

Ideologies in Northern Ireland are to an important degree embedded in political ritual and ceremony. Indeed much of their resilience and resistance to purely intellectual critique is due to this. We look at three examples of social practices which express, confirm and reproduce ideologies; in each case, ideological elaboration and contestation draws on underlying cultural and communal pre-understandings.

The symbolising of Protestant dominance and resistance: Orange marches. 'Orange' marches are central to the public culture in Northern Ireland.[81] The main marches are held on 12 July to commemorate King William's victory at the battle of the Boyne in 1690. In the Stormont period, the marches were granted the status of a state ceremony. Even today, the 12 July is a public holiday, and during the 'Twelfth week' (and week following) it is common for workplaces to close and people to take their summer holidays. But the entire summer is the 'marching season' and the marching bands spend the rest of the year practising and preparing for the season. In 1984, a year for which statistics are available,

---

[81] Not all loyalist marches are organised by the Loyal Orange Lodges: the Royal Black Preceptory and the Apprentice Boys of Derry also host important marches. We include them all under the category 'Orange'.

2,400 marches took place during a six-week period.[82] The vast majority of the marches (and almost all those permitted in central Belfast or in mixed-religion areas) are loyalist. Apart from the annual Twelfth march in Belfast, the venues of Orange marches change annually on a cyclical basis so that the entire area of Northern Ireland is ritually covered.

The marches are institutionalised, repetitive and highly ritualised.[83] Clothing, banners, music, routes and venues are closely regulated and 'traditional'. The solidary ritual marching of male Protestants re-enacts a 'public banding' tradition that began in the seventeenth century. The music, banners, slogans, names of the lodges and bands and speeches affirm the validity of the Protestant faith, the settler experience of siege and victory, and Ulster Protestant loyalty to the Crown and empire in times of war and peace. They express and reproduce a specific loyalist ideological tradition which defines itself as the core of the wider Protestant community. Indeed large numbers of the Protestant community are involved in the festival, at least as spectators. All the generations are present from the very young to the very old; women and children are prominent among the onlookers and present also among the marchers; the social types represented range from the respectable besuited Orangeman (the very old or very important travel in limousines) to a 'rough' element in the bandsmen and crowd; there are lodges from the South and from overseas; bandsmen with expensive brass instruments and ceremonial British military style costumes follow fife and drum bands with paramilitary associations.

The marching season is at once a communal celebration and a symbolic assertion of power over Catholics. These elements are inter-related – the communal cohesion which the marches evoke and renew are a condition of Protestant power. However the relative importance of the dominatory aspect varies greatly from march to march, locality to locality, and from one individual to another. In many cases it is latent rather than overt, emerging only in the event of Catholic challenge or opposition. When the dominatory aspect is activated the marches celebrate and legitimate the historical defeat of Catholicism and the continuing dominance of Protestants,[84] and more crudely convey to

[82] Commons written answer by Nicholas Scott to Mr Mallon, *Irish Times*, 20 July 1985.

[83] For descriptions, see Desmond Bell, *Acts of Union: Youth Culture and Sectarianism in Northern Ireland*, London, Macmillan, 1990; S. S. Larsen, 'The Glorious Twelfth: the politics of legitimation in Kilbroney', in Anthony P. Cohen, ed., *Belonging: Identity and Social Organization in British Rural Cultures*, Manchester, Manchester University Press, 1982.

[84] Protestant dominance must be preserved to prevent Catholic dominance. For one of Bell's respondents, the meaning of the marches was that 'they're not goin'te let the Taigs take over!'; Bell, *Acts of Union*, p. 109, cf. p. 127; Larsen, 'The glorious Twelfth', pp. 283, 288.

Catholics the solidarity, self-confidence and the brute force of organised Protestantism. There may be ritualised baiting of Catholics in the selection of march routes through 'Catholic' areas and the loud drumming outside churches or Catholic neighbourhoods. Catholics who live along a 'traditional route' may be confined for hours in their houses or streets (by police or simply from fear) up to a dozen times each summer. In some areas the struggle to maintain march routes against nationalist pressure for change is now a yearly test of loyalism's power and influence.[85]

In their dominatory aspect the marches are directed primarily against Catholics; they stress the permanence of the Catholic threat and the need for constant vigilance against it. But they also affirm the strength and defiance of loyalism within the Protestant community in the face of attempts to marginalise it. Unionists today are increasingly conscious of their dependence on the British state and international opinion. The marches – by their archaism, their politicised Protestantism and their settler mode of Britishness – subvert unionist attempts to set a normal tone of modern British life and politics in Northern Ireland. In this context the marches also remind the liberal and 'respectable' unionists who show disdain for loyalism of its power and resilience within the Protestant community, and of unionism's dependence on it if the union comes under threat.

The symbolising of Catholic resistance: the hunger strikes. The republican hunger strike of 1981 was symbolic action of a very different kind. The story is by now well known.[86] In June 1972, secretary of state for Northern Ireland (SOSNI) William Whitelaw had granted 'special category status' – including the right to wear civilian clothes – to prisoners convicted of terrorist offences. This policy was withdrawn in March 1976 as part of a package of measures intended to redefine the violence as 'criminal'. Republican prisoners refused to wear prison clothes and wore only a blanket, privileges were withdrawn and, after

---

[85] Intense feeling surrounded the marches and attempted reroutings in the mid-1980s in Portadown, in 1989 in Keady, in 1991 in Pomeroy, in 1992 on the lower Ormeau Road in Belfast; 1993 despite Irish government pressure there were no reroutings; in 1994 the routing of marches in Portadown was again in dispute; in 1995, there were again conflicts over the routing of marches in Portadown and on the lower Ormeau Road.

[86] For accounts see David Beresford, *Ten Men Dead: The Story of the 1981 Irish Hunger Strike*, London, Grafton, 1987; Liam Clarke, *Broadening the Battlefield*, Dublin, Gill and Macmillan, 1987; Padraig O'Malley, *Biting at the Grave: The Irish Hunger Strikes and the Politics of Despair*, Belfast, Blackstaff, 1990; Brian Campbell et al., *Nor Meekly Serve My Time: The H-Block Struggle 1976–1981*, Belfast, Beyond the Pale Publications, 1994.

increasing conflict with the warders, they began a 'dirty protest' in which they smeared their excrement on the walls of their cells. When two years of this protest had no effect on British policy the prisoners, against the advice of the republican leadership, began a hunger strike in October 1980; it ended in December, with no deaths, in the false expectation of British concessions. A second hunger strike began in March 1981 and over the next seven months, ten men died. Neither the strikers nor the British government gave way; the strike ended when the families of the strikers took them off their strike as soon as they lost consciousness.

The 1981 hunger strikes were public drama of great symbolic power and emotional intensity which gained world-wide attention. The struggle between prisoners and warders, republicans and British state, was symbolically fought out on the prisoners' emaciated bodies.[87] The symbolism tapped into foundational aspects of nationalist ideology: ancient Gaelic tradition, republican resistance to British rule at the turn of the century, Christian traditions of martyrdom. The religious resonances were particularly emphasised; wall murals in the Catholic ghettoes portrayed the suffering of the hunger strikers in imagery that evoked the death of Christ; Catholic clergy made similar comparisons before and during the hunger strike.[88]

The form of the hunger strikes increased their impact. The steady silent deterioration of the strikers within the prisons contrasted with the flurry of activity on the outside – the frantic attempts at mediation, the political protests and riots that followed each death. The ultimate individuality of the act – and the individuality of each hunger striker and his family was emphasised in the media – contrasted with the intensely communal experience outside where whole areas and communities waited for news. Funerals (the largest of which – that of Bobby Sands – was attended by 100,000 people) were communal rituals of mourning and protest.[89] The spacing of the dates on which each individual began his hunger strike, so that a new death would follow each period of mourning, highlighted the hunger strikers' determination and conviction and intensified the emotional effect on those outside. The endurance and courage shown by the strikers and the clarity of their action contrasted with the mundane, ordinary activities on the outside and made criticism

[87] Allen Feldman, *Formations of Violence: The Narrative of the Body and Political Terror in Northern Ireland*, London, University of Chicago Press, 1991, ch. 6.

[88] Denis Faul and Raymond Murray, 'Christ and the prisoner', *The Furrow*, vol. 31, no. 3, 1980; Denis Faul and Raymond Murray, 'H-Block and its background', *Doctrine and Life*, vol. 30, no. 11, 1980, p. 489; O'Malley, *Biting at the Grave*, p. 109.

[89] For descriptions, see John Conroy, *War as a Way of Life: A Belfast Diary*, London, Heinemann, 1988, pp. 170–80.

of the hunger strikes seem petty and vindictive. The willingness of the prisoners to take their own lives seemed to many if not to redeem their role in the taking of the lives of others, at least to prove that they were no ordinary criminals.[90]

The election of the first hunger striker to the Westminister parliament showed popular support for those on strike that went far beyond traditional republican support. A very wide range of public figures from the Catholic community argued that the political crisis in Northern Ireland and the exceptional legal procedures made a compromise – some form of special category status – appropriate.[91] The British refusal to compromise despite repeated appeals by Catholic church and Irish state symbolically constituted the British state as a common focus of opposition, a cold, distant power-centre, unresponsive to the suffering or the influence of any section of the Catholic or nationalist population;[92] it seemed to confirm the traditional nationalist view of the British role. Those who rejected the demands of the hunger strikers, as did many Catholics and almost all Protestants, were seen as siding with the state against the suffering individual: intense polarisation resulted within the Catholic community and between Catholics and Protestants.[93]

Unionists, for whom the legitimacy of the state and the criminality of republican terrorism were not in question, saw the hunger strikes as a strategic attack on the state, ordered and orchestrated by the IRA and backed by the whole Catholic community. Robin Eames spoke of the 'intensely felt reactions of those who have watched attempts to turn upside down the community's sense of values'.[94] Protestants were disturbed and incensed that the strikers could appear as victims while the real victims – the innocent people killed by republican terrorism – were being forgotten. The hunger strikes had symbolically reversed the

---

[90] Archbishop Eames notes that 'In a sense, the hunger strikers had achieved their special status'; Robin Eames, *Chains to be Broken: A Personal Reflection on Northern Ireland and its People*, London, Wiedenfeld and Nicholson, 1992, p. 44.

[91] Denis Faul and Raymond Murray, 'Christian humanism in prison', *The Furrow*, vol. 32, no. 3, 1981; Irish Commission for Justice and Peace, 'Statement on H-Block', issued 13 Oct. 1980, reprinted in *The Furrow*, Dec. 1980, vol. 31, no. 12, pp. 814–16, points 3, 5; letter from John O'Brien, CSSp to *Doctrine and Life*, vol. 30, 1980, 576–9; Ciaran McKeown, *The Passion of Peace*, Belfast, Blackstaff, 1984, p. 249; Faul and Murray, 'H-Block and its background'.

[92] Concern about the 'inflexible approach' of the state authorities was voiced by the European Court of Human Rights, May 1980, para. 64, by the Irish Commission for Justice and Peace in October 1980 and later by the Irish taoiseach, Garret Fitzgerald; see Garret Fitzgerald, *All in a Life*, Dublin, Gill and Macmillan, 1991, pp. 368–75. It was widely felt; O'Malley, *Biting at the Grave*, p. 144. It united Gerry Adams, Denis Faul, the Southern mediators, Ciaran McKeown, Seamus Deane.

[93] See O'Malley, *Biting at the Grave*, pp. 154–5.

[94] Eames, *Chains to be Broken*, p. 47; cf O'Malley, *Biting at the Grave*, pp. 165–89.

opposition between criminality and political principle, portraying the civilising modernity of the British state – with which unionists so identified – as barbarism.[95]

The political consequences of these events were momentous. Despite the dislike of a majority of Northern Catholics for the republican movement, the hunger strikes bonded the Catholic community to a greater degree than any event since the civil rights movement. The minority of Catholics who publicly rejected the strikers were subjected to communal harassment and marginalisation and were thereby confirmed in their rejection of communal politics and ideology. But the hunger strikes revitalised the republican movement and broadened its base socially and politically; the development of Sinn Féin as a political organisation dates from that period. For many in the South and outside Ireland the hunger strikes challenged the public image of IRA members as criminal psychopaths, portraying them instead as courageous if misguided idealists. Protestant incomprehension at this response indicated and extended the depth of division between the two communities.

Symbolising status change: the signing of the Anglo-Irish Agreement of 1985. On 5 November 1985, the taoiseach of the Republic of Ireland, Garret Fitzgerald and the British prime minister, Margaret Thatcher, signed the Anglo-Irish Agreement at Hillsborough Castle. A year earlier, Margaret Thatcher had rejected the report of the New Ireland Forum in a public interview. The manner of her rejection seemed to symbolise Irish powerlessness *vis-à-vis* Britain and was widely taken to be a personal humiliation for Garret Fitzgerald.[96] However, negotiations continued. The Irish government, which consulted with SDLP representatives throughout, finally reached an agreement which gave them some input into the government of Northern Ireland.[97] Politically and symbolically, it was an attempt to reconstitute an island-wide nationalist community from which republicans were excluded. The British state proposed to take this community as its junior partner in the governing of Northern Ireland.

The ceremonial signing of the Agreement was a conscious attempt by the two governments to symbolise the beginning of a new political era,

---

[95] Seamus Deane, *Civilians and Barbarians*, Field Day pamphlet no. 3, Derry, Field Day, 1983.

[96] Fitzgerald, *All in a Life*, pp. 523ff.

[97] Although less than they had initially proposed, they saw the Anglo-Irish Agreement as a major achievement; for further discussion see ch. 6; Brendan O'Leary and John McGarry, *The Politics of Antagonism: Understanding Northern Ireland*, London, Athlone, 1993, chs. 6 and 7; Fitzgerald, *All in a Life*, chs. 16, 17.

one in which the nationalist tradition was raised to a new status. The ceremony could have taken place in London, Belfast or even Dublin and could have been held in private. Instead it was held in Hillsborough Castle and was televised. Hillsborough is a scrupulously clean, neat and quietly prosperous Protestant village in the predominantly Protestant county of Down. Until 1973, Hillsborough Castle was the home of the governor-general, the queen's representative in Ireland, since then of the SOSNI. The village has an almost English feel, with families visiting the castle grounds and the main street lined with craft shops, tea shops and fashionable pubs. The choice of locale could not but maximise the symbolic impact of what was to come.

The taoiseach of the Republic of Ireland entered Hillsborough Castle as the formal equal of the prime minister of the United Kingdom to sign an international agreement that would give the Republic a role in the government of Northern Ireland. The solemn signing of the Agreement was televised. The taoiseach signed the Agreement in the Irish form of his name, part of his speech was in Irish and he declared that nationalists could now hold their heads high. It was a moment of triumph for Northern constitutional nationalism; meanwhile, unionist politicians waited outside the gates of the castle in the rain. Most Southerners missed the symbolism. In Dublin, people joked about the taoiseach's fluency in Irish. But for unionists it was devastating. Nationalism had intruded into the very heart of unionist and British Northern Ireland and displaced unionism at the queen's table. And there was no gratitude: the speech in Irish showed a rejection of British culture and, by implication, an affirmation and legitimation of the whole history of Irish nationalist rebellion.

For unionists, the symbolic seat of government had been taken over by their enemies. The implicit images – the fall of the besieged citadel, betrayal by the British who had sided with the Protestants' enemies against them, the triumph of the natives, or simply the ritual acknowledgement that Northern Ireland was no longer unambiguously British – crystallised themes from loyalist and unionist ideologies. Unionists' experience of marginalisation in the negotiating process, their wait outside the walls of the castle while their traditional Southern enemies were inside, starkly symbolised the reversal of their status and the triumph of the new nationalism.[98] Later, in the House of Commons, Harold McCusker of the UUP told how he had to beg 'like a dog' for a

---

[98] Eames, *Chains to be Broken*, p. 52; for the significance for Catholics, see Fionnuala O'Connor, *In Search of a State: Catholics in Northern Ireland*, Belfast, Blackstaff, 1993, p. 55.

copy of the Agreement as he stood outside the castle; then everything he held dear was 'turned to ashes in my mouth'.[99] Jim Allister of the DUP listened to the broadcast on his car radio and 'knew with all its consuming fury what it meant to be alienated in my own land'.[100]

Conclusion

Communal conflict is ideologically mediated. The two communities construct their histories in radically different ways and their image of the world and what is possible within it is shaped by these opposing historical narratives. In the recent period, the dominant, totalising ideological traditions have been reconstructed and now present themselves as open to dialogue, able to recognise and respect differences. However, ideological opposition remains intense, reproduced through the wider pattern of cultural division, social relations and communal conflict in Northern Ireland. The conflicting groups construct social practices which condense and crystallise ideological oppositions. The deconstruction of these oppositions is a precondition of wider social and political transformation. At the same time, ideology is interwoven with interests and ideological change will be contemplated only when it does not place vital interests in peril.

[99] Harold McCusker, quoted in *Sunday Tribune*, 1 Dec. 1985.
[100] Jim Allister, *Alienated but Unbowed: A Unionist Perspective on the Origin, Meaning and Future of the Anglo-Irish Agreement*, Carrickfergus, East Antrim DUP, 1987, p. 29.

5   The dynamics of conflict: politics

Partition was a pragmatic acknowledgement of the realities of economic and military power on the two islands at the beginning of the century (chapter 2). It also set the conditions for the renewal of the historical alliance between Irish Protestants and the British state, this time in the narrow ground of Northern Ireland. The reconstituted alliance was given institutional expression in the Government of Ireland Act of 1920 and in the conventions that grew up to regulate relations between Northern Ireland and Westminster. The new political arrangements would last for fifty years. In this chapter we look at the changing power relations underlying the British state/Protestant alliance and its institutional forms. We explain why the earlier settlement collapsed and why it has been so difficult to find an alternative.

The settlement of 1921

The reconstituted alliance between the British government and Northern Irish Protestants was a consequence of British policies, not their intent. The desire to keep Ulster within the empire was strong among sections of the British elite, but the overriding British priority was a stable Irish settlement distanced from British politics: in the Treaty negotiations and after, it became clear that a friendly home rule administration in Ireland as a whole was more attractive to the British government than respecting Ulster unionist wishes.[1] But the prior British decision not to force Northern Protestants into a home rule parliament, together with the determination to avoid overt British control anywhere in Ireland,[2] guaranteed that British governments would – more

---

[1] Nicholas Mansergh, *The Unresolved Question: The Anglo-Irish Settlement and its Undoing 1912–1972*, London, Yale University Press, 1991, pp. 124, 187; Bryan A. Follis, *A State under Siege: The Establishment of Northern Ireland 1920–1925*, Oxford, Clarendon Press, 1995, pp. 52–7.

[2] Mansergh, *The Unresolved Question*, pp. 120–33.

or less willingly – uphold the unionist interest in Northern Ireland. Ulster unionists would have control over the internal affairs of Northern Ireland, the constitutional settlement would be defended by the British state and unionists provided with the financial and legislative means of self-defence. The implicit condition was that the unionist government would manage Northern Ireland's affairs effectively and in line with wider British interests. The precise character and strength of this alliance was, however, unclear when the new state came into existence in 1921. In particular it was unclear how much control the Northern Ireland parliament would have over its internal affairs. There were, initially, two threats to that control.

One came from the South. The Government of Ireland Act of 1920 provided for all-Ireland institutions which, it was intended, would lead 'to the eventual establishment of a parliament of Ireland'.[3] The Anglo-Irish Treaty of December 1921 provided for a boundary adjustment 'in accordance with the wishes of the inhabitants'.[4] The former threatened the permanence of Northern Ireland. The latter threatened its territory, particularly in the nationalist majority counties of Fermanagh and Tyrone and in the border areas of south Down and south Armagh. In the event, civil war and its aftermath in the South weakened both the Free State's bargaining strength and the British interest in compromise with pro-Treaty 'moderates', delayed the appointment of a Boundary Commission until 1924, and enabled unionists to consolidate their position. The Council of Ireland never met, the Boundary Commission did not live up to nationalist hopes and finally collapsed.[5] At a meeting in December 1925 the British, Northern Ireland and Free State prime ministers recognised the finality of the 1921 boundary and formally transferred the Council of Ireland's functions to the Belfast and Dublin parliaments.[6]

The other threat came from the residual legislative powers of the Westminster parliament and its control of economic resources. Under the Government of Ireland Act the Westminster parliament retained responsibility for certain 'excepted services' and 'reserved services' and kept ultimate responsibility for the services devolved to the Northern Ireland government – education, health, personal social services, law and

---

[3] Jonathan Bardon, *A History of Ulster*, Belfast, Blackstaff, 1992, p. 477; for the provisions of the 1920 Act, see David Harkness, *Northern Ireland Since 1920*, Dublin, Helicon, 1983, pp. 4–5. Michael Connolly, *Politics and Policy Making in Northern Ireland*, London, Philip Allan, 1990, p. 31.

[4] Bardon, *History of Ulster*, pp. 484, 507.

[5] Harkness, *Northern Ireland*, pp. 39–40.

[6] Bardon, *History of Ulster*, p. 509.

order, housing, planning and economic development.[7] It was the central paymaster, in the interwar years allocating 80 per cent of Northern Ireland's budget.[8] Westminster had sufficient power to determine policy in Northern Ireland; much depended on whether it would use it.

Unionists early established Northern Ireland's independence of Westminister. Two events created precedents. The first, in early 1922, centred on the controversial activities of the Special Constabulary, a quasi-military police force some of whose members were engaging in violent unofficial attacks on Catholics; the second concerned the decision in 1923 to replace proportional representation in local elections with a plurality voting system.[9] Both raised the question of effective control in Northern Ireland; in each case, British attempts to change the decisions of the Northern Ireland government were abandoned in the face of resistance and threats of resignation by the Northern Ireland cabinet. A general precedent was established in 1923 when the Speaker at Westminster declared that questions on matters delegated to the Northern Ireland parliament must be dealt with in that parliament.

Having made its choice, the British government abided by it, keeping as close as possible an eye on finances but leaving the substance of policy-making to the government in Northern Ireland. From a British point of view it was not an ideal relationship. Claims that the Stormont government gerrymandered and discriminated were a source of some embarrassment; there was also concern about the amount of financial contribution to the Northern Ireland government and the lack of accountability. It had originally been envisaged that Northern Ireland would make a net contribution to the British exchequer but transfers from Britain to Northern Ireland soon became necessary, increasing dramatically with the institution of the welfare state after the Second World War.

No British government – except during the war years when there were attempts to bring the Free State into the war by offering constitutional

---

[7] 'Excepted services' included matters of imperial concern – the crown, the armed forces, trade agreements, currency, foreign affairs, the making of peace and war; 'reserved services' included the postal services, the Supreme Court and most forms of taxation. Bardon, *History of Ulster*, pp. 514–15; Harkness, *Northern Ireland*, p. 5; Connolly, *Politics and Policy Making*, p. 31.

[8] Harkness, *Northern Ireland*, pp. 5–6.

[9] Patrick Buckland, *The Factory of Grievances: Devolved Government in Northern Ireland, 1921–39*, Dublin, Gill and Macmillan, 1979, chs. 8, 10, 12; Michael Farrell, *Arming the Protestants: The Formation of the Ulster Special Constabulary and the Royal Ulster Constabulary, 1920–27*, London, Pluto, 1983, ch. 8; Paul Bew, Peter Gibbon and Henry Patterson, *The State in Northern Ireland, 1921–72*, Manchester, Manchester University Press, 1979 pp. 57–62.

change[10] – seriously contemplated change in these political arrangements. Apart from the likely reaction of unionists, the arrangements were
working tolerably well. Unionists appeared to be managing the affairs of
Northern Ireland with reasonable effectiveness and without too much
controversy, and they rallied to Crown and empire in the dark days
of the Second World War. For Churchill, this confirmed the position of
Northern Ireland within the United Kingdom: 'the bonds of affection
between Great Britain and the people of Northern Ireland have been
tempered by fire and are now, I firmly believe, unbreakable'.[11] In 1949,
the British parliament guaranteed the constitutional position of Northern
Ireland – change would not occur without the consent of the parliament
of Northern Ireland. Successive Conservative and Labour governments
refused to investigate civil rights and nationalist complaints.

The record of the Northern Ireland government during these years is
a matter of continuing dispute.[12] Its institutions, based largely on the
British model, were liberal democratic in form – there was a free press
and free elections. Protestants monopolised power but they did so as a
political majority elected by a demographic majority in a majoritarian
political system. Abuses existed however – modifications and manipu-
lations of the political system in order to increase the already considerable extent of unionist power – which seriously weakened the state's
claim to be a normal liberal democracy.

Changes in the electoral system were explicitly designed to increase
unionist power. The introduction in 1919 of proportional representation
based on the single transferable vote (PR–STV) and the redrawing of
local constituency boundaries had radically increased non-unionist
representation and given nationalists control of crucial local authorities.
Fermanagh county council refused to recognise the new Northern
Ireland parliament in 1921 and other nationalist authorities followed
suit.[13] This was a threat to both the authority and the boundaries of
the state. The unionist government responded by dissolving twenty-one
of these local authorities and giving their functions to government

---

[10] Bardon, *History of Ulster*, pp. 558–9.
[11] Harkness, *Northern Ireland*, p. 102.
[12] For a range of assessments of the government's record, see Tom Wilson, *Ulster:
Conflict and Consent*, Oxford, Basil Blackwell, 1989; John Oliver, 'The Stormont
administration', in P. J. Roche and B. Barton, eds., *The Northern Ireland Question: Myth
and Reality*, Aldershot, Avebury, 1991; Follis, *State under Siege*; Paul Arthur, *Government and Politics of Northern Ireland*, Harlow, Longman, 1980; B. O'Leary and
J. McGarry, *The Politics of Antagonism: Understanding Northern Ireland*, London,
Athlone Press, 1993; Michael Farrell, *Northern Ireland: The Orange State*, second edn,
London, Pluto Press, 1980.
[13] Bardon, *History of Ulster*, pp. 467–8, 499.

appointed commissioners.[14] They went on to abolish PR–STV in local elections and to redraw constituency boundaries. By 1927 unionists had regained their dominant position, recovering control of Derry Corporation and the county councils of Fermanagh and Tyrone.[15] In subsequent years they made further adjustments where and when appropriate – in Omagh in 1935, Derry in 1936, and Armagh in 1946. The electoral system used in elections to the Northern Ireland parliament was also changed – from PR–STV to a plurality system in 1929 – to strengthen Unionist Party control against the threat of the Northern Ireland Labour Party (NILP). The outcomes of subsequent elections became much more predictable: 3 out of 10 constituencies were uncontested in 1925, 33 out of 52 in 1933.[16]

Discrimination in housing and public sector employment was used to reinforce unionist control. It was most evident in local areas where the balance of power between the communities was finely tuned. Protestants were given privileged access to public authority housing; Catholic houses were located in electoral wards that were already majority Catholic and would not erode Protestant political majorities. Public sector jobs were allocated disproportionately to Protestants both at local and central levels. Catholic emigration was thereby encouraged and Catholic population increase contained.[17]

The Northern Ireland government gave itself security powers that were remarkably coercive by liberal democratic standards. In 1922 at the height of the IRA campaign the new parliament passed an emergency powers act – the Civil Authorities (Special Powers) Act – which gave the minister for home affairs (typically a hardline unionist) the power 'to take all such steps' necessary for 'preserving the peace', and allowed the delegation of this authority to the Royal Ulster Constabulary (RUC).[18] The law was renewed annually and (to avoid annual debate) made permanent in 1933. These powers were not always in use but were always available; internment existed in every decade from the 1920s to the 1970s, directed primarily, though not exclusively, against republicans.

---

[14] Ibid., pp. 499–51.

[15] J. H. Whyte, 'How much discrimination was there under the Unionist regime?', in Tom Gallagher and James O'Connell, eds., Contemporary Irish Studies, Manchester, Manchester University Press, 1983, p. 6.

[16] Brian M. Walker, ed., Parliamentary Election Results in Ireland, 1918–1992, Belfast, Institute of Irish Studies, 1992.

[17] Frank Wright, Northern Ireland: A Comparative Analysis, Dublin, Gill and Macmillan, 1987, p. 143 notes the unionist approval of this outcome.

[18] Powers explicitly mentioned included the banning of meetings and publications and internment and arrest without warrant; Harkness, Northern Ireland since 1920, pp. 29–30.

The security forces had their roots in Protestant communal defence organisations, they remained disproportionately Protestant and were frequently sectarian. The first branch to be created was the almost wholly Protestant Special Constabulary (A, B, and C Specials) formed to assist in the foundation of the state. Although formally created by a British civil servant, the existence and form of the Specials was a product of pre-existing Protestant mobilisation in the UVF – whole UVF units joined and their officers were given senior positions.[19] The B Specials – in 1922 numbering over 19,000 part-timers who kept their arms at home – subsequently became a permanent part of the security forces of the state.[20] The armed RUC, formed in 1922, was predominantly (and increasingly) Protestant but less overtly sectarian than the B Specials.[21] Both branches of the security forces received ready endorsement for their actions from the government and Catholic complaints about them were ritually dismissed.[22] The judiciary was also disproportionately Protestant, increasingly so as time went on; many of its members had close connections with unionism.[23]

The Orange Order was a powerful political force, nominating 25 per cent of delegates to the Ulster Unionist Council, the coordinating body of local unionist organisations which had authority over party policy. Unionist politicians joined the Order as a matter of course, marched in its parades and affirmed its beliefs in their speeches. Loyalists exercised constant vigilance to detect and deter possible Catholic threat and to guard against any softening of unionist or anti-Catholic principles. Although Protestants dominated in the civil service, particularly at the higher levels, even the most far-fetched allegations about Catholics getting preferential treatment were investigated.[24]

The ethos of the state was unambiguously and unashamedly sectarian. The unionist government repeatedly highlighted the constitutional question in elections and stressed the need for Protestant solidarity in the face of the Catholic threat. In the 1920s and 1930s, government

---

[19] Bardon, *History of Northern Ireland*, pp. 474–6; Follis, *State under Siege*, pp. 13–17; Brian Barton, *Brookeborough: The Making of a Prime Minister*, Belfast, Institute of Irish Studies, 1988, ch. 3.

[20] Farrell, *Arming the Protestants*; Follis, *State under Siege*, p. 131.

[21] A goal of one-third Catholic representation in the RUC was set at the outset, but it was never reached or actively pursued; in 1936 there were only 488 Catholics in the RUC out of a total of 2,849; Bardon, *History of Ulster*, p. 499.

[22] Farrell, *Arming the Protestants*, p. 158; Patrick Buckland, *A History of Northern Ireland*, Dublin, Gill and Macmillan, 1981, p. 51; Sir Arthur Hezlet, *The 'B' Specials*, London, Tom Stacey, 1972.

[23] Whyte, 'How much discrimination', p. 9.

[24] See Bardon, *History of Ulster*, pp. 497–9; Buckland, *History of Northern Ireland*, pp. 63–4; Whyte, 'How much discrimination', pp. 9–13.

ministers made blatantly sectarian appeals and the trend continued throughout the long premiership of Brookeborough.[25] The interests and concerns of the Orange Order, local unionist associations and the Protestant churches were carefully attended to. The demands of the United Education Committee of the Protestant Churches for what became in effect denominational education were accomodated.[26]

There was a degree of official tolerance of Protestant communal intimidation and violence against Catholics. Violence was at its height in the mass expulsions and killings of the early 1920s, but it continued well into the post-war period – attacks on Catholics returning from the Eucharistic Congress in Dublin in 1932 or celebrating the Fianna Fáil victory in the same year, the sectarian riots and attacks of 1935 and attacks on anti-partitionist campaigners in 1949. Protestants suffered in the communal violence, but Catholics invariably came out the worst.[27] There was also symbolic violence. Orange marches were frequently dominatory in their routes and symbolism and were not simply officially tolerated but officially sanctioned. Rare bans on unusually provocative marches were later rescinded under Orange pressure.[28]

These measures were explained and justified by the threat to the survival of the state – the Catholic minority's refusal to accept the legitimacy of the state and to participate wholeheartedly in it.[29] Unionists may have exaggerated the extent of the threat during the first decades of the state when Catholics were in disarray. But events from the 1960s onwards showed that in the long term the threat was real.

The Catholic challenge and the collapse of the settlement of 1921

Partition was a historic defeat for Northern Catholics and an acutely painful one. Initially they believed that the state would not last; that hope faded as unionist strength and British commitment became clear. Their efforts to undermine the state were a dismal failure. The attacks of republicans were countered by internment and loyalist retaliation; nationalist controlled local councils which refused to recognise the Northern Ireland parliament were abolished; teachers who refused to accept their salaries from the Northern Ireland administration had no

---

25 Bardon, *History of Ulster*, p. 538; Barton, *Brookeborough*, pp. 84–9; Buckland, *History of Northern Ireland*, p. 102.
26 Bardon, *History of Ulster*, pp. 501–5.
27 For examples, *ibid.*, pp. 494, 537–8, 540–1, 600–1.
28 Buckland, *History of Northern Ireland*, p. 71; Bardon, *History of Ulster*, p. 609.
29 Barton, *Brookeborough*, pp. 78–86.

alternative when the money from Dublin ran out. The hope that the Southern government would succeed in undermining the Northern state was dashed by its role in the Boundary Commission and subsequent recognition of the existing boundaries. Their last hope ended when De Valera showed that he lacked either the means or the will to effect change.

By then Catholics had embarked on the difficult task of adjusting to their new status as a minority in a state whose existence they opposed and which was determined to keep them under control. Belfast Catholic businessmen were the first to seek an accomodation with the new order.[30] They were followed by the Catholic church, anxious to ensure that vital church interests in education were defended.[31] Nationalist politicians swung between abstentionism and participation in the parliament, where they were singularly ineffective in the face of unionist dominance of legislation and debate. The Catholic population as a whole kept their distance from the new state.

Their political position was very difficult. Initially they were united only in broad Irish nationalist culture and aims. They were deeply divided in political interests and attitudes and far from a coherent political community. Their position in the economy and class structure was weak, their middle class small, socially conservative and for the most part ill-prepared for active political leadership. Their dependence on their church for social and political organisation meant that they were confined by its religious priorities.[32] They were divided on political strategy – whether to offer some form of recognition to the state in return for a better deal, or whether to oppose it and await outside aid. Emotions of anger and resentment – at themselves, at Protestants and at the South that had abandoned them – and contradictory tendencies towards deference and defiance impeded a calculated, strategic response to their dilemma.

Internal weaknesses were compounded by lack of external allies. After Michael Collins' death, the Cumann na nGaedheal government in the South distanced itself from Northern Catholics.[33] When Fianna Fáil came to power, its response to Northern nationalist demands was

---

[30] Eamon Phoenix, *Northern Nationalism: Nationalist Politics, Partition and the Catholic Minority in Northern Ireland 1890–1940*, Belfast, Ulster Historical Foundation, 1994, pp. 193–7.

[31] Mary Harris, *The Catholic Church and the Foundation of the Northern Irish State*, Cork, Cork University Press, 1993, ch. 6.

[32] Harris, *Catholic Church*, pp. 91–2; T. J. Campbell exemplifies the strong Catholic element in nationalist politics in the 1920s and 1930s; see T. J. Campbell, *Fifty Years of Ulster: 1890–1940*, Belfast, The Irish News, 1941.

[33] Cf Phoenix, *Northern Nationalism*, chs. 7, 8.

uneven, more often reflecting Southern than Northern priorities. Sympathetic British Labour politicians founded the 'Friends of Ireland' in 1945, and some sixty-six Labour MPs defied the whips on the Ireland Bill of 1949.[34] However their effectiveness was hampered by the convention that the affairs of Northern Ireland were not the concern of the Westminster parliament.

By the 1950s the failure of Nationalist Party politics was evident and alternative forms of political organisation were developing. Some were willing to offer qualified recognition of the legitimacy of the state in return for greater access to it; the first formal public articulation of this position was by G. B. Newe at a Social Studies Conference in 1958.[35] Some attempted to modernise nationalist political organisation and strategy and create a constructive nationalist opposition in Northern Ireland with policies on all the core social and economic issues: National Unity and the National Democratic Party were formed with these aims in 1959 and 1965 respectively.[36] Support for republicanism grew in the early 1950s and an armed campaign against partition began in 1956; the abject failure of this border campaign, which was formally ended in 1962, led many republicans to turn away from militarism to a new, more socially oriented political strategy.[37] These tendencies continued to develop through the 1960s. However a new departure temporarily united these diverse strands in a single mass movement – the demand for civil rights.

The civil rights movement and its impact

The civil rights campaign began in the mid-1960s with the formation of a number of small groups (largely Catholic with some liberal Protestant support) who attempted to achieve reform by documenting, publicising and lobbying for an end to abuses – discrimination in jobs and housing, unfair electoral procedures (in particular gerrymandering), and the

---

[34] Bob Purdie, '"The Friends of Ireland": British Labour and Irish nationalism 1945–49', in Tom Gallagher and James O'Connell, eds., *Contemporary Irish Studies*, Manchester, Manchester University Press, 1983.

[35] See David Kennedy, 'Whither northern nationalism?', *Christus Rex*, vol. 13, no. 4, 1959.

[36] Bob Purdie, *Politics in the Streets: The Origins of the Civil Rights Movement in Northern Ireland*, Belfast, Blackstaff, 1990, pp. 52–60; Ian McAllister, 'Political opposition in Northern Ireland: the National Democratic Party, 1965–1970', *Econonomic and Social Review*, vol. 6, no. 3, 1975; Michael McKeown, *The Greening of a Nationalist*, Lucan, Co. Dublin, Murlough Press, 1986, ch. 3.

[37] Farrell, *Northern Ireland*, ch. 9; Henry Patterson, *The Politics of Illusion: Republicanism and Socialism in Modern Ireland*, London, Hutchinson, 1989, ch. 4.

Special Powers Act.[38] Initially the methods were mild – letters, pamphlets, small local campaigns – and largely ineffectual. However the summer of 1968 saw the first of a series of civil rights marches which were to become increasingly provocative. The new tactics proved dramatically successful. In just over a year the movement had provoked a political and security crisis in the Stormont government and had brought the British government into the policy-making process on the side of reform. The new-found effectiveness of Catholic politics was the product of changes on three levels: changes in underlying power relations, conjunctural factors during the decade of the 1960s (including the form of the state and the climate of international opinion) and the specific character of the civil rights campaign.

The partition settlement reflected the power relations of the early part of the century – the strength of Ulster Protestants relative to Irish nationalists and the British government, and of the British government relative to Irish nationalists. This balance of power had significantly changed by the 1960s.

First, the strength of Northern Protestants relative to the British government had weakened. The Northern Ireland economy had become increasingly dependent on the British exchequer to fund its new industry programme, its investment in infrastructure and its expanded social services and there was irritation in Britain at the size of the subvention and the lack of financial accountability. British memories of war-time support had faded by the 1960s and there was increasing concern at reports of gerrymandering, job discrimination and triumphalist use of British national symbols. Ambivalence about unionists and Northern Ireland was most pronounced in the Labour Party, whose leader, Harold Wilson, had always made clear his sympathy for Irish unity.

Second, Southern Ireland had grown in economic and political strength. Its commitment to modernisation, to a more moderate and pragmatic nationalism and its openness to external (including British) investment brought about a much better climate of relations between the British and Irish governments. Both countries had applied for membership of the EEC in 1962 and expected quite soon to be members of it. The Republic had become an active member of the United Nations. The radical difference between the United Kingdom as a second-rank world power and the Republic as a small and peripheral country remained, but the gap had diminished following developments in the Republic and the decline in British power and prestige from its height at the beginning of the century.

[38] Purdie, *Politics in the Streets*, ch. 3.

Third, the political capacity of Northern Catholics had grown. By the 1960s they had matured as a political community, separate from the South. A new generation of political leaders was emerging, born in Northern Ireland, products of the new welfare state and the confidence of the 1960s, impatient with the Nationalist Party's ineffectual policies and its political dependence on the South and on the church.[39]

The development of the Keynesian welfare state in post-war Northern Ireland gave new incentives and new opportunities for Catholics to challenge the 1921 settlement. The persistence of unionist particularism in the context of an expanded state was multiplying the occasions for Catholic grievance and anger at a time when their political capacity had grown. Moreover the issues which emerged as grievances – housing, industrial location, regional development, jobs in the public sector – impacted on all levels of the Catholic community; since they did not raise the question of sovereignty, they could form the basis of a unified political movement.

At the same time, the changing political and economic order was generating tensions within the Protestant community.[40] Increasing dependence on the British exchequer and on outside industry demanded some moderation of the anti-Catholic and anti-nationalist rhetoric and practice of the unionist government; increased centralisation was threatening the powers of local unionist elites. The newly moderate tone of Unionism had few implications for policy but, in combination with the threat to local power bases, it alarmed loyalists. A new and charismatic champion of the Protestant interest emerged – the Reverend Ian Paisley. These internal divisions would greatly reduce the Stormont government's room for manoeuvre in response to the civil rights movement.

Internationally, there was a new concern with civil and minority rights. The 1950s and 1960s provided models of non-violent protest: the Black civil rights campaign in the US, the struggle against apartheid in South Africa, the campaign against the Vietnam war in the United States and the student riots of May 1968 in France and elsewhere in Europe. Demonstrations and marches were publicised world-wide through the new communications medium of television. The campaign for civil rights in Northern Ireland was part of this international trend; as such, it secured much wider internal and international support than could traditional nationalist protest.

[39] Farrell, *Northern Ireland*, pp. 239ff.; also Kennedy, 'Whither northern nationalism', p. 271.
[40] Paul Bew, Peter Gibbon and Henry Patterson, *Northern Ireland 1921–1994: Political Forces and Social Classes*, London, Serif, 1995, ch. 4 and pp. 171–85.

The demand for civil rights and the marches caught the public imagination and drew a popular Catholic response which surprised even veteran campaigners. Unionists found the form of the protest deeply disturbing. The injustices highlighted by the civil rights movement had long been criticised in nationalist propaganda, but now the criticism was liberal democratic rather than nationalist in form. Nationalists and republicans were active in the campaign but so too were individuals who had no strong views on the constitutional question, who would be happy with 'British rights for British citizens'.[41] The civil rights movement could not easily be fitted into unionist conceptual categories and they found it difficult to know how to respond to it: as old fashioned nationalism in a new guise or as a desire for greater equality within the union?

The tactic of the march increased the problems for unionists. Although an accepted, even celebrated, mode of non-violent protest in the 1960s, its role in Northern Ireland was problematic. Northern Ireland's geography was deeply sectarianised and the march had long been a Protestant weapon for asserting control over the public sphere. Civil rights marches which traversed Protestant territory, or indeed any territory not seen as exclusively Catholic, were perceived as a direct challenge. This flouting of the North's sectarian geography and Protestant dominance in the public sphere provoked loyalists and created communal flashpoints.

The security forces also faced difficulties in responding to the civil rights marches. They had been set up as much to contain a nationalist uprising as to engage in normal policing and the marches were ambiguous as to whether or not they were an attack on the state. Many in the RUC, and virtually all the B Specials, were defenders of the Protestant community first, defenders of the Protestant state second, and normal policemen third. The clashes between marchers and loyalists forced them to take sides, undermining any claims they had to be 'normal policemen'. The government was internally divided between those who saw the civil rights movement as a challenge to the state which had to be met head on, and those who believed that on grounds of principle or of pragmatism (in particular fear of pressure from the British government) that concessions should be made.[42] As the marches continued, the security situation deteriorated and the divisions widened.

The second march, in Derry on 5 October, was banned by home affairs

---

[41] Michael Farrell, ed., *Twenty Years On*, Dingle, Brandon, 1988.

[42] For an example of the former, see William Craig, interview with Richard Deutsch, *Études Irlandaises*, vol. 1, Dec. 1976, pp. 160–3.

minister William Craig but went ahead. The police batoned the demonstrators, and this was shown on television throughout the world. New civil rights organisations sprang up. The British government – without publicly breaching its non-interventionist stance – insisted on immediate reforms.[43] On 22 November, the prime minister of Northern Ireland, Terence O'Neill, announced a five-point reform programme which only partially satisfied civil rights demands, angered hard-line members of his cabinet and enraged loyalists.[44] In December O'Neill made a televised broadcast – 'Northern Ireland is at the Crossroads' – appealing for public support for his reform programme. Shortly afterwards he sacked his main cabinet critic, William Craig. Civil rights radicals in the student based People's Democracy (PD) were determined to keep up the pressure on the government and organised a march across Northern Ireland in January 1969. It was attacked by loyalists with security force collusion and, when the march was welcomed into Derry, loyalists and police attacked the Catholic Bogside district and Catholics were forced into explicit communal defence.

In the communal polarisation that followed, most of the Protestant support for civil rights fell away. O'Neill faced more criticism within his cabinet and party, and sacked more cabinet members. His attempt to secure moderate support for reform by holding an election in February 1969 backfired. The election showed the Unionist Party to be deeply divided; it also decimated the now relatively accomodationist Nationalist Party and brought civil rights radicals into politics. O'Neill resigned two months later: his successor, James Chichester-Clark, continued O'Neill's policies. The summer 'marching season' brought the crisis to a head; there was rioting in Derry on 12 and 13 August followed by large-scale rioting and shooting in Belfast. The government's capacity to keep order had broken down and British troops were called in.

Break-down

The most important effect of the crisis was to show that unionists could no longer manage the internal affairs of Northern Ireland effectively and without undue controversy. In retrospect, the entry of British troops proved the first step in dismantling the alliance between the Protestant community and the British state. Initially, however, the old model was

---

[43] Ken Bloomfield, *Stormont in Crisis: A Memoir*, Belfast, Blackstaff, 1994, p. 99.
[44] For details of the reform programme, see Michael J. Cunningham, *British Government Policy in Northern Ireland 1969–89: Its Nature and Execution*, Manchester, Manchester University Press, 1991, p. 19.

retained, and the British government worked through the Northern Ireland government which, under British pressure, pushed through reforms and attempted to maintain law and order.

The reform process already begun in November 1968 increased its momentum. The Cameron Report published in September 1969 reported that discrimination against Catholics was a major cause of the disturbances, and the government pledged to end discrimination in public employment. It also followed the recommendations of the Hunt Report of October 1969 to disarm and reform the RUC and to replace the B Specials with a new force – the Ulster Defence Regiment (UDR) – organised as a part-time regiment of the British army. The recommendations of the Macrory Report on local government reorganisation (published in May 1970) were also implemented. Twenty-six new local authorities were created, with elections based on PR-STV and full adult suffrage. In any case responsibility for housing, health and education was given to public boards; the new local authorities were left with responsibility only for recreational activities, the environment, cleaning and sanitation, registration of births, marriages and deaths. Incitement to hatred was outlawed, and the cabinet was broadened beyond the Unionist Party when David Bleakley of the NILP was appointed minister for community relations in 1971.

The reforms did not restore stability. The communal disturbances in August 1969 in Belfast had undermined the local equilibrium in working class areas; over 3,500 families – the majority of them Catholic – were intimidated from their homes in August and September 1969.[45] Each community now struggled for territory, mobilising in local defence groups, creating 'no-go' areas where security forces were excluded, and engaging in communal intimidation and attack. Both communities rioted and petrol-bombed the security forces. For Catholics, this was a continued combative assertion of civil rights demands and a challenge to the state; for Protestants violence was an attempt to reassert their control and to vent their anger.[46]

The situation continued to deteriorate. The republican movement split.[47] The Provisional IRA took the traditional republican militarists – most of the politically aware republicans went with the Official IRA – and provided a channel for Catholic communal anger and resentment.

[45] John Darby, *Intimidation and the Control of Conflict in Northern Ireland*, Gill and Macmillan, 1986, p. 58.
[46] Sarah Nelson, *Ulster's Uncertain Defenders: Loyalists and the Northern Ireland Conflict*, Belfast, Appletree, 1984, pp. 87–93; W. H. Van Voris, *Violence in Ulster: An Oral Documentary*, Amherst, University of Massachusetts Press, 1973, pp. 98–9.
[47] Patterson, *Politics of Illusion*, ch. 5.

The Provisionals emerged as Catholic communal defenders against Protestant attack and began to prepare themselves for a military campaign against the Northern state. State security was the responsibility of a Joint Security Committee composed of British and Unionist members, but the Unionist government was increasingly the stronger voice. Catholics were subjected to harsher security policies than were Protestants.[48] The British army proved as capable of harassment, intimidation and violence and as slow to admit fault as the RUC had been in the past. In July 1970, the Falls Road curfew, in which five civilians died, marked a decisive step in the alienation of Belfast Catholics from the British army and confirmed a growing support base for the Provisional IRA.

In autumn 1970 the Provisional IRA began an offensive campaign consisting of killing members of the security forces and bombing civilian targets. The campaign intensified in 1971. The Ulster Defence Association (UDA), a Protestant paramilitary organisation, was formed and its membership grew rapidly. Communal rioting and attacks continued. Mainstream unionists were horrified at the apparent impunity with which nationalists could attack the state and maintain 'no-go areas' outside its control. Protestant pressure for internment without trial grew. It was introduced on 9 August 1971, directed solely at the nationalist community and accompanied by the mistreatment and torture of internees. It immediately produced an increase in street violence, intimidation and in Provisional military activity: the death rate in 1971 rose from 34 in the period before 9 August to 140 in the period after.[49]

Moderate Catholics had been strongly opposed to the IRA but were disturbed by the harshness of security policy and the targeting of nationalists. As the impetus for reform slowed and the emphasis shifted to security, their opinions hardened. The SDLP welcomed government proposals in June 1971 for reforms designed to permit greater Catholic participation in the process of government through representation on committees. But in July 1971 it withdrew from Stormont in protest at the refusal of the British government to hold an inquiry into the army killing of two unarmed Catholics in Derry; internment a month later inflamed all Catholic opinion.

---

[48] The police tended to charge Catholics with 'riotous behaviour' and Protestants with the lesser charge of 'disorderly behaviour'. Catholics were also subject to harsher army searches; Buckland, *History of Northern Ireland*, p. 150; Desmond Hamill, *Pig in the Middle: The Army in Northern Ireland 1969–1985*, London, Methuen, 1985, pp. 31ff.

[49] Paul Bew and Gordon Gillespie, *Northern Ireland: A Chronology of the Troubles 1968–1993*, Dublin, Gill and Macmillan, 1993, p. 37.

On 30 January 1972, following a government decision to take a tougher security line, British paratroopers shot dead thirteen unarmed demonstrators at an anti-internment march in Derry. The impact on British, Irish and international opinion was profound and it provoked a fundamental change in British policy. Stormont was prorogued on 24 March 1972.[50] Executive power was transferred to a secretary of state for Northern Ireland (SOSNI), a member of the cabinet who would preside over a 'mini-cabinet' of junior ministers appointed to administer Northern Ireland government departments. A new Northern Ireland Office (NIO) was created and staffed at the highest levels by British civil servants. From now on Northern Ireland legislation would be dealt with at Westminster, virtually all of it through Orders in Council.[51]

The proroguing of Stormont marked the end of the British policy of effecting reform through the unionist government adopted in 1969, the end of the constitutional experiment of devolved government begun in 1921, and – most fundamentally – the end of the alliance between the British state and Northern Irish Protestants on which that experiment had been based. The alliance had become unsustainable: Protestants were no longer capable of orderly and effective administration in Northern Ireland and the British government could no longer afford to back them. A new approach to the government of Northern Ireland would have to be found.

The search for a settlement

Direct rule was initially intended as a temporary measure, a means of reconstituting structures of government for Northern Ireland that would again allow the British government to distance itself from Northern Ireland. But a new settlement was difficult to find. There followed a succession of failed initiatives. William Whitelaw's power-sharing executive and all-Ireland council of 1973–4 was brought down by the Ulster Workers' Council strike; Merlyn Rees' constitutional convention of 1975 failed to reach agreement; Roy Mason's bilateral talks of 1977 found no basis for devolution; Humphrey Atkins' conference of 1980 was indefinitely adjourned; James Prior's Assembly of 1982 sat for three years but was boycotted by the SDLP and for periods by the UUP and was never granted executive or legislative power.[52] Only the Anglo-Irish

---

[50] Bloomfield, *Stormont in Crisis*, pp. 162–7.
[51] See Brigid Hadfield, 'The Northern Ireland constitution', in B. Hadfield, ed., *Northern Ireland: Politics and the Constitution*, Buckingham, Open University Press, 1992, pp. 6–7.
[52] For further detail and discussion, see Cunningham, *British Government Policy*.

Agreement of 1985 – which did not depend on the agreement of the communities in Northern Ireland – survived.

The difficulty of finding a solution arose in part from the irreconcilable goals of the two communities. From the early 1970s, the minimal nationalist demand was power-sharing with 'an Irish dimension': the SDLP's wider aim was a united Ireland by consent, and it favoured 'condominium' or joint authority as a proximate aim. Republicans sought an immediate British withdrawal and Irish unity. Unionists refused to accept any erosion of their constitutional position; one strand of unionism was willing to contemplate power-sharing, most were not.

A further problem lay in changing power resources. The British government, as in 1920, sought to minimise its own involvement by devolving administration to local representatives with the capacity to govern effectively: this strategy meant identifying and working through the local balance of power. But with the collapse of the power structure which had been in place for fifty years the new balance of power was difficult to read. All parties to the conflict tended to overestimate their capacity to achieve their goals.

A defining moment came early. In 1973 the new British SOSNI, William Whitelaw, proposed as an alternative to Stormont a devolved assembly with executive power-sharing and a Council of Ireland.[53] The British parliament was overwhelmingly in favour, as were the SDLP and Alliance parties. The more moderate tendency in the Unionist Party did not reject the proposals (although they did not unambiguously accept them) and made up almost half of those elected in the Assembly elections of June 1973. The Assembly convened in July, and a power-sharing executive was agreed in November. It took office in January 1974 after a compromise agreement was reached on a Council of Ireland (less powerful than nationalists had wanted, more than unionists desired, and balanced by Irish government recognition that change in the status of Northern Ireland depended on majority consent).

From the outset unionists opposed to power-sharing disrupted the work of the Assembly; in January 1974 they forced the power-sharing faction out of the Unionist Party; they turned the Westminster election of February 1974 into a unionist plebiscite which they won resoundingly. The power-sharing executive continued to function and loyalists moved to bring it down by a mass strike which began on 14 May. It was coordinated by the Ulster Workers Council (UWC), an umbrella group

---

[53] *Ibid.*, pp. 45–56.

of loyalist trades-unionists and paramilitaries. Initially the strike depended for its effectiveness on intimidation but it soon gained the support of a wide range of unionist opinion including farmers, professionals and even civil servants.[54] The support of industrial power workers proved crucial; as they cut the supply of power the economic life of the province gradually came to a standstill. The executive, without control of security, could do nothing. The British army could have intervened, but the cost of conflict with loyalists would have been high and the new Labour government was convinced that the executive was doomed.[55] After fourteen days the unionist members of the executive resigned and the British government prorogued the Assembly. In October another British general election led to the overwhelming victory of unionists opposed to power-sharing.

All parties took lessons from the fall of the executive. The British government discovered the balance of power between loyalism and liberal unionism. The Irish government learned that the British government was unwilling to confront the loyalists and saw the problems it would face from a militant, mobilised, uncontrollable Protestant population in the event of a British withdrawal.[56] Northern nationalists became aware of the limits of their power; they had brought down Stormont but they could not secure a minimally acceptable replacement. Moderate unionists learned the depth of communal opposition to power-sharing. Mainstream unionists subsequently discovered the limits of their power when they found that their capacity to bring down a settlement of which they disapproved could not be mobilised to impose one of their choice – British governments consistently rejected the unionist preference for a new majority controlled devolved assembly and executive and in 1977 an attempt to impose such a settlement by another strike failed to gain public support.[57]

The UWC strike not only illustrated the balance of power, it affected and changed it. For unionists, the strike was an act of self-definition, of communal self-constitution outside the framework of the state from which they had been dislodged, an expression of Protestant solidarity that healed some of the divisions which had opened up during the previous period. The SDLP was crucially weakened, with internal differences on political strategy and a divergence between the SDLP and

---

[54] See Patrick Shea, *Voices and the Sound of Drums: An Irish Autobiography*, Belfast, Blackstaff, 1981, pp. 200–1; Merlyn Rees, *Northern Ireland: A Personal Perspective*, London, Methuen, 1985, pp. 77–8.
[55] Hamill, *Pig in the Middle*, pp. 145ff.; Rees, *Northern Ireland*, pp. 71, 77, 82.
[56] Garret Fitzgerald, *All in a Life*, Dublin, Gill and Macmillan, 1991, pp. 244, 271–2.
[57] Bew and Gillespie, *Northern Ireland: A Chronology*, pp. 118–21.

the Irish government emerging. The experience led John Hume to begin building external alliances which would strengthen Northern nationalism.

In the wake of the UWC strike the British government continued its strategy of working with and through the local communities, but it now sought to 'Ulsterise' the conflict. It reduced the British army presence on the streets and increased the numbers of locally based security forces. It sought to treat the violence as 'terrorism' and deal with it by the civil law rather than in a quasi-military fashion. Internment was phased out and replaced by special non-jury courts. It also intensified its security measures. The new policies carried a cost. The stronger security measures led to a series of human rights abuses: police interrogations, controversial killings by the security forces, allegations of collusion between the security forces and the loyalist paramilitaries.[58] The policy of criminalisation provoked a republican campaign for 'political status' culminating in the hunger strikes of 1981 which won unprecedented world publicity and sympathy for republicans and led directly to the political rise of Sinn Féin. Violence continued and communal polarisation deepened.

Alarmed at the growing strength of republicanism, Garret Fitzgerald as taoiseach convened a New Ireland Forum to forge a new constitutional nationalist consensus. It was to rest on the principle of communal and cultural equality for the nationalist and unionist traditions. This principle, its report claimed, necessitated a move beyond an internal Northern Ireland settlement.[59] Under pressure from the American and Irish governments the British government began to rethink its strategy, widening the context of resolution of the conflict to the island as a whole, and to the British–Irish relationship.[60] The first concrete expression of the new strategy was the Anglo-Irish Agreement of November 1985.

The Agreement reiterated the guarantee of Northern Ireland's constitutional status, dependent on the will of a majority in Northern Ireland, but it also recognised the island-wide identity of Northern nationalists and gave the Irish government a role in policy-making and a permanent presence in Northern Ireland in the Anglo-Irish Secretariat. The precise

---

[58] Amnesty International, *Political Killings in Northern Ireland*, London, 1994; T. Hadden, K. Boyle and C. Campbell, 'Emergency law in Northern Ireland: the context', in A. Jennings, ed., *Justice Under Fire: The Abuse of Civil Liberties in Northern Ireland*, London, Pluto, 1988, see table 1.1, pp 4–5.

[59] New Ireland Forum, *Report*, Dublin, Stationery Office, 1984, pp. 7, 17–19.

[60] Bew, Gibbon and Patterson, *Northern Ireland 1921–1994*, pp. 204–14.

understanding of the Irish government role was ambiguous but it was, in Garret Fitzgerald's words, 'more than consultative'.[61] In these ways, it not only recognised the island- and British Isles-wide context of the problem but brought more fully into play the balance of power at these levels.

For unionists, the Agreement was close to disaster. It emphasised the conditional nature of Northern Ireland's position within the United Kingdom. It gave the government of the Republic a direct say in the running of Northern Ireland, thereby separating the process of government in Northern Ireland from other parts of the United Kingdom and increasing the power of Northern nationalists. It established at intergovernmental level what unionists had resolutely resisted at regional level: power-sharing and institutional expression of the Irish dimension. Most of all it signalled the shift in the focus of British thinking from Northern Ireland to the island of Ireland as a whole. For many it was the end of the union as they had known it.

The Protestant community mobilised to bring down the Agreement. There was no attempt to repeat the UWC strike of 1974, but unionists held protest marches, mass demonstrations, a day of industrial action; they collected over 400,000 signatures, petitioned the queen, and challenged the legality of the Agreement in the courts in Britain and in the Republic. Unionist MPs at Westminster resigned their seats and stood for re-election to legitimate their opposition to it (in the process losing a seat to the SDLP); when re-elected they refused to meet with the SOSNI or to enter talks about devolution until the Agreement was removed. They encouraged civil disobedience in the form of a rent and rates strike. A new paramilitary organisation – Ulster Resistance – was formed to oppose the Agreement. Attacks on Catholics increased and evidence of collusion between security forces and paramilitaries would later emerge.[62] Unionist resistance succeeded in slowing up or preventing some of the promised reforms, particularly in the security area, but the Agreement remained in place.

Two years after the signing of the Anglo-Irish Agreement, unionists moved from protest to politics. The UUP and the DUP jointly proposed an alternative to the Agreement – a form of non-executive devolution in which power would be shared at committee level and in which unionists,

[61] O'Leary and McGarry, *Politics of Antagonism*, p. 226 and ch. 6; Cunningham, *British Government Policy*, pp. 172–80; on the ambiguities, see Jennifer Todd, 'Equality, plurality and democracy: Justifications of proposed constitutional settlements of the Northern Ireland conflict', *Ethnic and Racial Studies*, vol. 18, no. 4, 1995.
[62] Amnesty International, *Political Killings*, pp. 23–47.

as the majority, would maintain overall control.[63] This proposal prepared the way for 'talks about talks' to reach a political settlement.

Peter Brooke, SOSNI, initiated a three-stranded talks process – concerned with relations within Northern Ireland, between North and South and between the United Kingdom and the Republic – in January 1990. Procedural difficulties meant that interparty discussions did not begin until May 1991; they made little progress and were suspended in July. Underlying these difficulties were deep disagreements in aims. Unionists saw the talks as a way of transcending the Irish government's role in Northern Ireland, albeit at the cost of conceding power-sharing to Northern nationalists. Nationalists in the SDLP had little interest in an internal settlement which would remove the symbolic and practical benefits of the Irish government's role: they saw the talks as an opportunity to widen discussions to the constitutional framework.[64] Bridge-builders and the British government saw them as a way to achieve devolution within the Anglo-Irish framework agreed in 1985.

The difference in aims became explicit in the second phase of talks, reopened by the new SOSNI, Patrick Mayhew, in April 1992. The Unionist and Alliance parties and British government reached broad agreement on power-sharing structures within Northern Ireland in the Strand 1 talks. The SDLP's proposals – for a direct executive role for the Republic and the European Community in the government of Northern Ireland – highlighted nationalists' refusal to consider the internal administration of Northern Ireland in isolation from the wider context. They were seen by unionists and NIO officials as 'ludicrous' and 'offensive' and led to deadlock.[65] The talks moved onto Strand 2 (North–South relations) with even less progress: unionists and the Irish government were in sharp conflict over Articles 2 and 3 of the Irish constitution. The talks ended in early November 1992. Unionists subsequently refused to meet the Irish government. The talks process, however, had highlighted the Irish government's increasing role in the conflict.

Meanwhile a new initiative was underway to secure an IRA ceasefire. By the mid-1980s republicans had reached the upper limits of their

---

[63] Unionist Task Force Report, *End to Drift*, 1987, 'Parent document', circulated among the unionist parties in 1987, published *Irish Times*, 3 July 1991.

[64] Ed Moloney's articles in *Sunday Tribune*, 26 May, 30 June 1991. In the latter an SDLP member is quoted as saying 'A lot of us won't be too unhappy when this ends. Our attitude is we have a Rolls Royce in the garage. Why should we want to buy a Cortina with no window wipers?'

[65] Paul Arthur, 'The Mayhew talks 1992', *Irish Political Studies*, vol. 8, 1993; Fionnuala O'Connor, *In Search of a State: Catholics in Northern Ireland*, Belfast, Blackstaff, 1993, p. 143.

political support in the North and were clearly failing in their attempt to build a political base in the South. The Anglo-Irish Agreement did not undermine their core support but it isolated them politically and raised questions about the continued necessity of an armed campaign. Republicans began to debate alternative political strategies from 1986. They entered discussions with the SDLP in 1988; indirect contacts with Charles Haughey's Fianna Fáil government were initiated at around the same time and continued by Albert Reynolds when he became taoiseach in 1992. The loss of Gerry Adams' seat in the 1992 Westminster elections was further impetus for a change in strategy. Discussions between SF, SDLP and representatives of the Irish government led to an agreed document which was sent to the British government. The following year saw a long exchange of letters between the IRA and the British government on the prospects of a negotiated end to violence.

In September 1993, apparently because of the slowness of the British response, Gerry Adams and John Hume announced agreement on a set of principles which centred on a recognition of the Irish right to national self-determination, an acceptance that this right can only be exercised through agreement, and a commitment by the governments to work towards such agreement. A peace process must 'ensure that any new agreement . . . respects the diversity of our different traditions and earns their allegiance and agreement'.[66] The principles at once assert the necessity of change, deny unionists a veto on it but give them a full say in its direction. Hume and Adams claimed their principles could form the basis of an immediate peace settlement.

These principles were forwarded to the Irish government for inter-governmental attention. They were initially publicly rejected by both governments, then redrafted and, after further Irish/British negotiation, partially incorporated into the Downing Street Declaration (DSD) by the British and Irish prime ministers in December 1993.[67] The DSD acknowledged a right to self-determination on the island of Ireland to be exercised by agreement on the island and committed both governments to work towards such agreement. It also affirmed the right of a majority in Northern Ireland to consent, or withhold consent, to change in the

---

[66] Joint statements of Hume and Adams, Sept. 1993; John Hume, *Irish Times* 5 Jan., 31 Jan. 1994, and Gerry Adams *Irish Times*, 14 Jan. 1994.

[67] For changing Irish government formulations, see Irish Foreign Minister Dick Spring's 'Six Principles' of October 1993 (reported *Irish Times* 29 Oct. 1993) which highlighted the need for unionist consent, later adapted in an address to the Johns Hopkins University School of Advanced International Studies, 17 Nov. 1993, reported *Irish Times*, 18 Nov. 1993 which emphasised the need for the consent of both communities.

(constitutional) status of Northern Ireland. Each government gave differing formulations of the rights involved (chapter 11).

The UUP, in parliamentary alliance with the British Conservatives, initially accepted the DSD, as did the SDLP and Alliance parties, while the DUP rejected it and SF sought clarification. Loyalist violence increased and became explicitly proactive. There followed nine months of clarification for SF: the Irish government, but not the British, was explicit that nationalist consent was as necessary as unionist to any new settlement; Irish-Americans came in as 'persuaders'. On 31 August 1994 the IRA announced a complete cessation of military activity. Within a week, the Irish taoiseach, Albert Reynolds, met Gerry Adams and was photographed clasping his and John Hume's hands. Unionists – who feared that the British prime minister, John Major had given concessions to the IRA – noted the emergence of a 'pan-nationalist alliance'. Five weeks later, the loyalist paramilitaries also announced a cessation of violence.

The two governments developed their joint proposals for a political settlement. In March 1995 they published two documents (the Frameworks Documents) which were intended as a basis for all-party negotiation. The joint British-Irish Framework Document at once guaranteed that consent by a majority in Northern Ireland was necessary for constitutional change (paragraph 17) and recognised the absence of minority consent for the constitutional status quo (paragraph 18). It gave practical effect to the island dimension by proposing North–South bodies with executive and harmonising functions – although the precise nature of these institutions and their dynamic potential was left unclear – while maintaining an Irish government role in a modified Anglo-Irish conference. The parallel British document proposed for Northern Ireland a devolved legislature and executive with power-sharing and safeguards for the minority.

Nationalists welcomed the documents, more or less guardedly. Unionists – both UUP and DUP – rejected the documents, seeing in them a deeply unwelcome focus on the Irish context, evidence of Britain's lack of commitment to the union, and an attempt to curb their rightful powers as a majority in Northern Ireland.[68] The British government stressed, to unionists in particular, that the proposals were for discussion by the parties, not a blueprint to be imposed on them. Unionists set out to reverse the new direction of policy, the SDLP to consolidate it, SF to accelerate it.

---

[68] For example, John Taylor, *Irish Times*, 9 Mar. 1995

It is too soon to say if the conditions for a settlement have now emerged. Political goals remain opposed even if the parties' political strategies have changed. Talks must now cope not just with the opposed demands of the SDLP for a stronger, and the unionists for a weaker, Irish dimension, but with the radically conflicting demands of SF for an end to the unionist veto on constitutional change and the loyalists for an immediate end to nationalist pressure for constitutional change. If the Frameworks Documents form the basis of a settlement, it will be because they give a new – and ambiguous – arena in which to fight for these opposed goals.

Power and the conditions for a settlement

The suspension of violence and commitment to talks came from a reassessment among all parties of the balance of power and their prospects of achieving their minimal goals. What is the balance of power today, how stable is it and is it conducive to a settlement?

Communal power in Northern Ireland

In assessing the balance of power between the two communities in Northern Ireland we distinguish between institutional and structural power. The former refers to power derived from the occupancy of institutional positions; the latter refers to power derived from the possession of demographic, economic, political or ideological resources.

Institutional power. Protestants continue to predominate in elective positions. The nationalist parties have increased their share of the vote to over a third of first preference votes but unionists currently hold 13 of the 17 Westminster seats, two of the three European Parliament (EP) seats, and control 15, to nationalists' 6, of the 26 local councils: for nationalists this is a marked improvement on the past but one that does not fully reflect their share of the vote.[69] Unionists have used their Westminster seats to forge informal coalitions with the government in power – this was particularly important in the Labour administration of 1974–9 and in the 1992–7 Conservative

---

[69] O'Leary and McGarry, *Politics of Antagonism*, pp. 190–1; Joseph Ruane and Jennifer Todd, 'The social origins of nationalism in a contested region: The case of Northern Ireland', in John Coakley, ed., *The Social Origins of Nationalist Movements: The Contemporary West European Experience*, London, Sage, 1992, pp. 191–4; Paul Carmichael, 'The 1993 local government elections in Northern Ireland', *Irish Political Studies*, vol. 9, 1994, 143–4.

administration.[70] Unionist electoral strength confers legitimacy on their views, provides moral backing for Northern Ireland's position in the United Kingdom and is a warning to both British and Irish governments of the continuing strength and political solidarity of the Protestant community there.

Protestants still predominate in the apparatuses of state. The upper echelons of the Northern Ireland Civil Service and the judiciary remain disproportionately Protestant.[71] The security forces are overwhelmingly Protestant; over 90 per cent of the RUC and even more of the RUC reserve and UDR are Protestant.[72] The policy of 'Ulsterisation' embarked on in 1975 increased the numbers of locally recruited security forces and strengthened their identification with the Protestant community: UUP security spokesman, Ken Maginnis, has spoken of the UDR as a 'moderate Protestant army'.[73] It does not appear that the 1992 merging of the UDR with the Royal Irish Rangers in a new Royal Irish Regiment has significantly changed this. The area of greatest Catholic gains has been on the public boards which have taken over responsibilities previously exercised by local authorities – the Northern Ireland Housing Executive (NIHE), the Health Boards and Education Boards – but this depends on ministerial appointment of Catholics and nationalists to balance the unionists nominated by the local authorities.

Institutional power – in the civil service, the judiciary and the security forces – matters. It feeds into British strategies and institutional biases and tends to preclude the challenging of institutionalised 'common sense' that might be more likely from those who share the perceptions of the Catholic community. Senior Northern Irish civil servants, whose advice has been important in shaping the views of British ministers and NIO officials, have shared in the political culture of the Protestant community and have had a particular sensitivity to what Protestants

[70] Paul Dixon, '"The usual English double talk": the British political parties and the Ulster Unionists 1974–1994', Irish Political Studies, vol. 9, 1994.
[71] Brice Dickson, 'Northern Ireland's troubles and the judges', in Hadfield, ed., Northern Ireland, pp. 132–3.
[72] Census 1991, reported in A. M. Gallagher, R. D. Osborne and R. J. McCormack, Fair Shares? Employment, Unemployment and Economic Status, Belfast, Fair Employment Commission, 1994, p. 30, tables 3.4, 3.5.
[73] Ken Maginnis, quoted in Irish Times 16 Oct. 1985; cf. Anne Mandeville, 'La professionalisation d'une unité de maintien de l'ordre, étape de la secularisation du système politique nord-irlandais? Le cas de l'Ulster Defence Regiment', paper presented to conference, 'L'Irlande: vers une société laïque', Centre Universitaire d'Études Irlandaises, Paris, 22–3 May 1992, forthcoming in Paul Brennan, ed., La Sécularisation de l'Irlande, Caen; Andy Pollak, articles on the UDR in the Irish Times, 15, 16, 17 Oct. 1985.

would and would not accept.[74] Northern Ireland judges have shown no explicit Protestant bias and have been somewhat more more critical of the security forces than have the British Courts of Appeal.[75] Nonetheless, a mainly Protestant judiciary is less likely to engage in the radical questioning appropriate to a judicial system based on emergency law.

Protestant predominance within the security forces is also important. Put crudely, it means that one community polices the other. The actions of the police are answerable to higher authority but provisions for monitoring security force actions and securing redress in the event of abuse are far from satisfactory. A Police Authority, Police Liaison Committees and later a Commission of Police Complaints, all with civilian members, have been created but with inadequate powers. The British government's dependence on local (mainly Protestant) security forces, prison officers, and public servants more generally has limited the degree of reform that it has deemed possible.

Structural power. The sources of structural power are demographic (adult population size), ecological (location in strategically important areas), economic (control over crucial economic resources), political (strategic external alliances, organisational resources), ideological (a developed world view capable of carrying moral force in argument) and military (the exercise and threat of force). In each respect, Protestants' advantage remains considerable, but there has been erosion.

Protestants make up over 60 per cent of the adult population. However Catholics' demographic strength is increasing; now they are 43 per cent of the population as a whole.[76] The disparity in the birth rate may be falling, but so too is the disparity in emigration rates. Protestants continue to be located in the geographically strategic and economically most important parts of Northern Ireland – the traditional heartland of the Lagan Valley, the richer east of the province and the Belfast hinterland. But outside that they are losing ground. Only eleven of the twenty-six council areas have large Protestant majorities which have not been eroded in the last twenty years (Lisburn, with a safe but falling Protestant majority, makes twelve).

---

[74] Ewart Bell, quoted in Michael Connolly and Sean Loughlin, 'Policy making in Northern Ireland', in M. E. H. Connolly and S. Loughlin, eds., *Public Policy in Northern Ireland: Adoption or Adaptation*, Belfast, Policy Research Institute, 1990, p. 11; Bloomfield, *Stormont in Crisis*, pp. 254–5; Fitzgerald, *All in a Life*, p. 556.

[75] Brice Dickson 'Northern Ireland's troubles', pp. 136–7.

[76] The data on demographic strength is from the 1991 census as analysed in R. J. Cormack, A. M. Gallagher and R. D. Osborne, *Fair Enough? Religion and the 1991 Population Census*, Belfast, Fair Employment Commission, 1993, section 2, pp. 13–15.

Protestants have lost control of Derry City and are in process of losing control of Belfast City: Catholics, 34.1 per cent of Belfast's population in 1971, are now 45 per cent. The increasing numbers of local districts have moved from roughly equal population proportions in 1971 to definite Catholic majorities: Cookstown, Magherafelt, Moyle, Down, Dungannon, Fermanagh, Limavady – while Armagh and Craigavon, together with Belfast, have moved from a definite to a marginal Protestant majority. If present trends continue, Catholics will have the potential to gain power in a majority of local councils even before they form a majority in Northern Ireland as a whole.

Protestant military strength remains decisive. Large numbers of Protestants have been trained in arms through their membership of the security forces and they have substantial quantities of legally held weapons. There is no corresponding military experience or tradition among Catholics, the vast majority of whom have stayed clear of republican militarism; relatively few have legally held weapons. Protestants west of the Bann are strategically vulnerable, but the distribution of population in the east, with a Protestant majority ringing Catholic areas in the city of Belfast, favours Protestants.

As the majority community Protestants are still the dominant political force. It is their constitutional preference – membership of the United Kingdom – which is institutionalised and the majority preference that is guaranteed by both British and Irish governments. Catholics have partially compensated for their minority status by improved political organisation, more effective mobilisation of their vote, and by external alliances – with the Southern government, Irish-Americans, the British Labour Party and within the European Union. At the same time, the British government has distanced itself from its traditional alliance with unionists. The result – an increasing Irish input into Northern Irish politics and an increasing emphasis by the British government on the Irish context of the conflict – has increased the political capacity of Northern Catholics.

Catholics succeeded in claiming the moral high ground in the civil rights period and, the IRA campaign notwithstanding, have retained it. They have tapped into contemporary international norms of civil and human rights, pluralism and post-nationalism, with an ease that unionists have lacked. Only in the recent period has a new generation of unionist intellectuals begun to challenge this with, as yet, limited success in the international arena (chapter 10).

Despite these gains Catholics remain vulnerable. Much of their advance has come from the British government's commitment to executive-style reform in Northern Ireland. That commitment was in part an attempt to remove support from the IRA. The IRA ceasefire has increased nationalist solidarity within Northern Ireland and may bring a new set of highly politicised, radical and able working-class activists into the political process. Whether the British commitment to reform will long survive the end of the IRA campaign is less clear. The most important Catholic gains – the Anglo-Irish Agreement and the 1989 Fair Employment Act – were won for them by their external allies – the Republic, the British Labour Party, the United States and less directly, the European Union. This makes Catholic power dependent on the vagaries of politics elsewhere, in particular on the unpredictable course of American politics. This dependence has increased with the suspension of the IRA armed campaign.

Protestants are less externally dependent in their power resources. Their power rests on their dominance within the economy, their moral case as the democratic majority, their numbers and *in extremis* their military capacity. They are, however, vulnerable in one respect. The power of social disruption is a weapon of last resort. It is a poor defence against the multiplicity of minor reforms which are slowly and gradually eroding their position. It is also two-sided. If Protestants are too disruptive they could find themselves in confrontation with the British government and unwittingly provide it with the opportunity to withdraw. Catholic power is greatest in the wider Irish and international context and they have been able to use it to force through policies against unionist resistance. But even in the wider arena, the balance of power does not unambiguously favour Catholics and their position is vulnerable to changes in political interests and priorities.

The power balance on the island of Ireland

The balance of power between the two island-wide communities – Catholic/nationalist and Northern Protestant/unionist – is difficult to determine since it is not directly tested. Unionists focus their political efforts within Northern Irish and British institutions and minimise direct contact with the South. The Irish state avoids direct challenge to unionists, not least because it might be met by loyalist violence. There is only one terrain where the two communities meet and oppose each other and where their relative power is directly tested – in their relations with the British government.

There is no doubt that, in general, the position of unionists has weakened significantly since the beginning of the century, and more recently since 1969. They are no longer the progressive economic force on the island as they were for so long; the Southern Irish economy is now more dynamic and less dependent (chapters 6, 9). The unionist community is without a devolved parliament or government; Irish nationalism is now represented by a sovereign state whose economic and cultural resources and whose role in the EU and other international organisations allow it an influence on international opinion far beyond that of unionists. Moreover the increasing emphasis on the Irish context of the problem highlights unionists' demographic weakness – they may represent 59 per cent of the population of Northern Ireland but a mere 20 per cent of the island as a whole.

Unionists are by no means powerless, however. British insistence on the legitimacy of Northern Ireland as a political entity and of majority opinion there gives them some international standing. They also exploit with some effectiveness the weaknesses on the nationalist side – the illiberal and authoritarian aspects of the Irish state which challenges some of its pluralist claims, the weaknesses in its economy, the divisions between Northern and Southern nationalism. Moreover their military resources, even if much less than those of the Irish state, are not negligible in an Irish context. Culturally and ideologically the South is non-militaristic, and its small standing army is experienced in peace-keeping rather than in combat. It could not easily contain loyalist militancy and does not have the heart, even if the ability, to take on loyalists in their own north-eastern territory. In any case, economic and wider political considerations rule out such an undertaking.

On the one ground where the power-balance between unionists and nationalists is now tested – in their relations with the British government – the evidence of increased nationalist strength is unmistakable. At the time of partition the island-wide nationalist community lost all influence over British policy in Northern Ireland and power was delegated to the unionist community. This situation has dramatically altered. The unionist role as local agents of British rule and administrators of central policy was formally abrogated in 1972; decision-making is now concentrated in London and since 1985 the Irish government enjoys a privileged consultative role. The Irish government also plays a leading role in the search for a settlement and the principles of the New Ireland Forum Report – pluralist equality of the traditions – have framed successive British–Irish initiatives.[77] The Irish context of the conflict is now central to the search for a solution, as evidenced by the Downing Street Declaration of 1993 and the Frameworks Documents of 1995 (chapter 11). The major power-holder is still, however, the British

---

[77] Todd, 'Equality, plurality, democracy'.

government; the crucial arena of power is not – as yet, at least – the island of Ireland but the British Isles.

Power in the British Isles

Power in the British Isles is clearly and obviously unbalanced. The United Kingdom is a world power, if now one of second rank; the Republic of Ireland is a small neutral state. The Irish state has a significant influence on British policy in Northern Ireland only because the interests of the larger state make cooperation desirable. That influence, and British–Irish cooperation more generally, is conditioned and limited by British interests. When the British government is determined on a course of action, Irish government representations have limited relevance. In 1981, after repeated exchanges with the British government on the hunger strikes, the then taoiseach, Garret Fitzgerald, noted that 'There was simply nothing to be gained by pressing the British government any further; we should just have to live with the consequences of the way they had handled the situation'.[78]

This situation has changed in some degree in the recent period. The Irish government is now in a better position to have its representations heard with the commitment of both governments in the Anglo-Irish Agreement to make 'determined efforts' to resolve intergovernmental disagreements. The Frameworks Documents propose to strengthen this commitment. The increasing involvement of the government of the United States in the search for a resolution of the conflict has also introduced an important counterbalance to British power (chapter 10). But at the level of the British Isles, the imbalance of economic, political and military power between the British and Irish governments remains stark. Only if the British government irrevocably defines Northern Ireland as an area of Irish, rather than British or British–Irish, concern will this imbalance cease to be relevant. To date, the moves in that direction have been partial, ambiguous and reversible.

The current balance of power

The past twenty-five years have seen both continuity and change in the balance of power. Do nationalists now have the power resources to push successfully for real change? This was Gerry Adams' view at the time of the IRA ceasefire and it was one of the considerations in the IRA's

---

[78] Fitzgerald, *All in a Life*, p. 375.

decision to suspend its military operations.[79] In fact the present balance is very hard to call. Protestants retain a clear power advantage but it is decreasing; today it is more effective in vetoing constitutional change than in slowing – still less halting or reversing – the process of reform. The influence of the government of the Republic has grown to a point where the boundaries between the 'external' and the 'internal' in respect of Northern Ireland have become blurred. However ultimate control remains in the hands of the British government and further Catholic gains depend on continued state-sponsored reform. The wider international context is increasing in importance and Catholics are benefiting from it; but it remains a 'wild card' whose long term impact is difficult to predict (chapter 10). As in the past the crucial determinant of policy is the British government; but the British government also takes note of pressures from Northern Ireland, the Irish government and international bodies and their implications for its own interests. So close and unstable a power balance encourages Catholics to press for further gains and Protestants to resist and to retrench their position.

The meaning of political power

Power remains a crucial focus for communal relations in Northern Ireland[80] and has many levels of meaning. There is, first, the immediacy of power, the pleasure or satisfaction derived from dominance and defeat of the Other. For one young Apprentice Boy, the point of the Orange marches is to show that 'we won' 300 years ago.[81] For some young republicans, there was a pleasure in the violent destruction of Belfast city centre and of the 'normal' patterns of life in Northern Ireland. These attitudes may not be widespread in either community, but if few pursue power for its own sake, many will fight to ensure that the other side does not have it.[82]

Secondly, there are the immediate material benefits of power. For many Protestants, they are measured in their safety from IRA attack, their continued presence in their traditional neighbourhoods, their access to jobs, their ability to pursue their traditional marches. For many

---

[79] Adams, *Irish Times*, 29 Aug. 1994

[80] The focus on power is quite explicit among both communities. Denis Faul and Raymond Murray, 'The alienation of Northern Ireland Catholics', *Doctrine and Life*, vol. 34, no. 2, 1984, pp. 63–4; Steve Bruce, *The Edge of the Union: the Ulster Loyalist Political Vision*, Oxford, Oxford University Press, 1994, p. 46; A. T. Q. Stewart, *The Narrow Ground: Aspects of Ulster, 1609–1969*, London, Faber and Faber, 1977, p. 180.

[81] Desmond Bell's film, 'Redeeming History', produced for Channel 4 television, 1990.

[82] Cf. Wright, *Northern Ireland*, pp. 122, 234–5.

Catholics the benefits are measured in their economic opportunities, their freedom from security force harassment, their ability to have Orange marches rerouted away from Catholic areas, their ability to celebrate their own tradition openly, without being made to feel like trouble makers.

Thirdly, political power has a symbolic aspect. For both communities it is interwoven with cultural identity. The very existence of Northern Ireland is important to Northern Protestant identity. It is their place in the world, where they belong. It is an expression of their will and power, created in deference to their wishes, developed to fit their needs and defended with their blood. Northern Ireland today is as they made it. To dismantle it or to remove their stamp from it is to rob them of their birthright, of their past as well as their present. Thus Ian Paisley's comment that the prospect of an Irish flag flying over Stormont would be a planned deliberate insult to 'Ulster's dead and Ulster's living'.[83] For Catholics, the symbolic meaning of Northern Ireland is quite different. It symbolises a historic defeat, not just of Northern Catholics but of the island-wide community of which they form part. At its most immediate and pressing, getting out from under Protestant dominance is a precondition of their self-respect as a community. The exercise of power is a concrete expression of their recovery, a redemption of past defeat.

Fourthly, there is an important normative dimension to the power struggle. For Protestants, the struggle to maintain the existence of Northern Ireland is a matter of democratic principle. The state is a fully legitimate one based on the will of the majority of the population and it merits loyalty from all its citizens. It should function now – as in all democracies – according to the will of the majority of its people. For Catholics, the struggle to erode Protestant power is a matter of justice. Northern Ireland was established by force, against the wishes of the majority on the island and the minority in the new state: it systematically subordinated Catholics for decades. It can only win Catholic allegiance through a just settlement in the form of full equality with the Protestant community, with the Catholic aspiration to Irish unity given equal weight to the Protestant commitment to the union and the future constitutional position of Northern Ireland left open.

Finally, power has wider strategic implications. Both communities perceive the present conflict as part of a historical process whose outcome may be the destruction or continued subordination of their community. For Protestants, power within Northern Ireland is an

---

[83] Paisley reported in *Irish Times* 18 June 1986.

essential defence against the Catholic majority on the island of Ireland as a whole. Thus a UDA spokesman:

The vast majority of Protestants have been unwilling to share power with Catholics not because of their religion but because they consider them to be Irish nationalists intent on the destruction of Northern Ireland in pursuit of a united and overwhelmingly Catholic Ireland . . . Protestants fear that if Catholics are allowed any authority or position of influence within the political framework of Northern Ireland, they will use it to undermine Northern Ireland's position within the United Kingdom.[84]

For Catholics also, power is important in the achievement of wider communal goals. For the vast majority the first and most important aim is to ensure that they will never again be treated as they were during the decades of Stormont rule. At the very least, formal equality of power within Northern Ireland is necessary for this, and most Catholics now believe that a strong Southern involvement is necessary to balance Protestants' superior power resources within Northern Ireland. Some Northern Catholics see the acquisition of power in a longer and more radical frame of reference. Gaining control within Northern Ireland is a first step to ending partition, reintegrating with the nationalist community on the rest of the island and achieving the complete independence of the Irish nation.

Conclusion

The search for a political settlement continues. The obstacles are twofold. First, the communities are deeply divided in their political goals and aspirations. Unionists seek to halt, and if possible reverse, the erosion of their dominant position. They offer, at most, limited power-sharing and North–South contacts in return for an end to Irish government involvement in Northern Ireland's affairs and unambiguous acceptance of the legitimacy of the union. Nationalists seek to consolidate their gains and lay the basis for further advance. Their minimal demand is full power-sharing, North–South bodies with executive power, a continued role for the Irish government in Northern Ireland, and acceptance of the legitimacy of their Irish identity and nationalist aspirations.

Second, the balance of communal power is unstable and the political climate is one of ambiguity and uncertainty. Each community seeks a

---

[84] Charles Graham with John McGarry, 'Codetermination' in John McGarry and Brendan O'Leary, eds., *The Future of Northern Ireland*, Oxford, Clarendon, 1990, p. 163.

settlement which will improve its overall position; each fears an outcome which will leave it weaker than before. Each community is negotiating for the future as much as the present. The institutional power gained in an advantageous settlement will be available to extend the community's structural power; power lost in a disadvantageous settlement may never be regained. Each community accepts the need for compromise, but not at any price.

6   The dynamics of conflict: the economy

The conflict in Northern Ireland has an economic aspect.[1] Unequal access to economic resources is an important source of Catholic grievance; the political power of Protestants is underpinned by their economic power; the policies of the British government first helped maintain, then moderate, and more recently erode Protestant economic power. To stress the role of economic factors is not to argue that economic motives have primacy over political; there is not a stark opposition between the 'economic' and the 'national' or 'constitutional'.[2] On the contrary, for both Protestants and Catholics there is an interpenetration of material, symbolic and strategic meanings which blurs the boundaries between the economic, political and cultural domains.

Origins of Protestant economic power

English assertion of control over Ireland in the sixteenth and seventeenth centuries was not motivated primarily by economic considerations but economic interests were involved – Ireland would be an outlet for excess population in England and an opportunity for speculative investment

---

[1] Writers who attribute importance to the economic dimension of the conflict include David J. Smith and Gerald Chambers, *Inequality in Northern Ireland*, Oxford, Clarendon, 1991, and Paul Bew, Peter Gibbon and Henry Patterson, *The State in Northern Ireland 1921–1972*, Manchester, Manchester University Press, 1979.

[2] Some commentators posit such an opposition and see the primary cause of conflict as 'nationalism' rather than inequality; see Paul Compton, 'Employment differentials in Northern Ireland and job discrimination: a critique', in P. J. Roche and B. Barton, eds., *The Northern Ireland Question: Myth and Reality*, Aldershot, Avebury, 1991. p. 43, and Christopher Hewitt, 'The roots of violence: Catholic grievances and Irish nationalism during the civil rights period', in *ibid*. Hewitt's article is largely a reprint of his 'Catholic grievances, Catholic nationalism and violence in Northern Ireland during the civil rights period: a reconsideration', *British Journal of Sociology*, vol. 32, no. 3, 1981; for a critical response to that article, see Denis O'Hearn, 'Catholic grievances, Catholic nationalism: a comment', *British Journal of Sociology*, vol. 34, no. 3, 1983; the debate continued in subsequent issues of the journal.

while economic development would make English government in Ireland self-financing and could yield a surplus to the Crown. It was also clear that the settlers required a firm economic base if they were to carry out their intended political role. That base was established by transferring ownership of the land from Catholic to Protestant, by progressive displacement of Catholic tenants and by creating Protestant dominated networks of towns and trades.

This development went farthest in Ulster which saw the largest numbers of settlers and the widest extent of native clearance.[3] On foot of official and private plantations Protestants came to dominate the more fertile regions of the province, particularly the Lagan, Bann and Foyle basins, while Protestant (largely Presbyterian) traders, manufacturers and artisans dominated the port and inland towns. As elsewhere, Protestants owed their initial base to government sponsorship and protection, but in Ulster they quickly built on their initial resources. Ulster was the least developed Irish province in the early seventeenth century; by the end of the eighteenth century, largely due to the linen industry, east Ulster was supporting a denser population at a higher level of income then anywhere else in Ireland.

In the nineteenth century, east Ulster became the sole region of Ireland to industrialise on any scale and came close to retaining its population at a time when the rest of Ireland was experiencing a catastrophic decline. Ulster in the late nineteenth century was the world's leading centre for mechanised linen production, it was a major exporter of textile machinery and by the early twentieth century it possessed the world's largest shipyard. Belfast was the fastest growing city in the British Isles in the later nineteenth century; many smaller provincial towns – Lurgan, Portadown, Dungannon – also became important centres of industry. The development of east Ulster owed much to the influx of entrepreneurs and capital from England and Scotland but it was also a local achievement and an overwhelmingly Protestant one.

By the end of the nineteenth century Protestants controlled the vast bulk of the economic resources of east Ulster – the best of its land, its industrial and financial capital, commercial and business networks, industrial skills. Their dominance was due in part to their own effort and enterprise – Baker stresses 'the eighteenth-century capital and initiative

---

[3] For the economic history of Ulster, see Philip Robinson, *The Plantation of Ulster: British Settlement in an Irish Landscape*, Dublin, Gill and Macmillan, 1984; Peter Roebuck, ed., *Plantation to Partition: Essays in Ulster History in Honour of J. L. McCracken*, Belfast, Blackstaff, 1981; Jonathon Bardon, *A History of Ulster*, Belfast, Blackstaff, 1992; Liam Kennedy and Philip Ollerenshaw, eds., *An Economic History of Ulster 1820–1939*, Manchester, Manchester University Press, 1985.

of the Presbyterian entrepreneurs, and supported by the puritan ethos of education, apprenticeship, and self-help of the nineteenth century non-conformist migrant'.[4] It was due also to the cumulative effect of inter-generational transmission within families – and therefore within the Protestant community – of property, skills, networks of contacts and influence. But Protestant dominance was also achieved by displacing Catholics from resources and by restricting their access to the new positions becoming available.

The motivation for displacing and/or excluding Catholics varied. At times it was economic – the belief that Protestants would make better tenants or workers – or social – an expression of family, friendship or local solidarities. At other times politics was more important – for example the series of expulsions of Catholics from the Harland and Wolff shipyards in 1886, 1893, 1898, 1912 and 1920 in response to growing nationalist pressure for independence. At times economic and political concerns were conjoined – the expulsions of Catholic weavers from Co Armagh in 1795 at a time of increased Catholic competition and political assertiveness.[5] Those who engaged in exclusionary behaviour may not always have done so willingly; Protestant landlords and industrialists were frequently indifferent to the religion of their tenants and workers but came under pressure from co-religionists.[6]

Displacement and exclusion helped produce the economic marginal-isation of Catholics but cultural, educational and religious factors also played a role.[7] Whatever the causes, the effect is clear. Catholic tenant farmers found themselves concentrated in the poorer and upland areas or as small holders or farm labourers on better land. Catholics came late to the domestic linen industry and failed to advance to the higher levels. Some Catholic merchants built fortunes but a Catholic industrial bourgeoisie did not develop. A Catholic middle class emerged but it was small and concentrated in the professions and in the shopkeeping and liquor trade.[8] Catholic industrial workers were located dispro-portionately at the lower levels.

---

[4] Sybil E. Baker, 'Orange and Green, Belfast 1832–1912', in H. J. Dyos and Michael Wolff, eds., *The Victorian City: A New Earth*, vol. 2, London, Routledge Kegan Paul, 1973, p. 803.

[5] Bardon *History of Ulster*, p. 226.

[6] For example, Orangemen in Armagh attacked the property of mill owners and linen manufacturers who continued to employ Catholics in 1795; see Peter Gibbon, *The Origins of Ulster Unionism: The Formation of Popular Protestant Politics and Ideology in Nineteenth Century Ireland*, Manchester, Manchester University Press, 1975, pp. 39–40.

[7] See W. H. Crawford, 'The Ulster Irish in the eighteenth century', *Ulster Folklife*, vol. 28, 1982.

[8] Gibbon, *Origins of Ulster Unionism*, p. 92.

The Catholic experience is reflected in their position in Belfast at the end of the nineteenth century. Catholics were 'more heavily weighted in the unskilled than the skilled trades, more likely to be manual than white-collar workers. They were, for example, 47 percent of the barefoot women spinners, but 29 percent of the "superior" women weavers; 41 percent of the dockers, but 7 percent of the shipwrights; 32 percent of the general labourers, but 13 percent of the commercial clerks.'[9] Belfast Catholics also suffered relative demographic decline, their proportion of the population of Belfast falling from over 40 per cent in 1841 to 25 per cent in 1901. Similar decline, either demographic or economic, is evident in other smaller industrialising towns.[10]

Protestant economic power in the Stormont period

Protestants were in firm control of Northern Ireland's economic resources from partition until the 1960s. They were dominant at all levels of the private sector including the crucial areas of industry and finance. They controlled the apparatus of state and – within the limits of Northern Ireland's delegated powers – public policy at regional and local levels. They were the dominant presence in the major agricultural and business organisations, professional associations and influential informal networks. They had higher levels of education and training than Catholics. They were the majority of the population, spatially concentrated in the areas of most developed infrastructure.

In such circumstances retaining control was relatively easy. Economic power tended to be self-reproducing with property, skills, networks of contacts and influence transmitted intrafamilially and therefore intracommunally. The new firms in the 1950s and 1960s sought out the areas with the best infrastructure – in practice Protestant dominated – for economic reasons. The prevailing economic philosophy of 'growth centres' pointed to the wisdom of directing further public investment to these areas.[11] Hiring practices typical of the period – taking existing workers' relatives or shop stewards' references, preferring ex-servicemen, advertising first in the immediate neighbourhood, stressing the 'right' attitude to authority – ensured that Protestants rather than Catholics would be hired.

[9] Sybil E. Baker, 'Orange and Green', p. 802.
[10] For a study of the variations, see A. C. Hepburn, 'Catholics in the north of Ireland, 1850–1921: the urbanization of a minority', in A. C. Hepburn, ed., *Minorities in History*, London, Edward Arnold, 1978.
[11] See Tom Wilson, *Ulster: Conflict and consent*, Oxford, Basil Blackwell, 1989, ch. 11.

Such practices shaded into explicit discrimination, however. Some Protestant employers assumed Catholics were 'not to be trusted', were 'shifty, idle and unreliable, and fit only to be employed on unskilled work'.[12] Catholics were assumed to be more resentful of authority, more likely to be troublemakers or to have 'a chip on the shoulder'. Some employers were reluctant to employ Catholics lest this upset customers or other workers.[13] Others would not appoint Catholics to senior positions because they thought that Protestants would not 'work well under Catholic supervision' or because of Catholics' 'nationalist sympathies' – Barritt and Carter compare the latter to an English employer's doubts about hiring a communist as a manager.[14] Others believed that Catholics could not be trusted with business secrets, would gossip about the firm's business, have no regard for the truth, and would 'pack' the firm with other Catholics.[15]

Discrimination in the public sector was most conscious and systematic where the Protestant position was vulnerable. Whyte notes that the worst offenders were local authorities in the area of precarious unionist control west of the Bann, followed by other local authorities, and then the Northern Ireland civil service.[16] In the marginal constituencies west of the Bann, local unionists made explicit calls to reduce Catholic electoral strength by refusing jobs thus encouraging Catholic emigration and by refusing sales of land or letting of houses so as to deny Catholics the (property based) local government franchise.[17] Unionist politicians monitored the numbers of Catholics appointed in the civil service and informal quotas were adhered to, with 80–85 per cent Protestants put forward to selection boards.[18] The already small proportion of Catholics in the higher ranks of the civil service declined in the 1920s and 1930s

[12] D. P. Barritt and Charles F. Carter, *The Northern Ireland Problem: A Study in Group Relations*, Oxford, Oxford University Press, 1962, p. 94.

[13] *Ibid.*, pp. 100–1.

[14] *Ibid.*, pp. 101–2. Significantly the unwillingness of Protestants to work under Catholic supervision was not taken to imply a negative attitude to authority.

[15] *Ibid.*, p. 102.

[16] Whyte, J. H. 'How much discrimination was there under the Unionist regime?', in Tom Gallagher and James O'Connell, eds., *Contemporary Irish Studies*, Manchester: Manchester University Press, 1983, p. 14; Patrick Buckland, *A History of Northern Ireland*, Dublin, Gill and Macmillan, 1981, p. 63; for a defence of public employment practices during the Stormont period, see John Oliver, 'The Stormont administration', in Patrick J. Roche and Brian Barton, eds., *The Northern Ireland Question: Myth and Reality*, Aldershot: Avebury, 1991.

[17] Frank Gallagher, *The Indivisible Island*, London, Victor Gollanz, 1957, pp. 206, 221, 245.

[18] Fair Employment Agency, *Investigation into the Non-Industrial Northern Ireland Civil Service*, Belfast, FEA, 1983, appendix 4, p. v.

and by the 1940s and 1950s there were no Catholics in the top fifty-five positions.[19]

Protestant attitudes to discrimination varied. Some were opposed to it either on principle or for pragmatic reasons.[20] For others, doing business with, hiring and helping 'ones own' were normal and natural practices in which they assumed – with some justification – that Catholics also engaged. Some advocated discrimination on the grounds that Catholics were disloyal and a threat to the state. Brooke justified his famous 1933 call 'to employ good Protestant lads and lassies' wherever possible on the grounds that 'Roman Catholics were endeavouring to get in everywhere and were out with all their force and might to destroy the power and constitution of Ulster. There was a definite plot to overpower the vote of Unionists in the North.'[21] Originally articulated at a time of political tension, the sentiment was an undercurrent throughout the Stormont years.

Many, however, denied that discrimination existed at all, or if they accepted that it did, saw it as the exception rather than the rule. In Rose's 1968 survey, 74 per cent of Protestants denied that discrimination existed; of these 65 per cent thought complaints should be investigated 'fully confident that investigation would vindicate their position'.[22] Some saw talk of discrimination as 'the work of trouble-makers in the Catholic community', as ill-disguised nationalism, or simply Catholic 'whingeing'.[23] Protestant economic advantage, if it was acknowledged at all, was attributed to the working of market forces, the harder work and loyalty of Protestants, their modernising ethos and education system.

The converse of Protestant advantage was Catholic disadvantage. There was little sign of improvement in the Catholic position over the period. In a study of occupational mobility in Belfast between 1901 and 1951, Hepburn concludes that there was no narrowing of the gap between the two communities and 'the Catholic position was a less

---

[19] Patrick Buckland, *The Factory of Grievances: Devolved Government in Northern Ireland, 1921–39*, Dublin, Gill and Macmillan, 1979, p. 20; Whyte, 'How much discrimination', p. 9.

[20] Brian Barton, *Brookeborough: The Making of a Prime Minister*, Belfast, Institute of Irish Studies, 1988, p. 79; Brian Faulkner, 'Ireland Today', article published in *Aquarius*, 1971, reprinted in David Bleakley, *Faulkner: Conflict and Consent in Irish Politics*, London, Mobrays, 1974.

[21] A. C. Hepburn, *The Conflict of Nationality in Modern Ireland*, London, Edward Arnold, 1980, p. 164; Barton, *Brookeborough*, p. 81.

[22] Richard Rose, *Governing without Consensus: An Irish Perspective*, London: Faber and Faber, 1971, pp. 272–3; 19 per cent of Protestants agreed that there was discrimination; 4 per cent reported personal knowledge of it.

[23] *Ibid.*, pp. 272–3; Sarah Nelson, *Ulster's Uncertain Defenders: Loyalists and the Northern Ireland conflict*, Belfast, Appletree, 1984, p. 72.

favourable one at every level'.[24] Cormack and Rooney reach a similar conclusion for Northern Ireland as a whole.[25] In some respects the Catholic position worsened; between 1911 and 1971, the proportion of unskilled Catholics increased while that of Protestants decreased; Catholic male unemployment was slightly less than that of Protestants in 1911, but considerably higher in 1971.[26]

Catholic disadvantage also showed in a higher rate of emigration. Barritt and Carter estimate that while Catholics made up a third of the population they made up 55–58 per cent of emigrants for the period 1937 to 1951; Compton estimates 60 per cent for the period 1951–61, 54 per cent for 1961–71.[27] Differential emigration counteracted the high Catholic birth rate, although it was not sufficient to prevent an increase in the Catholic proportion of the population from the 1930s.

The 1971 census provides a comprehensive picture of the Catholic position at the close of the Stormont period. The community as a whole was by no means impoverished but there were clear differences between Catholics and Protestants. Catholics were underrepresented in key occupational sectors: administration and management, engineering and allied trades, clerical and professional; they were more likely than Protestants to be in less skilled, lower status jobs, at a lower status/ supervisory capacity in them, in lower social classes; their unemployment rate was over twice that of Protestants.[28]

The weakness in the Catholic position was due to many factors. They were disproportionately located in the poorer regions and in social classes with high unemployment rates. They had lower levels of educational

[24] A. C. Hepburn, 'Employment and religion in Belfast, 1901–1951', in R. J. Cormack and R. D. Osborne, *Religion, Education and Employment: Aspects of Equal Opportunity in Northern Ireland*, Belfast, Appletree, 1983, p. 63.

[25] R. J. Cormack and E. P. Rooney 'Religion and employment in Northern Ireland: 1911–1971', unpublished paper.

[26] Bew, Gibbon and Patterson, *State in Northern Ireland 1921–1972*, p. 167; Cormack and Rooney, 'Religion and employment', table 3.

[27] Barritt and Carter, *The Northern Ireland Problem*, p. 108; Paul Compton, 'The changing religious demography of Northern Ireland: some political considerations', *Studies*, vol. 78, no. 312, 1989, p. 398.

[28] Edmund A. Aunger, 'Religion and occupational class in Northern Ireland', *Economic and Social Review*, vol. 7, no. 1, 1975; E. A. Aunger, 'Religion and class: An analysis of 1971 census data', in R. J. Cormack and R. D. Osborne, eds., *Religion, Education and Employment: Aspects of Equal Opportunity in Northern Ireland*, Belfast, Appletree, 1983; Fair Employment Agency, *Industrial and Occupational Profile of the Two Sections of the Population in Northern Ireland: An Analysis of the 1971 Census*, Belfast, FEA, 1978; R. L. Miller and R. D. Osborne, 'Religion and unemployment: Evidence from a cohort survey', in Cormack and Osborne, eds., *Religion, Education and Employment*, p. 78.

attainment.[29] They were reluctant, in part for political reasons, to seek entry into the RUC or even the civil service.[30] Political defeatism carried over into the economic arena. They suffered both from the reality and the anticipation of discrimination. Their reaction to their situation ranged from resentment to bitterness.[31] The vast majority of Catholics – 74 per cent – believed that discrimination existed; 36 per cent claimed personal knowledge of it; only 13 per cent said it did not exist.[32]

Economic dependence and Protestant economic power

At the time of partition the economy of east Ulster had long been integrated into wider British, imperial and world markets. Most of the inputs for its industrial economy were imported; Britain took the bulk of its agricultural produce and most of its industrial exports. The sources of capital and enterprise were, however, to an important degree local. The success in building a strong regional economy had been crucial in securing partition – in backing the Ulster Protestant threat of building a state of their own if necessary. But the pre-partition period was to be the high point of east Ulster's economic independence; in the period that followed – and in particular after the Second World War – the economy became increasingly dependent.[33]

Dependence had several strands: farmers came to depend on government price and income supports; the traditional indigenous industries were declining and being replaced by branch plants, mainly of British companies; the growing public sector relied on an increased British subvention. Increasing dependence was due in part to the difficulty of renewing a small, peripheral regional economy with limited control over policy at a time when the national economy was itself in difficulty. But it was also a product of wider economic processes: reliance on the state was becoming the general pattern in European agriculture; reliance on foreign investment reflected the increased scale of industrial production and the emergence of a new territorial division of labour; the subvention

---

[29] For a review of relevant research, see A. M. Gallagher, *Employment, Unemployment and Religion in Northern Ireland. The Majority Minority Review, No. 2*, Coleraine, University of Ulster, Centre for the Study of Conflict. 1991.

[30] Whyte, 'How much discrimination', pp. 10–12.

[31] Ultach, 'The real case against partition', *The Capuchin Annual*, 1943; G. B. Newe, 'The Catholic in the Northern Ireland community', *Christus Rex*, vol. 18, no. 1, 1964, pp. 31–5.

[32] Rose, *Governing without Consensus*, p. 272.

[33] See Liam O'Dowd, 'Development or dependency? State, economy and society in Northern Ireland', in P. Clancy, S. Drudy, K. Lynch and L. O'Dowd, eds., *Irish Society: Sociological Perspectives*, Dublin, Institute of Public Administration, 1995.

from Britain reflected the growing role of western states in social and regional redistribution.

The post-war growth in the British subvention followed the commitment of the British government in 1938 to fund public services in Northern Ireland at the same level as elsewhere in the United Kingdom. The Northern Ireland government had sought to maintain parity from 1922 but lacked the resources to do so and found it difficult to tap into central funds. The implementation of the parity principle after the war coincided with the creation of the British welfare state. Per capita public spending in Northern Ireland increased and its local impact was considerable, although it still lagged behind other parts of the United Kingdom through the 1960s.[34]

The increased dependence of the Northern Ireland economy had far-reaching implications. As the state's role expanded, the universalist criteria used by the British state contrasted and clashed with the particularist concerns of the Northern Ireland government and the public nature of the issues made the contradictions more difficult to manage. The *laissez-faire* policies followed by Brookeborough's government in the 1950s restricted the occasions for conflict; the further expansion in the state's role in the 1960s – in housing, education, public utilities, industrial location, urban and regional development and direct employment – made conflict unavoidable.[35] The political exigencies of the new situation led to a more moderate and modernising rhetoric among unionists, led by Terence O'Neill. Some important policy changes followed, for example the recognition in 1964 of the Northern Ireland Committee of the Irish Congress of Trade Unions. However there were political limits to reform.

The crisis of the late 1960s set Northern Ireland on a path to ever deeper dependence. Direct rule was followed by a major expansion in the British state's role in the economy. Public sector employment increased from just under 25 per cent of total employment in 1970 to around 39 per cent in 1992; if the employment effects of heavy public expenditure in agriculture and industry are included, the figure is likely to exceed 50 per cent.[36] Public expenditure underwent a corresponding increase as did the proportion represented by the subvention from the British

---

[34] Wilson, *Ulster: Conflict and Consensus*, pp. 83–4; Michael Smyth, 'The public sector and the economy', in Paul Teague, ed., *The Economy of Northern Ireland: Perspectives for Structural Change*, London, Lawrence and Wishart, 1993, pp. 122–3.

[35] See Liam O'Dowd, Bill Rolston and Mike Tomlinson, *Northern Ireland: Between Civil Rights and Civil War*, London, CSE Books, 1980; for a defence of government policies at this time, see Wilson, *Ulster, Conflict and Consent*, chs. 11–13.

[36] Smyth, 'The public sector and the economy', pp. 124–5.

exchequer. In the late 1960s the subvention lay between 5 per cent and 10 per cent of public expenditure in Northern Ireland; by the late 1980s it was about one third and represented more than a fifth of personal income before tax.[37] The gap between public expenditure in Northern Ireland and public revenue in 1992/3 was just over £3 billion, or £2,000 per head of population.[38]

The dramatic growth in the public sector and in public spending occurred for several reasons. One was the principle of parity in social provision. Northern Ireland still lagged behind the rest of the United Kingdom at the time Stormont was abolished. The establishment of direct rule led to a rapid drive to eliminate this. Subsequent growth – which brought per capita spending in Northern Ireland to a level beyond that of the rest of the United Kingdom – was in response to Northern Ireland's distinctive economic, demographic, administrative and political circumstances.[39] A second reason was the political violence. The expansion in employment in the security and prison services was by far the most significant growth in public employment, particularly following the policy of 'Ulsterisation'. Rowthorn and Wayne estimated that by 1985 there were almost 20,000 employed in the local security forces and an additional 10,000 in security-related employment.[40] Heavy costs were also involved in the payment of compensation and in reconstruction.[41]

A third reason was the decline in industry. The decline of the traditional industries – shipbuilding, engineering and textiles – continued; many of the new firms which came in the 1950s and 1960s closed; attempts to generate or attract new industry met with little success. Employment in industry fell from 38.5 per cent of total employment in 1973 to 27.2 per cent in 1991. The new jobs in the public sector – particularly in the security forces – only partially compensated for the loss of industrial jobs. Unemployment increased from 9.1 per cent in 1979 to 16.1 per cent in 1982 to 18.6 per cent in 1986, falling back to 14.2 per cent by 1992.[42] This made further demands on public

---

[37] Thomas Wilson, 'Introduction' to R. I. D. Harris, C. W. Jefferson and J. E. Spencer, eds., *The Northern Ireland Economy: A Comparative Study in the Economic Development of a Peripheral Region*, London, Longman, 1990, p. 11.

[38] Smyth, 'The public sector and the economy', p. 134.

[39] Wilson, 'Introduction', pp. 11–12.

[40] Bob Rowthorn and Naomi Wayne, *Northern Ireland: The Political Economy of Conflict*, Cambridge, Polity, 1988, p. 112; cf. Brendan O'Leary and John McGarry, *The Politics of Antagonism: Understanding Northern Ireland*, London, Athlone Press, 1995, p. 203.

[41] See O'Leary and McGarry, *Politics of Antagonism*, pp. 44–6.

[42] Clifford W. Jefferson, 'The labour market', in Harris, Jefferson and Spencer, eds., *The Northern Ireland Economy*, p. 160, table 6.9 for averages for 1979, 1982, 1986; Vani Borooah, 'Northern Ireland: typology of a regional economy', in Teague, ed., *Economy of Northern Ireland*, p. 5, for figures for Feb 1992.

expenditure – in unemployment benefit, to bring new jobs and to help maintain the industrial jobs that remained.[43]

The effect of these changes was greatly to reduce Protestants' control of the commanding heights of the Northern Ireland economy. The decline in the old indigenous industries and the growth in branch companies and in outside takeovers reduced their control over the private sector. The abolition of Stormont removed their power to make public policy; decisions in the vastly expanded state sector were now made, or directly supervised, by the British government. Protestants remained, however, a powerful presence at the influential middle levels of the public and private sectors. Here too there was pressure on their position in the form of a demand for 'fair employment'.

The politics of fair employment

The demands of the civil rights movement included an end to discrimination in housing and public sector employment. The conflict over housing was resolved by the creation of a new centralised body – the Northern Ireland Housing Executive (NIHE) – charged with allocating houses and increasing the housing stock. Discrimination in employment was to prove a more difficult problem to resolve. The civil rights movement had focused on discrimination in the public sector, but there was also discrimination in the private sector and – even more problematic – a high degree of structural economic inequality between the communities.

Discrimination in the public sector was acknowledged to be a problem by the Stormont and British governments in November 1968 and the five-point plan agreed by them included provision for a parliamentary commissioner for administration (PCA) to investigate allegations of discrimination; the 'Downing Street Declaration' of August 1969 set down the principle of 'equality of treatment and freedom from discrimination as obtains in the rest of the United Kingdom irrespective of political views or religion'.[44] The new PCA (who also filled the new position of commissioner for complaints) had the power to monitor companies tendering for public contracts and (in 1971) to require of them an undertaking not to practice religious discrimination in the performance of the contract.[45] In fact few cases of alleged discrimination

---

[43] O'Dowd, 'Development or dependency', p. 135.
[44] Quoted in Standing Advisory Commission on Human Rights (SACHR), *Religious and Political Discrimination and Equality of Opportunity in Northern Ireland: Report on Fair Employment*, London, HMSO, 1987, p. 9.
[45] *Ibid.*, 9–10.

in employment were brought before the commissioner and none was upheld.[46]

None of these measures promised to tackle the range of discriminatory practices, much less the extent of economic inequality, but political pressure for more radical measures was limited. All sides hoped that the problem would be resolved by increased economic development rather than policies that might benefit one community at the expense of the other. The SDLP urged constructive economic policies, job creation and cross border schemes rather than measures to counter discrimination or undo its effects.[47] However they noted continuing discrimination in the civil service and the issue was taken seriously by the Southern government in the leadup to the Sunningdale conference.[48] Sinn Féin's economic thinking at the time centred on economic strategy in a future *Éire Nua*.[49]

The next major initiative came after direct rule. In August 1972 the British government appointed a working party (under the chairmanship of ministers in the Northern Ireland Office) with representatives from business and labour (but not the Northern Irish political parties) to consider ways of preventing discrimination in private sector employment. Its report recommended the creation of an agency to investigate complaints of discrimination, to urge and advise organisations on how best to achieve equality of opportunity, and to engage in research. It rejected quotas but advocated affirmative action; it also stressed the need for a general increase in employment. The 1973 Northern Ireland Constitution Act prohibited discrimination on political or religious grounds. It also established a permanent committee, the Standing Advisory Commission on Human Rights (SACHR) to advise the SOSNI on the adequacy of the law in preventing discrimination and to coordinate the activities of relevant agencies.[50]

The incoming Labour administration did not give the issue of fair employment priority and it was not until 1976 that legislation was put in place. The Fair Employment (NI) Act (1976) incorporated most of the working party report's recommendations. It declared direct

---

[46] Michael J. Cunningham, *British Government Policy in Northern Ireland 1969–89: Its Nature and Execution*, Manchester, Manchester University Press, 1991, p. 34.

[47] *SDLP News*, 1.4, Jan. 1973; *Social Democrat*, 1 Mar. 1976, 1 Aug. 1976; H. Logue in *Fortnight*, 121, 130, Feb. 1976, July 1976. Cunningham points out that early developments in fair employment policy were not the result of direct political pressure from the nationalist parties; Cunningham, *British Government Policy*, pp. 83, 130.

[48] *SDLP News*, 1.4, Jan. 73; Garret Fitzgerald, *All in a Life*, Dublin, Gill and Macmillan, pp. 201.

[49] E.g *Republican News*, 19, 26 Mar. 1972, 9, 16 Apr. 1972.

[50] Cunningham, *British Government Policy*, pp. 83–5.

discrimination in public and private sector employment illegal and sought to counter the effects of past discrimination by fostering a voluntary approach to fair employment. Progress was to be monitored and furthered by an independent public agency, the Fair Employment Agency (FEA), whose goal was to promote equality of opportunity and the elimination of discrimination, to undertake research on the barriers to this, and to investigate individual complaints.[51]

The 1976 Act had the support of the Conservative Party but provoked much criticism from unionists: according to one (quite moderate) unionist MP, the FEA would be 'the stamping ground of the professional agitator and the trouble-maker'.[52] Unionists particularly objected to its publication of statistics which 'have created imagined grievances and have been an incitement to social unrest'.[53] Any highlighting of the religious composition of the workforce was seen as introducing sectarian considerations into the workplace, and likely to lead to quotas or affirmative action which would discriminate against Protestants.[54] Unionist fears were intensified by British policies. The government's refusal to include the ailing Harland and Wolff and Short and Harland in its nationalisation programme for the shipbuilding and aircraft industries (although the firms were massively subsidised and later taken into public ownership) was taken as evidence for British economic withdrawal from Northern Ireland.[55]

In fact the powers of the FEA were limited, it was understaffed and took a cautious line in view of the prevailing economic conditions; R. G. Cooper, the chairman, was conscious of the difficulty of enforcing fair employment in a period of recession and closures.[56] The Agency defined its role in terms of education, exhortation and moral pressure rather than enforcement.[57] For example, employers who accepted the principles of the new legislation could sign a 'Declaration of Principle and Intent' and advertise themselves as Equal Opportunity employers; from 1982 those seeking government contracts were required to sign it. Over 50 per

---

[51] *Ibid.*, 130–4.

[52] Jim Kilfedder, *Newsletter*, 17 Feb. 1976, quoted in John Doyle, 'Workers and outlaws: Unionism and fair employment in Northern Ireland', *Irish Political Studies*, vol. 9, 1994, p. 52.

[53] UUC report for 1980, p. 4, quoted John Doyle, 'Workers and outlaws: Unionism and fair employment in Northern Ireland', MA thesis, Politics Department, University College Dublin, 1992, p. 113.

[54] Doyle, 'Workers and Outlaws', 1994, p. 52; this argument was repeated later in the context of new FEA legislation, Doyle, 'Workers and Outlaws', 1992, p. 119.

[55] Cunningham, *British Government Policy*, p. 129.

[56] A. Pollak, 'The civil service investigation: the FEA's last chance?', *Fortnight*, no. 188, 1982, p. 11.

[57] Smith and Chambers, *Inequality in Northern Ireland*, pp. 239–40.

cent of those eligible signed the Declaration in the first year but the undertaking was self-regulated, and many of those who signed paid little attention to its provisions.[58]

The Agency investigated cases of alleged discrimination, but only a small percentage were upheld.[59] It had more success highlighting structural inequality in employment. Its commissioned research documented the extent and persistence of economic inequality between the communities and raised questions about some of the stock explanations for Catholic disadvantage – the absence of a work ethic, poor education.[60] Its investigations of individual firms and public bodies (which it published from 1982) showed striking disparities in many workforces and revealed some of the means by which Protestant dominance in the workplace was reproduced – informal recruitment networks, Protestant dominated recruitment boards, selection criteria.[61]

The Agency highlighted the issue of inequality and gave a new precision to political and academic debate about it. But it was having little practical effect on employment patterns and pressure began to build up for stronger measures. The returns of the 1981 census – first reported in the media in 1983 – indicated that the disparity between Catholic and Protestant employment patterns continued. Subsequent research confirmed this.[62] Research commissioned by SACHR showed no significant improvement in Catholic employment between 1971 and 1985. As before Catholics were more likely than Protestants to be unemployed and to experience long term unemployment: Catholic men were 2.5 times

---

[58] *Ibid.*, ch. 6; Cunningham, *British Government Policy*, p. 131.

[59] Seven per cent in 1979. FEA personnel attributed the low figure to the weak powers of the Agency; see Pollak, 'The civil service investigation', p. 9; by 31 March 1989, a total of 58 complaints had been upheld, 124 complaints were still outstanding, 215 had been withdrawn or not pursued, 28 had been judged to fall outside the scope of the act; Smith and Chambers, *Inequality in Northern Ireland*, p. 248.

[60] R. L. Miller, *Attitudes to Work in Northern Ireland*, FEA research paper no. 2, Belfast, Fair Employment Agency, 1978; R. C. Murray and R. D. Osborne, 'Educational qualifications and religious affiliation', in Cormack and Osborne, eds., *Religion, Education and Employment*.

[61] For examples, see FEA investigations into the Northern Ireland Electricity Service (1982), the Fire Authority for Northern Ireland (1984), the Ulster Museum (1986); R. G. Cooper, 'Chairman's Foreword', in D. Murray and J. Darby, *The Vocational Aspirations and Expectations of Schoolleavers in Londonderry and Strabane*, Belfast, FEA, 1980, p. 5.

[62] E.g. Tom Hadden, 'The census: not just a sectarian headcount', *Fortnight*, no. 195, 1983, p. 9; R. D. Osborne and R. J. Cormack, 'Unemployment and religion in Northern Ireland', *Economic and Social Review*, vol. 17, no. 3, 1986; R. D. Osborne and R. J. Cormack, *Religion, Occupations and Employment: 1971–1981*, Belfast, Fair Employment Agency, 1987; David Eversley, *Religion and Employment in Northern Ireland*, London, Sage, 1989; R. J. Cormack and R. D. Osborne, eds., *Discrimination and Public Policy in Northern Ireland*, Oxford, Clarendon, 1991.

more likely to be unemployed than Protestant men; Catholic women were 1.5 times more likely to be unemployed than Protestant women.[63] The disparity in unemployment rates held for all regions (although there was variation by local area), for every age group, in all the major sectors of the economy, and for men across all social classes.[64] Catholics were at relative disadvantage in job level, type of industry, class profile, income level and standard of living.[65]

In 1984 a campaign was launched in the United States by Irish–American political activists to persuade companies, state legislatures and municipalities considering investing in Northern Ireland to adhere to a much tougher set of fair employment principles – the 'MacBride Principles'. The campaign was modelled on the campaign directed in the 1970s at South Africa. It sought to make United States investment (by corporations, state or municipal governments) conditional on the adoption of the principles which included increased representation in the workforce for underrepresented groups, affirmative action measures (including training programmes for employees from the minority and targeted recruitment measures), the abolition of discriminatory measures in recruitment and layoff procedures, the banning of sectarian or provocative symbols from the workplace, security for members of minority groups travelling to and from work and at work, and timetables for these measures.[66]

The MacBride Principles campaign threatened American investment at a time when jobs were much needed and also highlighted the weakness of the British government's own legislation. The British and Irish governments opposed the campaign, as did the unionist parties and the leadership of the SDLP. However the campaign continued to make ground. It also had an effect on employment in Northern Ireland. Even before the MacBride principles were launched, Short Brothers PLC had been spotlighted as a firm in which Catholics were seriously under-employed and there was pressure on the American government to stop buying aircraft from the firm. In response Shorts, despite its traditionally Protestant and loyalist workforce and its situation in Protestant East Belfast, raised the recruitment of Catholic apprentices from 6 per cent to almost 25 per cent in the space of two years.[67]

---

[63] Smith and Chambers, *Inequality in Northern Ireland*, pp. 161–3, based on CHS data from 1983–5.

[64] *Ibid.*, pp. 164–8.   [65] *Ibid.*, pp. 165, 196–212, 343–4, 349–52.

[66] R. J. Cormack and R. D. Osborne, 'Disadvantage and discrimination in Northern Ireland', in Cormack and Osborne, eds., *Discrimination and Public Policy*, p. 16.

[67] FEA Progress report on third monitoring exercise in Short Brothers PLC, Dec. 1985, pp. 1–7; Cormack and Osborne, 'Disadvantage and discrimination', p. 15.

Pressure came from other sources. The Fair Employment Agency had long been aware that the 1976 act was inadequate, that it was being ignored even by firms the agency had investigated. Support for stronger measures also came from senior members of the civil service, the British Labour Party, SACHR and the ICTU.[68] The electoral rise of Sinn Féin alarmed the Southern government and drew its attention to fair employment as one way of assuaging the anger of working-class Catholics. With the administration of justice, it was the most frequently raised topic in meetings of the Anglo-Irish Conference and it was discussed on at least twelve occasions between 1985 and 1989.[69]

The British government responded to the growing pressure with a new code of practice in 1987 and in 1989 a new Fair Employment Act (NI). The 1989 Act outlawed not only direct but also indirect discrimination.[70] It gave greater powers of enforcement to the newly named Fair Employment Commission and broadened the range of legally acceptable compensatory measures, for example the targeting of specific groups in job advertising and training programmes. It made monitoring of the religious composition of the workforce (and, for the public sector and large private firms, of job applications) a requirement and it set up a new Fair Employment Tribunal to hear individual cases of discrimination. The legislation did not satisfy all those who had pressed for stronger measures. Timetables and targets were excluded despite arguments from the FEA, SACHR and others; there was no definition of the goal of 'fair participation in employment', and only limited affirmative action measures were explicitly permitted.

The British Labour Party played a central role in strengthening the provisions of the bill. The SDLP supported the aims of the new legislation and attempted to get stronger measures to balance past discrimination but let the Labour Party make most of the detailed suggestions. Sinn Féin, which supported the MacBride Principles, pressed the SDLP – unsuccessfully – to take a joint stance on the issue. Most unionists were reluctant to oppose the bill as a whole, lest this further cast them in a bad light.[71] However the predominantly unionist

---

[68] Richard Jay and Rick Wilford, 'Fair employment in Northern Ireland: a new initiative', *Irish Political Studies*, vol. 6, 1991, pp. 26–9.

[69] Cunningham, *British Government Policy*, p. 230.

[70] Indirect discrimination was defined in terms of unjustifiable employment requirements or conditions which in effect disadvantage one community; for alternative definitions of 'indirect discrimination' which were fought out in the debates over the bill, see Jay and Wilford, 'Fair employment', p. 29 and Christopher McCrudden, 'The evolution of the Fair Employment (Northern Ireland) Act 1989 in parliament', in Cormack and Osborne, eds., *Discrimination and Public Policy*.

[71] Doyle, 'Workers and outlaws', 1994, p. 54; Jay and Wilford, 'Fair Employment', p. 27.

Confederation of British Industries (Northern Ireland) opposed it behind the scenes, and unionist politicians opposed specific measures, particularly those which the FEA and SACHR felt necessary to strengthen the legislation – monitoring and targets. They argued that the old FEA had been selective and one-sided in its investigations,[72] that compulsory monitoring would lead to affirmative action and 'discrimination against Protestants' since otherwise there would be no point in collecting the information.[73] Some unionist politicians were vocal in their opposition: Roy Beggs and William McCrea contested the statistics on inequality arguing that there was no proof that it existed; Peter Robinson accepted that a differential existed, but denied that the reason for it was discrimination.[74]

The new legislation represented a major advance over the 1976 Act and has intensified the pressure for change. However American pressure has not abated; MacBride campaigners have been able to use the monitoring returns and the FEC's yearly reports to strengthen their case. By early 1995 forty cities and sixteen states had passed resolutions or legislation supporting the MacBride Principles and pressure continues.[75] For example, in early 1995 New York City's pension fund was using its new investments in British companies with subsidiaries in Northern Ireland to apply the MacBride Principles there;[76] at the same time a bill was being presented to Congress mandating that no United States company based in Northern Ireland may export its products to the United States without a certificate saying it is in compliance with the MacBride Principles.[77]

Economic inequality, 1971–1991

There were significant differences in the economic status of Catholics and Protestants in 1971. How much has changed? Changes in the census categories do not permit systematic comparison between the 1971 and 1991 censuses, but some conclusions can be drawn. In their overview of the 1991 census, Gallagher, Osborne and Cormack stress continuity in both the structure of the labour market and in the pattern of Catholic disadvantage; however they also point to change in strategically important areas – particularly at the level of the middle classes – and

---

[72] Doyle, 'Workers and outlaws', 1992, pp. 120–1.
[73] *Ibid.*, p. 119.   [74] *Ibid.*, pp. 123–4.
[75] *Irish Times*, 3 Jan. 1995.
[76] *Sunday Business Post*, 1 Jan. 1995.   [77] *Irish Times*, 3 Jan. 1995.

see evidence 'that significant change in the labour market is starting to occur'.[78]

Catholic numbers as a proportion of the total population continued to rise – from 36.8 per cent in 1971 to 43.1 per cent in 1991; the rate of increase was particularly rapid in the 1980s. Catholics formed 31 per cent of the economically active population in 1971; they formed 39.9 per cent of the economically active population in 1991 and 43.9 per cent of those under 35.[79] Cormack et al. attribute much of the Catholic increase to a fall in Catholic emigration and suggest that 'Protestants have formed a larger proportion of more recent out-migrants'; however, reliable calculations of relative rates of emigration are not yet available and there is some evidence that emigration may still be disproportionately Catholic.[80]

Catholics in 1971 were more than twice as likely to be unemployed as Protestants. The disparity persisted through the 1980s; it has recently declined for males but increased for females. In 1971 Catholic men were 2.6 times more likely to be unemployed than their Protestant equivalents and remained at that level through the mid-1980s; in 1991 the ratio had fallen to 2.2 – 28.4 per cent for Catholics and 12.7 per cent for Protestants. The ratio for Catholic women was 1.9 in 1971 and declined to 1.5 in the mid-1980s; in 1991 it was 1.8 – 14.5 per cent for Catholics and 8 per cent for Protestants.[81] In addition, Catholics were much more likely than Protestants to be among the more recent and long-term unemployed and to be on a government training scheme. As in the past, the disparity in unemployment was evident in most parts of Northern Ireland and at each level of educational qualification, particularly for males.[82]

The social class profile of Catholics has traditionally been weaker than that of Protestants, particularly for males. In 1971, 21 per cent of

---

[78] A. M. Gallagher, R. D. Osborne and R. J. Cormack, *Fair Shares? Employment, Unemployment and Economic Status*, Belfast, Fair Employment Commission, Belfast, 1994, reprinted March 1995, p. 84.

[79] *Northern Ireland Census of Population 1971; Religion Tables*, Belfast, HMSO, 1975 and *Northern Ireland Census of Population 1991; Religion Report*, Belfast, HMSO, 1993, own calculations; Gallagher et al., *Fair Shares*, p. 55.

[80] R. J. Cormack, A. M. Gallagher and R. D. Osborne, *Fair Enough? Religion and the 1991 Population Census*, Belfast, Fair Employment Commission, 1993, p. 14; Paul Compton and John Power, 'Migration from Northern Ireland: a survey of New Year travellers as a means of identifying emigrants', *Regional Studies*, vol. 25, no. 1, 1991.

[81] R. Osborne and R. Cormack, 'Religion and the labour market: patterns and profiles', in Cormack and Osborne, eds., *Discrimination and Public Policy*, p. 57; Cormack et al., *Fair Enough?*, pp. 21–2; Gallagher et al., *Fair Shares?*, pp. 55–6.

[82] Cormack et al., *Fair Enough*, p. 35, and pp. 47–51; Gallagher et al., *Fair Shares*, p. 55.

Catholic males were in the categories 'Professional, managerial' and 'Lower grade, non-manual'; 33 per cent of Protestant males were in these categories.[83] Strict comparison with 1991 is not possible, but the general tendency persists. In 1991, 29.6 per cent of Catholic males were in the categories 'Professional', 'Managerial and technical' and 'Skilled non-manual' compared to 39.9 per cent of Protestants; the difference for women remains less marked – in 1991 55.7 per cent of Catholic women were in these categories compared to 61 per cent of Protestant women.[84] A comparison of the under- and over-35 age cohorts in 1991 showed little evidence of generational change.[85]

Differences continue in respect of employment status but they have diminished in extent. Catholic self-employed males remain less likely to have employees than Protestants, but the difference has reduced greatly since 1971 and is now slight; the proportion of self-employed Catholic females with employees now exceeds that of their Protestant equivalents.[86] Among employees, Protestant males continue to be much more likely than Catholics to be managers, especially in large and extra-large concerns, and to be in the category 'professional employees'; for Catholic women underrepresentation is greatest in smaller concerns. However the Catholic position has improved noticeably since 1971 in these respects, and the Catholic underrepresentation among foremen/supervisors which was apparent in 1971 had disappeared by 1991.[87] The increase in the proportion of managers and administrators who are Catholic continues – from 30.5 per cent in 1990 to 34.4 per cent in 1993.[88]

Occupational differences remain important. In 1971 Protestant males were overrepresented in security related services, management and administration, and skilled engineering; Catholic males were overrepresented in lower-status manufacturing and construction. This pattern persists. In 1991 Protestant males were overrepresented in the same three occupations, Catholic males in skilled construction, labouring, and on government employment and training schemes. As in 1971, Catholic women in 1991 were overrepresented in personal services, health and teaching, Protestant women in clerical occupations. Catholics in general continued to be overrepresented in occupations

---

[83] Osborne and Cormack, 'Religion and the labour market', in Cormack and Osborne, eds., *Discrimination and Public Policy*, table 2.2, p. 54.

[84] Gallagher et al., *Fair Shares?*, tables 2.1, 2.2, p. 15.

[85] *Ibid.*, pp. 13–14.

[86] Cormack et al., *Fair Enough?*, table 6.4, p. 29.

[87] *Ibid.*, table 6.5, p. 30.

[88] FEC, *A Profile of the Northern Ireland Workforce. Summary of the 1994 Monitoring Returns;* Monitoring Report no. 5, Belfast, FEC, 1995, p. 37, table 4.

servicing their own community, including 'teaching and legal occupations'.[89]

Catholics and Protestants differed in their relative participation in the different industrial sectors. The traditional pattern of over and underrepresentation has persisted, but with significant changes in its extent. For Protestant men the areas of overrepresentation in 1971 were (in descending order) metal manufacturing, public administration and defence, other manufacturing, energy and water supply, finance, banking and insurance, medical and veterinary services. They were overrepresented in most of these in 1991 but to a lesser extent; the exceptions were public administration and defence, where overrepresentation increased, and medical and veterinary services, where it changed to underrepresentation. Catholic male overrepresentation in construction and other services diminished and in agriculture, forestry and fishing changed to underrepresentation; the extent of overrepresentation in transport and communication, extractive industries and education services increased, and Catholics were now overrepresented in medical and veterinary services.[90] Over the same period Catholic female overrepresentation in 'Other manufacturing' almost disappeared while that in education and medical and veterinary services increased further; Protestant female overrepresentation in other services increased.[91]

For Gallagher et al. the census data indicate that Catholic men have moved beyond the church controlled educational sector to find employment in the tertiary sector and in educational administration; they have also benefited from employment opportunities created by changes in medical technology.[92] More generally they draw out the significance of the Catholic increase in white-collar, professional, managerial and administrative occupations:

The increase in the Catholic middle class has involved an expansion into occupations beyond those identified as 'servicing' the Catholic community – teachers, doctors, lawyers and priests. Now Catholics are also substantially represented amongst accountants and other financial service professionals, middle managers, middle ranking civil servants, architects and planners and university and further education lecturers. Much of the Catholic middle class expansion has taken place in the public sector and in areas of expanding opportunities in private sector concerns.[93]

Catholics remain underrepresented in almost all of these areas, but their position has improved considerably. At the same time, Gallagher et al.

---

[89] Gallagher et al., *Fair Shares?*, p. 21, cf. pp. 21–7.
[90] *Ibid.*, pp. 45–53, figure 4.5.   [91] *Ibid.*, fig. 4.6, p. 59.
[92] *Ibid.*, p. 47.   [93] *Ibid.*, pp. 83–4.

draw out a striking continuity with the past – 'the stubborn nature and scale of the unemployment differential'.[94]

It is clear that the erosion of Protestant economic power at the middle levels has been less significant than their loss of power over the commanding heights of the economy and state. The Catholic middle classes have made ground, moving beyond occupations serving their own community and rising to positions of authority in the public sector. But they still have a considerable distance to go before they achieve proportionate representation in these occupations and even farther before they reach a level equal to Protestants in the economy.

The labour market is, however, becoming more volatile. The intensification of pressure from the MacBride Principles campaign and the strengthened Fair Employment Act of 1989 is reducing economic inequality at the middle levels.[95] With the ceasefires, there is the possibility of a scaling down of the numbers in the security forces and prison services which would increase Protestant unemployment and increase competition in the labour market; Catholic willingness to work in firms with a strong loyalist presence might also increase. Catholic demographic patterns are also changing. The present rapid growth in Catholic numbers makes fair employment a 'moving target'[96] but there are indications that the disparity in the birth rates is now reducing. Relative emigration rates are a further crucial and unpredictable variable. There are also the macro variables – the performance of the British economy, the scale of the British subvention, the effects of the ceasefires on inward investment and of the measures to promote indigenous industry.

These factors make long term – and even short term – changes impossible to predict. Catholic progress has been uneven and the Catholic position remains vulnerable. R. G. Cooper of the FEC has affirmed that if inequality is to be eliminated, it is necessary 'for greater efforts to be made by the Commission, employers, trade unions and the Government'.[97] By implication, if current pressure slackens, the recent trend towards greater equality could be reversed.

---

[94] Ibid., p. 84.
[95] On the increased representation of Catholics at managerial and professional levels, see R. G. Cooper, 'Chairman's Foreword', Profile of the Northern Ireland Workforce, Monitoring Report no. 5, 1994.
[96] Cormack et al., Fair Enough, p. 18.
[97] R. G. Cooper, 'Chairman's Foreword', A Profile of the Northern Ireland Workforce. Summary of the 1993 Monitoring Returns, Monitoring Report no. 4, Belfast, FEC, 1994.

The sources of economic inequality

The difficulty of predicting change in the pattern of inequality is heightened by the complexity of the forces which produce and reproduce it. Different kinds of forces have been identified: structural (differences in geographical and class location), cultural (differences in levels of education and skills), political (relationship to the state) and strategic (in particular direct and indirect discrimination).[98] The picture that emerges from research thus far is of a cumulative historical process in which these factors have combined in an over-determining way to produce and reproduce inequality.

The origins of economic inequality lie in the seventeenth century when it was created as a matter of government policy. Once inequality had become embedded in the social and territorial structure and Catholic and Protestant were separated into different cultural and political worlds, it became self-reproducing. A similar interaction and overdetermination (no longer state-led) operated in the nineteenth century. Population increase, the spread of the market, industrialisation and urbanisation began to break down the segmentation of the earlier period. New economic positions were opening up and Catholics were seeking entry to them. Their poorer economic circumstances and lower education levels placed them at a competitive disadvantage and this was further reinforced by discrimination – restrictions on entry and periodic expulsions – particularly in respect of the high status engineering industries. As the century progressed, Catholics in Belfast – males in particular – found themselves in disproportionate numbers at the bottom levels of the social structure, cultural disadvantages compounded by structural ones.[99]

After partition Protestant economic power continued to be self-reproducing but was further reinforced by discrimination made possible by Protestant control over the state. Catholic disadvantage was compounded by relatively poor educational provision which arose in part from lower levels of state funding for Catholic schools. Jobs servicing the Catholic community at once provided employment for Catholics and reduced the pressure on Protestant resources. However the expansion of the public sector in the post-war period raised Catholic expectations of gaining access to the new positions becoming available.

---

[98] For an overview of the debate, see Eversley, *Religion and Employment*, pp. 1–2 and 218–19; also Gallagher, *Employment, Unemployment and Religion*, pp. 49–61.

[99] A. C. Hepburn, 'Work, class and religion in Belfast, 1871–1911', *Irish Economic and Social History*, vol. 10, 1983.

The discriminatory Protestant response played a central role in the crisis of the late 1960s.

Today, the British government's commitment to redressing Catholic inequality is on a scale that is historically unprecedented. It does not mean that equality is assured; many of the forces making for inequality may be beyond the reach of present policies. Indeed it is on this point – the causes of inequality and the appropriateness of government policies – that contemporary debate takes place.[100] The debate is highly politicised. Arguments which stress discrimination as a cause of inequality appear to attribute moral blame to Protestants. Structural arguments are either of a 'no fault' kind or place the responsibility on Catholics for their situation, as do many cultural and political arguments. On the one hand, stronger government sanctions against discrimination are urged, on the other, fair employment legislation is held to be at once inappropriate in its direction, unjust in its implication of blame and ineffective.[101]

The debate has tended to take an inappropriate either/or form, centring on whether inequality is due to structural factors or to discrimination. As we have seen, the historical pattern has been one of the dynamic interaction of structural, political and cultural factors and discrimination. A similar interaction is likely at present and makes all the more difficult the identification of one major cause of inequality. For example, structural factors certainly play some role in inequality. Catholics are disproportionately located in localities where unemployment levels are high;[102] in social classes and in sectors of the economy (for example the construction industry) with high unemployment rates;[103] in (young) age groups where unemployment is high;[104] they have higher fertility levels than Protestants, and unemployment rates increase with the number of dependent children.[105] In general, the Catholic demographic structure is an unfavourable one with high numbers of entrants to the labour market and low numbers retiring.[106]

---

[100] Eversley, *Religion and Employment*; Gallagher, *Employment, Unemployment and Religion*.

[101] Compton, 'Employment differentials'; Smith and Chambers, *Inequality in Northern Ireland*.

[102] The correlation is most striking at the local council level and below. Compton, 'Employment differentials', p. 59; David Eversley, *Religion and Employment in Northern Ireland: Additional Tables*, Belfast, FEA, 1989 shows this clearly.

[103] Compton, 'Employment differentials', pp. 59, 61–3; cf. Smith and Chambers, *Inequality in Northern Ireland*, pp. 164–6, 167–9.

[104] Smith and Chambers, *Inequality in Northern Ireland*, pp. 166–7; Compton, 'Employment differentials', p. 68.

[105] Smith and Chambers, *Inequality in Northern Ireland*, p. 176.

[106] Eversley, *Religion and Employment*, ch. 4 and p. 234.

Structural factors do not, however, explain the whole of the differential. Catholic rates exceed Protestant ones for all parts of Northern Ireland, all classes, (almost) all sectors of the economy, all age groups, and (almost) all family sizes.[107] Moreover, the ways in which structural factors operate require further specification. For example, the disadvantages of a particular geographical location may arise from the fear of working in a nearby Protestant-dominated area because of intimidation or the 'chill factor', or from poverty or the lack of car-ownership.[108] Catholic fertility presents itself as a problem not *per se* but because Catholics are seeking entry into a stagnating and partially segregated labour market in which there are many more Catholic entrants than exitants.[109]

Educational differences also play some role. Catholic school-leavers have traditionally had lower levels of educational achievement than Protestants, with a lower proportion leaving with A-levels and a higher proportion leaving without qualifications; they also placed less emphasis on scientific and technological subjects. The disparity with respect to A-levels reduced significantly between 1975 and 1987 but the disparity for those without qualifications increased; it was particularly great for males.[110] The traditional subject bias has also persisted. But differences in education themselves reflect wider structural and political differences between the communities – in the class profile, the Catholic bias towards occupations that serve the needs of their own community (itself related to their exclusion from other sectors), the relative underfunding of Catholic schools which has only recently been redressed.

Political factors are still demonstrably important in one respect – in the serious Catholic underrepresentation in security-related jobs, now such an important source of employment in Northern Ireland. Robert Cooper of the FEC notes that if Catholics were proportionately employed in such occupations, the male unemployment differential would drop from 2.2 to 1.7.[111] Several factors have been involved here, including Catholic dissent from the Northern Ireland state, the fear of communal ostracism and IRA attack, the 'chill' factor coming from the general ethos of the security forces and from some Protestants within them. The position now is more hopeful, but Catholic attitudes to participation in the

---

[107] Smith and Chambers, *Inequality in Northern Ireland*, pp. 164–96.
[108] Eversley, *Religion and Employment*, pp. 196–8, 214–15.
[109] *Ibid.*, pp 53–5; Smith and Chambers, *Inequality in Northern Ireland*, pp. 191–3.
[110] R. D. Osborne, R. J. Cormack and A. M. Gallagher, 'Educational qualifications and the labour market', in Cormack and Osborne, eds., *Discrimination and Public Policy*, p. 99.
[111] Gallagher et al., *Fair Shares*, p. 5.

security forces are dependent on an acceptable political settlement, including reform of the police. Moreover a permanent peace would drastically reduce the size of the security forces, with inevitable effects for Protestant unemployment figures.

Discrimination, the major focus of government policy, undoubtedly plays some role in producing the disparity in unemployment but its importance is unclear and attempts to measure it have generated controversy. Smith and Chambers use a logistic regression model to assess the contribution of class, family size, age, location and education to the disparity and ascribe the large unexplained residual to discrimination and unequal opportunity.[112] Compton, in a discussion which dismisses the importance of discrimination, uses standardisation techniques to assess the contribution of four variables (age, geography, social class, industry) to unemployment and finds an unexplained residual of just 18 per cent.[113] Also controversial is the form which discrimination may take, in particular the role of indirect discrimination, and the appropriate means to combat it. As we have seen, indirect discrimination – in the form of habitually segregated labour markets or the chill factor – may itself be central to structural sources of inequality.

In fact the controversy about discrimination may exaggerate its political significance. Catholics have made much of the issue of discrimination but their sense of economic grievance arises ultimately from their inequality of condition. If discrimination is the crucial factor and the measures adopted to deal with it are effective, economic inequality will disappear. If discrimination proves not to be the main source of inequality, attention will soon focus on its other determinants and if these are structural, political or cultural, the political problem becomes even more serious. Presumably more radical policies will then be demanded and pressure applied until the inequality is removed. Government measures to eliminate discrimination have involved it in a high level of 'civil surveillance' by normal British standards, which some already regard as intolerable.[114] More radical measures would exacerbate this tendency.

The attitudes of Protestants are very important here. Many have opposed the fair employment process. Some deny any need for it; others

---

[112] Smith and Chambers, *Inequality in Northern Ireland*, pp. 176–87.

[113] Paul Compton, 'Employment differentials', p. 65; for an overview and critique of the substantive and methodological differences between Compton and Smith and Chambers, see Anthony Murphy with David Armstrong, *A Picture of the Catholic and Protestant Male Unemployed*, Employment Equality Review Research Report no. 2, Belfast, Central Community Relations Unit, 1994.

[114] See Compton, 'Employment differentials', pp. 70–1, 76.

accept measures to ensure equality of opportunity for individuals, but not equality of outcome for the two communities. Unionist politicians have lobbied against legislative change, employers have ignored directives, workers have sought to block change by threats or intimidation. Protestant opposition certainly slows movement towards equality. They may have lost overall control of the economy and state but they remain a powerful presence at the middle levels. Their opposition stems in part from an awareness that the more ground they cede, the more vulnerable they are to further pressure. An agreed political settlement might change their attitudes, but it is far from certain.

The meaning of economic inequality

Economic inequality, its causes and its reform matter so much to both communities because inequality carries with it vital material, symbolic and strategic meanings.

At the most basic level, economic inequality is important because it impacts on the economic well-being of the individual, the family and the local community. It affects one's access to employment, to an acceptable wage or salary, to an adequate level of living, the possibilities for providing for one's children, the quality of life in one's neighbourhood. This is particularly important to the working class which bears the brunt of poverty and unemployment, but it is important also for the middle classes preoccupied with status and life-style. In Northern Ireland, the slow development of the economy and the high rate of unemployment mean that policies which increase Catholics' access to employment or income are likely to be at the expense of Protestants. There is therefore a zero sum quality to the communal struggle for resources and even those individual Catholics and Protestants whose immediate welfare is unaffected by policies of reform may be concerned about the future or their children's prospects.

Economic inequality also has a symbolic and moral meaning that relates to community identity and history. For Protestants their superior economic standing is a symbol of their historical achievement in Ulster which validates in turn their rights and their sense of moral worth as a community. If they came as settlers to Ulster they earned their right to be there by the reclamation of its land and development of its resources beyond anything which the native population had, or would have, done. They deeply resent the Catholic assertion that their achievement was based on no more than the stealing of Catholics' resources or exploitation of the Catholic population. Their stronger economic position today is due to their enterprise, hard work, superior way of living, their Protestantism and for some, God's favour. Protestants' superior wealth and resources today are a reward for past effort and sacrifices, a core component in their identity and perception of the right ordering of relations in the world.

The Catholic view is in stark contrast. For Catholics, their economic position is a symbol – a symptom and a reminder – of their historic and continuing marginalisation as a community. They are deeply angered by the Protestant assumption that Ulster was barren and empty until the settlers arrived and developed it, by the Protestant refusal to acknowledge the discrimination of the Stormont period and by Protestant arguments that Catholics are poor because they lack the Protestant work ethic or opt for social security rather than a job. They view such attitudes as rationalisations for dispossession and discrimination. For Catholics, challenging the economic status quo is part of their refusal to accept the irreversibility of their past defeat; achieving economic equality with Protestants would signify their recovery and redemption as a community in one domain at least.

There is, finally, a strategic level of meaning. Protestants have long viewed their security on the island as dependent on their regional demographic and economic strength. Their industrial success in the nineteenth century not only gave them an incentive to remain in the United Kingdom, it gave them the resources to ensure it. In the Stormont period, their economic control enabled them to counter the Catholic demographic challenge by ensuring that emigration would be disproportionately Catholic. Strategically little has changed, except that Protestants now face a run-down economy and a British government trying to force them to give way to Catholics and in so doing to undermine the economic base that ensures their continued membership of the United Kingdom. Inevitably they resist. As one rural unionist put it, 'why should you give jobs and houses to people who are trying to take you over?'[115]

Catholics have a corresponding set of strategic concerns and an opposed set of interests. They are conscious that had they had access to houses and jobs on the same basis as Protestants after 1921 they would probably now be the majority community in Northern Ireland, able to exert major control over its future, perhaps even to undo partition.[116] They are aware that their political and cultural standing depends on

115 Reported by Graham MacFarlane, quoted in Aileen Cronin, 'War and Peace: A study of hostility and harmony in Northern Ireland', University College Dublin Politics Department, MA thesis, 1979, p. 63; cf. Darby, *Intimidation*, p. 47.
116 Cf. Frs. D. Faul and R. Murray, 'The alienation of Northern Ireland Catholics', *Doctrine and Life*, vol. 34, no. 2, 1984, p. 64.

strengthening their position within the Northern economy. One view influential in SDLP circles in the mid-1980s was that fair employment legislation could not directly affect the unemployment ratio but would bring more Catholics into decision-making positions and thus alter the overall direction of policy.[117] But more is at stake than progress within Northern Ireland; a firmer Catholic hold on the economy, a growth in the Catholic population and the intensification of North–South economic links could lay the basis for Irish reunification. There is no guarantee that if Catholics had such economic power they would use it to abolish partition – the practical economic consequences of being part of the United Kingdom or the Republic of Ireland would be weighed – but for the first time they would have a choice in the matter.

Conclusions

The economy is a crucial arena of conflict in Northern Ireland. The Catholic position is one of relative disadvantage; Protestants are stronger at all levels. But Protestant economic power has declined significantly over the past twenty-five years. Economic dependence and direct rule have relocated the higher levels of economic decision-making outside Northern Ireland; anti-discrimination measures have weakened the Protestant position at the middle levels. Catholics have gained ground and the signs are that this will continue. But the pace of change is slow. The British government's determination to prevent active discrimination is not in doubt, but its commitment to, and capacity to achieve, full economic equality between the communities is less certain.

Also uncertain are the effects of economic equality were it to be achieved. Some commentators imply that it would remove a major – perhaps the major – source of conflict. We are less certain. At the symbolic and strategic levels the economic, the cultural and the consti-tutional are inextricably intertwined. Economic power is a resource for political and cultural struggle, and if conflict in those areas continues there is every reason to believe that it will be reflected in continued competition in the economic domain.

[117] Jay and Wilford, 'Fair employment', pp. 22–3.

7 　 The dynamics of conflict: culture

Culture – identity, values, norms, ethos, world view, sense of place in history and in the world – provides another arena for conflict in Northern Ireland. Conflict has centred on the ways in which cultural differences between the communities have been inscribed in public relations of hierarchy and control.[1] It is fought out in the symbolic practices of the public sphere and in the meanings embodied in the state and public institutions. In this chapter we trace the development of cultural conflict, assess the communities' relative cultural status and power and the meanings of cultural conflict today.

The making of Protestant cultural dominance

English control in Ireland in the sixteenth and seventeenth centuries was secured culturally as well as militarily and politically. The Protestant religion, the English language and English notions of civility and order were to be dominant in Ireland, ideally accepted by the majority of the people but at the very least the culture of the economic and political power-holders. English – and to a lesser extent Scottish – settlers were to be the agents of this acculturating process and they became the embodiment of English/British culture in Ireland. This process took a distinctive form in Ulster. There the clash between settler and native cultures was particularly sharp and the extent of native displacement greatest. A culturally complex social world emerged. English influence was predominant among the aristocracy and gentry throughout Ulster;

---

[1] These are issues which have become increasingly important in other fields of study; see, e.g., Pierre Bourdieu, *Outline of a Theory of Practice*, trans. R. Nice, Cambridge, Cambridge University Press, 1977, ch. 4; Michel Foucault, *Power/Knowledge*, ed. C. Gordon, Brighton, Harvester, 1980; Eric Hobsbawm and Terence Ranger, eds., *The Invention of Tradition*, Cambridge, Cambridge University Press, 1983; Edward Said, *Orientalism*, Harmondsworth, Peregrine, 1985; for an overview of the issues in Northern Ireland, see Lucy Bryson and Clem McCartney, *Clashing Symbols*, Belfast, Institute of Irish Studies, 1994.

Scottish influence was strong among the middle classes, particularly in the east. Gaelic-Irish culture and its successor hybrid culture (chapter 2) remained important at the lower social levels, in the remoter areas and on Ulster's borders. Urbanisation in the nineteenth century brought these different strands – and the tensions between them – into the towns, Belfast in particular.

Partition enabled the dominant community in the North – as in the South – to tighten its cultural control over the public sphere, to infuse it more fully with its values, ethos, symbols and historical understanding. In both parts of Ireland, separatist policies were pursued. Southern nationalists sought to differentiate their culture from the wider British one; Northern unionists sought to differentiate 'Ulster' or 'Northern Ireland' from the rest of the island and from 'Irishness'. There were however differences in the conditions for a coherent cultural project – in the stability, permanence and independence of each state, the extent of cultural consensus among the dominant community, the size of the dissenting minority and the intensity of its dissent. In the South, a distinctive and independent culture emerged (chapter 9); in the North, cultural politics became a central arena of conflict.

Cultural politics: Protestants

Protestants in Northern Ireland after partition were divided about what their culture was and what, if anything, they wanted it to become. Some saw it as a distinctive strand within the wider Irish weave. Others stressed its English or Scottish origins. Still others emphasised Ulster's regional distinctiveness and its blend of British and Irish cultures. Some took questions of cultural distinctiveness seriously; others saw such concerns as an expression of the nationalism they had been struggling against. The unionist cultural project reflected this diversity. It had three aspects – to separate Northern Ireland from the rest of the island and strengthen its relationship to Britain, to allow the different strands of Protestant culture and identity to coexist in harmony, and to contain Northern Catholic cultural self-expression. The new official public culture was pluralist and inclusive in respect of Protestant differences and exclusionary with respect to the Catholic minority.

Separatist tendencies were neither as deep nor as developed within unionist as within nationalist culture. However the desire to separate Northern Ireland from the rest of the island was quickly elaborated. From the foundation of the state, unionists defined the two parts of Ireland as different places, separate from and alien to each other. Politicians and journalists were careful to avoid statements that implied that North and South were part of a single larger entity and the unionist public was quick to criticise any such implications.[2] 'Ulster' – Northern Ireland – was conceived as a society in its own right within the United Kingdom – not as a 'smaller and more backward England, but as a country, like Scotland, with some articulation of its own'.[3]

Attempts were made to define this 'cultural articulation'. Ulster Protestants could not easily lay claim to a distinctive 'Ulster' artistic tradition and there were only a few serious attempts to create one; unionists were, in any case, more concerned to distance themselves from the 'Irish' tradition with which before partition they had vaguely identified than to develop an alternative.[4] They stressed instead the distinctiveness of the Ulster (Protestant) character – honest, plain-spoken, hardworking – and Ulster's progressiveness in economy and science – the shipyards, linen, industrial development, the Protestant contribution to science and medicine.[5] However the main cultural foci of the new state were Protestantism and Britishness.

Protestantism was all-pervasive in the public culture: in the street preachers, the missions, the Protestant Sundays, the public prominence of the Orange Order.[6] Unionist governments systematically identified the state with this culture and the Protestant churches reciprocated. There was an interrelation of unionism and Orangeism and Orange celebrations and marches enjoyed public status. Attention was given to representations from Protestant clergy, who were also present (in considerable numbers) on each of the boards of management of the state schools. It was accepted by both church and state that the Protestant clergy would make political pronouncements and state symbols were often present in Protestant churches. Politicians affirmed the 'Protestant' nature of the state,[7] and spoke of 'Ulster', 'the Ulster people' or even 'the people' to refer only to Protestants.[8]

---

[2] Rex Cathcart, *The Most Contrary Region: The BBC in Northern Ireland 1924–1984*, Belfast, Blackstaff, 1984, pp. 64–7, 141–2.

[3] *News Letter* radio correspondent, 1936, quoted Cathcart, *Most Contrary Region*, p. 76.

[4] *Ibid.*, pp. 65–6, 130; however, some writers and artists, notably John Hewitt, Sam Hanna Bell and William Conor contributed to the emergence of a distinctive Ulster tradition in the arts.

[5] *Ibid.*, pp. 141, 138; cf. Jennifer Todd, 'Two traditions in unionist political culture', *Irish Political Studies*, vol. 2, 1987, p. 13, for the general cultural importance of this theme; Terence Brown, 'British Ireland', in Edna Longley, ed., *Culture in Ireland: Division or Diversity?*, Belfast, Institute of Irish Studies, 1991, p. 76.

[6] See Robert Harbison, *No Surrender*, London, Faber and Faber, 1966, for one auto-biographical description.

[7] Dennis Kennedy, *The Widening Gulf: Northern Attitudes to the Independent Irish State 1919–1949*, Belfast, Blackstaff, 1988, p. 143.

[8] E.g. Jonathon Bardon, *A History of Ulster*, Belfast, Blackstaff, 1992, p. 513.

British symbols and rituals were also pervasive. Symbols of the Crown and the British connection – the flag, the royal family, the national anthem, national commemoration days, royal birthdays and weddings, the whole inherited paraphernalia of titles, trappings and awards – were part of the public culture. King George V's opening of the Northern Ireland parliament in 1921 was a major occasion for public celebration. Events in Protestant and in British history were fused; the Somme came to be a landmark both of Ulster loyalism and of Ulster loyalty to Britain; Orangeism was seen in a wider British and imperial context.[9] The benefits of the British connection were repeatedly stressed, and the study of British and world geography and history displaced the study of Ireland. The United Kingdom became the reference point for all meaningful comparison and norms; comparisons with the South were made only to demonstrate the latter's inadequacies.[10]

The Protestant and British ethos of Northern Ireland, the Protestant character of the 'Ulster' people and their triumph over nationalism, were constantly reiterated in statements in parliament, in public speeches at Orange celebrations and on other public occasions. Opportunities to make particularly powerful cultural statements were grasped. The new parliament building at Stormont, opened in 1932, was the architectural embodiment of Craig's earlier wish: 'There must be a dignity about our Parliament ... so that no opponents at any time dare come forward and say of that great structure . . . that is only a small affair, and we can easily sweep it to one side.'[11] The imposing building, in classical style with lavish interiors, was situated on a hill, approached by a long wide avenue and fronted by a large statue of Carson in defiant posture. It dwarfed in scale and grandeur the town house of the Duke of Leinster which served as the parliament building in Dublin.

Unionist cultural politics had considerable success. The internal cultural tensions within the Protestant community were contained although by no means eliminated. Over time, the Protestant sense of the island and of being part of an island-wide culture diminished; the sense of closeness to Britain increased, particularly after the Second World War. For some, the weakening of links with the South brought a sense of

---

[9] R. McNeill, *Ulster's Stand for Union*, London, John Murray, 1922, p. 13; Bardon, *History of Ulster*, p. 540.

[10] Kennedy, *Widening Gulf*.

[11] Quoted in Nicholas Mansergh, *The Unresolved Question: The Anglo-Irish settlement and its undoing 1912–1972*, London, Yale University Press, 1991, pp. 248–9; in similar vein, Hugh Pollock, minister of finance, saw Stormont as 'the outward and visible proof of the permanence of our institutions; that for all time we are bound indissolubly to the British crown', quoted Bardon, *History of Ulster*, p. 513.

loss, an unwelcome narrowing of perspective.[12] Some attempted to lessen the 'widening gulf': the Irish Assocation was founded in 1938; the Ulster Folk and Transport Museum was established in 1958 and serves the whole of the historic province of Ulster; the Institute of Irish Studies in Queen's University Belfast was founded in 1965. But many more viewed the severing of links with relief – it strengthened Ulster defences against a reGaelicising, hostile South.

A distinctive Northern Irish Protestant culture emerged, a blend of Protestant and provincial British values. It stressed respectability, uprightness, honesty, order, respect for authority, work ethic, cleanliness and tidiness, modesty and informality in social relations, social and political conformity. There was an unquestioned belief in the superiority of this culture to the one emerging simultaneously in the South. It became an integral part of Protestant identity, functioning as 'cultural capital' in relations with the state and in the search for employment or electoral office.

Unionists were willing to ignore Catholic culture as long as its expressions were not overtly political, did not impinge on Protestant expression or threaten the cultural construction of the state. Politicised Catholic symbols like the Tricolour were restricted from public display and nationalist parades or anniversary celebrations were always liable for bans or attacks. The teaching of the Irish language in schools was not proscribed but neither was it facilitated and its place on the timetable was restricted;[13] it was never used in state, public or even most mixed religion occasions. There were no official restrictions on Gaelic games, but the BBC ended broadcasting of GAA results in 1934 after unionist protests.[14]

Too assertive a public display of any aspect of Catholic culture could also provoke a hostile response from loyalists and from the security forces. There were many examples of RUC and loyalist harassment of individuals participating in GAA games. Eamonn McCann tells of Frankie Meenan who, stopped by the police in 1957 and asked his name, replied 'Proinsias Ó Mianáin, tá mé ag dul abhaile' [Francis Meenan, I am going home] and was taken to Crumlin Road jail and held without

---

[12] Cf. Brown, 'British Ulster', p. 76; cf. Todd, 'Two traditions', p. 16, for a continuing, although diminished, sense of island identification.

[13] Mary Harris, *The Catholic Church and the Foundation of the Northern Irish State*, Cork, Cork University Press, 1993, pp. 228–30.

[14] In 1946, the BBC began again to broadcast the results, but in deference to Protestant sabbatarian sensitivities, on Mondays, the day after the matches were played. Cathcart, *Most Contrary Region*, pp. 66, 141–2.

trial for seven months.[15] 'Surly' looks directed at the security forces or local unionists, sitting or fidgeting during the national anthem, or – at more elevated social levels – refusal to attend a royal garden party, were taken as deliberate affronts which unionists were likely to reciprocate or punish.

In 'mixed' gatherings Catholics were expected to be sensitive to Protestant feelings – to show respect for the queen or the Union Jack, to avoid speaking about the pope or the South; this concern was seldom reciprocated. There are innumerable examples of petty insensitivities from these years as well as some celebrated public ones. In 1922, the security forces searched Cardinal Logue's car and examined his private papers; in May 1969 Terence O'Neill commented that 'if you treat Roman Catholics with due consideration and kindness they will live like Protestants in spite of the authoritarian nature of their church'.[16]

Such asymmetry in cultural esteem might occur without a deliberate intent to define power relations or to wound, although it often had that effect: in politicised contexts, it was both the intent and effect. Some Protestant politicians took pride and pleasure in thinking up remarks they knew would be offensive to Catholics or adopted a robustness of style that paid scant regard to Catholic sensitivities. Thus in 1923 Unionist MP Dehra Chichester (later Dame Dehra Parker) justified the requirement that those paid by local authorities or state take an oath of allegiance: 'it was only right that those who paid the piper should call the tune and . . . the tune they wanted was the National Anthem'.[17]

There was some softening in Protestant attitudes to Catholics in the 1960s – a decade which saw unionist expressions of sympathy on Pope John XXIII's death, tolerance of the 1916 celebrations and Terence O'Neill's meeting with Irish taoiseach, Seán Lemass. However it was uneven. In these years, the new town between Lurgan and Portadown was named Craigavon, the new bridge over the Lagan was named Queen Elizabeth Bridge (this was a compromise, the first unionist proposal, Carson Bridge, being deemed too provocative), a riot was provoked when the police removed a Tricolour from the republican election offices on Divis Street, and the Rev. Ian Paisley held up and mockingly described a Catholic Host in a televised debate at the Oxford Union to demonstrate the idolatry and superstition of Catholicism.

[15] Eamonn McCann, *War in an Irish Town*, 2nd edn, London, Pluto, 1980, pp. 10–11.
[16] A. C. Hepburn, *The Conflict of Nationality in Modern Ireland*, London, Edward Arnold, 1980, p. 182.
[17] Harris, *Catholic Church*, p. 148.

Cultural politics: Catholics

Catholic culture had many aspects: religious activities like mass going, devotions and pilgrimages, a focus on familial and communal values, an interest in Irish history and culture, a set of political and national symbols. Whatever the form, most Catholics felt unable to express it in a free, spontaneous and self-confident way in 'mixed' settings, for Protestants did not hide their perceptions of Catholic culture as foreign, subversive, inferior or simply out of place in Northern Ireland, or indeed any modern society. This sense of restriction extended even to such seemingly trivial matters as using an 'Irish' name out loud in the street, saying openly that they were going to mass or revealing an interest in Irish history or culture.[18]

Catholics found such constraints oppressive, but they had no satisfactory mode of response. They could attempt to persuade Protestants that they were mistaken about the subversive and/or inferior and/or exclusivist nature of Catholic culture, but at the cost of yielding to their adversaries the moral high ground and without much chance of success. They could openly challenge unionist dominance but at a price, as the experience of Francis Meenan indicates. More passive means of resistance – withholding of consent, 'acting stupid', being 'spiritually and silently insurgent'[19] – carried a cost in terms of pride and self-respect. Many tried to avoid the problem by remaining spiritually within their community. But this option – Purdie described it as *'being* Irish' rather than uniting Ireland[20] – carried the price of living in a cultural ghetto.

Catholics' position was made all the more difficult by the strains in their relationship with the South. For many Catholics, to travel to the South and find full public support for their values and symbols was a culture shock at once liberating and reassuring.[21] Many took 'refuge' there annually on occasions of ritualised offensiveness such as 'Twelfth week'. Others had a sense of grievance that the South had first excluded, then ignored and finally abandoned them. Still others were less than

---

[18] Interviews.
[19] The quotes are respectively from Eddie MacAteer, quoted in Bob Purdie, *Politics in the Streets: The Origins of the Civil Rights Movement in Northern Ireland*, Belfast, Blackstaff, 1990, p. 41, and Denis Donoghue, *Warrenpoint*, quoted in Patricia Craig, ed., *The Rattle of the North: An Anthology of Ulster Prose*, Belfast, Blackstaff, 1992, p. 289.
[20] Bob Purdie, 'The Irish Anti-partition League, South Armagh and abstentionism', *Irish Political Studies*, vol. 1, 1986, p. 76.
[21] Desmond Fennell, *The Northern Catholic: An Inquiry*, an extended version of a series of articles published in the *Irish Times*, 5–10 May 1958, Dublin, Mount Salus Press, n.d., p. 12.

impressed at the society emerging in the South and found unqualified cultural identification with Southerners more and more difficult.[22]

Catholics did not experience Northern Irish society as uniformly oppressive. Virtually all found the cultural forms of the state and the unionist political establishment alienating; offensive remarks, whether in public or in private, cut deep and were remembered. But not all aspects of the public culture of Northern Ireland were equally problematic. Catholics and Protestants shared some cultural roots and a similar relationship to an increasingly important international mass culture. Both communities could identify with the cultural assumptions implicit in the British welfare state. For many Catholics, it was unionist rather than British symbols which were offensive: in 1966, Republican Labour councillors gave 'eager support' to the naming of the Queen Elizabeth Bridge.[23] There were also many aspects of Protestant culture which Catholics respected and admired.

The crisis of 1969–72 was fuelled in part by cultural inequality but it was not motivated by strong cultural nationalist assumptions. On the contrary, the most striking aspect of the civil rights movement was its sharing of aspects of global protest and youth culture and the fact that it pointedly ignored traditional cultural issues. The slogan 'British Rights for British Citizens' may have been ironical, but that it was possible at all indicates the extent to which cultural questions had been (temporarily) shelved. The marches, provocative to unionists because they deliberately ignored sectarian constructions of territoriality, symbolically united the diverse cultural strands in the Catholic community – culture-blind youthful idealists, traditional nationalists and those who were willing to manipulate cultural tensions to provoke a crisis in the state.

Though temporarily shelved, cultural questions were never far away. The economic and political demands of the civil rights movement – for equality in respect of jobs, houses, votes and the law – had deep symbolic and strategic meanings (chapters 5, 6) that went beyond the more immediate ones that the civil rights movement emphasised. If the political crisis had been averted, the deeper meanings might not have come into play. Once the crisis began, however, it was almost inevitable that conflict would extend to everything that divided the communities and defined relations between them.

Once the deeper meanings were tapped, they came quickly to the fore.

---

[22] Michael McKeown, *The Greening of a Nationalist*, Lucan, Co. Dublin, Murlough, 1986, p. 20; Fennell. *Northern Catholic*, pp. 12–13; cf. ch. 9 below.

[23] Ian Budge and Cornelius O'Leary, *Belfast: Approach to Crisis: A Study of Belfast Politics 1613–1970*, London, Macmillan, 1973, p. 163.

As conflict intensified, the complex structure of controls, silences, evasions and acquiescences which had served to contain cultural conflict was broken and the depth of mutual hostility was laid bare. Cultural inequality took on a new and much more intense meaning.

The British intervention and the changing cultural context

The British government's intervention in 1969 on the side of reform had little immediate impact on the cultural terms of the conflict, but the long term consequences have been considerable: government policies have increasingly focused on cultural divisions, the terms of public debate about the conflict have changed and Northern Ireland has experienced more intense metropolitan influence. The effect has been a widening of cultural differences within each community.

Changing policies: from community relations to cultural traditions

The cultural dimension of the conflict and the depth of the communal division were recognised by the British government. It was also accepted that greater public recognition of 'Irish culture' would be necessary to secure Catholic allegiance, and that political stability depended on achieving a level of mutual cultural tolerance and respect between Protestant and Catholic.[24] The implicit aim of government policy was to create a place for Irish culture within a reformed Northern Ireland in which the two communities were reconciled. From August 1969, a series of measures aimed at reducing sectarianism and improving community relations were put in place. A Community Relations Commission (CRC) (with an equal number of Protestants and Catholics) and a Ministry of Community Relations were established. A Prevention of Incitement to Hatred (NI) Act was passed in 1970 based on race-relations legislation in Britain. The CRC supported intercommunity and inter-schools contact, community development programmes in local communities, and research. The most ambitious attempt to create a place for nationalist culture, however, was the power-sharing executive and Sunningdale Agreement of 1973–4 which formally recognised the separateness of the two identities and allegiances. Ironically, it was the power-sharing executive which abolished the CRC in 1974 (on the grounds that it was no longer necessary) and the Ministry for

---

[24] For a clear statement of one of the assumptions underlying policy, see Merlyn Rees, *Northern Ireland: A Personal Perspective*, London, Methuen, 1985, p. 332.

Community Relations was merged with the Ministry of Education in 1975.[25]

Throughout the remainder of the 1970s and early 1980s, community development and community workers were funded by district councils but there was no systematic or explicit policy on cultural division or community relations. The aims of greater cultural tolerance and improved community relations were sometimes undermined by government policies, particularly in the security area, sometimes implemented as a byproduct of other reforming initiatives. The policy of appointing Catholics to public boards, equal employment legislation, and the entry of Catholics into positions of authority, power and social prominence (including such substantially trivial roles as television presenters or newreaders) showed that being Catholic was no longer a barrier to social advance. Support was made available for some forms of Catholic cultural activities through the traditional music section of the Northern Ireland Arts Council, and in the increasing attention shown to the Irish language and Gaelic games by the BBC. The Community Murals and Community Arts projects of the mid to late 1970s were formally egalitarian as between the communities but also principledly non-political, excluding both unionist and nationalist political symbolism.[26] There was also an official tolerance of public expressions of militant nationalism in nationalist districts that would have been unthinkable in the Stormont period – wall murals glorifying the republican armed struggle became prevalent in Catholic areas of Belfast and Derry from 1981.[27]

A new phase of policy making followed the Anglo-Irish Agreement, explicitly designed to foster contact and cultural tolerance, equality and pluralism between Protestant and Catholic. The Catholic and nationalist tradition was put on a more equal footing with the Protestant and unionist. The right to fly the Tricolour and the Union Jack were subject to the same constraints of public order, Irish language signs were legalised, sectional political and cultural symbols (unionist as well as nationalist) were banned from areas of work. A Central Community Relations Unit was set up in 1987, with the role of monitoring government policy for its effects on community relations; it also funds research

25 Michael J. Cunningham, *British Government Policy in Northern Ireland 1969–89: Its Nature and Execution*, Manchester, Manchester University Press, 1991, pp. 35–6, 133; A. M. Gallagher, 'The approach of government: community relations and equity', in Seamus Dunn, ed., *Facets of the Conflict in Northern Ireland*, London, Macmillan, 1995, pp. 27–31.

26 Bill Rolston, *Politics and Painting: Murals and Conflict in Northern Ireland*, London and Toronto, Associated University Presses, 1989, ch. 2.

27 *Ibid.*, ch. 3. In practice soldiers and police attempted to destroy the murals with 'paint bombs', *ibid.*, p. 101.

on the issue. A Cultural Traditions Group was established in 1988 to explore the cultural heritages of both communities in Northern Ireland and to foster mutual understanding. It has funded publications, cultural initiatives and held a series of conferences.[28] In 1990 it became a part of a new Community Relations Council, which grant-aids, advises and encourages groups involved in inter-community contact. There has been increasing government support for integrated education and, in 1989, cultural heritage and education for mutual understanding (EMU) became compulsory parts of the school curriculum.

At the same time, efforts were made to restrict activities which were thought to aggravate community relations. From 1985, tighter controls were placed on the routes of Orange marches. There was an attempt to direct Irish cultural activities into politically 'safe' channels. The government began funding Irish language programmes under the new Ultach Trust, while simultaneously cutting funding to the already flourishing Glór na nGael – its nursery schools were first to suffer. Funding was restored only after pressure from the Republic, Irish–American politicians, and the SDLP during the run-up to an election. Conway Mill, an adult education centre as well as a centre for new small businesses and other cultural activities, was considered to have too close links to republicanism. Financial support from the government and also from any organisations funded by or answerable to government – the Arts Council, the Workers Educational Association, Rupert Stanley College, the International Fund for Ireland – was cut off. There was again pressure from the government of the Republic, from American politicians and from John Hume and funding was eventually restored in 1995.[29]

The terms of public debate

These changes in policy were accompanied by a radical shift in the terms of public debate which itself reflected the new structure of political

---

[28] Among the books sponsored and published by Cultural Traditions Group are Maurna Crozier, ed., *Cultural Traditions in Northern Ireland: Varieties of Irishness*, Belfast, Institute of Irish Studies, 1989; Maurna Crozier, ed., *Cultural Traditions in Northern Ireland: Varieties of Britishness*, Belfast, Institute of Irish Studies, 1990; Maurna Crozier, ed., *Cultural Traditions in Northern Ireland: All Europeans Now?*, Belfast, Institute of Irish Studies, 1991. Martin McLoone, ed., *Culture, Identity and Broadcasting in Ireland: Local Issues, Global Perspectives*, Belfast, Institute of Irish Studies, 1991; Maurna Crozier and Nicholas Sanders, compilers, *A Cultural Traditions Directory for Northern Ireland*, Belfast, Institute of Irish Studies, 1992. Many more books have been funded or partially funded by the group.

[29] For descriptions of the cases, see The Political Vetting of Community Work Working Group, *The Political Vetting of Community Work in Northern Ireland*, published by Northern Ireland Council for Voluntary Action, 1990, pp. 13–14, 31–4.

authority. During the Stormont period the broadcasting media adopted an 'apolitical' stance uncritical of unionism and reflecting its basic presuppositions.[30] In the later 1960s they adopted the 'moderate centrism' of O'Neillite unionism. With British intervention, the British government became the 'centre' from which a 'balanced' representation of viewpoints was sought.[31] The conflict was defined as a communal one, with the British (and later the Irish) government's role seen as that of a neutral mediator, ensuring law, stability and an environment supporting moderation. This discourse came to predominate in the British and Irish broadcasting media and in most of the print media in Britain and the Republic, though not in Northern Ireland where newspapers have explicitly communal political perspectives and readerships.[32] The marginalisation of the extremes was further increased by the Irish and British broadcasting bans on Sinn Féin. Criticism of or dissent from government policy was not entirely absent, but it was kept within firm bounds.

Research too has changed in form. In the Stormont period, the intellectual work produced or sponsored by the state – census returns, resource surveys, parliamentary reports, reports of inquiries – confirmed in its presuppositions and concerns the British character of Northern Ireland and the permanence of the state. Academic work tended to avoid the issue of contemporary communal division, with one important exception – Barritt and Carter's *The Northern Ireland Problem: A study in group relations*, commissioned by the Irish Association.[33] Nationalist political tracts were countered by similar unionist writing, some of it state sponsored.[34]

Since 1969, the amount of research on or relevant to the conflict has grown enormously, much of it supported by government funding.[35] Very little of this literature is apolitical – as the debates and controversies occasioned by it attest – although its politics may be implicit rather

---

[30] See Cathcart, *Most Contrary Region*, for a history.
[31] Cf. David Butler, 'Ulster unionism and British broadcasting journalism, 1924–1989', in Bill Rolston, *The Media and Northern Ireland: Covering the Troubles*, London, Macmillan, 1991, p. 115; David Butler, 'Broadcasting in a divided community', in Martin McLoone, ed., *Culture, Identity and Broadcasting in Ireland*, pp. 100–1.
[32] Cf. Brian Trench, 'In search of hope: coverage of the Northern conflict in the Dublin daily papers', in Rolston, ed., *The Media and Northern Ireland*, 1991.
[33] D. P. Barritt and Charles F. Carter, *The Northern Ireland Problem: A Study in Group Relations*, Oxford, Oxford University Press, 1962.
[34] Nationalist publications in the 1950s were countered by series of government published unionist pamphlets, for example Lord Brookeborough, W. B. Maginnis and G. B. Hanna, *Why the Border Must Be: The Northern Ireland Case in Brief*, Government of Northern Ireland publications, 1956.
[35] Cf. Gallagher, 'The approach of government', pp. 37–8.

than explicit. Its underlying assumptions are liberal-reformist: the 'internal conflict model' is the dominant paradigm;[36] the main problem is seen as communal division; the broad framework of the state is taken as unalterable, although reform of specific policies may be urged.

The new terms of public debate mark a striking departure from the earlier period in their conscious attempt at balance. They do not endorse Catholics' aspirations to Irish unity; indeed they characterise them as 'unhelpful', 'unreasonable', 'outdated' or 'impossible'. On the other hand they endorse the legitimacy of more moderate reformist demands and, if republicans have felt demonised by the media, constitutional nationalists have appreciated the new channels open to them. In contrast, both unionists and loyalists have found the new situation deeply disturbing. The terms of public debate, supportive of their views for fifty years, have become at best neutral and often hostile. Unionists believe that their position has been wilfully misrepresented by radio and television presenters and academic researchers unsympathetic to their political views; until the recent ceasefires, loyalists felt as demonised and as marginalised as republicans.

Intensified metropolitan influence

These changes in policy and public discourse were part of a wider change that brought Northern Ireland more fully into the mainstream of British life – reflected in the new references to Great Britain as 'the mainland'. Symbolically as well as administratively the centre of power had moved from Belfast to London, from Stormont and the Northern Ireland civil service to Westminster and the Northern Ireland Office. The trappings of power and authority that once attached to the leading unionist politicians transferred to English secretaries of state and ministers who articulated a metropolitan British world view and perception of Northern Ireland. Official visits by royal dignitaries became more common; British notables chaired the succession of committees and boards set up to investigate aspects of practice in Northern Ireland. The embodiments of coercive power were no longer solely the Northern Protestant RUC and B Specials/UDR, but also English, Welsh and Scottish soldiers who saw themselves as outsiders and both communities as natives.

The political culture of the Northern intelligentsia changed. The language and know-how of British state apparatuses – from quangos to welfare rights – became increasingly important. Northern Irish civil servants were integrated into practices and norms which now stemmed

---

[36] John Whyte, *Interpreting Northern Ireland*, Oxford, Clarendon, 1990, ch. 9.

from London, and their reliance on British institutional and policy models increased.[37] Northern Ireland legislation continued to be distinguished from that of the rest of the United Kingdom, but there was now less tolerance for deviation from British norms. This was parallelled by closer party political contacts. Enoch Powell, defeated in his home constituency of Wolverhampton, sat as UUP member for South Down from 1974 to 1987; the Conservative Party offered candidates for the local elections in 1989; the Liberal Democrats established close links with the Alliance party and their leader campaigned for Alliance in the 1992 elections.

The new closeness between Britain and Northern Ireland went beyond the political elite. The people of Northern Ireland, long used to being ignored in the British media, now found themselves the subject of more or less constant comment. Increasing numbers of students – particularly Protestants but also Catholics – went to university in Great Britain. IRA operations in Britain and the subsequent arrests and trials brought the British judicial system under close scrutiny in Northern Ireland. Members of both communities in Northern Ireland had to reconstruct their cultural maps, and in some degree also their sense of imagined community.

Cultural differentiation: the Catholic community

The changes of cultural policy and context have opened up new divisions within the Catholic community. The Stormont government (in Catholic eyes, irreformable) was abolished. The British state claimed to offer a new pluralist and inclusionary beginning for all willing to work within its terms, while harshly punishing those who challenged it outside the law. Two sharply opposed cultural routes were now available to the Catholic community: one assimilative to the new values of the British state and increasingly distanced from the more politicised symbols of nationalist culture and identity; the other reactive, forcefully affirming Irish national identity against old and new forms of Britishness.

The Catholic community made its cultural choices in a complex context. Catholics' self-confidence had benefited from their success in breaking the unionist monopoly of power and winning international support. At the same time, the nature of Irish identity came into question, both because Protestants were more forcefully affirming their

---

[37] Michael Connolly and Sean Loughlin, 'Policy making in Northern Ireland', in M. E. H. Connolly and S. Loughlin, eds., *Public Policy in Northern Ireland: Adoption or Adaption*, Belfast, Policy Research Institute, 1990, p. 15.

Britishness and because the South was resisting involvement in the conflict. Republican violence cast the values of traditional nationalism into doubt for many. There were wider changes also – secularising, pluralist, internationalist and post-nationalist currents – some of them associated with the process of European integration.

Assimilation offered strategic economic benefits to those willing and able to avail of them. It also offered cultural benefits to those who perceived the Catholic cultural world as inward-looking and ghettoised, offering the promise of participating in a more universalistic metro-politan liberal culture. There was a price to pay. It required the acceptance in some degree of a British identity and the adoption of elements of the style of the existing, predominantly Protestant, middle class – British (in a regional Northern Irish form) with a strong Northern Protestant strain.[38]

For those who chose the option of resistance the price was much higher – those suspected of sympathy for republican violence were subject to economic and political marginalisation, harassment by the security forces, moral condemnations by political and religious leaders. Their reaction, consciously modelled on Irish cultural nationalism at the turn of the century, was to create an alternative hierarchy of cultural status and self-respect. Republicans, especially in working-class Belfast where nationalist cultural tradition had been weakest before the troubles, became strongly Irish-identifying, expressed most clearly in a new commitment to the Irish language.[39]

The majority of Catholics, very diverse in cultural affinities, class position and political preferences, kept their distance from either assimilation or resistance.[40] The reforms of the later 1980s – which sought to bring Irishness more systematically into the public sphere and to separate cultural from political and constitutional questions – have been directed at this group but their effects have yet to become clear.

Cultural differentiation: the Protestant community

The unionist state, pluralist and inclusive in respect of the Protestant community, had contained and partially reconciled Protestants' internal cultural differences. British intervention and the abolition of Stormont

---

[38] See Fionnuala O'Connor, *In Search of a State: Catholics in Northern Ireland*, Belfast, Blackstaff, 1993, chs. 2, 9, for discussion of the divisions and options open to middle-class Catholics today.

[39] Felim Hamill, 'Belfast: The Irish language', *Éire-Ireland*, vol. 21, no. 4, 1986; Rolston, *Politics and Painting*, ch. 3.

[40] E.g., see O'Connor, *In Search of a State*, ch. 9.

removed the principal institutional means by which Protestants had secured their unity-in-division.

British policies deepened Protestant division by redrawing the boundaries of inclusion and exclusion so as to divide Protestants. The old boundary had separated Protestant and Catholic; the new one separated 'moderates' and 'extremists'. The issue centred less on attitudes to violence than willingness to work within the new political framework. Loyalists – even those who eschewed violence – were outside the new boundary, unionists were within. But unionists also differed in their willingness to accomodate themselves to British policies. Some accepted the new direction; others totally rejected policies which brought nationalists into the heart of public decision-making and appeared to treat nationalism on a par with unionism.

British intervention widened Protestant divisions by disconfirming a major aspect of Northern Protestant identity – their Britishness. The Protestant community was subject to a highly contradictory form of cultural pressure.[41] For British politicians, unionists' identity as British was at best questionable, at worst a self-serving deceit. In British eyes, unionists lacked the traditional British virtues of tolerance and fair play, they were not patriots but, as Harold Wilson put it in 1974, 'spongers'. If they were genuinely British they would live up to British values of tolerance, fair play and compromise and concede rights to Catholics. In unionist eyes, however, the concession of such rights would undermine their position in the United Kingdom – to validate their claim to be British they were being asked to put their position within the United Kingdom in jeopardy.

The Anglo-Irish Agreement removed any ambiguity about British perceptions and intentions and the shock to Protestant confidence was acute, so severe that it took time before a serious reappraisal became possible.[42] By the 1990s a reappraisal, and further cultural fragmentation, was underway: some reaffirmed their traditional dual Ulster and British identity despite its negation by Britain; some assimilated to the new British norms while others reactively stressed their Ulster Protestant identity; some sought a way out of the impasse by rethinking the question of identity in terms of a new shared regional culture which could incorporative the assimilative tendencies within the Catholic

[41] Arthur Aughey has called it the Catch 22 for unionists. Arthur Aughey, *Under Siege: Ulster Unionism and the Anglo-Irish Agreement*, Belfast, Blackstaff, 1989, pp. 85–6.
[42] Robin Eames, *Chains to be Broken: A Personal Reflection on Northern Ireland and its People*, London, Weidenfeld and Nicolson, 1992, ch. 6; the Unionist Task Force Report, *End to Drift*, 1987, stated 'Few outsiders can understand the bitterness and indignation of unionists unfairly characterized as the guilty party in the Ulster conflict.'

community; some disclaimed any concern with questions of culture and identity which they saw as expressions of outdated nationalism.

Cultural inequality today

Cultural inequality was an integral feature of communal relations during the Stormont period. Today, Protestants have lost ground but they retain important reserves of cultural status and power.

Equality of cultural status

The first and most important expression of Protestants' dominant cultural status is the very existence of Northern Ireland. Ulster is the historic homeland of Northern Protestants; Northern Ireland is their home today. It exists as a separate and distinctive society because the Protestant community willed it so and was willing to make the ultimate sacrifice to achieve and defend it. Virtually all Northern Protestants share in the sense of achievement that springs from this: for some it gives quiet satisfaction and a sense of security; for others it symbolises triumph against their historic enemies and is a cause for celebration. All inter-action in Northern Ireland takes as its point of departure this primary and successful act of Protestant self-determination.

By the same token, the existence of Northern Ireland attests to a traumatic Catholic defeat. Northern Ireland came into existence in defiance of the wishes of Northern Catholics and most still refuse to accord it legitimacy. At the same time, the political existence of Northern Ireland was the condition of Northern Catholics' existence as a community. There is thus a deep and painful negation at the heart of the Northern Catholic communal identity which produces in turn a sense of alienation and anger.[43] One of our Catholic interviewees said Belfast is 'not my city', its 'theirs'. A contributor to the Opsahl Commission made the point more generally: 'I feel, as a Catholic, no sense of belonging to the fabric of society that makes up the official state of Northern Ireland.'[44] But increasingly Catholics also find it difficult to identify with the South; at a cultural level, the Catholic 'search for a state' is a search for a homeland.

The imbalance is evident in the cultural landscape of Northern

---

[43] It pervades the interviews and editorial voice of Fionnuala O'Connor's *In Search of a State*.
[44] Brian Gaffney, submission to Opsahl Commission, Andy Pollak, ed., *A Citizens' Inquiry: The Opsahl Report on Northern Ireland*, Dublin, Lilliput, 1993, pp. 360–1.

Ireland. This landscape was shaped by Protestants, mirrors their identity and confirms – indeed celebrates – their triumphs and victories. It is present in the plantation towns, Derry's walls, the ruins of planter castles, Anglo-Irish big houses, Protestant churches, the reclaimed rich farm land, the anglicised place names, the linen mills and towns, the cranes of Harland and Wolff which dominate the Belfast skyline. It is present also in the British-funded air of prosperity that obtains through much of Northern Ireland, in the motorways and new urban developments that mark the North as different from the South.

For Catholics, the history with which they can identify is not immediately available to them; it has to be excavated – in Seamus Heaney's images, 'delved' for or dredged up – and the narrative which reconstructs it is invariably one of defeat: ancient sites which survive only in the remoter areas, older settlement structures on which new ones have been superimposed, castles whose original Gaelic owners were replaced by settlers, place names once Gaelic now anglicised or indicating historic marginality (Irishtown) or plantation ownership (Draperstown, Salterstown), rich farming land lost to the settlers.[45] Reforms have made some changes but with much effort and limited results: Belfast can become a centre of Irish-speaking but only through arduous revivalist effort; Londonderry city council can rename itself, and even the city, as Derry, but the walls and the historic associations remain.

The British state is a powerful all-pervasive cultural presence throughout the United Kingdom: the Crown is embossed on a multitude of items, from banknotes to post-boxes to children's toys; monarchy is celebrated not just in ritual but in the attention given the royal family; social hierarchy exists in the plethora of titles, awards and honours; foundational narratives are embedded in the political tradition and institutions, norms embodied in canons of taste, the imagined community celebrated in the media. Recent reforms in Northern Ireland have had limited impact on its cultural presence. Irish flags may fly in Catholic areas but in Belfast city centre and on public buildings it is the British flag. Irish ministers may occasionally visit Northern Ireland, but it is British ministers, British channels of authority, British security forces, and British political mores which are the visible authorities.

The reforms since 1972 have shaken the confidence of the Protestant community in the British state and there is now a real fear of betrayal and abandonment. But the sense of the state's legitimacy remains, its

---

[45] Walter Benjamin sees this fragmentation and lost-ness as typical of the cultural heritage of the defeated: W. Benjamin, 'Theses on the philosophy of history', in *Illuminations*, ed. H. Arendt, Glasgow, Fontana, 1973.

right to exercise authority in Northern Ireland beyond question. For many the attachment is to the Crown and it is a deeply emotional one, founded in centuries-long service in peace and war. For others, there is a more cerebral identification with 'the idea of the union' or a sense of pride and admiration for its structures. Many criticise British government policies, are alienated from contemporary English cultural attitudes and are ambivalent about English power. But they accept the state as the legitimate expression of public authority; to serve it brings pride and self-respect.

For most Catholics, such identification is at best partial – limited to an uneven identification with the British socialist tradition, the norms of the welfare state or multiculturalism. There is no emotional attachment to the British state or its symbols, no identification with its forms or achievements. The national successes symbolised in authoritative British institutions have a quite different meaning for Catholics than for Protestants: the constitution itself, as defined by the Glorious Revolution, was secured through the defeat of Irish Catholics; British global influence required, allowed and justified British and Protestant dominance in Ireland; British military glory has had its local presence in heavily armed soldiers in housing estates in West Belfast. Northern Catholics have come to appreciate some of the benefits of the British state, but this is despite, not because of its symbolic expressions. For most Catholics, the structures of the Northern state and public sphere constitute 'chill factors';[46] participation entails a challenge to, perhaps erosion of, identity.

The Protestant economic and political power advantage in Northern Ireland enhances their communal self-esteem. Protestant cultural values and style and British identity are associated with – and seen by many as a precondition of – material success and political authority. Catholic values, style and Irish identity are the hall-marks of the underdog, a source of defiant pride for some but for others of embarrassment and shame. A key motivation for many upwardly mobile Catholics is to escape from their material and cultural origins. The existence of a few very successful and unambiguously culturally Catholic figures in Northern Ireland today has allowed more relativisation of these traditional associations, but still – whatever individuals' moral judgement or cultural choice – the social status associated with the differing cultures favours the Protestant.

Military power too has a cultural face – crude, unnuanced, often a

---

[46] Bernard Cullen, submission to Opsahl Commission, in Pollak, ed., *A Citizens' Inquiry*, pp. 355–6.

caricature of the culture in its articulated form. In the Stormont period, the B Specials and RUC were a symbol of the unionist state: Catholics might reject their unimaginative use of unionist power, seeing them as 'stupid in a profound, bovine and solemn manner'[47] but public status lay with the security forces. Today the security forces are more diverse but they retain a strong British identification in flags, symbolism and in their linkages with the royal family. At best, they share the culture embodied in the British state; at worst, they remain agents of Protestant and British control, still targeting nationalist dissent.[48]

Only in one area are the roles reversed. As 'Irish', Catholics identify with all the cultural achievements of the island – language, literature, music, dance, Gaelic games – irrespective of whether Catholics or Protestants created them. Few Protestants feel able to make the same identification. Some deny that they are 'Irish' at all; others identify only with the Protestant contribution to Irish culture but face the further difficulty of distinguishing between Protestant nationalist and Protestant unionist contributors; still others wish to identify with the whole culture of the island but feel unable in the face of the prior, more assertive, claim of Catholics.[49] In response, the Protestant community has a rich store of sarcasm and invective about Gaelic-Irish culture and nationalist aspirations, refusing to use the Gaelic forms of names or mispronouncing them to (in unionist ears) comic effect, describing Irish as a 'leprechaun language'.

Equality of cultural power

Protestant culture continues to be accorded higher status than Catholic culture, not least because of its relationship to the public sphere which Protestants largely created. However, Protestant cultural power – their ability to impose their values and ethos on the public culture of Northern Ireland – has declined.

Cultural power depends on access to strategic resources in the economy and state and on cultural capital – including education, self-confidence, self-esteem and articulateness. Protestants monopolised these resources in the Stormont years. Their culture was able effortlessly to impose itself in face-to-face interactions, in the ethos of organisations

---

[47] Deane, 'Why Bogside?', in Craig, *Rattle of the North*, p. 397.
[48] See Amnesty International, *Political Killings in Northern Ireland*, London, Amnesty International, British Section, 1994.
[49] For the importance and difficulty of the issue for unionists, see Arthur Aughey, *Irish Kulturkampf*, Ulster Young Unionist Council, Feb. 1995; John Wilson Foster, 'Who are the Irish?', *Studies*, vol. 77, no. 308, 1988.

and in public decisions. Catholics had fewer strategic resources; their culture was low in self-esteem, defensive, vulnerable, silent and resentful rather than rebellious in the face of Protestant cultural self-assertion.

This unequal power was structurally underpinned. Each community controlled its own sites of cultural reproduction – the family, the school, religious organisations, political parties, newspapers, cultural associations. But Protestants also controlled the public sphere – the state apparatuses, the industrial and financial sectors of the economy, the broadcasting media, higher education – and imbued them with a ethos which served further to reinforce their culture. Catholics had their own voluntary organisations, but it was an unequal contest.

British intervention brought radical change. Intervention and the later suspension of Stormont made a profound cultural statement, declaring that Northern Ireland was not a possession of Northern Protestants but of the British state and distancing the British state and people from the 'British culture' which had been institutionalised in Northern Ireland. The British government, not unionists, now implemented and institutionalised its understanding of British norms and values. The assertion of cultural power by the British government radically reduced Protestant cultural control in Northern Ireland though without a corresponding increase in Catholic control.

British policies have been designed to make the public sphere more neutral, to enhance cultural equity and, if possible, to achieve parity of esteem for both traditions in Northern Ireland. As we saw, their effect on the communities has been uneven. Loyalists now feel held in contempt by the British government and by many of their fellow Protestants, with the central expression of their culture – the Orange marches – increasingly restricted, tolerated only from fear of the consequences of banning them. The Protestant middle classes are well within the boundaries of the new more British-orientated public culture but many feel uncomfortable with the English cultural assumptions which underlie it. They retain strategic power resources, their cultural status and capital remain disproportionately high and they continue to exercise informal cultural power. But they are newly vulnerable, conscious of supervision by the British government, their ethos in danger of being relativised and open to criticism that before would have been inconceivable.

The new policies have benefited the Catholic community but their cultural power resources remain inferior to those of Protestants, and their cultural vulnerability greater. Many now participate fully in the state and public sphere but there remains a sense of uncertainty, of fitting into institutions whose ethos has been defined by Protestants and unionists, of having to check spontaneous self-expression.[50] Even those who have to some degree assimilated to British norms are likely to perceive an easy commonality of assumptions, language and symbols between the British government and unionists – from which they feel excluded – rather than the more subtle tensions and dependence of which unionists are conscious.

Those nationalists who have asserted cultural control at the local level and 'reclaimed' their localities from the official culture, as in West Belfast, have a strong and tangible sense of cultural empowerment in stark contrast to the experience of many Protestant local communities. A community worker on the Shankill Road noted that the 'Protestant retreat is all the sharper against the backdrop of a perceived Catholic community in the ascendant'.[51] However there is unevenness and contradictions in the nationalist advance in this respect. Some of the activities concerned – for example, republican war murals – symbolically separate the communities from the state, but many other culturally 'secessionist' activities benefit from or seek British government financial support. It is not clear if the spirit of political defiance would survive the institutionalisation of cultural parity of esteem in a reformed Northern Ireland.

The Catholic community has gained ground and this is reflected in an increased cultural self-confidence. The 'articulate' Northern Irish Catholic became a stereotype in the civil rights period: now it is the 'self-confident' Catholic.[52] Self-confidence is an important resource in relations with the British state and in the communal struggle; Catholic gains have had a culturally disabling effect on the Protestant community, which increasingly sees itself as the loser in the march of history.[53] At the same time, self-confidence is a volatile emotion and the extent of Catholic progress is often exaggerated. In the words of one non-nationalist Catholic 'I could go on reciting a long list of "chill factors" – ways in which manifestations of Britishness in the public and private life

---

[50] Interviews; O'Connor, *In Search of a State*, pp. 32–3; Pollak, ed., *Citizens' Inquiry*, pp. 360–1.

[51] Jackie Redpath, submission to Opsahl Commission, in Pollak, ed., *Citizens' Inquiry*, p. 354.

[52] See for example Lionel Shriver in Pollak, ed., *Citizens' Inquiry*, pp. 419–22.

[53] Arthur Aughey, 'The end of history, the end of the union', in A. Aughey et al., *Selling Unionism, Home and Away*, Ulster Young Unionist Council, 1995; Steve Bruce, *The Edge of the Union: The Ulster Loyalist Political Vision*, Oxford, Clarendon, 1994, ch. 2; Seamus Dunn and Valerie Morgan, *Protestant Alienation in Northern Ireland: A Preliminary Survey*, Coleraine, Centre for the Study of Conflict, 1994, p. 19.

of Northern Ireland either leave many of its citizens cold or excite more or less irritation'.[54]

The meaning of cultural inequality

Cultural inequality has multiple layers of meaning – practical, symbolic and strategic. It has immediate practical consequences for the members of each community. The cultural characteristics claimed by and/or attributed to the members of each community have important consequences for life-chances and personal and social experience – the likelihood of getting a job or being promoted, being treated well or badly by the security forces, being able to express oneself with confidence in a public setting, hearing one's culture spoken of with respect in public, having one's cultural symbols given a recognised place in the public domain or institutionalised at the level of the state, being taken as a serious or honest person in one's personal or business dealings, being able to insist on appropriate respect in interactions and to object when offence is given.

Cultural inequality between Protestants and Catholics means that these differences work systematically to the benefit of Protestants. Protestants still have prior claim on the cultural qualities (hard workers, straight in their business dealings) attractive to employers, the behavioural characteristics (law abidingness, respect for the institutions of the state) which merit respect from the security forces, the personal qualities (honesty, fidelity) deserving of trust and esteem, the right to take offence at symbols or aspirations different from their own. Catholics may challenge the assumptions on which these claims and attributions rest, but they do so in contexts where Protestants are much more likely to be in positions of authority and able to define Catholic opposition or counter-claims as politically motivated, as whingeing or simply another way of being offensive to Protestants.

Cultural inequality also operates at a more symbolic level – in the identity processes in terms of which each community builds up its view of the world, past and present, and validates its position within it. All historically deep communities engage in such processes. It is most difficult in divided societies, for the achievements celebrated by one community are frequently those which the other wishes to forget, the traumatic events to which one community returns obsessively may be

---

[54] Bernard Cullen, submission to Opsahl Commission, in Pollak, ed., *Citizens' Inquiry*, pp. 355–6; O'Connor, *In Search of a State*, ch. 9, suggests that many share this perception.

ignored or regarded as trivial by the other. Cultural inequality affects the capacity of each community to engage in these processes freely and on its own terms.

Each community in Northern Ireland has a past which demands constant remembrance and reinterpretation. Within little more than a generation the first Protestants to settle in Ulster faced a determined attempt to drive them out; a half century later they experienced another challenge. They survived but continued to live with the fear of a resurgent native Catholic population hostile to their presence; David Trimble refers to 'One of the enduring folk memories of the Ulster British people' as 'the fear of massacre'.[55] The traumatic nature of the Catholic experience is a matter of record – the conquest, plantation and subsequent long drawn out displacement, the recurring sectarian conflict in which almost invariably they came out the worst, their marginalisation within the emerging industrial economy, the sundering of their relations with their wider national community at partition, the long decades of subordination during the Stormont years.

Each community feels the need to forge an account of the past that vindicates its role in it and offers guidance for the future; each feels the need to defend that account in the face of the denials and contrary claims of the other community. This imperative underlies the attachment to the symbols, myths, celebrations and rituals which outsiders sometimes deplore as the source of the conflict. The processes are the same in both communities but the balance of past suffering is unequal as is the capacity to address it. As the winners in successive struggles, Protestants have more to celebrate; as the culturally dominant community, they have greater freedom to construct, sustain and validate their chosen identity; as the community which formed Northern Ireland in its own image, they have the material symbols of their past and present throughout the public sphere. As the losers, Catholics have more to come to terms with; they must do so from a position of continuing cultural inequality which precludes the distance necessary to accept the past; they have few public memorials which symbolise and objectify their past and present, and those they propose (for example, bilingual Irish/English signs) are opposed by unionists as offensive. If, for Protestants, the concern is to retain the conditions of their identity and self-respect as a community, for Catholics it is to secure those conditions.

A third level of meaning is strategic. The struggle to establish the public culture of Northern Ireland as 'British', 'Irish' or a mixture has political implications: the defence or erosion of the union and all it

---

[55] David Trimble, in Crozier, ed., *Cultural Traditions in Ireland*, p. 50.

entails. The struggle in Northern Ireland is in part psychological, a battle of wills in which identity and morale are crucial resources. Each community believes that if it 'goes under' culturally, political collapse will soon follow; each hopes that its cultural strength will convince the other that the contest is hopeless and that it is best to yield – that nationalism is on an inexorable rise, or that 'the dogs in the streets' know that Northern Ireland is going to stay British. Each measures ground lost and gained in culture as much as in employment or in elected representation. Each detail – the national anthem at Queen's University graduation ceremonies, the bilingual policy of the students' union – is seen as part of a wider pattern of victory or defeat.[56]

Protestants, in a position of relative advantage, sense danger in even the smallest concessions. Dominic Murray notes that Protestant parents resist any exposure of their children to Irish culture as if it would result in the loss of their Britishness;[57] Frank Millar senior has warned his fellow Protestants that 'Once you start going Paddy, you have to go all the way.'[58] Catholics, starting from a position of cultural marginalisation, favour the reforms and seek to extend them. They are also less fearful than Protestants that cultural contact will lead to assimilation. Their culture has shown itself resilient in the past and is in a stronger position at the level of the island as a whole.

There is also an external dimension to the cultural conflict. The judgements of outside observers are affected by the public culture of Northern Ireland – whether it *appears* British or Irish in its landscape, the character of its people, its social mores, its prevailing ethos.[59] For unionists the key reference group is the British government, for nationalists the South, but international opinion is important also. The fact that Northern Ireland is geographically part of the island of Ireland already biases judgement towards the Irish context; all the more important for unionists that to the observer it appear or feel culturally British, and for nationalists that it appear and feel culturally Irish. This depends in turn on the structure and symbolism of the public sphere – songs, flags,

[56] For example, Ian Paisley Jnr sees the British government as trying to 'wear down loyalist political resistance and determination to stay in the United Kingdom', *Sunday Business Post*, 2 Oct. 1994.

[57] Dominic Murray, *Worlds Apart: Segregated Schools in Northern Ireland*, Belfast, Appletree, 1985, p. 27.

[58] Frank Millar, Snr, in the context of Belfast City Council's refusal to give a civic reception to Lebanon hostage Brian Keenan (a Belfast Protestant with an Irish passport) on his release.

[59] Historically, too, political actors were very conscious of the external dimension; cf. Clare O'Halloran, *Partition and the Limits of Irish Nationalism: An ideology under stress*, Dublin, Gill and Macmillan, 1987, pp. 17–20.

rituals, monuments, names, language. In this sense the cultural struggle is part of the politics of legitimation.

Conclusion

Culture is one of the arenas of conflict in Northern Ireland and cultural inequality one of its important sources. The past twenty five-years have seen major changes in the nature and form of cultural inequality and the momentum of change has increased in the last decade. The achievements thus far have been mixed: inequality has been reduced but not removed, cultural relations between the communities have in some respects been ameliorated, while new sources of tension within each, and between each and the British state, have emerged.

8   The British context of the Northern Ireland conflict

There are contrasting views of Britain's role in the Northern Ireland conflict. For some, the conflict has its roots in a peculiarly Irish or Northern Irish context and Britain offers a progressive modern political arena within which it can be resolved. For others, the conflict derives from the British presence and is prolonged by it. In this chapter we show how the dynamics of the British state and wider British world have impinged on the conflict and assess the opportunities they offer for a resolution of the conflict.

The British state and British world

The British world is that wider political and cultural realm, brought into being by the expansion of the English/British state, which over centuries has felt the impress of English/British decision-making, institutions and culture.[1] It reached its greatest territorial extent and cohesion in the late nineteenth century when it embraced a quarter of the land surface of the globe. It now exists only in residual form. It was a distinctive political and cultural formation, one in which state- and empire-building went on simultaneously, and in which ethnic, national and imperial identities collided, coalesced and – in varying degrees and for differing lengths of time – fused.

The constitution

The British state developed less as a legal-rational structure than as a complex and uneven assemblage of structures, institutions and ritual practices. There has been no formal written constitution; statute law, made by and revocable by parliament, and established practice have

---

[1] See J. G. A. Pocock, 'British history: a plea for a new subject', *Journal of Modern History*, vol. 47, no. 4, 1975.

defined the constitutional parameters.[2] Nor has the constitution had clear territorial definition.[3] In practice, two constitutional spheres developed within the British world – one for the domestic or metropolitan sphere, another for the imperial or colonial.[4] The distinction was understood rather than formally asserted, but it was clear and only one territory – Ireland – was ambiguous between the two spheres.[5]

The domestic constitution derives from the settlement defined by the 'Glorious Revolution' of 1688. This brought to a close the religious conflicts of the sixteenth and seventeenth centuries and the political struggle between Crown and parliament. Moderate Anglican Episcopalianism and parliament each won qualified victory. Power now resided in the 'Crown in Parliament', a constitutional formula which enabled parliament to make statute law which did not bind its successors and gave it control over an executive whose powers originated in the Crown but would in time rest with the cabinet. The constitution made for a strong executive mode of government 'constrained by the wishes of the political community . . . represented . . . through Parliament'.[6] The potential excesses of such a concentration of executive power were countered by institutionalising (at first for elites, progressively for the wider population) the principles of consent, representation, respect for individual and local liberties and the rule of law. The assertion of the absolute sovereignty of the centre was accompanied by a withdrawal of central power from local affairs: an informal 'localisation of power' coexisted with central autonomy from local influence.[7]

The result was a constitution which Pocock has defined in terms of 'conservative enlightenment'. There was resistance at once to absolute power and to popular mobilisation: neither pope nor king, religious fanaticism nor popular sovereignty, absolute power nor decentralisation

---

[2] For more detail, see Patrick Dunleavy, 'Topics in British politics', in Henry Drucker, Patrick Dunleavy, Andrew Gamble and Gillian Peele, eds., *Developments in British Politics 2*, Houndsmills, Macmillan, 1988, pp. 330–1.

[3] Richard Rose, *Understanding the United Kingdom: The Territorial Dimension in Government*, London, Longman, 1982, pp. 48–50.

[4] Jack P. Greene, *Peripheries and Center: Constitutional Development in the Extended Polities of the British Empire and the United States 1607–1788*, London, Norton, 1990, pp. 67–8.

[5] Keith Robbins, *The Eclipse of a Great Power: Modern Britain 1870–1975*, London, Longman, 1983, p. 9.

[6] Philip Norton, 'The Glorious Revolution of 1688: its continuing relevance', *Parliamentary Affairs*, vol. 42, no. 2, 1989, p. 145.

[7] Greene, *Peripheries and Center*, pp. 62–3; Jim Bulpitt, *Territory and Power in the United Kingdom: An Interpretation*, Manchester, Manchester University Press, 1983, ch. 3; Bernard Crick, 'The English and the British', in Crick, ed., *National Identities: The Constitution of the United Kingdom*, Oxford, Blackwell, 1991, pp. 101ff.

were instituted.[8] Power resided in evolving representative institutions, in which traditional elites had strong formal and informal influence, not in 'the people'. But where extra-parliamentary demands were sufficiently strong and compatible with overall political stability, there was provision for responding to them and bringing existing institutions and practices into line with changes in the structures of power and political expectations.

The constitution which emerged in the colonies was quite different, both in terms of parliamentary and executive powers and of local and individual rights. It emerged more as a contract than as a theory of sovereign power and took the form of an evolving *modus vivendi* between settlers and metropolis which varied in detail for each colony.[9] It permitted, and typically implied, a division of rights and interests within the colony – between settler and native – of an order and importance inconceivable in Britain itself. In principle – and usually in practice – the interests of the metropolis took precedence over those of the settlers. Settler resentment was moderated by strategic considerations – economic interests, the superior military power of the metropolis and dependence on that power in the event of native pressure.

The contractual nature of the relationship implied a relative equality of status that fostered settler consciousness of their rights. In their understanding the contract was not subject to change without their consent.[10] The eighteenth century saw a reduction in the power of the central authority over local affairs in the North American colonies.[11] The attempt unilaterally to reassert that authority later in the century provoked resistance, rebellion and eventually secession. Policy in the nineteenth century was more flexible; the settlement colonies were allowed a very large measure of independence on the understanding they would remain satellites within the wider imperial system.[12] But the underlying metropolitan assumption throughout was that metropolis and colonies would remain distinct entities rather than evolve into a single united political community.

Ireland was to be the one exception to this and, significantly, the

---

[8] J. G. A. Pocock, 'Conservative enlightenment and democratic revolutions: The American and French cases in British perspective', *Government and Opposition*, vol. 24, no. 1, 1989.

[9] The pattern here derived from early experience in Ireland and continued into the second empire; see D. K. Fieldhouse, *The Colonial Empires: A Comparative Study from the Eighteenth Century*, London, Macmillan, 1982, pp. 59ff., 290ff.

[10] Greene, *Peripheries and Center*, pp. 61–2, 67ff., 75–6.

[11] *Ibid.*, pp. 71–6, 149–50.

[12] John Darwin, *The End of the British Empire: The Historical Debate*, Oxford, Basil Blackwell, 1991, p. 3.

experiment was to prove a failure. The dualistic nature of the British constitutional tradition provided two quite distinct constitutional options for Ireland – external control through British settlers and their descendants or integration into the consensual polity of the metropolitan centre. Both options were tried; neither was successful. The internal divisions in Ireland which made possible but ultimately unworkable the colonial constitution of the eighteenth century also set limits to the effectiveness of the metropolitan constitution in reconciling those divisions in the nineteenth century (chapter 2).

Core and periphery

The boundaries of the British world expanded and contracted as territories were acquired or relinquished. The domestic sphere also changed in its territorial extent. England was the irreducible core, although Great Britain developed a high degree of internal integration. Wales was annexed and later integrated almost fully into England. Scotland was integrated first by the union of crowns (1603) and later of parliaments (1707), although separate Scottish legal and educational institutions remained. England, Wales and Scotland were governed as a single state from 1707, but with some provision for local difference.

Ireland was viewed variously as a colony, conquered kingdom, sister kingdom, and region of an integrated British Isles; it was fully integrated for a brief period under the exceptional conditions of the Protectorate, then a separate kingdom under the Crown and subordinated to the British parliament, briefly given more autonomy, then integrated into the British parliamentary system, then given different forms of home rule.[13] British territories beyond the two islands were in a different category again.[14] The nature and dualistic structure of the constitution facilitated variation and change, defining a British world that was spatially expandable and contractable without constitutional upheaval at the centre.

The attitude underlying territorial acquisition was instrumental and pragmatic rather than nationalistic – territories were brought into the British world for economic, political, military or prestige benefits. Over time, as in the case of Scotland and Wales, instrumentalism could give way to a genuine sense of solidarity and obligation, strengthened by the

---

[13] For debates and discussion of the exact constitutional status of Ireland at different periods, see S. J. Connolly, *Religion, Law and Power: The Making of Protestant Ireland 1660–1760*, Oxford, Clarendon, 1992, pp. 105–14; H. G. Koenigsberger, 'Composite states, representative institutions and the American revolution', *Historical Research*, vol. 63, no. 148, 1989, pp. 144–5.

[14] Darwin, *End of the British Empire*, pp. 4ff.

sense of the island of Great Britain as a common homeland. Attitudes to the distant colonies (and particularly to the nineteenth-century acquisitions) were quite different. The territories were to be developed, secessionist tendencies contained and defended against outside attack, but only so long as the advantages – material or symbolic – of retention outweighed the costs. When this ceased to be the case, departure could be swift, moderated only by the aim of keeping the colony within the informal sphere of British influence.[15]

Here again Ireland was intermediary. Ireland was closer geographically and culturally than the distant colonies and the historical and social ties were much deeper. But it was a separate island and a different world, one in which British institutional and constitutional practices appeared to produce perverse results. Even after the Act of Union a sense of identification and solidarity was slow to develop as the British response to the famine of the 1840s made unambiguously clear. The following century, once strategic concerns had been met, the secession of the greater part of Ireland could be contemplated with equanimity, indeed relief.

Metropolitan instrumentalism was reflected in turn in differing forms and degrees of political legitimacy. Only in England did the state (as distinct from a particular dynasty) enjoy full and unconditional legitimacy, rooted in tradition and in ethnic identity. In Wales and Scotland, the state's Englishness was a source of tension. Legitimacy was more dependent on performance and adherence to norms of equity and redistribution; however the state profited from the historic depth of its presence and the sense of a common 'British' homeland. In Ireland, and even more so in the distant colonies, legitimacy remained fragile, conditional and uneven.

Britishness

The British world – whether Great Britain or beyond – was understood as one of separate peoples. English culture and political traditions were preeminent, but there was no question of other peoples being integrated into the English imagined community or of their specific cultural traditions being replaced by English ones. There was, however, a political and cultural coherence to the whole given symbolic expression in the concept of 'Britishness'. Used in this way the concept dates from the sixteenth and seventeenth centuries and appealed particularly to Welsh and Scots keen to keep their separate identities while forming a single kingdom with the English. Linda Colley describes how, in the

[15] *Ibid.*

eighteenth and early nineteenth centuries, a quasi-national popular notion of Britishness, closely intertwined with Protestantism, was forged within Great Britain through participation in empire and war.[16] It would retain that special reference; it would also integrate the newly enfranchised working class and become a vehicle of cohesion and identity for the empire as a whole in the later nineteenth century.

As an ideology of empire, Britishness had many of the characteristics of an 'official' state-centred nationalism in its assumption of the intrinsic superiority of British values, British civilisation and its concern to extend British influence and British pre-eminence. At its heart lay the monarchy. Itself one of the ancient English institutions of state, it was reinvigorated as a centre for popular national ritual in the later nineteenth century.[17] It became deeply imbricated in imperial glory and a symbol of the 'Greater Britain' defined by empire. Victoria became Empress of India in 1877, colonial leaders attended her diamond jubilee in 1897. But if the crown was the empire's most potent symbol, a veritable wealth of symbols and rituals were created – imperial motifs, exhibitions, great buildings, popular literature, children's board games. All served to create a sense of a 'greater British world' – expansive, modernising, civilising – binding the separate nations and classes of the United Kingdom and hundreds of separate peoples throughout the world into a cohesive whole.[18] Britishness was again renewed – to incorporate the colonies and dominions which aided in the war effort – in the two world wars.

Britishness was thus a richly textured concept, both flexible and functional, with shifting boundaries. It could be limited to the native English, Welsh and Scots or to all who lived in Great Britain; it could refer to settlers from Great Britain in Ireland or further afield, to native peoples who came to identify or give their loyalty to the British empire, to all who spoke the English language or identified Britain as the mother country. The nature and intensity of associated communal feeling varied. In a British world with domestic divisions and fluctuating imperial boundaries, such vagueness and open-endedness, expandability and contractability, were virtues rather than vices.[19] They made for a flexible

[16] Linda Colley, *Britons: Forging the Nation 1707–1837*, New Haven, Yale University Press, 1992; the Irish were largely excluded from this process, including, in the earlier period at least, Ulster Protestants, *ibid.*, p. 140.

[17] David Cannadine, 'The context, performance and meaning of ritual: the British monarchy and the "Invention of Tradition" c. 1820–1977', in Eric Hobsbawm and Terence Ranger, eds., *The Invention of Tradition*, Cambridge, Cambridge University Press, 1983.

[18] For examples and statements of this vision of imperial Britain, see J. H. Grainger, *Patriotisms: Britain 1900–1939*, London, Routledge and Kegan Paul, 1986.

[19] Bernard Crick, 'The English and the British', pp. 90ff.

strategy for the defence of British interests, British forces and British subjects abroad.

Britishness did not describe a particular culture but it was not without cultural substance. This substance had been made by the interaction of Scots and Welsh with the English regions.[20] It was embedded in a political order – the United Kingdom, reaching out to the empire – which was more than England despite English dominance within it. English culture gave a framework: the language of government and the public sphere was English, as was the political and constitutional tradition; the centre – culturally and politically – was London. But British culture was also Protestant, industrial, modernising, with a global rather than a European perspective. The monarchy was at once a traditional English institution and one which symbolised and incorporated a British multi-national and multiracial unity. British cultural practices and styles were widely exported, in architecture, sport, clothing, political institutions. In the colonies where the contrast between British and native traditions was often acute, 'British' became synonymous with 'modern' and 'civilised' and 'native' with 'backward' and 'inferior'; at home, and in sharp contrast, the concept was consciously being endowed with the aura of antiquity.[21]

Britishness defined a quasi-national and quasi-imperial community additional to, rather than a replacement for, a primary national or communal one – whether English, Welsh, Irish, American, Trinidadian, Gibraltarian. Other groups could be admitted to this inclusivist British identity without dislocating the values of its English core.[22] The peoples of the British Isles and empire perceived themselves as a family of nations complexly interlinked by ties of descent and/or commitment to shared symbolism, experiences, and shared cultural reference points. Yet no single British 'nation' developed, even in Great Britain. The term 'British' was used *tout court* only where indigenous traditions were weak (as in the Caribbean) or in settler colonies where British and native identities were sharply opposed.

The concept of Britishness – both national and imperial – had a compelling appeal for many Protestants in Ireland in the late nineteenth century. Its appeal was multilayered – a source of pride in shared ethnic

---

[20] Keith Robbins, *Nineteenth Century Britain: England Scotland and Wales. The Making of a Nation*, Oxford, Oxford University Press, 1989, p. 11.

[21] Cannadine, 'British monarchy'.

[22] Crick, 'The English and the British', p. 92; Peter J. Taylor, 'The English and their Englishness: "A curiously mysterious, elusive and little understood people"', *Scottish Geographical Magazine*, vol. 107, no. 3, 1991; John Osmond, *The Divided Kingdom*, London, Constable, 1988, chs. 6, 7.

origins, political association and imperial history with a people then at the zenith of its power and prestige in the world, a common cultural currency to mediate ever closer commercial ties within the United Kingdom and the empire and – above all – a justification and defence for the union now coming under increasing pressure from the claims of Irish nationalism. The capacity of Irish Catholics to identify with Britishness was much less. However committed some were to the empire, there were no ties of ethnic origin linking the Gaelic-Irish to the inhabitants of Great Britain. Nor could they ignore the fact that Britishness had come to Ireland in a Protestantising and imperial mode. For them, the increasing elaboration of British imperial imagery in the late nineteenth century added to the tensions surrounding the issues of conquest and colonisation and gave further impetus to Irish nationalism.[23]

Cultural hierarchy

The British world was unambiguously hierarchical and cultural status meshed with economic and political power. Viewed as a single entity the British Isles contained regional as well as national cultures,[24] but status, like power, was centred in England. In the dominant stereotypes, the English were advanced in the arts and sciences, law, economy and politics, rational and controlled; the Welsh, Scots and Irish were in different degrees emotional, unreliable, changeable, excitable, prone to violence.[25] This British Isles hierarchy carried forward into the colonies, but there it formed part of a more elaborate hierarchical system organised around a central divide of race.

The distinctions were based in part on a ranking of cultural and social systems, in part on the assumed attributes of racial difference. The criteria intertwined in the discourses which defined cultural hierarchy. The discourse of 'celticism' defined the cultures of the British Isles as complementary but not as equal.[26] English culture was taken to be deeper, more continuous and superior to all others. Irish, Scottish or Welsh culture might have imagination, verve and colour but they were seen as small scale marginal cultures, feminine, without the organising

[23] Scott B. Cook, 'The Irish Raj: social origins and careers of Irishmen in the Indian civil service 1855–1914', *Journal of Social History*, vol. 20, no. 3, 1987.

[24] Hugh Kearney, *The British Isles: A History of Four Nations*, Cambridge, Cambridge University Press, 1989, pp. 7–8; Robbins, *Nineteenth Century Britain*, p. 11.

[25] For the very negative stereotypes of the Irish, see John Darby, *Dressed to Kill: Cartoonists and the Northern Ireland Conflict*, Belfast, Appletree, 1983, ch. 1, pp. 21–41.

[26] David Cairns and Shaun Richards, *Writing Ireland: Colonialism, Nationalism and Culture*, Manchester, Manchester University Press, 1988, ch. 3.

ability, stamina or capacity to exercise power of the English. The dominance of English political traditions, the export of English political habits, and the failure of Ireland in particular to assimilate to them simply proved the point. Imperial 'orientalist' discourse played a similar function in North Africa, the Middle East and the Indian subcontinent;[27] in Africa, racist hierarchies were applied more crudely.

Interacting with these discourses were assumptions about the status of religion, language and political culture, expressed in a range of writings and attitudes. Anglicanism was more developed and superior to the various forms of dissent; almost all streams of Protestantism were superior to Catholicism; all forms of Christianity were superior to the non-Christian religions, though further distinctions were made between the great religious traditions and the animistic religions of more 'primitive' peoples.[28] The English language – as a vehicle of government, economy or science – was superior to the native languages of Scotland, Wales, Ireland or overseas colonies, and was most properly spoken in England itself. Private ownership of the means of production was more advanced than communal systems. English political habits and constitutional development were far superior to the oppositional politics typical of Ireland and other colonial systems.

The hierarchical model was partly resisted by the Scots, Welsh and Irish who differed also on how to rank each other. It was also internalised by them, both in a degree of deference and in a corresponding degree of insecurity and resentment. Resistance was the more difficult because so many features associated with the English – aristocracy, industrialisation, the language, the political tradition and party system, urbanisation – were by the nineteenth century integral, even dominant, parts of the Welsh, Scottish and Irish social systems.

Stability and instability

The extent of stability and instability in the British world differed between core and periphery. The seventeenth-century settlement did not bring all political challenge in Great Britain to an end, but subsequent challenges were weak. Jacobitism was a source of instability until its final defeat in the Highlands in 1745, but never posed a serious threat.

[27] Edward Said, *Orientalism*, Harmondsworth, Peregrine, 1985.
[28] Keith Robbins, 'Religion and identity in modern British history', in Stuart Mews, ed., *Religion and National Identity*, Oxford, Basil Blackwell, 1982; Eamonn Duffy, '"Englishmen in Vaine": Roman Catholic allegiance to George I', in *ibid.*; Colley, *Britons*, chs. 1, 8; Said, *Orientalism*.

The radical movements of the late eighteenth century evaporated with the French Revolution and war with France. Chartism in the 1830s and 1840s was repressed. The labour movement later in the century was integrated by reforms. The Scottish and Welsh home rule movements were simply ignored. This stability and continuity appear all the more impressive in the context of unprecedented economic change and a crisis-prone European continent.

Successful defence against external invasion was a necessary condition of this stability, but not a sufficient one. It owed much also to elite strategies of managing social, religious and territorial division – a complex blend of centralism and localism, a judicious mix of repression and accomodation on class and religious issues, a pragmatic, commercial approach to empire, a willingness on the part of the English partially to submerge their sense of national identity in a concept of Britishness open to the Scots and Welsh, a stress on the unity of the peoples of Great Britain against all other nations. It owed something also to the benefits of being the pioneers of industrialism and the opportunities and spoils of empire.

Conditions in the colonies were quite other. There the conflicts of race/ethnicity, class, creed, of rulers and ruled were sharper and there was less concern to hide them. Metropolitan attitudes and policies were instrumental, at best moderated by self-serving claims about bringing peace, order, civility and true religion to violent and backward peoples. Settler cooperation was based on self-interest and dependence. Settler–native relations were predicated on absolute divisions of status and power; exploitation was tempered only by paternalism. The conditions for harmony and stability so characteristic of the core were absent and accomodations proved at best short term. Sooner or later all the colonies asserted themselves and most broke away completely.

Again Ireland was a half-way house. It experienced much of the ruthless instrumentality of the colonial process elsewhere (though for more contingent reasons, chapter 2) and its subsequent divisions. But Irish differences always appeared – to the British at least – less inevitable and more reconcilable than those of the other colonies. The experiment of union was in part a strategic manoeuvre to counter separatist tendencies but it was also a genuine attempt to overcome division by integrating Ireland into the quite different culture and historical dynamic of the core. In practice the divisions had gone too deep to be contained in this way, still less overcome. Irish instability would run its course and the greater part of the island would secede. But, in hindsight, Irish secession appears less inevitable than that of the rest of the empire.

Contemporary Britain

The empire, which had existed for centuries and taken its most elaborate form at the start of the twentieth century, was gone within decades. The process began with the secession of southern Ireland from the United Kingdom in 1921; by the end of the 1960s it was virtually complete. Britain has had to reconstruct itself on post-imperial principles, constructing new relationships with its ex-colonies while negotiating a role for itself in the developing European Union. For the ex-metropolis, as much as for the ex-colonies, the process of adjustment to a post-imperial world has been a gradual and at times a difficult one. Britain's imperial past has left a powerful impress on its social and political structure. Many features of the constitution, political culture and habits of territorial management which were functional during the high tide of empire are problems today. To paraphrase Bernard Crick and generalise his insight, the end of empire 'transformed what had previously been a political virtue into an open wound'.[29]

Britain in a new world order

The end of empire and the weakening of the special relationship with the United States has required Britain to redefine its international role. But the transition from an imperial to a post-imperial role has only been partial. English/British world power and 'greatness' was achieved by seapower in a global arena and premised on the avoidance of continental European entanglements. Britain's special relationships were with the English speaking world with which it shared institutions and political culture as well as language: the relationship with the US was of special importance. That unique role fed into habits of thinking about British power and international strategy and into diplomatic activity. There has been no serious strategic rethinking of how to reconstitute a sense of national 'purpose' or 'greatness' in a changed international arena.[30]

In the recent period, British interests have turned towards the European Union. Habits of elite and public thought have not. British nationality was conceived in a British world – rather than a European – framework. 'Britishness' moved out from the core of England and Great Britain – the 'island race'– to the 'cousins' of the English speaking world. Continental Europeans, in contrast, were regarded as foreign. The

---

[29] Crick, ed., *National Identities*, p. 99.
[30] William Wallace, 'Foreign policy and national identity in the United Kingdom', *International Affairs*, vol. 67, no. 1, 1991, pp. 65, 70.

result is that even today 'our head is in Europe but our heart is still elsewhere'.[31]

These features of British political culture have had an important impact on British performance. Britain has failed to mark out a role in the EU appropriate to its size and status. It kept its distance from European integration in the immediate post-war period when its foundational structures were laid.[32] This permitted the creation of EU political instititutions and the development of EU law and of written constitutional rights in a manner not easily assimilable to Britain's tradition of parliamentary sovereignty and informal constitution, thus reinforcing the British perception of the EU as 'foreign'. Britain has been unable to counter the French/German control over the European agenda; forced periodically to block their moves, it has appeared half-hearted about the whole enterprise. Within the EU, it is among the most committed to the 'nation-state' and intergovernmental model of EU development and most opposed to the regional/federal model. It has not benefited economically from membership to the same degree as the other large powers, or succeeded – as France has – in using European cooperation to renew its power and influence in the world.

Without a clear alternative international role, the legacies of Britain's period of imperial global power retain considerable hold on attitudes, sense of nationality and national pride.[33] This has worked against a far-reaching, integrated reevaluation not just of Britain's international role but also of its economic strategies, political structures and national identity.

The economy

The history of the British economy has been inextricably linked to the history of empire, with the economic effects of the end of empire exacerbated by a succession of failures – the failure to renew the industrial infrastructure in the immediate post-Second World War period, to achieve the cooperation of capital and labour in building a prosperous economy, to draw back from an expensive international global power role which favoured financial over manufacturing interests.[34]

---

[31] *Ibid.*, p. 68.

[32] Robbins, *The Eclipse of a Great Power*, pp. 178–81, 259–64

[33] Patrick Wright, *On Living in an Old Country: The National Past in Contemporary Britain*, London, Verso, 1985.

[34] For the nature and causes of British economic failures, see David Coates, *The Question of UK Decline: The Economy, State and Society*, London, Harvester, 1994.

Throughout the twentieth century the British economy has been in relative decline. It remains the sixth largest economy in terms of total GDP. But whereas it enjoyed by far the highest level of national income per capita in the world in 1900, in 1985 it was thirteenth.[35] In 1900 British industrial exports constituted a third of world trade, by the 1980s they were less than a tenth.[36] In 1900 Britain was the leading financial power in the world, today it remains an important centre but significantly behind the US, Japan and increasingly Germany. Relative decline has been as evident in the post-war as in the earlier period.[37]

Decline has been sectorally uneven. There is little evidence of weakness in such areas as agriculture, financial services, the 'heritage industry' or tourism, or in British multinational industry. The main area of weakness is in indigenous manufacturing, one of the primary sources of British wealth and preeminence in the nineteenth and early twentieth centuries. Economic growth in the 1980s was particularly high in well-remunerated areas such as private financial services supported by a government policy emphasis on low inflation and a strong pound. It was also high in private consumer services (although often employment here was low paid). Output in manufacturing industry rose but the numbers employed fell sharply and labour released from declining manufacturing industry did not typically find its way into higher paid manufacturing or services; most of it entered poorly paid jobs in the service sector or remained unemployed.

The result was the exacerbating of class and region based inequalities. Many of the working-class gains of the 1950s and 1960s – in real income and in rights – were rolled back. The worst hit were in manufacturing and in the public sector. This inequality had a definite spatial form. The north (including east lowland Scotland, south Wales and north-east Ireland) and the midlands, the areas of industrial prosperity in the nineteenth and early twentieth centuries, were most affected by manufacturing decline.[38] More recent and more successful manufacturing has been concentrated in the south-east along with the new service sectors. Indeed for a period in the 1960s and 1970s areas which had never had

---

[35] Kieran A. Kennedy, Thomas Giblin and Deirdre McHugh, *The Economic Development of Ireland in the Twentieth Century*, London, Routledge, 1988, p. 14, table 1.1.

[36] Andrew Gamble, *Britain in Decline: Economic Policy, Political Strategy and the British State*, 3rd edn, London, Macmillan, 1990, p. 18, table 1.3; David Coates, *The Question of UK Decline*, p. 6, table 1.2.

[37] Coates, *Question of UK Decline*, p. 6, table 1.2.

[38] Doreen Massey, 'What's happening to UK manufacturing?', in John Allen and Doreen Massey, eds., *The Economy in Question*, Milton Keynes, Open University, 1988, pp. 59–62.

industry were doing better than the traditional industrial areas. On a increasingly visible North/South divide[39] were superimposed divisions between declining urban and industrial regions and more dynamic growth areas: within the prosperous south-east itself, new service and manufacturing industries have moved out of London.

Britain has little tradition of effective regional policy which might counter these trends.[40] Indeed government policies in the 1980s – the acceptance of the contraction of the industrial base, the welcoming of multinational capital on a *laissez faire* basis, monopoly and mergers policy – have exacerbated them.[41] In Britain as a whole, regional redistribution is mainly through social and welfare services – it is taxes and unemployment benefits, not regional economic planning, which redistributes wealth from one part of the country to another. Developed institutional frameworks for economic planning or European networking exist only in Wales, Scotland and Northern Ireland.[42]

The social and political impact of recent economic changes has been profound. There is a return (after a century and a half of eclipse) to the long historical prominence of the south-east as the economic core of Britain, indeed of the British Isles as a whole.[43] Deepset territorial antagonisms have been brought into play. There has been social disruption and breakdown of social control in the inner cities, increasing politicisation of local government in urban areas like London and Liverpool, a reemergence of Scottish and Welsh nationalisms, and a deeper political malaise in the depressed regions of England which lack the power, institutions or population to make their voice heard politically.

[39] Jim Lewis and Alan Townshend, 'Introduction', in Jim Lewis and Alan Townshend, eds., *The North-South Divide: Regional Change in Britain in the 1980s*, London, Paul Chapman, 1989, pp. 16–17.

[40] For a discussion of the recent history of Britain's regional economic policy see P. J. Damesick, 'The evolution of spatial economic policy', in Peter Damesick and Peter Woods, eds., *Regional Problems, Problem Regions and Public Policy in the UK*, Oxford, Clarendon, 1987; for more critical accounts, see Graham Day and Gareth Rees, eds., *Regions, Nations and European Integration: Remaking the Celtic Periphery*, Cardiff, University of Wales Press, 1991.

[41] See Jonathan Morris, Philip Cooke, Goio Etxebarria, Arantxa Rodrigues, 'The political economy of regional industrial regeneration: The Welsh and Basque "models"', in Day and Rees, eds., *Regions, Nations and European Integration*.

[42] Gareth Rees and Kevin Morgan, 'Industrial restructuring, innovation systems and the regional state in South Wales in the 1990s', in Day and Rees, eds., *Regions, Nations and European Integration*, p. 157.

[43] Kearney, *British Isles*, pp. 106ff.

The constitution

The state's failure to manage the post-imperial transition and the adjustment to a new economic order has had constitutional implications. Immigration from the ex-colonies and the rise of racism have raised fundamental questions of identity and citizenship. The breakdown of traditional mechanisms of social order and consensus in the context of a vastly expanded state has led to an increased reliance on coercive modes of social control.[44] The tendency towards an authoritarian state and the factors producing it are common to all modern Western societies,[45] but they have been exacerbated in Britain by the form and intensity of regional economic differences. Political party loyalties have become more region specific and the main parties no longer function to secure territorial integration and social consensus.

Margaret Thatcher's terms as prime minister in the 1980s brought many of these tensions to a head. The philosophy of One Nation seemed to have been abandoned by a party willing to rule from a southern English power base and ride roughshod over those who did not support it. The stress on consensus gave way to a 'politics of conviction' which claimed a complete monopoly of political virtue. Moderation was replaced by a politics of confrontation, most evident in the carefully planned victory over the miners. The traditional respect for individual liberty was eroded by the terms of the extended Official Secrets Act which decreased the accountability of state agencies and increased police powers and legal punitiveness.[46] The principle of respect for local rights appeared abandoned by the targeting of elected local authorities which opposed the power of the centre.

These developments convinced many – liberals and most on the left – of the fragility of traditional rights and liberties in the face of a determined executive power. The compatibility of the absolute sovereignty of the crown in parliament with individual liberties and rights came into question.[47] What parliament has given, it can take away and all rights appear insecure when the social consensus which has been the historical basis of British liberal freedoms is endangered. A range of demands for constitutional reform – bill of rights, electoral change to PR–STV,

---

[44] Paddy Hillyard and Janie Percy Smith, *The Coercive State: The Decline of Democracy in Britain*, London, Fontana, 1988.

[45] See Nicos Poulantzas, *State, Power, Socialism*, London, Verso, 1978; Claus Offe, *Contradictions of the Welfare State*, London, Hutchinson, 1984.

[46] Hillyard and Percy Smith, *Coercive State*, chs. 1, 3, 4, 7, 8.

[47] F. F. Ridley, 'There is no British constitution: a dangerous case of the emperor's clothes', *Parliamentary Affairs*, vol. 41, no. 3, 1988.

devolution all around in the United Kingdom – were put forward and for a period it seemed as if the pressure for wholesale constitutional review might become unstoppable.[48] The impetus for reform has slowed with the end of 'Thatcherism' but the underlying problems remain and the debate continues.

The stability of the union

The shrinking of the British world has thrown into sharp relief the stability of the United Kingdom itself. In the past, the union was held together by the strength of British industry, the power and prestige of the British state in the world, the opportunities of empire and by the belief that these benefits were being evenly spread throughout the United Kingdom. Economic and political decline, the end of empire, the renewed dominance of the south-east of England and more specific conflicts (for example over Scottish oil) are testing British solidarity at a time when regionalist alternatives to union are emerging within the EU. Scottish and Welsh nationalism have been on the increase – though unevenly – since the 1960s.

Thus far an accomodation has been reached with Welsh nationalism, in part because it has not traditionally been separatist: Saunders Lewis explained 'We must have self-government. Not independence. Not even unconditional freedom. But just as much freedom as may be necessary to establish and safeguard civilization in Wales.'[49] Since the 1979 referendum on devolution, Plaid Cymru's political nationalism has become still more attenuated. There has been no equivalent accomodation with nationalism in Scotland, whose stronger political and constitutional focus has more seriously challenged the wider British order. The 1979 referendum on devolution in Scotland failed to pass the 40 per cent threshold of population, but in the 1980s nationalism increased its strength and widened its social base.

The Labour Party and the churches have been important participants in this new phase of Scottish nationalism. The Scottish Nationalist Party (SNP) retains its strength and a range of Scottish-oriented arts and media have emerged.[50] Nationalist demands range from a desire for

---

[48] For discussion of a range of proposals see Philip Norton, 'The Constitution: approaches to reform', *Politics*, Sept. 1993. Dawn Oliver, 'Citizenship in the 1990s', *Politics*, Sept. 1993.

[49] Lewis in 1975, quoted in L. J. Sharpe, 'Devolution and Celtic nationalism in the UK', *West European Politics*, vol. 8, no. 3, 1989, p. 96.

[50] *Radical Scotland*, published between 1983 and 1991, was one of the most important political publications.

limited devolution to full regional autonomy within a more integrated EU to independence: at the end of 1990, 39 per cent of Scots favoured independence, 44 per cent home rule.[51] Broad-based nationalist statements, for example, 'A Claim of Right for Scotland' strongly challenge British constitutional practices, claiming the right to Scottish self-determination and appealing to long Scottish traditions of limited rather than absolute sovereignty. The political impetus has slowed in the recent period but Scottish nationalism remains strong.

Scotland's right to secede from the union appears not to be in question, but the pressure on it to remain is considerable. There is a commitment to the integrity of Great Britain, seen, for example, in Conservative Party statements, but there are also multiple institutionally based interests in maintaining the union.[52] The political elite has strong interlinkages throughout Great Britain, with Welsh and Scottish politicians prominent in all parties; the Labour Party has a particularly strong self-interest in preserving the union since it relies on Scottish and Welsh constituencies for its strength. Indeed there is fear of granting even a limited form of devolution to Scotland: 'Once there is an elected Assembly to speak on Scotland's behalf, the terms of the union will be a matter of continuous reinterpretation and legitimate dispute.'[53]

Pressure to regionalise the United Kingdom may increase, coming from above (the EU) or below (Scotland), but territorial change at the core of the British state will not be so easily accommodated as change on the periphery has been, and it will not readily be conceded.

Britishness and cultural hierarchy

The concept of Britishness has adapted to the end of empire, but retains much of its earlier form. It remains important, seldom as a sole identity, but – a significant minority of Scots excepted – as an addition to a primary identity.[54] It also retains its ambiguity. Goulbourne has traced the move from an imperial to traditional nationalist and ethnic notions

---

[51] Robert McCreadie, 'Scottish identity and the constitution', in Crick, ed., *National Identities*, p. 55.

[52] James Cornford, 'Towards a constitutional equation', in Crick, ed., *National Identities*.

[53] *Ibid.*, p. 163.

[54] James G. Kellas, 'The social origins of nationalism in Great Britain: the case of Scotland', in John Coakley, ed., *The Social Origins of Nationalist Movements: The Contemporary West European Experience*, London, Sage, 1992, p. 172, table 9.1; John Osmond, 'Coping with a dual identity', and Owen Dudley Edwards, 'Wales, Scotland and Ireland', in John Osmond, ed., *The National Question Again: Welsh Political Identity in the 1980s*, Llandysul, Gomer, 1985; Crick, 'The English and the British'.

of Britishness.[55] In the traditional nationalist notion, Britishness is now limited to the residents of Great Britain (and more dubiously Northern Ireland) of all ethnic origins. In the ethnic notion, Britishness is restricted more severely to the indigenous English, Scots and Welsh (a subsection of Northern Ireland Protestants may also sometimes be included). In any of these references, it may carry only political resonances – acceptance of British political traditions and identification with the symbolism of the British state – or stronger cultural substance.

Much of the traditional cultural substance of Britishness has survived the demise of empire. David Coates notes with some sharpness: 'to be British is to be white and powerful internationally, tolerant, moderate and reasonable at home . . . to be British establishes a point of contact and identification that transcends the divisions of class, gender and religion, in a common unity against the inadequate foreigner and in a common heritage of national pride and imperial glory'.[56] In a similar vein Goulbourne notes the failure to construct an inclusivist notion of British nationality which integrates the wider British experience (the legacy of the colonised as well as colonisers) with white, island-centred cultural and political traditions.

Even within Great Britain, Britishness is only ambiguously inclusivist. A *Guardian* editorial in 1990 stated that to recognise oneself as British means 'we accept the permanence of the English dominated constitutional settlement of this island'.[57] The editorial writer went on to affirm that this 'English dominated settlement' is 'in no way necessarily antagonistic to or incompatible with . . . [r]espect and nurture of minority cultures'.[58] Framing the relationship between the cultures in this way serves only to highlight the lower status of the 'minority cultures'. What applies to the constitutional settlement applies equally to language, the media, the writing of history, cultural criticism, the agencies of cultural transmission and revision, in all of which the English presence is dominant not just demographically but in the definition of cultural norms. Cultural nationalism has widened the space available for autonomous cultural expression in Wales and Scotland, but these nationalisms are relegated to the status of 'harmless eccentricities',[59]

---

[55] Harry Goulbourne, *Ethnicity and Nationalism in Post-Imperial Britain*, Cambridge, Cambridge University Press, 1991.
[56] David Coates, *The Context of British Politics*, London, Hutchinson, 1984, p. 196.
[57] *Guardian* editorial, 8 May 1990, in Crick, ed., *National Identities*, pp. 168–9.
[58] *Ibid.*, p. 169.
[59] In Northern Ireland, in contrast, nationalism is seen as a 'nasty aberration'; Cornford, 'Towards a constitutional equation?', p. 157.

while their more successful literary achievements are appropriated to the general category of 'English' (or at best, British).

English certainties are being challenged more effectively from within than without. The dominant cultural debate in Britain today is about the making of cultural hierarchies, of class, religion, ethnicity, region, and the role of canonical texts and images in perpetuating or subverting these. Important historical work on radical and conservative notions of patriotism and liberty complements sophisticated excavations of the meanings of contemporary symbolically charged events and deconstructions of the canons of English literature.[60] Immigrant minorities have looked to a redefinition of Britishness/Englishness which acknowledges the intertwining of English and Indian or Pakistani culture while denying white English dominance.[61]

It is increasingly accepted that the notion of Englishness is relational, defined against its others (internal, Celtic or colonial), hiding internal structures of domination and complex, contested hierarchies. This is, for the most part, an opening and egalitarianising of a dominant culture by an intellectual elite within the core. The agenda is critical, but set from the centre not from the peripheries. From this perspective, Scottish, Welsh and Irish concerns are merely parochial, 'tiddliwinks' as an English professor is reported to have described an interest in Irish politics.[62]

Past and present

The British experience of historical change is, by European standards, remarkably gradualist. In no other European society does the *ancien régime* appear so intact. To an important extent, Britain retains the traditions of 'state-craft' – the understandings, the political procedures and practices, the cultural values – formed in and through the process of state and empire building.[63] Continuity is celebrated and reinforced in state rituals and symbols of past glories and traditional authority – the

---

60 Hugh Cunningham, 'The Conservative party and patriotism', in Robert Colls and Philip Dodd, eds., *Englishness: Politics and Culture 1880–1920*, London, Croom Helm, 1987; Bill Schwarz, 'Conservatism, nationalism and imperialism', in James Donald and Stuart Hall, eds., *Politics and Ideology: A Reader*, Milton Keynes, Open University Press, 1986; Robert Eccleshall, *British Liberalism: Liberal Thought from the 1640s to the 1980s*, London, Longman, 1986; Dennis Smith, 'Englishness and the liberal inheritance after 1886', in Colls and Dodd, *Englishness*; Wright, *On Living in an Old Country*; Raphael Samuel, ed., *Patriotism: The Making and Unmaking of British National Identity*, 3 vols., London, Routledge, 1989.
61 Hanif Kureishi, 'London and Karachi', in Samuel, ed., *Patriotism*, vol. 2.
62 Personal communication to one of the authors.
63 See Bulpitt, *Territory and Power*, p. 3.

great totalising symbol is the monarchy, but there is also parliament and the constitution, the memory of empire and the commonwealth. Celebrated too are the enduring qualities of the British people in their defence of their 'historic freedoms' and 'island home'.[64] The image of an unchanging, traditional Britain was, paradoxically, renewed during the 1980s by a political leader whose policies were dramatically changing British social structure but whose language and international stance harked back to another age.

The integrating power of traditional British political culture has been partially undermined by new forms of social and political conflict together with the more general corrosive tendencies of post-modernity. The unceasing crises of the actual – as distinct from symbolic – royal family appear symptoms of deeper problems in the public culture. Increasing numbers express their sense of distance from the traditional symbols and rituals.[65] For many on the left, they are no longer acceptable forms of social integration, at once eliding contemporary social divisions and reproducing hierarchical forms of political management and cultural status. Some look to ethnic pluralism, others to a new egalitarian constitution with a post-nationalist as well as post-imperial form of citizenship, integrated by egalitarian and functional institutions, not traditional symbols. As yet, no alternative has emerged, not least because the political framework and habits of statecraft embody the continuity with tradition that the symbols celebrate.

Britain has negotiated the post-imperial transition by emphasising traditional continuities. In Northern Ireland a harder transition is occurring without the possibility of such traditional legitimation. The British emphasis on continuity – the traditional conservative nation and British rituals – feeds into and emphasises the unionist/nationalist division. Change – the new liberal and pluralist currents – provides material for intra-unionist conflict on political strategy without bridging communal divisions. As in the past, the modes of political integration used to resolve conflict and manage change in Great Britain are ineffective in the face of Irish social divisions.

The United Kingdom and the conflict in Northern Ireland

'It is doubtful whether any party to the Northern Ireland conflict has shown such a desire as the British government to reach a settlement

---

[64] Tom Nairn, *The Enchanted Glass: Britain and its monarchy*, London, Hutchinson Radius, 1988; Wright, *On Living in an Old Country*.
[65] Samuel, ed., *Patriotism*, vol. 2; Nairn, *Enchanted Glass*; Osmond, *The Divided Kingdom*.

consonant with generally accepted principles of political equity, or pursued so rocky a penitential path, strewn with the debris of successive "political initiatives", towards it.'[66] Charles Townshend overstates the case but his view usefully balances the criticisms that Ireland is low on British priorities and that the problem persists because of British indifference, inconsistency or inappropriate policies.[67]

Both judgements, however, focus too narrowly on issues of policy and intent. The British state is not simply a maker of policy, it is a framework of institutions and meanings, the embodiment of a political tradition and the centre of a wider British world. Its habits of territorial management, its constitution, its wider economic structure and culture impinge directly on the Northern Ireland conflict. In this section we look at the place of Northern Ireland in the post-imperial British world, the impact of British policy patterns on the dynamics of conflict and the longer term prospects of conflict resolution within a British context.

Northern Ireland within the United Kingdom

In constitutional theory, Northern Ireland is an integral part of the United Kingdom. In the perceptions of the British political elite, however, it is 'a place apart', differentiated by its geography, history and culture. It is seen as part of a larger entity – the island of Ireland – which has its own complex historical dynamic and a political culture profoundly different to that of Great Britain.[68] It is a place where things are done differently, one to which the (more sensible and rational) British way cannot easily be exported.[69] Northern Ireland might be separated from Great Britain by a narrow channel, but as Merlyn Rees put it, he did not want his colleagues to think that 'because Ulster was near, it was somehow British'.[70] Reginald Maudling's comment was more blunt – 'What a bloody awful country'.[71] Powerful sections of the political elite favour increasing Irish government input into administration as a means, not

---

[66] Charles Townshend, *Political Violence in Ireland: Government and Resistance since 1848*, Clarendon, 1983, p. 396.

[67] For example, Padraig O'Malley, *The Uncivil Wars: Ireland today*, Belfast, Blackstaff, 1983, p. 254.

[68] Margaret Thatcher, *The Downing Street Years*, London, Harper Collins, 1995, p. 385.

[69] Merlyn Rees, *Northern Ireland: a personal perspective*, London, Methuen, 1985, p. 41; Roland Moyle quoted in B. O'Leary and J. McGarry, *The Politics of Antagonism: Understanding Northern Ireland*, London, Athlone, p. 171; William Whitelaw, *Whitelaw Memoirs*, London, Aurum, 1989, pp. 78–9, 122.

[70] Rees, *Northern Ireland*, p. 321.

[71] Paul Bew and Gordon Gillespie, Northern Ireland: *A Chronology of the Troubles 1968–1993*, Dublin, Gill and Macmillan, 1993, p. 28.

simply of reconciling the Catholic minority to the state, but of insulating Northern Ireland from British political trends.[72] British governments assume that the future of Northern Ireland may (some believe should) lie within a united Ireland.[73]

There is ample evidence that the wider British public shares these assumptions. In two recent polls, around half of the British public believes that Northern Ireland should leave the United Kingdom.[74] Brendan O'Leary notes the 'widespread British enthusiasm to be rid of Northern Ireland, but indifference as to the means or the consequences' and points out that 'The "Irish dimension" is so strongly entrenched in the minds of the Great British public that more of them think the Irish government should have a major role in the affairs of Northern Ireland than think the same should apply to their own government.'[75]

Northern Ireland is at best on the margins of the British moral consciousness. Tragic events, deaths and atrocities there have shocked and saddened people in Great Britain, but as the suffering of fellow citizens or neighbours, not of kith and kin. It is also on the margins of the political culture. The legal framework and activities of the British security forces in Northern Ireland – internment without trial, 'inhuman and degrading treatment', 'shoot-to-kill', collusion with paramilitaries, supergrass trials – have not been seen as threats to civil liberties in Britain but as a response to a peculiarly Irish situation. Despite the manifest relevance of Northern Ireland to British debates on the economy, the constitution, cultural pluralism, vestiges of empire, the future of the left, the meaning of Englishness or Britishness, these debates have been conducted with studied disregard for the conflict there.[76]

The perception of Northern Ireland as separate, different, ultimately detachable, has been concretised in a wide range of policies and assumptions: the great reluctance by the main political parties in the United Kingdom to organise in Northern Ireland; the willingness to administer affairs of state in Northern Ireland with minimal representation of the local population; the acceptance of a situation in which a 'loyal' community polices a 'disloyal' one, and does so in part as a regiment of the British army; the official leniency given to soldiers responsible for the

---

[72] Paul Bew, Peter Gibbon and Henry Patterson, *Northern Ireland 1921–1994: Political forces and social classes*, London, Serif, 1995, pp. 170–1, 211–13.

[73] *Ibid.*, pp. 168–70.

[74] MORI/Irish Times poll reported *Irish Times* 27 Jan. 1992. Gallup polls commissioned by Joseph Rowntree Reform Trust 2–8 July 1991, in Brendan O'Leary, 'Public opinion and Northern Irish futures', *The Political Quarterly*, vol. 63, no. 2, 1992.

[75] *Ibid.*, pp. 146, 159–60.

[76] For example, the important leftist journal *New Left Review* did not publish any articles on Northern Ireland through nearly 25 years of violent conflict.

deaths of civilians in controversial circumstances; the statements – sometimes slips of the tongue – of British politicians and military that compare Northern Ireland with former colonies.[77] It does not affect all aspects of government policy; Northern Ireland is administered economically and socially as if it will remain a permanent part of the union. Yet even this may begin to change if the North–South institutions sketched in the joint British–Irish Framework Document are given real powers.

Unionists are shocked and distressed at the British government's self-defined 'neutrality' on the constitutional question, its lack of 'selfish strategic interest' in Northern Ireland. Sir Patrick Mayhew – often seen as a secretary of state with unionist sympathies – is seen by unionists as 'a senior Cabinet minister, in charge of a department of State, that has no particular policy to pursue. No mention of defending the integrity of the Kingdom, not even a personal expression of what the constitutional position of Northern Ireland should be.'[78] Yet unionist demands for a more permanent constitutional place are unlikely to be met. The lack of territorial definition of the British constitution and the post-imperial strategy of accepting majority local opinion as to constitutional status preclude unconditional defence of present British national boundaries. Even Scotland, with which there is much closer cultural and political identification than with Northern Ireland, would be granted independence if a clear majority unambiguously demanded it. And more effort would be expended to keep Scotland in the union than Northern Ireland. The long-term practice of insulating Northern Ireland from British politics and the cultural exclusion even of Northern unionists from the core 'British' imagined community, place Northern Ireland 'on the edge of the union'.

The British context and the dynamics of conflict

The structure of the British state, its approach to territorial and economic management and its cultural substance have important effects on the conflict in Northern Ireland, intensifying the struggle between the communities.

The territorial structure of the British state and its approach to

---

[77] Cf. Peter Brooke's analogy with Cyprus, reported *Irish Times*, 8 Nov. 1989; Nicholas Fenn, British ambassador to Ireland, asserted that 'for Britain, the North is not now a colonial issue', *Irish Times*, 10 Aug. 1991.

[78] Reg Empey, 'Climate of submission', Ulster Unionist Information Institute, Issue no. 10, Feb 1993, p. 1; cf. Jim Allister, *Alienated but Unbowed: A Unionist Perspective on the Origin, Meaning and Future of the Anglo-Irish Agreement*, Carrickfergus, East Antrim DUP, 1987, p. 14.

territorial management – once functional in the empire and still functional in Great Britain – exacerbate conflict in Northern Ireland. First, the post-imperial principle of respecting the constitutional preference of the majority exacerbates communal division in Northern Ireland. The communities there are partially defined by their constitutional preference and each feels trapped and threatened by the fixed constititutional preference of the other. Given the close demographic balance, each finds in the majoritarian guarantee an added reason for maintaining communal solidarity and increasing communal demographic strength. Thus constitutional conflict feeds into communal conflict, and what might otherwise be a rational assessment of costs and benefits turns into a bitter struggle for communal power.

Second, the traditional British strategy of territorial management involves working with and through local power holders. This strategy allows the British state to insulate itself politically from Northern Ireland but it also encourages the communities to focus on power and on power struggle. During the Stormont period the British government took the Protestant community as its local ally and supported its monopoly of power. The break with this policy after 1969 did not stem simply from a penitential desire to make amends to Catholics, but from a recognition that power relations had changed and Catholics had to be accomodated. Such a strategy of territorial management encourages each community to try to maximise its power the better to harness the power of the British state to gain advantage over the other. The effect is intensified communal conflict.

Third, the strategy of working through local power relations has taken on a new and more complex form since the 1980s. British policy makers now view Northern Ireland more explicitly as the historical residue of a wider Irish conflict and the emphasis is on addressing the conflict in the island context. From this standpoint, by bringing the Southern state into the task of conflict management the British state has harnessed the power relations on the island to counter an imbalance of power in Northern Ireland – it has widened the political arena, incorporated the Irish government as local power broker and thereby provided Northern Catholics with additional support in their struggle against unionist control.

By thus reconstituting the political arena, in large part in response to nationalist pressure, the British government has contributed to the redefinition of the conflict from an internal Northern Ireland to a wider Irish one. There is every reason why this shift should alarm the Protestant community; the purpose of partition was to enable them to escape the logic of their status as a minority on the island. As British policy focuses more on the island context, partition becomes problematised and its permanence comes more into doubt. It is thus all the more important for Protestants not simply to halt further Catholic gains, but to reverse the process. Catholics respond by pressing their demands with still greater insistence.

In the economic sphere, British strategy in Northern Ireland includes a strong fair employment policy designed to equalise not just the economic opportunity of the two communities but their economic condition – to remove the unemployment differential and differences in income and status among the employed. To date, success has been limited. But both communities now feel that their just rights have been disregarded (chapter 6), and the conflict-laden meanings of economic inequality have been accentuated.

The limitations of British policy in this area owe much to weaknesses in the British economy. Policies of fair employment cannot in themselves remedy the imbalance in employment; economic expansion is also necessary.[79] But the state of the British economy does not provide a favourable context for such expansion. The public sector in Northern Ireland is already more highly developed than anywhere else in the United Kingdom and further expansion of public employment is neither economically defensible nor politically feasible. The British high-paid private service sector is regionally concentrated in south-east England, and the potential for dispersing this to Northern Ireland is very limited. British manufacturing industry is in decline even in areas which offer more promising locations to prospective employers than Northern Ireland. A strong regional development policy would help, but would be limited in its effects without a wider recovery in British industry. In the absence of a more productive local economy, the British state has expanded its role as supplier of subventions to industry, provider of public sector and security force work, and of unemployment and sickness benefits. Economic dependency has nurtured in turn a culture of dependency which prevents serious thought about alternatives.

British cultural norms and perceptions are embodied in state institutions, rituals, and administrative practices, in the authoritative norms of public discourse, in mass culture and in the very fact of union. We have seen that they function as cultural resources for the Protestant community (chapter 7); for the Catholic community it means having to struggle not just against Protestant cultural domination but against the wider British cultural context. Some of the new post-imperial and

---

[79] See R. G. Cooper, in the chairman's foreword to the FEC, *Annual Review 1992–3: The Year in Summary*, p. 3.

pluralist themes in British culture challenge the meanings some Protestants ascribe to 'Britishness' and point to ways in which Catholics and Protestants in Northern Ireland can find cultural common ground; they are the point of departure for Catholic unionism and for some of the current attempts to reconstruct unionism within the Protestant community. Even in Britain, however, the new themes are developing unevenly and are being articulated within a traditional cultural hierarchy. To those in Britain now preoccupied with class, regional and gender hierarchies and with the challenge of creating a public culture that can accomodate a multiracial as well as a multinational society, the different forms of communities and cultural concerns in Northern Ireland seem both anachronistic and parochial. Even the more progressive elements of British political culture, then, are easily turned to particularist use, resonating with older unionist traditions in stressing the civilising qualities of (the new) Britishness in contrast to the authoritarian, mono-lithic parochialism and backward qualities of Irishness.

It is frequently pointed out that the Britishness of unionists is not always, or even usually, recognised by the 'mainland' British. For some it is residence that disqualifies: Northern Protestants may be the descendants of British settlers in Ireland and members of the United Kingdom, but they have long resided outside the British homeland (Great Britain). For others it is political or cultural values: they may be loyal to the Crown but they do not subscribe to British norms of tolerance, fairness and compromise. For others it is ethnicity – Northern Protestants are Irish. Even for Mrs Thatcher, unionists' patriotism was 'too narrow'.[80] But while this distancing and exclusion affords Catholics some satisfaction, it feeds Protestant insecurity and makes them less, not more, willing to compromise.

Finally, both communities suffer from their subordinate status within the wider British cultural hierarchy, concretised in the accents, speech codes and habits of authority of English people exercising power in or over Northern Ireland. A shared feeling of cultural marginalisation and alienation sometimes unites Protestants and Catholics; at other times the challenge to cultural self-esteem finds an outlet in cultural intolerance towards the other community.

The British context and the prospects of conflict resolution

We have seen that the institutions and policy patterns of the British state tend to intensify communal conflict in Northern Ireland. But these are

[80] Thatcher, *Downing Street Years*, p. 385.

short-term effects. Is the British context favourable or unfavourable to the resolution of conflict in the longer term? We argue that it is ambiguous and contradictory rather than simply positive or negative and that its potentially positive aspects cannot readily be used for conflict resolution.

The British constitutional tradition is in many ways inappropriate to Northern Ireland. The virtues of the British constitution – the merging of liberal freedoms with traditional authority – presuppose social consensus. In Northern Ireland, where both Protestants and Catholics lack trust in British institutions and authority, where there is a habit of opposition to state authority rather than integration into it, and where one community (the Catholic) believes that social stability and established practices serve only the interests of the other (the Protestant), such conditions do not exist. The 'top-down' concept of sovereignty implicit in the British constitution impedes the search for radical forms of local democracy which might permit greater communal equality. On the other hand the very character of the constitution – the fact that it is unrestricted by written rules or territorial definitions, developed in an age when the distinction between domestic and colonial spheres was still fluid – facilitates potentially fruitful experimentation in Northern Ireland.

The deep-rooted structural weaknesses in the British economy make difficult fundamental economic restructuring in Northern Ireland and impede progress towards economic equality; this problem seems set to persist. On the other hand the small scale of the Northern Irish economy compared to the relatively rich and powerful British economy makes possible a high level of public funding. The EU has vast resources but cannot direct them to one small area or use them in the same way. The Republic of Ireland will never be able to mobilise the level of resources available to the much larger British state and has yet to demonstrate that a more autonomous local or island based economic strategy offers a real alternative to the economic benefits of the union.

We have seen that British culture is changing, that new critical, pluralist and post-imperial themes are emerging which may in time offer a more egalitarian set of cultural norms and identities on which both communities in Northern Ireland can draw. On the other hand the pace of change is slow and its pattern is not all one way – as we saw, imperial themes enjoyed a recovery in the 1980s after the relative egalitarianism of the 1960s and 1970s.

It is possible that the positive elements may strengthen in the future. Constitutional revision may become more radical – it may lead to a displacement of traditional authority (and the monarchy) from its central role, a view of the people rather than the Crown in Parliament as sovereign, a stress on popular democracy and it may open up new opportunities for local political restructuring. The economy may renew itself. The imperial legacy may finally give way to an egalitarian, open and inclusivist notion of Britishness which, while different from Irishness, would no longer be oppositional to it. A more positive approach to European integration and a regionalised United Kingdom within a federal EU would open up further political possibilities for Northern Ireland. But all of this is for the long term, if at all.

There is a further, ultimately more serious, problem. Even if these changes were to occur there is no guarantee that their positive potential would be realised in Northern Ireland. The British context has to be understood not simply in its own terms but relationally – in respect of its meaning and function in Northern Ireland. The communal conflict is in large measure *about* the British context – whether the British connection should exist at all, and in what form. Moreover, each community is orientated to that context not with a view to harnessing its potential to moderate the conflict but to advance its own interests. That tendency alone will be sufficient to counterbalance the potentially beneficial effects of the changes discussed above. Paradoxically, the full potential of the British context to improve relations in Northern Ireland can only be realised when the intensity of conflict has been reduced and the conditions of conflict are being dismantled by other means and in other arenas.

9   The Republic of Ireland and the conflict in Northern Ireland

In contrast to Britain – a post-imperial state adjusting to its decline from world economic and political preeminence – the Republic of Ireland is a post-colonial state seeking to overcome the legacy of the past and to realise its foundational goals. We look at the ways in which it has conceived and pursued its national project, at the changes in its public culture and in attitudes to partition. Finally we look at the ways in which Southern society, culture and politics impact on the conflict in the North and the potential that exists within the Irish context for resolving the conflict.

Independent Ireland's national project

From its foundation, the policies of the Southern Irish state were framed within a consciously pursued national project which had wide public support. The goal was to establish political, cultural and economic independence from Britain, to protect and develop a distinctive Irish culture, to develop the economy and to secure a respected place for Ireland in the international community of nations. The project had a decolonising and a modernising aspect. The decolonising strand sought to dismantle the British legacy in Ireland and to build a new and authentically Irish state and society; the modernising strand sought to develop Ireland as a modern society fully in line with contemporary Western European norms. The two sets of goals usually harmonised but could conflict – for example, if decolonisation demanded distance from Britain, modernisation frequently demanded close contact. Emphases and priorities within the project, and the degree of commitment to it, differed between groups and over time. Decolonisation was given priority during the first decades of the new state; in the 1960s the emphasis shifted to modernisation. The drive to modernise continues, but there is also concern to complete the task of decolonisation.[1]

[1] Works which stress the continued importance of the colonial legacy include: Raymond Crotty, *Ireland in Crisis: A Study in Capitalist Colonial Undevelopment*, Dingle,

The initial conditions for the pursuit of this national project were less than favourable. Irish nationalists had a long tradition of constitutional politics and an Irish administration was already in place. But they had no direct experience of the process of government and the new state was almost bankrupted by the civil war. The economy had long been a structurally peripheralised region of the British Isles, with very limited industry and a banking system that served mainly to channel funds to British financial markets. Its population had been falling for more than seventy years; moderate levels of income per head and social stability were made possible by high levels of emigration.

British cultural influence on Ireland had gone very deep. The public and political sphere had been anglicised for centuries, English was the only serviceable language for the vast majority of the people, the country's institutions and legal system had all been fashioned according to English models. The social agents of the anticipated cultural trans-formation – the Catholic middle and lower-middle classes – had a distinctive culture, but one which had developed in a partly assimilatory, partly reactive way within a British dominated public sphere (chapter 2). The consensus on national aims was considerable but far from total; the civil war and the divisions that followed reflected real ideological dif-ferences about the society's goals and how they should be pursued.[2] There were well-established vested interests – the Catholic church, property owners, the Gaelic revival movements – with their own agendas which sometimes harmonised, sometimes conflicted with the national one.

Independence and a distinctive Irish culture

The new state fell far short of the republic originally intended by the revolutionaries. It had dominion status within the British Common-wealth; its formal head of state was the king; it had a Crown appointed

Brandon, 1986; John Waters, *A Race of Angels: Ireland and the Genesis of U2*, Belfast, Blackstaff Press, 1994; Desmond Fennell, *The State of the Nation: Ireland since the Sixties*, Swords, Ward River Press, 1983; Declan Kiberd, 'The elephant of revolution-ary forgetfulness', in Máirín Ní Dhonnchadha and Theo Dorgan, eds., *Revising the Rising*, Derry, Field Day, 1991; for a discussion of related issues, see Joseph Ruane, 'Colonial legacies and cultural reflexivities', *Études Irlandaises* (Numéro hors série), 1994.

2 Tom Garvin, *The Evolution of Irish Nationalist Politics*, Dublin, Gill and Macmillan, 1981, chs. 9–12; J. Prager, *Building Democracy in Ireland: Political Order and Cultural Integration in a Newly Independent State*, Cambridge, Cambridge University Press, 1986; Richard Sinnott, 'Interpretations of the Irish party system', *European Journal of Political Research*, vol. 12, 1984.

governor-general; elected representatives were required to take an oath of allegiance to the Crown; the constitution provided for appeal (in limited circumstances) from the Irish Supreme Court to the Privy Council; the British retained garrisons in three ports. The Cumann na nGaedheal governments of the 1920s worked to widen the freedom attendant on dominion status at the commonwealth conferences of 1926 and 1930, facilitating the more radical removal of the constitutional trappings of Britishness in the 1930s by De Valera.[3]

In the six years that followed his accession to power De Valera abolished the oath of allegiance to the Crown, removed the right of appeal to the British Privy Council, reduced the power of the governor-general and then abolished the position, relocated Ireland's relationship to the Crown and Commonwealth in the sphere of Ireland's foreign policy, drafted a new constitution without consultation with Britain and negotiated British withdrawal from the ports.[4] The achievement of full sovereignty was expressed and symbolised by Ireland's decision to remain neutral during the Second World War. The final severing of constitutional links with Britain took place in 1949 with the declaration of a Republic and departure from the commonwealth.

In other respects the new state remained within the British political orbit and British politics were a constant point of reference. There were constitutional innovations but the basic model was British: cabinet government, common law, a majoritarian political culture. Yet the Irish system gradually acquired its own unique features and the Irish political and administrative class developed a firm sense of its autonomy and power. If Britain has remained the principal external model for legislation and institutional reform this is due more to institutional similarities between the two political systems and established channels of communication than to a psychology of dependence. Anglo-Irish relations remain at the centre of Irish foreign policy concerns, but for practical political and economic reasons, and as part of an extensive network of foreign policy arenas created by EU membership, wide-ranging trading contacts and participation in international bodies.

The new government quickly established the institutions and instruments of an independent economy, but the task of reducing the structural and financial links between the Irish and British economies

---

[3] Nicholas Mansergh, *The Unresolved Question: The Anglo-Irish Settlement and its Undoing 1912–1972*, London, Yale University Press, 1991, pp. 268–307.
[4] *Ibid.*, chs. 13, 14.

was more difficult.[5] At the time of independence the Irish economy was little more than a region within the wider British one: 90 per cent of its exports and almost 70 per cent of its imports were to or from Britain; only 10 per cent of the population was employed in manufacturing industry.[6] The protected nature of European agricultural markets and the proximity and openness of the British market militated against any immediate search for new export markets. The development of new industry was limited by the small size of the domestic market and weaknesses in infrastructure; the dependence of existing industry on exports raised doubts about industrialisation behind tariff barriers. Concern about the international standing of the new currency led to the maintenance of strict parity with sterling.

A more determined effort to reduce dependence was made in the 1930s. The government embarked on a policy of self-sufficiency, seeking to build an indigenous industrial sector behind tariff barriers. The policy had some success – industrial employment grew by an average of 6 per cent per year and industrial output increased – but did not change the fundamental relationships.[7] Agricultural output declined and employment in the economy as a whole fell.[8] The tariffs damaged the older export-oriented industries; the new industrial sector (in which there was substantial British involvement) exported little, and that mainly to Britain.[9] By the end of the 1950s the British market still took 75 per cent of Irish exports; Britain remained the key destination for Irish emigrants; Irish currency was still pegged to sterling; Irish trade union and business practices remained heavily influenced by British models.

Change came in the 1960s. Irish tariff barriers were lowered and foreign investment was actively pursued. In time the United States became the main source of foreign investment and multinationals in

---

[5] Basil Chubb, *The Government and Politics of Ireland*, 3rd edn, London, Longman, 1992, pp. 227–32; Ronan Fanning, *The Irish Department of Finance 1922–58*, Dublin, Institute of Public Administration, 1978; Brian Girvin, *Between Two Worlds: Politics and Economy in Independent Ireland*, Dublin, Gill and Macmillan, 1989, ch. 2.

[6] Kieran A. Kennedy, 'The context of economic development', in John H. Goldthorpe and Christopher T. Whelan, eds., *The Development of Industrial Society in Ireland*, Proceedings of the British Academy, 79, Oxford, Oxford University Press, 1992, pp. 10–11; James Meenan, *The Irish Economy since 1922*, Liverpool, Liverpool University Press, 1970, p. 76; J. J. Lee, *Ireland 1912–1985: Politics and Society*, Cambridge, Cambridge University Press, 1989, pp. 109–11; Lars Mjøset, *The Irish Economy in a Comparative Institutional Perspective*, Dublin, National Economic and Social Council, 1992, p. 113, table 6.2.

[7] Kieran A. Kennedy, Thomas Giblin and Deirdre McHugh, *The Economic Deveolopment of Ireland in the Twentieth Century*, London, Routledge, 1988, p. 47.

[8] Meenan, *Irish Economy*, pp. 41, 52.

[9] Kennedy, Giblin and McHugh, *Economic Development*, pp. 44ff.

Ireland produced for world markets. The proportion of Ireland's exports going to Britain fell rapidly, from 75 per cent in 1960 to 35 per cent in 1988.[10] From the 1970s the EU emerged as a critical arena of political and economic decision-making. The link with sterling was broken when Ireland joined the European Monetary System in 1979. A significant minority of Irish emigrants now go to EU countries rather than to Britain.

The new state set out to nurture a distinctive Irish culture. The formal symbols of Britishness in the public domain – the national anthem, the Union Jack, statues, monuments, some street and town names – were removed and replaced by Irish equivalents. It was a gradual process – a statue of Queen Victoria was still in position in front of Dáil Éireann in the 1940s – but was more or less complete by the end of the 1940s. Most of the cultural effort centred on the revival of the Irish language through the schools. Irish was made a compulsory subject with the hope that soon all education would take place through Irish. The policy was resisted by teachers on general educational grounds and was later scaled down. The numbers reporting an ability to speak Irish increased in successive censuses but competence varied and the numbers of native speakers continued to fall, from about 200,000 in 1922 to 100,000 in 1939 to 50,000 in 1964.[11] A new history curriculum replaced the previous emphasis on Britain and the empire with a focus on Ireland, and to a lesser extent Europe (minus England); there was also a practice (encouraged by the primacy given to the Irish language) of downgrading English literature relative to Irish and other international literatures.[12]

Gaelic games were promoted as the national games, but in fact needed no official support. Irish music and dance did less well against British and American imports; despite clerical condemnations, the new music and dance forms spread rapidly from the 1920s. Consumption of English and American books, periodicals and films was high; censorship kept out those that had sexually explicit content but most of what was produced during this period had little such content to begin with. In business practice, public administration, scholarship, architecture and fashion, British influence was very strong.[13]

[10] Kennedy, 'Context of economic development', pp. 11–12.
[11] Lee, *Ireland*, p. 134.
[12] John Coolahan, *Irish Education: Its History and Structure*, Dublin, Institute of Public Administration, 1981, pp. 38ff., 75; D. H. Akenson, *A Mirror to Kathleen's Face: Education in Independent Ireland 1922–1960*, Montreal, McGill-Queens University Press, 1975, chs. 3, 8.
[13] Lee, *Ireland*, pp. 89–90, 92–3, 105, 260–1; Terence Brown, *Ireland: A Social and Cultural History 1922–79*, Glasgow, Fontana, 1981, p. 206.

There have been important changes in the cultural arena since the 1960s. The internationalisation of the economy, increased travel and the development of mass communications have increased exposure to outside cultures. American and continental European influence has grown considerably. At the same time British influence remains deep and pervasive. American influence is mediated and partially offset by a perception of the United States as a distant and fantastical place with only tangential bearing on people's immediate situation. The EU is an important channel of cultural influence, but continental Europe is still an exotic terrain and the language barriers are formidable. In contrast, and despite ambivalence, the relationship with England remains close and multistranded.

There is now less concern at governmental level with promoting a distinctively Irish culture. The government offers material and moral support for 'Irish' cultural activities but more in response to public demand and the need to support the arts than as a deliberate policy of promoting the 'national' culture. Indeed it is difficult to see in government policy today any overall view of – or even interest in – what Irish culture is or should be. The government's retreat from this area does not imply a diminished public preoccupation with Irish culture or with questions of identity. On the contrary, public concern with such matters has grown.[14]

Finally, there has been a move away from fixed notions of Irish culture to exploring what it could be or may be in process of becoming. The most striking example is Irish soccer, once the symbol of all that was 'non-Irish'. Today the Irish international soccer team – half-Irish half-English with an English manager – is taken to symbolise the world-wide spread of the Irish people, the rediscovery of the children of past emigrants and their discovery of their homeland, and, more contentiously, the transition from a 32 to a 26 county nationalism.[15] The team's supporters – depicted as passionate, fun-loving, carousing but well behaved – are thought to present the face of modern Ireland to the world – warm, likeable, responsible, internationalist – an example to all other countries, and especially to England.

[14] An Coiste Comhairleach Planála/The Advisory Planning Committee, *The Irish Language in a Changing Society*, Dublin, Bord na Gaeilge, 1986, chs. 2, 9.
[15] Dermot Bolger, 'In High Germany', in D. Bolger, *A Dublin Quartet*, Harmondsworth/London, Penguin, 1992; Michael Holmes, 'Symbols of national identity and sport: the case of the Irish football team', *Irish Political Studies*, vol. 9, 1994, pp. 95–7.

Economic development

The new state started with some economic strengths. Income per head was average by international standards, the infrastructure was relatively developed and the state was a net creditor. But the main industry – agriculture – was low-input/low-output in form, the small manufacturing sector was based largely on food and drink, the bulk of exports consisted of agricultural commodities and went to one market. Perhaps most important, the peripheral form of this economy, which had developed alongside the most precociously capitalist economy in Europe, was deeply entrenched.

Growth in the economy was slow and uneven (Table 5). There are different assessments of this performance, but the dominant view stresses its weakness. Kieran Kennedy describes the performance for the whole period 1913 to 1987 as at best 'mediocre' with performance during the first decades particularly bad.[16] Ireland kept pace with British growth levels, but at about three-fifths the level of income per head, and the United Kingdom had 'the worst record in Europe over the period in terms of the growth both of output and output per capita'.[17] Compared to the rest of western Europe, Ireland fell seriously behind. D. S. Johnson and Liam Kennedy come to different conclusions.[18] Making different assumptions about Ireland's GDP per capita in 1913 and taking into account the rapid growth at the end of the 1980s, they conclude that in comparison with other EU countries Ireland's performance over the period 1913–91 – and for all decades within it except the 1950s – was 'modal' rather than mediocre. Viewed as a whole it is the slow growth decade of the 1950s which stands out as the aberration which depressed the measured performance of the economy for the whole period.[19] Emigration rates were high in the 1920s, considerably reduced in the 1930s, rising again in the 1940s. Since then they have been inversely proportionate to growth rates: peaking in the 1950s, slowing down in the 1960s, reversing in the 1970s, rising again in the 1980s.[20]

Whatever the assessment of Ireland's overall growth rate, there is little doubt that progress toward remedying the structural limitations of the

---

[16] Kennedy, 'Context of economic development', p. 9.
[17] Ibid., p. 7.
[18] D. S. Johnson and Liam Kennedy, 'The two economies of Ireland in the twentieth century', in T. W. Moody, F. X. Martin, F. J. Byrne and W. E. Vaughan, eds., *A New History of Ireland*, vol. VII, Oxford, Oxford University Press (forthcoming).
[19] Ibid.
[20] Kennedy, Giblin and McHugh, *Economic Development*, p. 140, table 7.1.

Table 5. *Average Annual Growth Rates, Republic of Ireland*

	Total real product	Real product per capita
1926–38	1.3	1.4
1938–50	1.1	1.0
1950–60	1.7	2.2
1960–73	4.4	3.8
1973-85	1.7	0.5

Source: Kennedy, Giblin and McHugh, *The Economic Development of Ireland*, table 8.2, pp 118–19.

economy was slow. Investment in Irish agriculture was growing from the early 1950s but it remained a low-input/low-output system; an indigenous industrial sector grew up behind tariff barriers from the 1930s and imports from Britain had declined, but the new industry was inefficient and had little capacity for export or further growth; in 1950, 80 per cent of Irish exports still consisted of agricultural commodities; 87 per cent of Irish exports still went to the British market; the population continued to fall.[21]

After 1960, some of the structural problems of the economy were overcome, in particular dependence 'on one slowly-growing market (the UK) and on one slowly-growing product (food)' and weaknesses in managerial and industrial skills.[22] Industrial output expanded and became more diversified. Exports of manufactures grew from 19 per cent of total exports in 1960 to 64 per cent in 1985.[23] But new problems have emerged. Irish agriculture is now heavily dependent on EU supports. The indigenous industry established behind tariff barriers failed to adapt to free trade conditions and attempts to foster new indigenous industry in the 1980s have met with limited success. Most of the expansion in industrial exports has come from foreign firms which have been attracted to Ireland by generous grants and tax rebates, repatriate their profits and have limited linkages to the rest of the economy.[24]

Rapid expansion in public expenditure after 1973 was unsustained by growth in the economy or taxation and led to a dramatic increase in

[21] Kennedy, 'Context of economic development, p. 12; Desmond A. Gillmor, *Economic Activities in the Republic of Ireland: A Geographical Perspective*, Dublin, Gill and Macmillan, 1985, pp. 20–2.
[22] Kennedy, 'Context of economic development', p. 22.
[23] Kennedy, Giblin and McHugh, *Economic Development*, pp. 184–5.
[24] *Ibid*, pp. 239–41.

government borrowing. The ratio of national debt to GNP went from 54.5 per cent in 1973 to 142.2 per cent in 1986.[25] It has since fallen to about 96 per cent (1994) but servicing the debt remains a serious drain on public resources. The rate of unemployment increased from 5.2 per cent in 1972 to over 17 per cent in the mid-1980s where it has since hovered.[26] The fall in the birth rate in the 1980s is expected to bring down the unemployment rate, but not until the next century.[27] The expense of financing both debt and unemployment has restricted further the scope for state action to promote development. This has increased dependence on EU funding which, in the late 1980s, represented close to 7 per cent of GNP. The future of such transfers is now uncertain while competitive pressures are increasing in the single market.[28]

A place among the nations

There is a widespread view of the new state as inward-looking in the decades after independence. The image is in many ways misleading. Neither society or state was isolationist by way of general principle. On the contrary, the new state was committed to playing an international role appropriate – more accurately disproportionate – to its size.[29] Its purpose was at once to realise the nationalist dream of Ireland taking its 'place among the nations' and to pursue specific policy goals – the consolidation of Ireland's independence, the enhancement of national prestige, an end to partition, economic benefits. The Irish government played an important role in the British Commonwealth during the 1920s and participated actively in the League of Nations from 1921. Wartime neutrality and the refusal to become part of NATO reflected specific concerns (internal stability, partition, the dangers of military alliances) rather than a general isolationism. Ireland applied for membership of the United Nations in 1946, was a member of the OEEC from 1948 and

---

25 *Ibid.*, p. 89; Mjøset, *Irish Economy*, p. 383.
26 Richard Breen, Damian F. Hannan, David B. Rottman and Christopher T. Whelan, *Understanding Contemporary Ireland: State, Class and Development in the Republic of Ireland*, Dublin, Gill and Macmillan, 1990, p. 144.
27 Cf. Kennedy, 'Context of economic development', p. 23.
28 Revenues under the CAP represented almost 5 per cent of GNP in 1987; ERDF represented 5.6 per cent of the Irish public capital programme the same year; structural funds in 1987 were less than half a percent of GNP but the increased structural funds from 1989–93 can be estimated at around 2–3 per cent of GNP; Rory O'Donnell, 'Regional policy', in Patrick Keatinge, ed., *Ireland and EC Membership Evaluated*, London, Pinter, 1991, pp. 66–8.
29 Patrick Keatinge, *A Place among the Nations: Issues of Irish Foreign Policy*, Dublin, Institute of Public Administration, 1978.

the Council of Europe from 1949 and joined the UN in 1955. The policy of neutrality remains, but Irish soldiers have played a part in UN peace-keeping operations since 1960.

Ireland's international role has further expanded since 1960.[30] The internationalisation of the economy entailed a corresponding increase in supportive diplomatic and consular activity. Membership of the EU brings government ministers and the higher echelons of the civil service into close contact with their opposite numbers in other member states. The Irish government holds in rotation the presidency of the Council of Ministers. The outbreak of conflict in Northern Ireland led to closer links with the British government and, from the 1980s, the United States government. The Irish government has continued its role in UN peace-keeping forces and in international aid. In line with such developments, the current president – Mary Robinson – has maintained a high international profile.

The increased external orientation of Irish society is not limited to government. Irish farmers and industrialists are highly conscious of developments in the international economy; a small number of Irish firms have themselves become multinationals. Irish human rights and environmental groups are integrated into international networks. People in general, the young in particular, participate in a global media-based culture. Irish sports and music stars aspire to success at an international level. Irish writers stress the international context of their work. Irish aid agencies are active in many parts of the world, often following in the steps of Irish missionaries of the past. The resurgence of emigration in the 1980s has renewed Irish ethnic communities abroad and the Irish self-perception as a diaspora community.

The 'success' of independence

Internal judgements on the success of (Southern) Irish independence vary enormously and the public culture is at once volatile and self-critical. There is pride in the fact that the new state survived a bitter civil war and achieved stability and democracy, in contrast to other new European states which emerged in the post-1918 period or more recent post-colonial states. On the other hand there is frequent criticism of the present political system. The criticisms tend to be ones commonly applied to western liberal democracies (an over-extended state, a lack of public accountability, a lack of political principle, corruption) which in

---

[30] Paul Sharp, *Irish Foreign Policy and the European Community: A Study of the Impact of Interdependence on the Foreign Policy of a Small State*, Aldershot, Dartmouth, 1990.

Ireland are seen as symptoms of a distinctively Irish malaise. The state of the economy receives more attention and more criticism. The 1980s were a traumatic decade with mounting unemployment, public indebtedness, renewed emigration and a growing realisation that many of the problems thought solved in the 1960s and 1970s remained. The 1990s have brought a return to growth, cautious optimism, predictions of long-term improvement and of convergence with other EU states. But for the moment the perception is of an economy with deep-rooted problems. In the cultural domain, there is pride in the vigour and resilence of Irish literature, drama, music and (more recently) dance and in the emergence of greater openness and pluralism, but concern about the survival of a distinctive Irish culture in the longer term.

Few believe that the potential of independence was fully realised, but there is no regret that it was fought for and achieved and there is no support for reversing the process.[31] Nor is there evidence of a general desire to reproduce the dependence of the British years within the European Union.[32] The Irish record among the highest scores for national pride in the EU,[33] the fundamental thrust of the culture remains nationalist and realising the potential of independence remains the underlying goal of public policy. From that standpoint at least, independence has been a complete success.

Religion, nationalism and the changing public culture

Catholicism and nationalism pervaded the public culture during the first decades of the new state. The boundaries of the dominant political and religious communities – the Irish nation, the Catholic people – coincided; the Protestant minority, British in identity and unionist in politics, was on the margins. All the churches were confirmed in their control over areas in which they claimed special competence, particularly education, but it was the social teaching and moral guidelines of the Catholic church which were reflected in legislation and in the 1937 constitution. The Eucharistic Congress of 1932 was a celebration of both national and religious deliverance. Catholic bishops and clergy enjoyed social prominence, their pronouncements were treated with respect by political leaders and reported extensively in the newspapers; their Protestant counterparts kept a low profile. In the one serious clash

---

[31] Micheál MacGréil, *Irish Political Attitudes and Opinions*, Maynooth, Survey and Research Unit, St Patrick's College, 1992, p. 32, table 16, question 7.

[32] *Ibid.*, p. 79, table 34, questions 2, 4.

[33] Michael Fogarty, Liam Ryan and Joseph Lee, *Irish Values and Attitudes: The Irish Report of the European Value Systems Study*, Dublin, Dominican, 1984, p. 157, table 13b.

between Catholic church and government during this period – the Mother-and-Child Scheme – the government backed down.[34]

Catholicism was as prominent in the popular as in the official domain. These were years of intense public and private Catholic devotionalism. Religious activity was more or less constant – processions, the honouring of saints' feast days, parish retreats, public and family rosaries, confraternities, the building of shrines to the Blessed Virgin, collections for the Catholic missions overseas, the placing of pictures of the Sacred Heart and statues of the Blessed Virgin and saints in the home, pilgrimages to Knock, Lourdes and Fatima. The high ratio of clergy and nuns to laity was visible not simply in the official statistics but at almost all public gatherings.

Nationalism exercised a similar dominance over the public sphere and affairs of state. All the leading politicians were veterans (or relatives of veterans) of the war of independence. Their political speeches and commemoration ceremonies stressed the dark days of the past, and celebrated the years of freedom struggle and the final victory. National and local newspapers reported their activities and speeches. Newspapers, books, pamphlets and the folk tradition recounted episodes from the past – the famine, evictions, attacks on landlords, the land war, the war of independence. Statues and memorials were erected throughout the country. A determined effort was made to revive the Irish language. The primary political cleavage derived from a division within the nationalist movement, and party competition worked within nationalist assumptions.[35]

The strength of Catholicism and nationalism rested in part on the overwhelmingly rural and small town nature of the society. Over half of the country's workforce was employed in agriculture in 1920 and over a third in 1960; over two-thirds lived in rural areas in 1926 and over half in 1961.[36] It was a period of rapid constitutional and institutional development but much of the substance of everyday life centred on more private and local issues – family, work (or the lack of it) and community – and was lived within local boundaries. For a large majority, their understanding of the world and their response to developments at national level were mediated by the nature of the society in which they lived – local, rural, familial, familiar.

[34] J. H. Whyte, *Church and State in Modern Ireland 1923–1970*, Dublin, Gill and Macmillan, 1971, especially chs. 2, 7, 8.
[35] Garvin, *Evolution of Irish Nationalist Politics*, chs. 9, 10; Richard Sinnott, 'Interpretations of the Irish party system'.
[36] Mjøset, *Irish Economy*, p. 114, table 6.2; Meenan, *Irish Economy*, pp. 184–5, table 6.2 (rural areas = less than 1,500 population.)

Clerical dominance met little resistance in small-scale family-centred rural communities where Catholic views on marriage and sexuality were in close harmony with the requirements of a family-farm economy. Nationalists could more easily disseminate their view of Irish history and current policies in communities where long folk memories kept ancient religious and ethnic grievances alive. But the role of elites must not be exaggerated and the strength of Catholicism and nationalism cannot be accounted for by limited horizons, domination or manipulation; both were firmly rooted in popular sentiment and would survive, in modified form, the transition to a new kind of society in the 1960s.

The position of Southern Protestants during the early period was very difficult. The years of the Anglo-Irish conflict and civil war had been traumatic and large numbers of Protestants left for the North or Britain immediately after independence, some by choice, some as part of military withdrawal and administrative reorganisation. As a proportion of the population of the 26 counties, Protestants fell from over 10 per cent to 8 per cent between 1911 and 1926 and to 5 per cent by 1961.[37] Those who remained retreated into a separate world of family and friends from which Catholics were largely excluded.

Southern Protestants were internally differentiated – Bowen distinguishes farmers and rural townsmen, 'West Britons', the lower and middle classes of the cities, and identifies Protestants in the three Ulster counties as a distinct group.[38] But they shared some common concerns. One was demographic. Between 1926 and 1961 the Church of Ireland fell from 5.5 per cent to 3.7 per cent of a total population that had itself decreased by 5 per cent since 1926.[39] The main source of the decline was emigration. Protestant emigration rates in the post-war period were lower than those of Catholics but the effects on a scattered and demographically fragile community were more serious. It was further aggravated by a low marriage rate (uncompensated, as among Catholics, by very high fertility rates) and from the 1940s by a rising rate of marriage to Catholics, around 16 per cent in 1961.[40]

By and large, Protestants did not feel oppressed, but they felt politically and culturally marginalised. They had a British identity and allegiance and had been unionist in politics. The new state was nationalist, committed to removing all remaining vestiges of Britishness

---

[37] K. Theodore Hoppen, *Ireland since 1800: Conflict and Conformity*, London, Longman, 1989, p. 241.
[38] Kurt Bowen, *Protestants in a Catholic State: Ireland's Privileged Minority*, Dublin, Gill and Macmillan, 1983, ch. 7.
[39] *Ibid.*, p. 21.
[40] *Ibid.*, pp. 29–31, 40–1.

from its public life and to re-Gaelicisation. The reaction of most Protestants was to insulate themselves from the new political and cultural order and to keep the expression of their views to the private realm.[41] They could not do so completely and the policy on the Irish language was a particular source of grievance.[42] The tensions softened only as nationalist political rhetoric and the policy of re-Gaelicisation moderated, and Protestants moved away from a British identity and allegiance to a cultural and political identity as Protestant Irish.

State support to Protestant schools and hospitals was relatively generous, but in other respects the political climate was inhospitable. The provisions in the constitution of 1922 which promised to protect Protestant interests (large constituencies, executive appointments to the Senate, the possibility of appeal from the Irish Supreme Court to the British Privy Council) were eroded over time or abolished. Much of the new state's legislation echoed Catholic moral and social teaching; the preamble to the constitution of 1937 implicitly identified the Irish people as Catholic and nationalist. Particular events highlighted Protestant vulnerability. In 1932 the appointment of a Protestant as county librarian in Mayo was opposed by the local council on religious grounds and the person was transferred to Dublin. In 1952 the Supreme Court declared the commitment made under the Catholic church's *Ne Temere* decree – the written promise by a Protestant married to a Catholic to rear the children as Catholic – to be legally binding.

Protestants had however one very important resource – their privileged position within the economy. They were disproportionately represented in the professions, among large farmers and in the private sectors of finance and industry, particularly its higher echelons.[43] They sought to maintain their privileged position in these domains by direct and indirect discrimination in favour of their own community.[44] Catholics objected to the more blatant forms of discrimination and complained privately about its less blatant forms, but took no legislative or political action against it. They concentrated their attention on the new positions opening up in the state from which Protestants by and large kept their distance.

From the 1960s the ideological certainties and consensus of the first decades of the state were dissolving. The public culture remained Catholic and nationalist, but became more liberal in tone and style; it

---

[41] *Ibid.*, ch. 3, esp. pp. 58–9.
[42] Akenson, *Mirror to Kathleen's Face*, ch. 8; Bowen, *Protestants in a Catholic State*, pp. 59–60.
[43] R. F. Foster, *Modern Ireland 1600–1972*, London, Penguin, 1988, p. 534.
[44] Bowen, *Protestants in a Catholic State*, pp. 96–103.

also became more contested. The change had socio-structural roots. Between 1961 and 1985 the numbers employed in agriculture more than halved.[45] Ireland became an urban society, increasingly socially differentiated. The middle class (upper and lower) expanded from 23.2 per cent of the (male working) population in 1961 to 38.9 per cent in 1985, with the more rapid rate of expansion at the higher level.[46] The state underwent rapid expansion in both numbers employed and economic importance; total public expenditure expanded from 32 per cent of GNP in 1960 to 67 per cent in 1985.[47] The advent of television and changes in radio amounted to a revolution in public broadcasting; newspapers became much more important as vehicles of public criticism.

These changes coincided with a succession of new developments which challenged the old Catholic nationalist order: the Second Vatican Council and the decline in religious vocations, the opening up of the Irish economy, the collapse of the Northern Ireland state and the onset of endemic paramilitary violence, the entry into the European Economic Community, the unprecedented increase in the level of unemployment and in the national debt, the emergence of a class of 'super-rich' and a large affluent middle class alongside considerable poverty, the pressure of the feminist movement, changes in family and sexual behaviour, the politicisation of issues of sexuality, contraception, abortion and divorce. Political and religious elites became more divided, the public sphere more fragmented and contentious. The ideological effect was a clear differentiation of Catholicism and nationalism, with each fragmenting internally.[48]

Traditional Irish Catholicism is today very much a residual and international developments in Catholicism – liberal, neo-conservative, radical – are amply reflected in religious life. An increasingly vocal anti-clerical and secularising tendency has also emerged. Within the church itself, divisions have emerged between the hierarchy and more liberal clerics and religious orders, and between the clergy and the laity, with women – lay and religious – playing an increasingly important role in criticising traditional and neo-conservative forms of religion. These religious struggles are partially overlain by an emergent feminist consciousness

---

[45] Breen, Hannan, Rottman and Whelan, *Understanding Contemporary Ireland*, p. 57, table 3.2.

[46] *Ibid.*, p. 57, table 3.2.

[47] Kennedy, Giblin and McHugh, *Economic Development*, p. 87.

[48] See Joseph Ruane, 'Secularization and ideology in the Republic of Ireland', in Paul Brennan, ed., *La sécularisation de l'Irlande*, Caen, forthcoming. See also Liam O'Dowd, 'Intellectuals and the national question in Ireland', in Graham Day and Gareth Rees, eds., *Regions, Nations and European Integration: Remaking the Celtic periphery*, Cardiff, University of Wales Press, 1991.

which is strongly opposed to traditionalist and neo-conservative Catholicism.

Nationalism has also differentiated. Traditional nationalism has given way to a more liberal variant which has now the greatest claim to being the dominant ideology; it retains the foundational goals of the state (including Irish reunification), but pursues them in a modernising, moderate, realistic, pragmatic and outward looking way. There is also 'revisionism', harshly critical of traditional nationalism (though national-ist in many of its underlying assumptions) and of the policies of the post-independent state and Catholic church; it seeks root-and-branch reform in a 26-county context, including a more secular – or at least pluralist – public sphere. Revisionism has in turn produced its own reactions in the form of neo-traditional and decolonising nationalisms. Other ideological tendencies (themselves internally differentiated) now cross-cut the national and religious ones – feminism, socialism and ecologism. Public ideological debate has been intense and frequently bitter.

Catholicism and nationalism – in their more liberal variants – remain the dominant ideologies and retain strong institutional power bases. The Catholic church possesses a formidable communications system through the local parish, weekly sermons and high (though falling) levels of attendance at mass. It retains control over most of the school system and, despite the falling numbers of clergy and nuns, has resisted government pressure to loosen its grip. Nationalism is embedded in the party system, in national cultural organisations, in school curricula and – most of all – in the very existence of the state itself.

The public sphere is, however, much less pervaded by Catholic and nationalist symbols than before. Public forms of Catholic religious expression continue – the Angelus on RTÉ radio and television, public processions, the reporting of the pronouncements of bishops – but on a lesser scale. The last great public celebration of the struggle for Irish independence was in 1966. The change is in part a shift from the public to the private domain – the public devotional concept of Catholicism has given way to a more private and family-centred one; a similar reticence has grown up about the expression of nationalist sentiments. There is a new unease and uncertainty towards nationalism and Catholicism, in part an effect of the conflict in Northern Ireland, in part of wider international developments, including European integration.[49] Some

---

[49] Michael P. Hornsby-Smith, 'Social and religious transformation in Ireland: a case of secularisation?', in Goldthorpe and Whelan, eds., *Development of Industrial Society*; Joseph Ruane, 'Ireland, European integration and the dialectic of nationalism and post-nationalism', *Études Irlandaises*, vol. 19, no. 1, 1994.

now see Catholicism and nationalism as symbols of a backwardness and cultural oppressiveness that took over when the British left, if not before. Southern Protestant numbers continued to fall during the 1960s, recovered somewhat during the 1970s, and declined again during the 1980s.[50] Emigration remained an important source of decline but the primary cause now appears to be intermarriage. The rate of intermarriage increased very rapidly from the 1960s despite the efforts of parents and clergy to prevent it. By 1979 estimates of the numbers of Protestants marrying Catholics were as high as 40 per cent.[51] The Catholic church no longer asks Protestants who marry Catholics to promise to rear the children as Catholic, but requires the Catholic partner to promise to try to ensure that.

The protected Protestant economic and social world has been substantially eroded. Some Protestant firms failed; others merged with Catholic ones or were taken over by outside firms, bringing to an end the discriminatory practices of the past.[52] Protestant schools, social and sports clubs have opened up to Catholic participation or have merged with Catholic ones.[53] Trinity College, Dublin, has become increasingly Catholic in its student body and staff; its first Catholic provost was appointed in 1991; since the 1970s its representatives on the Senate have included Catholics. The *Irish Times* changed its profile in the 1960s from a largely Protestant to a mixed Protestant–Catholic newspaper; its first Catholic editor was appointed in 1986. Protestants are effective in pressure group politics when important interests are at stake, particularly in education and health. But very few are active in party politics, and those who are do not seek to represent Protestants as a distinct group in the society.

The opening up of previously sheltered Protestant sectors is due in part to the fall in Protestant numbers and problems of viability. It is also due to a considerable improvement in Catholic–Protestant relations. Changes in Catholicism since Vatican II have softened religious divisions. The emergence of a liberal and pluralist nationalism open to both communities has moderated political division. The growth in the numbers and self-confidence of the Catholic middle class has reduced status tensions. There has also been a conscious effort to improve relations, not least to show the people of Northern Ireland and beyond how much better interdenominational relations are regulated in the

---

[50] Hoppen, *Ireland Since 1800*, p. 241; Bowen, *Protestants in a Catholic State*, pp. 25ff.
[51] *Ibid.*, p. 42.
[52] *Ibid.*, ch. 4.
[53] *Ibid.*, chs. 6, 7; F. S. L. Lyons, 'The minority problem in the 26 counties', in Francis MacManus, ed., *The Years of the Great Test*, Cork, Mercier, 1967, pp. 92–103.

South. In practice, however, the past has not been entirely forgotten and ambivalence and cultural unease remain.

The decline in Protestant numbers, the very high level of inter-marriage, the erosion of their protected economic base and the entry of Catholics into previously guarded Protestant social domains may suggest a community on the point of disintegration. The future is more open than this implies. The Protestant ethos is being diluted but Catholic exposure to it also means enhanced Protestant cultural influence in the wider society. Important sections of the Catholic middle class aspire to values – freedom of conscience, individualism, liberalism, pluralism – which they explicitly associate with Protestantism. Much will depend on numbers; if Protestants succeed in maintaining themselves demographically their cultural influence within the South is likely to grow in the years to come.

Attitudes to Northern Ireland and the question of partition

Partition had profound implications for the form of the new Irish state. It gave it a distinct spatial, economic, demographic, religious and political profile, shaping its culture, identity, institutions and sense of community. The people of the South of Ireland emerged as an imagined community in their own right, the immediate one for most Southerners, Catholic and Protestant. However, while the previous dominant imagined communities – the island-wide ethnic community of Irish Catholics and the more pluralist 'Irish nation' – lost some of their solidarity and cohesiveness, they did not disappear. They were sustained by the activities of the churches and cultural organisations who continued to operate on an all-Ireland basis after partition as well as by the *idea* – common to Catholics and most Protestants – of Ireland as a single entity.[54] Today Southerners, like Northerners, live in multiple overlapping communities whose salience in any given situation depends on the issue. We look first at Southern Catholic, then at Southern Protestant, attitudes.

Southern Catholics

Partition bequeathed to the South a complex and contradictory legacy – Irish independence had been achieved/not achieved, the struggle with

---

[54] Duncan Morrow, 'Warranted interference? The Republic of Ireland in the politics of Northern Ireland', *Études Irlandaises*, vol. 20, no. 1, 1995, pp. 130–4.

Britain was over/not over, 'Ireland' was 26 counties/32 counties, the people of Northern Ireland were/were not 'Irish', the state was permanent/impermanent. Southern attitudes have been based on two broad assumptions which coexisted in tension. One is that nationalists, North or South, could do little (militarily or otherwise) to avoid partition or, once established, to bring it to an end. Nor was it incumbent on them to take major steps – still less to make important sacrifices – to do so. Unionists had defied the democratic wish of the Irish people as a whole and Britain had supported them. It was there that the problem lay and there that it had to be resolved.

The second assumption was that partition was damaging and destructive to the whole of Ireland and reunification would bring certain benefits. This attitude would prove surprisingly resilient. No Southern political party or authoritative body – ecclesiastical, economic, cultural – has ever publicly supported partition or argued against reunification; some newspaper columnists have begun to do so in recent years, but no newspaper has adopted this as editorial policy. Popular opinion supports this view. Despite the conflict of the past twenty-five years, opinion polls since 1970 show a fluctuating but increasing majority – in 1991, 82 per cent – having unity as an aspiration, with decreasing numbers disapproving of unity.[55] Well over a third of the Southern public has unity not just as a (low intensity) aspiration but as a policy preference, with well over half having it as a first or second policy preference.[56]

The sources of support for reunification are sometimes attributed to 'nationalist irredentism' but they are more complex and varied than that. There was a sense of pain at the sundering and rupturing of what was for nationalists the ancient and unbroken – and natural – unity of Ireland. There was also guilt at the abandonment of Northern Catholics to a state where it was quite clear they were being ill-treated. There was anger that unionists – who had made their contempt for Irish nationalism and its project unambiguously clear – had challenged them and had won and that Britain still occupied part of Ireland. But there were also pragmatic concerns, in particular the belief that the new state was weaker fiscally

[55] Peter Mair, 'Breaking the nationalist mould: the Irish Republic and the Anglo-Irish Agreement', in Paul Teague, ed., *Beyond the Rhetoric: Politics, the Economy and Social Policy in Northern Ireland*, London, Lawrence and Wishart, 1987, pp. 89–90. *Irish Times*, 23 Apr. 1991; *Irish Political Studies*, vol. 7, 1992, data section, p. 160, question 2; Mac Gréil's data show a slightly lower figure, but the questions are ambiguous as between aspiration and policy preference; see Mac Gréil, *Irish Political Attitudes*, p. 32, table 16, question 1 and 2.

[56] B. O'Leary, 'Public opinion and Northern Irish futures', *The Political Quarterly*, vol. 63, no. 2, 1992, pp. 147–8; in 1993, 41 per cent had unity as a first policy preference; *Irish Political Studies*, vol. 9, 1994, p. 210; poll by MRBI Nov. 1993.

and economically because it had been deprived of the island's traditional industrial sector. There was also partition's legacy of contradictory attitudes and orientations which was culturally and psychologically disturbing and which precluded easy relations either with Northerners or with the British.

Partition did however bring practical benefits, even if it was not easy to acknowledge this. It meant a society that was virtually homogeneous culturally and ideologically and that was spared the political and religious rancour that characterised the North. It brought a higher degree of political stability than would otherwise have been possible. The South conformed much more to the nationalist under-standing of Ireland and the Irish nation – as rural, nationalist, Catholic – than did the island as a whole and it was possible to implement a strongly nationalist programme without fear of internal resistance or external criticism. Partition also gave particular interest groups – the Catholic church, Gaelic revivalists, industrial protectionists – a degree of control over public policy they could not have had in a unified Ireland. However, it was the costs rather than the benefits of partition which exercised the public mind.

The South rejected partition but was obliged to accomodate itself to it. The government was faced with the responsibility of building a state and could not do this in a condition of permanent uncertainty about its boundaries. Nor could it long sustain the policy of Michael Collins of attempting actively to destabilise Northern Ireland; quite apart from the likely British response, the civil war showed how precarious was its own stability. There was also a psychological aspect – partition was an open wound that had to be closed. The solution the South chose was to distance itself from the North and to resist attempts by Northern nationalist politicians to involve it.[57] The strategy of distancing evoked ambivalent feelings and it was difficult to implement. But over time it became easier. The two societies went their separate ways and Southerners recognised less and less of their own experience in that of Northern Catholics.[58]

The outbreak of conflict in 1969 was contradictory in its effects. On the one hand it made Southerners much more aware of the experience and aspirations of Northern Catholics; on the other hand it revealed the difficulties each had in understanding and empathising with the other. The conflict was deeply disturbing for the South. It reopened issues –

---

[57] Clare O'Halloran, *Partition and the Limits of Irish Nationalism: An Ideology Under Stress*, Dublin, Gill and Macmillan, 1987, pp. 29–30, 95–6 and chs. 4, 5.
[58] Cf. MacGréil, *Irish Political Attitudes*, p. 23, table 12, question 1.

partition, sectarianism, the British role in Ireland – which had been put to one side rather than resolved. The violence shocked and repelled; the Arms Crisis, bombs in Dublin and Monaghan and later the hunger strikes made it clear that if more serious conflict broke out it would not be confined to the North.

The distancing of the earlier period was no longer possible but involvement or close identification were also avoided. The North was never far from the public consciousness and was a constant subject of media reporting and comment. Interest remained: the detailed survey on Southern attitudes to the conflict carried out in 1978 reported that 75 per cent of respondents declared themselves 'interested' in it.[59] Feelings about the conflict were strong; discussions about it – even among those who declared themselves indifferent – frequently became emotionally charged. But most debate was confined to the media. Foreign visitors reported their shock at how little discussion there was; Northerners visiting the South found themselves without listeners if they insisted on talking about the conflict; Southerners who revealed too serious an interest were regarded with some suspicion; there were complaints to RTÉ and to newspaper editors for giving too much coverage to Northern Ireland. By the 1980s, media interest had declined and coverage centred mainly on the violence.[60]

Public discussion, when it took place, was frequently ill-informed and stereotypes abounded. Northerners were trouble makers, backward, prone to violence, terrorists or potential terrorists, extreme and unreasonable; they were fighting a religious war or a war against the British that everyone else on the island had forgotten about.[61] The conflict between the communities had been going on for centuries and would always be there; the obvious solution was compromise, but each community was too blind, too fanatical or too much under the control of its politicians to see that. The conflict arose from the fact that Catholics had been ground down and given no rights whatever; alternatively, both communities were at fault – Protestants trapped in a 'siege mentality', Catholics forever 'whingeing' and 'whining', satisfied with nothing.

The combination of silence and ill-informed comment had a degree of

59 E. E. Davis and Richard Sinnott, *Attitudes in the Republic of Ireland Relevant to the Northern Ireland Problem*, Dublin, Economic and Social Research Institute, 1979, p. 37, table 3.
60 Brian Trench, 'In search of hope: coverage of the Northern conflict in the Dublin daily papers', in Bill Rolston, ed., *The Media and Northern Ireland: Covering the Troubles*, London, Macmillan, 1991.
61 MacGréil, *Irish Political Attitudes*, p. 29, table 14; see also the writings of newspaper columnists such as Eoghan Harris, Eamonn Dunphy and Kevin Myers.

official sanction. The government imposed restrictions on the reporting of the conflict by RTÉ in 1972; the major political parties rarely made Northern Ireland an election issue and, when in opposition, endorsed the government's broadcasting restrictions; leading politicians showed themselves little better informed about the conflict than the wider public. But there were other reasons for the inadequate public response. There was an acute awareness of having insufficient information or understanding to comment usefully on the situation. There was emotional distress at the endless killings, the funerals and the grieving of relatives. There was frustration at the apparent unwillingness to compromise when – it seemed to most – compromise was a fair and honourable solution.

More self-interestedly, there was fear of the conflict spreading South and a belief that the conflict was blocking progress on the island as a whole. There was shame at the image of Ireland that was being projected internationally. There was a sense of being morally and politically compromised by a conflict which Southerners believed was not of their making and resentment at Northern imputations that they were also to blame. Many were angry that important components in Southern nationalist identity – the celebration of 1916, rebel songs, the positive image of the war of independence, the tricolour – had become disvalued or politically suspect. There was a sense of powerlessness *vis-à-vis* the unionists and the British government, and a renewed sense of guilt about Northern Catholics. There was also guilt (as well as relief) that the South did not care more than it did about what was happening to either community in the North.

In this context it is striking that over the period the aspiration to Irish unity remained strong. Reconciliation was the priority and consent was stressed, but the aspiration remained.[62] Its continued strength was all the more impressive in the face of the arguments against unity now elaborated in the Southern media. It was argued that the aspiration was irredentist; it derived from the map image of Ireland; it was more concerned with territory than people; it was a fantasy that took no account of economic or political obstacles; it was retained for purely sentimental reasons or because there was no real prospect of its being realised; it was giving aid and comfort to the IRA and aggravating unionist fears about the future thereby exacerbating the conflict.[63]

---

[62] *Irish Political Studies*, vol. 9, 1994, p. 209, questions 1, 5; poll by MRBI Nov. 1993. An earlier poll showed that while 82 per cent hoped for Irish unity, an equal percentage were willing to postpone unity if it helped bring about an internal settlement in the North (IT/MRBI *Irish Times*, 23 Apr. 1991); see also references in footnotes 55, 56.

[63] Padraig O'Malley, *The Uncivil Wars: Ireland Today*, Belfast, Blackstaff, 1983, pp. 73ff., 96–7, 357–8; see also columnists in the *Sunday Independent*.

Why has the aspiration to unity persisted? Irredentist ideas – in particular the sense that the island is a natural unit – play some role though less now than in the past. There is also a belief that Northern Catholics will never get justice except in a united Ireland, or that the conflict will continue until unity is achieved.[64] Many believe in the economic potential of unity – the single island-wide economy that will draw on the talents and resources of the island as a whole. There are also many who, disenchanted with the fruits of Catholic nationalism, see in Irish unity the best hope for a liberal and pluralist Ireland. Others see it as a way of clearing the ground for other political agendas. Overall the spirit animating the desire for unity is more pragmatic and conditional than in the past, with more stress on its tangible benefits and a willingness to wait until they are likely to be delivered. From that standpoint the persistence of the aspiration to unity is less mysterious than it might first appear – it bears more than passing resemblance to the desire to create a united Europe.

Southern attitudes to the North and to Northerners changed dramatically in the wake of the ceasefires. The change was led from the top. In the months before the ceasefires, broadcasting restrictions were eased and the references of the Southern government to republicans became more moderate and conciliatory; politicians began to use a language – of self-determination and national rights – which they had avoided for two decades. The wider public (at least those who noticed) found the new policies confusing, even alarming, but when their logic and rationale became apparent in the form of an IRA ceasefire their attitude quickly changed. They accepted the official line that a new situation now obtained and that it was time to revise old attitudes and opinions. The virulent anti-republican rhetoric of the previous period was deemed unnecessary and outdated; continued attempts to marginalise or demean Sinn Féin (as on the first appearance of Gerry Adams on RTÉ's *Late Late Show*) were seen as mean-spirited, backward-looking and harmful to the cause of peace.

The ceasefires led to a new openness in the South to the North and to Northerners. There was less resort to stereotypes and clichés, less moralism, more interest and concern to understand. The 'war' (a term associated with republicans and never used while violence continued) was over; it was time to move on. There was greater solidarity with Northern nationalists but also an interest in unionism, particularly in the new loyalism, and a concern to be constructive in furthering a settlement.

[64] Cf. Micheál McGréil, *Irish Political Attitudes and Opinions*, St Patrick's College, Maynooth, 1992, p. 23, table 12, question 3.

The years of silence and censorship have, however, left huge gaps in understanding and many unrealistic expectations.

Southern Protestants

Southern Protestants, particularly in the recent period, share many of the general features of Southern Catholics' political orientation to the North, but there are some differences. They are particularly marked in the case of Protestants in the three Ulster counties of the Republic, outliers of the historic Ulster Protestant community. Partition cut them off from that community and some felt deeply betrayed by it.[65] They have absorbed much of the political and cultural ethos of the South and give their allegiance to the Republic, but their sense of a shared identity with Northern Protestants remains strong. They have kinship and friendship links across the border, many have gone to work in Northern Ireland or found spouses there and their clergy are often from the North.[66] The conflict is of immediate concern to them and they understand what is at stake in it for Northern Protestants; many see Northern Ireland as the best guarantee of the survival of Protestantism in Ireland. A significant proportion favours the union, and most would oppose any attempt to pressure or force unionists to accept Irish unity.[67] Some actively support unionism or loyalism, but cautiously and discreetly.[68]

Protestants elsewhere in the Republic feel much more detached from their coreligionists in the North. Religious, business, friendship, kinship and organisational ties remain, but Southern Protestants do not identify with the strong Scottish and Calvinist strains in Northern Protestant culture; in accent and cultural style they are 'Southern Irish', critical of many aspects of Southern society but comfortable within it. Their contacts with Northern Protestants and their historical experience as a Protestant minority of British stock mean that they are better placed than other groups to hear and appreciate the arguments on both sides. Despite this – or perhaps because of it – they have tended to remain silent on the conflict and on partition.

---

[65] John M. Barkley, *Blackmouth and Dissenter*, Belfast, Whiterow, 1991, pp. 152–3.

[66] Kurt Bowen, *Protestants in a Catholic State*, Dublin, Gill and Macmillan, 1978, p. 68; see also Barkley, *Blackmouth and Dissenter*. Davis and Sinnott, *Attitudes in the Republic of Ireland*, pp. 112ff.

[67] In 1978, 41.3 per cent of border Protestants favoured retaining the union; 29.3 per cent favoured some form of Irish unity; Davis and Sinnott, *Attitudes in the Republic of Ireland*, p. 49, table 12.

[68] Bowen, *Protestants in a Catholic State*, p. 170; cf. Sam McAughtry, *Down in the Free State*, Dublin, Gill and Macmillan, 1987, p. 78.

Southern Ireland and the conflict in Northern Ireland

The contribution of Southern Ireland to the conflict in Northern Ireland is a matter of contemporary debate.[69] Some argue that the aspiration to unity, the constitutional claim and ambivalence about the use of coercion to achieve Irish unity have intensified the 'siege mentality' of unionists and strengthened their resistance to reform; in their view the South should keep its distance from Northern Ireland, remove its constitutional claim and concentrate on 'putting its own house in order'. Others – and this includes the majority in the South – insist that conditions in the South contribute little if anything to the conflict. If unionists are fearful of the South this is because they are out of touch with developments there – in particular the emergence of an open and pluralist society and the abjuring of Irish unity by any means other than consent.

We argue, first, that the nature of Southern society is more problematic for Northern Protestants than most Southerners realise. Second, a policy of distancing from the North is not now – if it ever was – a practical option for the South; the pressure of a politically mobilised Northern Catholic community cannot be ignored. Third, even limited Southern involvement has destabilising consequences for Northern Ireland.

Northern Protestants and the South

Northern Protestant perceptions of the South derive from their own cultural and political experience. Their culture has been shaped by Protestantism and by Scottish, Ulster regional and Irish traditions, overlain more recently by British provincialism. Their dominant political concern has been to secure the support and protection of the British government in their struggle with Catholic nationalism. This has given Protestant political culture a markedly different cast to that of Catholics. In particular, political independence – as opposed to a degree of regional autonomy – has a low (or even a negative) value in Northern Protestant culture. They accept their status as a region of a much larger state and society whose wider political goals they take as given – leaving 'high politics' to the British political elite and attending to it only insofar as it impinges on their interests and concerns. Their experience of state building was limited to the formation of a devolved government with limited powers and even this was desired primarily for strategic reasons.

---

[69] O'Malley, *Uncivil Wars*, pp. 83–4, 357–8; throughout the 1980s, Vincent Browne's editorials in the *Sunday Tribune*, the letters page of the *Irish Times* and columnists in the *Sunday Independent* give some indication of the debate in the South.

The project that the South has been engaged in – the building of an independent self-determining sovereign state – strikes no empathetic chord among Northern Protestants; for some its appeal is simply a mystery. Even those who see some merit to independence consider the cost to be too high – higher rates of unemployment and emigration, poorer roads, lower levels of health and social services, restrictive laws on censorship, contraception, divorce and abortion. Northern Protestants' perceptions of the South are further influenced by a concept of what the Southern state represents. In their eyes it is no more and no less than the political embodiment of the Catholic-nationalist tradition on the island – a tradition which they have feared and opposed for over a century, and in its communal form for much longer. Many Southerners protest that this is a narrow and outdated view of the Republic today – that their state is no longer the Catholic-nationalist creation of the De Valera years but is modern, progressive and pluralist, a state with which Southern Protestants (by and large) express their satisfaction. Few Northern Protestants are convinced by such arguments.

There are, however, important differences in emphasis and approach among Northern Protestants in their attitudes to the South. We distinguish in ideal-type terms three broad orientations which individuals may hold in varying degrees. The first – echoing loyalist ideology – is unremittingly hostile: the South is a Third World country; its economy is bankrupt; its politics are those of 'banana republic'; it is dominated by the Roman Catholic church; its people are manipulative, devious and untrustworthy; its culture is parochial, introverted and backward; it is a 'very sick country';[70] Southern Protestants have been denied a real say in public life and their numbers have been reduced to a fraction of their original size; Southern Catholics have an ingrained hostility to Northern Protestants and will defeat and destroy them if ever they get the opportunity. Contact with them is dangerous and should be kept to a minimum.

The second orientation is not actively hostile to the South; it simply regards it as a foreign country like, say, France or Germany or – as some more pointedly remark – some country in Africa. This is taken

---

[70] W. Martin Smyth, 'A Protestant looks at the Republic', in John Fairleigh, et al., *Sectarianism: Roads to Reconciliation*, Dublin, Three Candles, 1975, quoted in A. C. Hepburn, *The Conflict of Nationality in Modern Ireland*, London, Edward Arnold, 1980, p. 193; for more examples, see Todd, 'Two traditions', pp. 7, 19. John Taylor evoked images from this orientation and the following one when he declared: 'I'm an Ulsterman not an Irishman – I don't jig at crossroads or play Gaelic football', in *Beyond the Fife and Drum*, Report of a conference held on Belfast's Shankill Road, October, 1994, Newtownabbey, Island Publications, 1995.

as self-evident, requiring no further elaboration. Whether it is of long standing or a product of partition is seen as irrelevant; it exists now and is deeply felt. The dominance of this orientation is compatible with quite extensive business dealings or political connections in the South, occasional holidays there, recognition of the positive features of Southern society, even openness to further institutionalised linkages should these be of mutual benefit. As with any foreign country, however, knowledge and interest are detached, identification absent.[71]

The third orientation is much more open-minded towards the South; Protestants who hold it are likely to visit the South, have business dealings there and may have lived there for a time.[72] This orientation sees the South as another jurisdiction and as culturally different, but not 'foreign' in the normal meaning of the term. Those who hold it are aware of the traditional Northern stereotypes of the South but do not uncritically endorse them; they may indeed actively contest them on the basis of knowledge and experience. Their own criticisms of the South are nuanced, problems are seen in context, misunderstandings are open to correction, 'positive' changes in the South are acknowledged.

Each perspective implies a different attitude to Irish unity. The first acknowledges a common Irish heritage but in the form of a permanent struggle between two mutually antagonistic communities. Unity would be a disaster, a final historical defeat which would marginalise and finally eliminate Protestants from the island. If it occurred, the struggle for survival would necessarily be renewed within the new state. The second approach denies an island-wide Irish community or the possibility of one; Northern Protestants are British and Irish unity would remove them from their national community and relocate them in a foreign state. It would not be acceptable; if it occurred Northern Protestants would be a British ethnic minority within the new state.

The third approach is more open to recognising commonalities between North and South, whether economic or cultural. It acknowledges an Irish identity but one that is quite different from the Catholic Irish identity; it does not share the nationalist definition of the 'Irish nation'; a single island-wide community does not now exist and, while it might be constructed, it would have to take account of the diverse nature of the Irish experience. This approach typically opposes unity but not because it would represent communal defeat or because of an irrevocably British identity. It is simply that there are few if any positive arguments for unity given the weakness of the Southern economy, the

---

[71] This attitude was evident in some of our interviews with Alliance Party supporters.
[72] Examples range from the late Senator Gordon Wilson to the McGimpsey brothers.

dominance of the Catholic church, the stress on Gaelic culture, the hostility of many in the South to Northern Protestants and their insensitivity to Protestant culture and concerns. If all that were to change – and most doubt that it will – unity is not inconceivable and it would be possible for Northern Protestants to participate fully in a public sphere reconstructed on genuinely pluralist lines.

Most Northern Protestants internalise the constitutive elements of more than one orientation and, depending on context and circumstances, are capable of very different responses. Which orientation dominates depends in part on developments in Southern society. Threat or pressure from the South (including for some the permanent threat of Articles 2 and 3 of the Irish Constitution) can produce stereotypical perceptions in otherwise openminded Protestants; unexpected consideration can break through the stereotypes of the most bigoted; particular events or reactions in the South may emphasise its foreignness (for example the abortion and divorce referenda of 1983 and 1986) or suggest underlying affinities (for example, the pluralist ethos projected by Mary Robinson).[73]

Northern Catholic attitudes to the South

Northern Catholic attitudes to Southern Ireland have long been marked by ambivalence.[74] On the one hand, there was a tendency to idealise the South as a place where their deepest aspirations were being realised, where they could enjoy full public respect and could give free rein to their cultural and religious identity. On the other hand, that society abandoned them to an intolerable position within Northern Ireland and ignored their appeals for help. The idealised view is rarely heard today. Northern Catholics now tend to be critical of the kind of society the South has built – they point to the poor quality of its public services, its lack of respect for individual rights, the level of social inequality, the lack of seriousness or of principle in its politicians.

Consciousness of the limitations of Southern society pre-existed the troubles; it was given a new edge by the Southern response to the conflict. Northern Catholics of all political persuasions have been

---

[73] See, for example, *Alliance News*, Interparty talks supplement, Nov.–Dec. 1992, p. 6, for a very positive reaction to President Mary Robinson's inaugural speech.

[74] Eamon Phoenix, *Northern Nationalism: Nationalist Politics, Partition and the Catholic Minority in Northern Ireland 1890–1940*, Belfast, Ulster Historical Foundation, 1994, pp. 254ff., 271ff., 333ff.; Desmond Fennell, *The Northern Catholic: An Inquiry*, Dublin, Mount Salus Press, 1000; Fionnuala O'Connor, *In Search of a State: Catholics in Northern Ireland*, Belfast, Blackstaff, 1993, ch. 7.

shocked and offended by this response. Instead of sympathy and support they frequently met indifference or hostility, resistance to their view of events, accusations that they and not Northern Protestants or the British state were the root cause of the conflict, assertions that 'one lot is as bad as the other'.[75] Southern attitudes were often inferred from the media, but many had wounding personal experiences – being turned away from a pub when their accent was heard, being treated as likely trouble-makers by the police. The more republican minded have been the most critical – of the Irish government's 'collaboration' with Britain, its 'obsession' with violence, its harassment, imprisonment and extradition of republicans, its support for 'revisionism', of the wider population's acquiescence in this.

Structural developments over the past thirty years have also divided Northern Catholics and Southern Catholics. Up to the 1960s they had much in common. Both shared a sense of historical displacement, a predominantly rural, Catholic and nationalist background and the polit-ical aims of Irish national unity and independence. Southern society and its project were immediately comprehensible to Northern Catholics; Southern Catholics intuitively understood the difficulties Northern Catholics faced in Northern Ireland. Since the 1960s the South has become an urban society and one in which the state plays an increasingly important role; it is still Catholic and nationalist but there are several versions of each and the dominant liberal versions are hard to pin down; wealth and seventy years of self-government have given confidence to the middle class and diminished (though not quite eliminated) their sense of historical displacement and anti-Britishness; independence and unity remain goals but are pursued differently than before; the society has become more outward looking and internationalist – for the middle class the fascination is with 'Europe' and the United States not with Britain or Anglo-Irish affairs.

During the same period Northern Catholics have been wholly absorbed in their efforts to reconstruct (or to dismantle) Northern Ireland. Their struggle has brought them into much closer contact with the British state, requiring accomodations that they resisted in the past. Some have adopted British state norms which they now apply in their evaluation of the South. The upwardly mobile middle class in particular has partially assimilated to the dominant Protestant culture and accepted its traditionally critical view of the South: many women, too, have become used to the more liberal British laws in relation to divorce and abortion, have benefited from British educational grants and feel

---

[75] O'Connor, *In Search of a State*, p. 228.

correspondingly distanced from the South. For many Northern Catholics the South is uncharted territory, uncongenial, different, even foreign.

Differences and difficulties remain, but the ceasefires have reopened possibilities of improved relations. One observer writing before the ceasefires considered that the rift between Northern and Southern Catholics may some day be final – 'separation from the South all over again, and this time by mutual consent'.[76] This seems much less likely now. Southern attitudes were deeply coloured by the IRA's campaign. The suspension of that campaign led to much more positive attitudes towards Northern Catholics and this has been (though perhaps to a lesser degree) reciprocated; the variety of business and other institutional initiatives now being contemplated should also intensify the links and further improve relationships.

There is, moreover, a crucial strategic consideration which ties Northern nationalists to the South – their dependence on the Southern government to counteract their minority status within the North. That interest has strengthened since the ceasefires. The armed campaign gave a powerful political weapon to Northern Catholics, even to those who detested it and wanted it stopped. It meant that there could be no return to stable majority rule in Northern Ireland. That weapon was set aside in part in exchange for Southern government support. Northern Catholics cannot now afford to distance or alienate themselves from the South. For its part, the Southern government has also learned that it cannot, as it did for so long, ignore Northern Ireland or neglect the concerns of the Northern Catholic community.

The Southern government and the Northern Ireland conflict

The Southern government's policy of distance and detachment from Northern Ireland and Northern Catholics during the Stormont years was to have serious long-term consequences. It contributed to the conditions under which Northern Catholics mobilised as a separate political community, turned to violence when their efforts at reform failed and were able to sustain indefinitely their campaign of violence. The Southern government played an initial role in arming and training the Catholic community for self-defence, but without any anticipation of the proactive IRA campaign that was about to begin. When it began the government was horrified and frightened. The campaign was concentrated in the North – and the Southern government was

[76] *Ibid.*, p. 271.

determined that it remain so – but it threatened the authority of government in the South and created the conditions for all-out conflict on the island.

The Southern government had only limited means at its disposal to intervene in the new situation. Northern Ireland was the primary locus of the conflict, but it had no jurisdiction there and – at this time – had very limited influence over the British government. It exercised some influence over constitutional nationalism in the North, but little or none over republicanism. Its policy had two strands. The first and more important centred on security – to defend its own integrity as a state and the well-being of its own (Southern) citizens.[77] The second was to strengthen constitutional nationalism in the North as an alternative to republicanism by offering it moral and political support and by pressing for reforms. Successive Irish governments hoped for a return to peace and stability. All questions of Irish unity were shelved; the prospect of a possible British withdrawal in 1974 created alarm in a Southern government fearful of attempting to exercise authority over the loyalists who had so recently brought down the power-sharing executive.[78]

The relative emphasis on security and reform varied over time. The parties and personalities in government mattered but less than the quite radical differences in party attitudes and rhetoric on the North would suggest;[79] more striking is the continuity of Northern policy despite frequent changes in government. For much of the 1970s, a time when the Irish government's influence over the British government was weak, the emphasis was on security. The government introduced new offences against the state legislation, special courts and specialised units within the Gardaí and special branch; it established closer cooperation with the British security forces and became more moderate in its criticisms of security practices in the North; it restricted access by republicans to the media, toned down the nationalist ethos of the state and made repeated denunciations of nationalist violence; it made extensive diplomatic efforts to undermine republican political and financial support in the US.

These measures successfully contained republicanism in the South; in the North they carried a price. The perception that the Southern state was more interested in defeating republicanism than in defending or advancing the position of Northern nationalists helped consolidate support for the IRA among the most disadvantaged sections of the

[77] Cf. B. O'Leary and J. McGarry, *The Politics of Antagonism: Understanding Northern Ireland*, London, Athlone, 1993, p. 236.

[78] Garret Fitzgerald, *All in a Life*, Dublin, Gill and Macmillan, 1991, pp. 244ff.

[79] See Richard Sinnott, 'The North: party images and party approaches in the Republic', *Irish Political Studies*, vol. 1, 1986.

Northern Catholic population who perceived them as the only group seriously concerned about their problems. Weaknesses in the Southern government's channels of information hid the extent of communal support for the IRA until the hunger strikes and electoral rise of Sinn Féin made it clear. The policy of defeating republicanism continued – indeed intensified – but more effort was now devoted to strengthening constitutional nationalism by pressing for reform. This was facilitated by changes in British policy in the early 1980s and the new emphasis on intergovernmental relations.

The primary achievement of this new departure was the Anglo-Irish Agreement of 1985. The Agreement did not end – or even significantly erode – support for Sinn Féin which may indeed have peaked before it was signed.[80] But it brought the Irish government directly into the political process, giving it the right to represent the Northern nationalist community at the intergovernmental level. In so doing it strengthened the morale and political weight of constitutional nationalism. The centrality of the Irish government to the search for a political solution became even more clear in the series of 'three-stranded' talks between 1990 and 1992. It became clearer again with the success of the peace process.

The possibility of such a process arose from talks between the SDLP and Sinn Féin begun in 1988 and later continued by John Hume and Gerry Adams, but its success depended on the positive response of the Irish government. The IRA's campaign would be suspended but only in return for guaranteed access by Sinn Féin to the political process and support from the Southern government for at least some republican ideals. This condition was met and in less than a year – between 1993 and 1994 – the Southern government radically revised its public and private stance towards republicans and achieved its goal of an IRA (and loyalist) ceasefire. In doing so it has locked itself into an even more central role in Northern Ireland's affairs. A return to the politics of ignoring Northern Ireland is now inconceivable.

The stated goals of Southern government are to resolve the historic conflict on the island of Ireland and to 'bring all the people of Ireland together' by peaceful means in an agreed constitutional settlement: 'threat' and 'coercion' are explicitly eschewed.[81] It proposes a series of constitutional, institutional and structural reforms within Northern Ireland to enable Catholics to participate fully in public life and, through

---

[80] Paul Bew, Peter Gibbon and Henry Patterson, *Northern Ireland 1921–1994: Political Forces and Social Classes*, London, Serif, 1995, p. 219.
[81] Downing Street Declaration, paragraph 6.

264 The dynamics of conflict in Northern Ireland

closer links between North and South, to give expression to their wider
Irish identity. At the same time, to meet the concerns of unionists, it
formally guarantees that Northern Ireland will remain part of the United
Kingdom as long as a majority so wishes and it pledges to change 'any
elements in the democratic life and organisation of the Irish State' that
appear to offer a 'real and substantial threat to their [Unionists'] way of
life and ethos' or are not 'fully consistent with a modern democratic and
pluralist society'.[82]

The Southern government presents these policies as balanced and
even-handed. In practice, if implemented, they would represent a
considerable gain for Northern nationalists. The Southern state is now a
power broker of significance and its increasing involvement in Northern
Ireland is affecting the balance of symbolic and strategic resources
available to each community, to the advantage of Catholics. That is why
Catholics support Southern involvement and Protestants fear and resist it.

Ireland as a context for resolving the Northern Ireland conflict

The expanding role of the Southern state in the affairs of Northern
Ireland is from another angle the increased integration of Northern Ireland
into the wider Irish context, a development that parallels its increased
integration into the United Kingdom. The Irish context is even more
strikingly contradictory in its implications for the conflict than the British
one.

The Irish context is now the most important arena in which the
conditions of conflict are reproduced. This is not to underestimate the
British state's role in the conflict in the past or today. But the interests
which once motivated it to manipulate and (later) strategically to
manage communal division in Ireland have now largely disappeared
(chapter 11). The legacy of division in Ireland remains. It is rooted in an
overdetermined clash of religion, ethnicity, culture and national identity
and in the threat which each community poses to the identity and vital
interests of the other. It is most intense in Northern Ireland, but it is its
continued presence at the level of the island as a whole that reproduces
the intensity of conflict in Northern Ireland (chapter 11). This
communal division is at the heart of the conflict and resolving it is a
precondition of peace, stability and reconciliation on the island and (if it
survives as a distinct political entity) within Northern Ireland.

Far from conditions being favourable to reconciliation at the level of

---

[82] *Ibid.*, paragraphs 6, 7.

the island, however, there is a strong dynamic for conflict in the current situation. Notwithstanding the changes in Southern society and politics over the past decades, the South remains both unappealing to unionists and a danger to their interests and identity. Despite this, unionists are under increasing pressure to engage more closely with the South. This is a product not of Southern demands for reunification but rather of pressure by Northern Catholics for equality of political, economic and cultural conditions with Northern Protestants. Unionists do not accept the legitimacy of Northern Catholic demands, but Catholics have – for the present at least – the support of the Irish (and to a lesser extent, the British) government and the international community (chapter 10).

There is more to unionist resistance than the question of the legitimacy or otherwise of Catholic demands. Unionists fear that, regardless of constitutional guarantees, the equalising of communal relations in Northern Ireland will erode their power within Northern Ireland and their position on the island. They believe that they will find their choices increasingly confined, their traditional preferences no longer tenable, their political and even their demographic strength eroded. They accept that no attempt will be made physically to force them into a united Ireland, but they fear that the gradual erosion of their position will some day make it morally or politically impossible for them to say no to unity. For that reason they oppose any changes in Northern Ireland which might hasten that day. But their resistance to change is, from a Northern Catholic standpoint, an insistence on continued Protestant dominance.

There is, therefore, a central contradiction to be addressed. The minimal demand of Northern nationalists is for equality of status with unionists and this both requires and implies closer political and institutional links between North and South. For unionists, any movement in this direction is a threat to their vital interests and they oppose it. The Southern government has no wish to put pressure on unionists, and is concerned about the political and security implications of so doing. But it also finds it impossible to ignore the concerns of Northern nationalists. Nationalist sentiment and considerations of social justice play some role in this; more importantly, the government believes that to distance itself from Northern Ireland is to invite continuing political instability and the renewal of violence.

This contradiction makes the island context at once the crucial arena for resolving the conflict and the one most fraught with difficulty. Chapter 11 will outline our proposals for dealing with it.

10   The international context

From the outset, the conflict in Northern Ireland has had an international dimension. International opinion and interventions by international organisations and other governments have influenced the policies of the British and Irish governments and the expectations of the two communities in Northern Ireland. Outside responses have been shaped in part by the perception that the conflict does not fall into a neat category to which international norms and principles of law can unambiguously be applied. We begin by exploring the historical roots of this 'category problem' and its implications. We then consider the consequences of the increasing role of the United States and European Union in the conflict.

British–Irish relations in international context

The history of British–Irish relations can be viewed within two quite different comparative frames of reference: as an interface–periphery conflict arising from two competing European state- and nation-building processes, or as a colonial conflict which happens to be in Europe but which is more characteristic of the legacy of European colonialism elsewhere.[1] The comparative frame used has important practical and political consequences. Interface-periphery conflicts are now regulated by recognising existing frontiers, by intergovernmental agreements and the legal protection of minority rights. In contrast, settler–colonial conflicts are resolved by the departure of the colonial power and the acceptance by the settlers of their minority status.

---

[1] For discussion of this issue in the context of Northern Ireland today, see Ian S. Lustick, *Unsettled States, Disputed Lands: Britain and Ireland, France and Algeria, Israel and the West Bank–Gaza*, Ithaca, Cornell University Press, 1993; John McGarry and Brendan O'Leary, *Explaining Northern Ireland: Broken Images*. Oxford, Basil Blackwell, 1995, ch. 8; Liam O'Dowd, 'New introduction', to Albert Memmi, *The Colonizer and the Colonized*, London, Earthscan, 1990.

The ambiguities surrounding British–Irish relations have their roots in two interrelated aspects of European development. One is its multipolar nature – the fact that Europe developed as a complex structure of over-lapping and interlocking political, economic and cultural power centres. The second is the uneven involvement of the European states in the colonisation of the non-European world. All of Europe was touched by the consequences of European colonialism from the fifteenth century, but only some of Europe's political centres were directly involved and the impact of colonialism was mediated – in a sense 'Europeanised' – by Europe's multipolarity. In order to grasp the implications of this dualism for British–Irish relations we draw on Stein Rokkan's attempt analytically to map Europe's multipolar structure by means of a 'geoethnic, geo-economic, geopolitical' model of European development, and on Immanuel Wallerstein's model of a European created 'capitalist world-system'.[2]

Rokkan's central concern is with Europe's uneven pattern of state- and nation-building. He identifies a central 'city belt' in late medieval Europe, consisting of the central plains and alpine territories and stretching from Italy to the Baltic. In the middle ages this was the most advanced region of Europe, with a well developed agricultural economy, a strong network of cities, linked together culturally through a common religion. But state-building was impeded by the existence of many urban centres and the power of the church. Instead it began on the coastal plains on the western edges of the city belt (Spain, France, England) where monetisation was greatest, resources for state building were easily extractable and the emergence of strong centres was not impeded by other competing centres. The second phase began on the landward side of the central belt: Sweden, Austria and Prussia. Meanwhile the city belt saw either early consociations e.g. Netherlands, Belgium, Switzerland, or political fragmentation (Italy, Germany). State-building there was not completed until the nineteenth and twentieth centuries. Nation-building began in the sixteenth century. It was most rapid in the northern reformation territories where processes of vernacularisation and the use of print were most developed.[3] The combination of early state- and nation-building in the northern and central coastal states produced 'empire-nations' seeking with varying degrees of success to incorporate

[2] Stein Rokkan, 'Territories, centres, and peripheries: toward a geoethnic–geoeconomic–geopolitical model of differentiation within western Europe', in Jean Gottman, ed., *Centre and Periphery: Spatial Variations in Politics*, London, Sage, 1980; Immanuel Wallerstein, *The Modern World System*, 3 vols., London, Academic Press, 1974, 1980, 1988.

[3] Rokkan, 'Territories, centres and peripheries'.

more than one ethnic group.[4] Nation-building was delayed in the territories dominated by the counter-reformation church, where the outlook remained supranational until the nineteenth century.

The Atlantic states developed as 'empire-nations' in another sense. From the fifteenth and sixteenth centuries they were exploring and colonising the shores of west Africa and the New World; very soon this was extended into the Indian ocean and beyond. A 'modern world-system' was coming into being that would link structurally all parts of Europe and an increasing part of the globe.[5] The resources the Atlantic states thus acquired increased their strategic advantages within Europe; the city state region – even Holland which, geographically, was initially well placed – lost ground; state and infrastructural development farther to the east regressed. The long-term impact of this unevenness eventually bore poisonous fruit in the two great crises of adjustment in the European state system represented by the first and second world wars.

The history of Europe is not simply that of its major political and cultural centres; it is also that of the multiplicity of smaller territorial entities, of regions and minor ethnic groups who in varying degrees dissolved in, or were subordinated by, the new states or survived as peripheries on their margins. Rokkan distinguishes four types of peripheries: first, the seaward peripheries to the west and north of the coastal plains, some of which (for example, Brittany) were 'failed centres' which experienced a degree of state-building prior to external incorporation; second, the interface peripheries between the areas of major state formation (for example, Lorraine and Alsace, Alto Adige/South Tyrol); third, the landward peripheries to the east; fourth, the enclave peripheries.[6]

Europe's colonies were also varied. In some (North America, Australia) the local population was destroyed or displaced and replaced by European settlers; in others (west Africa, India, the West Indies) the existing population, or a replacement, remained the majority and there was acculturation on both sides; in still others (southern Africa, Algeria) the settlers were a minority but large and demographically self-sustaining. Colonial institutional forms typically owed something to local traditions; more important was the impress of the administrative systems, national cultures and economic needs of the colonising

---

[4] Stein Rokkan and Derek W. Urwin, *Economy, Territory, Identity: Politics of West European Peripheries*, London, Sage, 1983, fig. 2.2, p. 31.

[5] Wallerstein, *Modern World System*.

[6] Rokkan, 'Territories, centres and peripheries', table 9.4.

power.[7] But the influence was not simply one way – colonisation impacted back on the colonisers (and through them to all of Europe), shaping their economies, political institutions and self-perceptions.

Decolonisation took place in two broad waves. The first occurred at the end of the eighteenth century and was limited to the New World; the second – consisting in most cases of territories acquired in the nineteenth century – took place in the twentieth century. Decolonisation sometimes occurred painlessly and with little loss of life; at other times – where vital imperial interests were thought to be at stake or European settlement had been substantial – it was long drawn out, bitter and bloody. In all cases it left in the host society a profound institutional and cultural legacy and also an emotional one – typically an ambivalent mix of respect and resentment towards the colonial power and hostility to colonialism as a process.

State- and nation-building and colonialism within the British Isles form a subset within this wider pattern. England followed the general pattern of the coastal states, developing both as an empire-nation and a colonising power. But its island status uniquely afforded it the option of minimising its continental involvements and concentrating its attention on its wider trade and colonial interests. Its developing sense of cultural identity reflected this. The very early and strong sense of English nationhood (which Protestantism later greatly reinforced) became a core around which developed a more inclusive British identity – partly national, partly imperial – that was capable of unlimited expansion to include the other nations of Great Britain, Ireland and the peoples of the empire (chapter 8).

The distinctiveness of the Irish experience derives in part from its location on Europe's North Atlantic periphery but more importantly to its exposure to two quite different force-fields – one 'European' (which made it similar in some respects to Scotland, Wales, Brittany or Galicia), the other 'colonial' (giving it some of the characteristics of the settler colonies of the New World). Weak indigenous state development left Ireland vulnerable to medieval penetration by Norman-English settlers, and their colony remained loyal to the English crown. In the sixteenth and seventeenth centuries the English attempt to impose its rule over the whole of Ireland and to establish the reformation led to resistance from the native Irish and the descendants of the medieval settlers. The English responded with renewed conquest and colonisation and Ireland found itself ambiguously located between the colonial and metropolitan

---

[7] Wallerstein, *Modern World System*. Eric Wolf, *Europe and the People Without History*, Berkeley, University of California Press, 1982.

spheres of the emerging British world (chapters 2 and 8). An attempt in the nineteenth century to integrate Ireland fully into the metropolitan sphere was to prove a failure.

Ireland's structural dualism has shown itself in many ways. The Protestant–Catholic religious divide was both a local variation on the European pattern and a functional equivalent to ethnicity or colour in separating native majority from settler minority. The English goal of 'civilising' Ireland was at once an expression of the 'civilising process' at European level and a central theme in English/British imperialism. Both the American war of independence and the French revolution struck immediate chords in Ireland; the Hungarian nineteenth century struggle against Austrian domination was seen as a model by Irish nationalists, so also was that of the Boers against the British in South Africa; the Irish struggle for independence was used as a model by other subordinated nationalities in Europe and by native populations in the colonies.

The dualism inherent in the Irish experience has important consequences for outside responses to the conflict in Northern Ireland. If the conflict is viewed in the context of European state- and nation-building, it is an interface–periphery conflict and the solution lies in the recognition of existing borders (or their modification with the consent of the governments and the local population), intergovernmental agreements and the legal protection of minority rights. If it is viewed in the context of British empire-building, the conflict is a colonial one; the solution lies in British withdrawal and the acceptance by the Protestant settler-minority in the north of Ireland of the will of the majority on the island. The ambiguous nature of British–Irish relationships makes impossible any unequivocal declaration that the conflict is of one kind or the other.

This ambiguity also precludes the ready application to Northern Ireland of standard international norms for regulating disputes. Consider the problems in applying the principle of self-determination. Gallagher points to the difficulties. A number of United Nations resolutions, in 1960, 1966 and 1970 have 'pronounced the right of all "peoples" to self-determination,' but they also insist that 'this does not confer any right to dismember the territorial unity of any existing state'; at the same time they give no indication which of these two rights – that of self-determination and of territorial integrity – should take precedence.[8] The problem arises in part because 'the 1960 declaration . . . was made deliberately vague on key issues because it was intended to assert that

---

[8] Michael Gallagher, 'Do Ulster unionists have a right to self-determination?', *Irish Political Studies*, vol. 5, 1990, p. 14.

people living in the colonies of the European powers had a right to end their colonial status, while simultaneously wanting to ensure that no right of secession was bestowed on people living in independent states'.[9] But it is on precisely this issue that Ireland's dualism turns. The island as a whole can be viewed as a colony which at the time of independence was unjustly divided to accommodate a settler minority, a practice which the UN now strongly opposes; alternatively the Republic can be seen as a secessionist segment of the British state, the legitimacy of whose secession can be questioned and which in any case does not have the right to insist that the rest of the island follow its example.[10]

The European response to this category problem is mediated by the principles and aspirations underlying the project of the European Union. One of the principles of the 'new Europe' is that nationalist irredentisms should no longer be entertained and that majority-minority conflicts should be resolved by according minority rights rather than by boundary revision. There is, therefore, no support for Southern Irish aspirations to Irish unity in the face of unionist opposition. But European opinion is also influenced by considerations that derive from the complexity of the Irish case. One is that the colonial dimension in British–Irish relations makes the Northern Ireland conflict qualitatively different from other European border conflicts such as Alto-Adige/South Tyrol or Schleswig and may require unusual measures to address it. A second is a ready sympathy with the situation of Northern Catholics as a minority which has suffered at the hands of an overbearing majority.

Wider international perceptions of the conflict, shaped by a quite different historical dynamic, are quicker to stress the colonial dimension, to entertain doubts about Northern Ireland's foundational legitimacy and to sympathise with Northern nationalists.[11] American perceptions derive in part from the US's own experience of shaking off British metropolitan control, as well as from its project of dismantling the British empire to secure access to its territories and to replace it as the preeminent power in the world; this perception is further reinforced by Irish-Americans who view the conflict unambiguously as the legacy of British colonialism. A similar anti-imperialist attitude animates sympathy for Irish nationalism elsewhere in the world, particularly where the struggle against colonialism has been recent. The nature and extent of the identification was dramatically revealed in the world-wide

[9] *Ibid.*, p. 14.

[10] Kevin Boyle and Tom Hadden, *Ireland: A Positive Proposal*, Harmondsworth, Penguin, 1985, pp. 27–8.

[11] Adrian Guelke, *Northern Ireland: The International Perspective*, Gill and Macmillan, 1988, ch. 1.

response to the death on hunger strike of Bobby Sands. Despite their different interpretations, therefore, both the European and international responses to the conflict have converged in a common sympathy for the Northern Catholic community.

If international norms provide no clear direction for the resolution of the conflict, they are more directly applicable to specific abuses of human and civil rights which have arisen in its course. Amnesty International has monitored events in Northern Ireland since the beginning of the current conflict and its report on the ill-treatment of internees in 1971 gave an important impetus to the Irish government to take the case to the European Court of Human Rights. An Amnesty report in 1977 alleging ill-treatment of political suspects in the Republic led to a change in police procedure. In the late 1970s its criticisms of RUC interrogation methods contributed to the setting up of the Bennett Commission and to the suspension of arms sales from the United States to the RUC.[12] Amnesty's interventions during the 1980s and 1990s have included reports on political killings in Northern Ireland and ill-treatment of suspects in custody; these have formed the basis of submissions to UN Committees and have been taken up by senior American politicians.[13] More recently the United States-based Helsinki Watch published several critical reports on civil liberties issues, later cited in the State Department's Human Rights report for 1994.

The effect of such pressure depends on the willingness of the governments to accede to it; both governments have tended initially to resist it. From 1957 until 1984 the United Kingdom entered a derogation to the European Convention on Human Rights with respect to Northern Ireland.[14] During that period, claims against Britain could only be on the grounds of non-derogable rights, for example, freedom from torture or discrimination. When the British government removed its derogation in 1984, four individuals who had been detained under the Prevention of Terrorism Act immediately entered a claim against it. In 1988 the European Court of Human Rights declared parts of the Act – those allowing the authorities to hold terrorist suspects for up to seven days without charge – to be in breach of the Convention. Britain immediately declared a derogation from the Convention on the issue the legality of which was challenged but upheld by the European Court in a judgement

[12] Guelke, *Northern Ireland*, p. 140.
[13] Amnesty International, *Political Killings in Northern Ireland*, London, Amnesty International British Section, 1994; St Patrick's Day statements by the Friends of Ireland, *Irish Times*, 18 Mar. 1992, 18 Mar. 1993.
[14] Guelke, *Northern Ireland*, pp. 165ff.

in May 1993.[15] Similarly the Irish government resisted acceding to the European Convention on the Suppression of Terrorism because of its provisions on extradition; it eventually did so in 1986 following the signing of the Anglo-Irish Agreement.[16]

The precise impact of international opinion and judicial processes on the conduct of the two governments is difficult to assess; expert opinion is divided.[17] As we have seen the governments have been quick to adopt evasive strategies when their interests so dictated. However Guelke argues that such pressures have acted as a constraining influence on the options open to the British government: for Britain, it has been important to sustain the claim that the Northern Ireland conflict is being dealt with according to the norms of a Western European democracy, rather than of a colonial power; thus the harsh security measures advocated by unionists have been ruled out.[18] More direct influences on the policy process have come from the United States and to a lesser extent the EU.

The American connection, 1969–1995

The influence of the United States on British–Irish relations is as old as the United States itself. The American rebellion served as a political model for Irish Protestant assertiveness against the British government in the 1770s and 1780s; the *idea* of America as a land of freedom and opportunity became an ideal in terms of which conditions in Ireland were judged; Irish emigrants in the post-famine period brought with them an intense hatred of Britain and nurtured the hope that the growing power of the United States could be used to free Ireland from British rule; Irish-Americans played a crucial role in the birth of Fenianism and its financing; Irish-American funds sustained the war of independence and American pressure went some way to redressing the imbalance of power between the British state and Irish nationalists in the treaty negotiations; there was Irish-American financial support for the IRA's border

---

[15] In March 1991, the European Commission of Human Rights declared admissable the complaint that the United Kingdom's derogation on seven-day detention was unlawful, but the eventual judgement (Brannigan-McBride, 26 May 1993) was in Britain's favour.

[16] Guelke, *Northern Ireland*, pp. 169–70.

[17] Kevin Boyle, 'The Irish question and human rights in European perspectives', and Torkel Opsahl, 'Some comments on Kevin Boyle's contribution', in Harald Olav Skar and Bjørn Lydersen, *Northern Ireland: A Crucial Test for a Europe of Peaceful Regions*, Norwegian Foreign Policy Studies no. 80, Norwegian Institute of International Affairs, 1993.

[18] Guelke, *Northern Ireland*, pp. 166–8.

campaign in the 1950s; the Black civil rights marches provided the model for the Northern Ireland civil rights movement – the march from Belfast to Derry in January 1969 was consciously modelled on the march from Selma to Montgomery, Alabama.

Despite – or perhaps because of – these historical connections, the American government's initial response to the current conflict was to resist any involvement; the first public statement of interest by an American president was not until 1977. In the early years, it was Irish republicans who drew effectively on the 'American connection'. When the crisis broke, they immediately reactivated the American support networks dormant since the end of the border campaign. They had considerable success. Holland reports that an American arms network sent between 2,000 and 2,500 guns and a million rounds of ammunition to the IRA before it was broken.[19] The Irish Northern Aid Committee (NORAID), established in 1970 to raise money for republican causes, had sent at least $3 million to Ireland by 1986, and it is alleged that other undeclared money was used to buy arms for the IRA.[20] During that period the IRA developed other sources of money and weapons, but without the initial support from the United States it is doubtful whether it would have succeeded in launching its campaign and making it self-sustaining.

Republicans also organised politically in the US. In 1974 NORAID, the Ancient Order of Hibernians (AOH) and other groups formed the Irish National Caucus (INC) to lobby actively for Irish reunification.[21] Its relationship to the campaign of the IRA was unclear but understood by many to be sympathetic if not actively supportive; however in the late 1970s its dominant figure, Fr Frank McManus, publicly distanced it from NORAID, the IRA and support for violence.[22] The INC continued to stress the goal of Irish unity but also became increasingly active on human rights issues, focusing attention on the security forces and on job discrimination; it was the prime mover in launching and ensuring the success of the MacBride Principles in the 1980s. Earlier, in 1977, it had helped form the Ad Hoc Congressional Committee on Irish Affairs, the first significant mobilisation of support for Irish nationalism at the level of Congress, and a body which reached politicians outside the traditional confines of Irish-America. The Ad Hoc Committee remains a marginal group but it has had some notable successes, including the propaganda

---

[19] Jack Holland, *The American Connection*, Dublin, Poolbeg, 1989, p. 112.
[20] Adrian Guelke, 'The United States and the Northern Ireland question', in Brian Barton and Patrick J. Roche, eds., *The Northern Ireland Question: Perspectives and Policies*, Aldershot, Avebury, 1994, pp. 191–6.
[21] Holland, *American Connection*, p. 117.   [22] *Ibid.*, p. 142.

coup in 1979 of having the State Department suspend its sale of guns to the RUC on the grounds that they were engaged in human rights abuses.

The growing influence of the INC and the Ad Hoc Committee provoked the Irish government into developing an Irish-American network of its own. The Irish government had strongly opposed NORAID and was deeply distrustful of both the INC and Ad Hoc Committee – not simply on the grounds of their ambiguous relationship to the IRA but because they were lobbying for the traditionalist nationalist aim of reunification at a time when constitutional nationalist opinion had distanced itself from that aim. To counter the increasing influence of these groups, John Hume and the Irish government established links with four of the most senior Irish-American politicians – Edward Kennedy, Hugh Carey, Tip O'Neill and Daniel Patrick Moynihan. Their first public intervention was a speech on St Patrick's Day 1977 which condemned IRA violence and opposed the giving of money to organisations supporting it. Their intervention made little impression on committed republican supporters, but it influenced moderate Irish-American opinion and over time the 'four horsemen' (as they were called), in close liaison with the Irish government and the SDLP, succeeded in curtailing – though not ending – the influence of NORAID, INC and the Ad Hoc Committee.[23]

The 'four horsemen' were not simply concerned with blocking the activities of the more radical groups; they also sought the active involvement of the American government. Presidents Nixon and Ford had both refused to take a political stand on the conflict; they declared it an internal British matter and a problem first and foremost of violence. The election in 1976 of a Democratic president, Jimmy Carter, with a public commitment to support human rights throughout the world, opened up new possibilities. In 1977 the 'four horsemen' persuaded him publicly to commit the United States government to offer aid to Northern Ireland in the event of an agreed settlement. The statement was regarded as a breakthrough, establishing for the first time that Northern Ireland was a legitimate subject of American government concern.[24]

Carter's defeat in the 1980 election appeared to bring this development to an end. Ronald Reagan, a Republican, was far more concerned with international terrorism than with human rights and, despite Irish government and Irish-American pressure, refused to intervene during the hunger strikes. His arrival saw the temporary renewal of the 'special

---

[23] Holland, *American Connection*, p. 130.
[24] Paul Arthur and Keith Jeffery, *Northern Ireland since 1968*, Oxford, Basil Blackwell, 1988, pp. 84–5.

relationship' between the United States and the United Kingdom governments with American support for the British government in the Falklands war and British support for American attacks on Libya; a close personal relationship developed between Reagan and Thatcher based on a shared economic and political philosophy. Irish government diplomatic efforts continued, however, as did pressure by moderate Irish-Americans, now as part of a broad Friends of Ireland group.

Their efforts met with success. In 1984 Reagan publicly praised the work of the New Ireland Forum after its rejection by Margaret Thatcher, and raised the matter of Northern Ireland with her in their meeting in late December. American government opinion had now seriously entered the political equation and played an important role in the process leading to the signing of the Anglo-Irish Agreement in 1985.[25] Reagan's public welcome of the Agreement – where, in company with Tip O'Neill, he quoted Jimmy Carter's earlier promise of American aid in the context of a peaceful settlement – was a public expression of continuing American concern with the conflict. It was also evidence that presidential concern could transcend American party divisions.

The 1980s and 1990s saw increasing and more broadly based activity in the United States on Northern Irish issues. The MacBride Principles campaign on fair employment progressed rapidly, gave wide publicity to conditions within Northern Ireland and won support far beyond the Irish-American constituency. By 1995 over sixteen states and forty major cities had ratified the principles. There was increasing concern with human rights issues arising from the conflict, reflected in March 1990 in the holding of an official hearing by the Congressional Human Rights Caucus on the case of the Birmingham Six. Traditionally this body concerned itself with violations by the Soviet Union, South Africa and Cuba.

The Anglo-Irish Agreement itself extended American interest in Northern Ireland. American financial backing of the Agreement through the International Fund for Ireland (IFI), though very small in American terms, required monitoring and debates on new donations and on IFI practices.[26] It also allowed American political principles to be applied directly to Northern Ireland. For example, the IFI initially accepted British and Irish security force assessments of what projects were paramilitary-oriented and denied grants accordingly.[27] However such political vetting, with its refusal to give public evidence of its allegations,

[25] Holland, *American Connection*, pp. 145–6; Guelke, *Northern Ireland*, p. 147.
[26] *Fortnight*, 316, 1993, p. 15.
[27] Charles Brett, *Irish Times*, 1, 2 Jan. 1991; Niall Kiely, *Irish Times*, 21 Aug. 1990.

was seen as unacceptable in the United States where access to information is a civil right and met with criticism from Democrats and Republicans alike.[28]

The growth of a bi-partisan – Democratic and Republican – concern with Northern Ireland owes much to changes in the form and relative importance of the Irish-American vote. Long-term changes in the social profile of Irish-Americans, who have been moving out of the urban working class, have combined with more recent changes in voting patterns and Irish-Americans are now as likely to vote Republican as Democrat. Its floating vote now makes the Irish constituency important not just in local politics but increasingly in presidential elections. In 1984 and 1988, Democratic presidential candidates responded to the Irish-American lobby by making commitments on behalf of Northern Ireland Catholics. Even George Bush, an inactive president on the Irish question, declared his support for fair employment and further investment in Northern Ireland.[29]

This tendency has developed farther again during the recent period. Private research by Clinton before the 1992 elections showed that in certain key states 'Irish issues had come up with surprising regularity', and he committed himself to ' "take a more active role" in working to achieve peace and justice in Northern Ireland'.[30] 'Irish Americans for Clinton-Gore' were an important part of his election campaign and his preelection commitments on the Irish question – to appoint a peace envoy, to grant a visa to Gerry Adams, to support the MacBride Principles – were, reportedly, informed by policy consultations with the Irish embassy and Edward Kennedy's office.[31] After his election, Clinton further cemented his administration's links with the Irish-American constituency and with constitutional nationalism in Ireland by appointing Jean Kennedy Smith as ambassador to Ireland.

The role of Irish-Americans – and, through their influence, the American government – has increased further with the launching of the peace process. Businessmen as well as politicians were central actors: William J. Flynn, chairman and chief executive of Mutual of America insurance company and chairman of the National Committee on American Foreign Policy, organised a conference in New York for February 1994 and invited the leaders of the five Northern Ireland political parties to attend – Flynn's full-page advertisements in the *New*

---

[28] Sean Cronin, *Irish Times*, 7 May 1990.
[29] *Irish Times*, 19 Mar. 1992.
[30] Mary Holland, *Irish Times*, 29 Oct. 1992.
[31] Conor O'Clery, *Fortnight*, no. 312, 1992, pp. 8–9.

York Times and *Washington Post* stated 'Peace for Northern Ireland is within their grasp!' It proved the opportunity for intense and successful Irish-American lobbying for a visa for Gerry Adams: the granting of the visa against strong British opposition showed the willingness of Clinton's administration to take an independent line on Northern Ireland.[32]

In August 1994, three prominent Irish-Americans – William Flynn, Bruce Morrison and Niall O'Dowd, a businessman, an ex-Congressman and a journalist – went to Northern Ireland and convinced Sinn Féin that Irish-American support and pressure would ensure that republican and nationalist aims would be kept on the political agenda in the event of a republican ceasefire. This was confirmed after the ceasefire in a series of American government decisions against British opposition: in October 1994 to withdraw the White House ban on contacts with Sinn Féin, in March 1995 to allow the party to fundraise in the United States and to invite Gerry Adams to the White House for the St Patrick's Day celebrations. The principles behind these decisions were American government support for the peace process, for constitutional politics and for a fair settlement of the conflict on the terms of the Downing Street Declaration.

Clinton's commitment to and knowledge of the Northern Ireland situation goes beyond that of any previous president; in part, it reflects his need for a foreign policy success; it also appears to have a personal aspect. His involvement, however, is the culmination of a long-term tendency toward greater United States involvement in the Northern Ireland conflict. This tendency is unlikely to be reversed. Apart from the new strength of the Irish-American lobby, there has been an important change in underlying American assumptions: Northern Ireland is now not merely a domestic matter for the British government but an issue of legitimate American concern.

In recent months the American government has emphasised strongly its non-partisanship in the conflict – its concern with the rights and well-being of both communities in Northern Ireland. In practice, American government involvement and American pressure generally have strengthened the hands of nationalists. This is in line with a traditional American sympathy with Irish nationalism (see above); but it owes much also to the effectiveness with which Irish-Americans have used the language of American public life to state their case – equal opportunities, civil rights, freedom of expression, pluralism – and mobilised multiethnic coalitions to advance their programme. Unionists

---

[32] Cf. James Adams, 'Kneecapped! How Gerry Adams's US visit crippled the "special relationship"', *Sunday Times*, 6 Feb. 1994.

have been much less effective. The contrast is not simply one of political capacity; the Catholic case lends itself more easily to articulation in those terms.

There is little likelihood that the American connection will diminish in importance in the years to come. The Irish-American lobby is now led by established and powerful politicians and successful businessmen. The social and political mobility of Irish-Americans increases their electoral leverage, as does their demographic concentration in a small number of states. Both Republican and Democratic presidents now have an incentive to sustain an interest in Ireland. But there may also be a structural dynamic at work. The first tentative commitment of a United States president in 1977 to give financial support to an agreed settlement in Northern Ireland has now grown to the point where the presidency has become an integral part of the search for a political settlement. There is an economic dimension to that increased involvement – Father McManus has spoken of the 'foreign policy nexus between US dollars and job discrimination', arguing that American investment in Northern Ireland has opened the way to American political involvement because 'US tax and investment dollars in Northern Ireland is the business of Americans'.[33]

The European Union

In the multipolar, conflictual pattern of European historical development, Ireland has counted for very little in the strategic considerations of the continental powers. History and geography placed Ireland firmly within the English sphere of influence and English claims to jurisdiction over it were not challenged. It was potentially a base from which to launch an attack on England but attempts so to use it were rare, on a small scale and unsuccessful. There was sympathy for Irish Catholics and nationalists, but strategic interests rather than sentiment dictated the policies of European states towards Ireland.

Considerations of national strategy and sentiment have not now disappeared but today they operate within the legal and political framework of the European Union (EU)[34] and are circumscribed by and expressed in terms of its pluralist and reconciliatory goals. The formation of the EU has not radically transformed Europe's traditional state

---

[33] *Irish Times*, 3 Jan. 95.
[34] We use the new name, European Union, throughout the discussion, except when the reference is unambiguously and solely to periods when it was known as the European Community (EC) or the European Economic Community (EEC).

structures. Thus far it represents a new socio-spatial layer superimposed on the multipolar structure of the past; national identities and interests are still extremely important and the lineaments of traditional conflicts remain visible within the new order (as the response to German reunification clearly revealed). The formation of the EU has improved relations between member states, including between Britain and Ireland. It has also made available new strategic resources for the parties to the conflict in Northern Ireland – the two states and and the two communities. It has not, however, provided a dramatically new context for resolving the conflict.

The EU and the conflict in Northern Ireland

When EEC membership first emerged as an option for the Republic in 1960 the government saw it as a potential route to Irish reunification. By the time membership came about – in 1973 – Northern Ireland was in the throes of violence and Irish unity was off the immediate political agenda for constitutional nationalists. For the Irish and British governments the priority was to find some means of ameliorating relations between the communities in Northern Ireland, though without compromising their differing constitutional claims and aspirations. For their part, the communities were concerned to use whatever means European integration might provide to defend or advance their vital interests. For the two states, the EU provided a context in which they would acquire the experience and skills to address the conflict in a more cooperative way; for the two communities it became an extension of the domestic battle-field.

In principle the EU's founding ideals – in particular the goal of transcending European interstate and border disputes – provided some basis and rationale for an active policy in respect of Northern Ireland. In practice both the Commission and Council were determined to keep their distance from it.[35] Constitutionally the conflict was internal to the United Kingdom and therefore the EU had no competence to intervene. But in addition, neither Commission nor Council considered there was much they could do to improve matters and both were concerned that, if they overstepped the mark, they could threaten the far more important matter of ensuring progress in EU integration. No pressure came from either government for any other policy.

---

[35] This and following information is drawn from interviews with a number of Commission officials in 1993. See also Jacques Delors's clear statement in Belfast, reported *Irish Times*, 4 Nov. 1992.

The Commission adopted the view that, while it could not intervene directly, it could perhaps alleviate some of the economic problems which were exacerbating the conflict. It responded generously to applications for aid under existing programmes and supported cross-border programmes; in January and March 1995, it announced additional EU funding as part of the 'peace dividend' in response to the peace process. From time to time there have been decisions with a more political slant. Thus in 1978 the European Council agreed to three European parliament seats for Northern Ireland – a significant overrepresentation compared to the rest of the United Kingdom – to ensure a voice for the nationalist community in Northern Ireland in the parliament. In all such decisions, the Commission and Council have followed the lead of the two governments and have acted only when there is agreement between them.

This response, and more generally the *modus operandi* of EU institutions, have encouraged cooperation and agreement between the British and Irish governments. The consequences have been important. Intergovernmental and administrative contact and cooperation at EU level and the formal equality of Irish and British representatives within the EU have helped break the older patterns of Anglo-Irish relations and have made a bilateral approach to Northern Ireland more plausible and attractive. The notion of pooled sovereignty – though not formally accepted – has framed many proposals for government of Northern Ireland. All this helped pave the way for the institutionalised cooperation of the Anglo-Irish Agreement;[36] in many respects, the Anglo-Irish Secretariat at Maryfield is modelled on the European Commission.[37] Similar principles underlie the proposals contained in the Frameworks Documents.

The European Parliament has adopted a much more interventionist stance than either the Commission or the Council of Ministers; it has also been an arena in which the representatives of the two communities

---

[36] Garret Fitzgerald notes the constant meetings and contacts with British counterparts within the EU in *All in a Life*, Dublin, Gill and Macmillan, 1991; see also Dennis Kennedy, 'The European Union and the Northern Ireland question', in Barton and Roche, eds., *The Northern Ireland Question: Perspectives and Policies*, pp. 177–8; Patrick Keatinge, 'Foreign policy', in P. Keatinge, ed., *Ireland and EC Membership Evaluated*, London, Pinter, 1991, pp. 156–8.

[37] John Hume, *London Review of Books*, 2 Feb. 1989; Hugh Logue's submission to the Opsahl Commission, in Pollak, ed., *A Citizens' Inquiry*, pp. 213–14; also John P. Loughlin, 'The Anglo-Irish Agreement: federal arrangement or affirmation of the nation-state?', paper presented at the World Congress of International Association of Federal Centres, College of Europe, Bruges, 1989; Kennedy, 'European Union', pp. 183–5, notes, however, that the fact that Anglo-Irish institutions apply only to Northern Ireland not to the archipelago makes the EU analogy only partial.

in Northern Ireland and their supporters in the Republic and Britain have sought to advance their particular interests. This tendency developed only after the first direct elections to the parliament in 1979. The first attempts by Northern and Southern Irish MEPs to raise matters relating to the conflict were unsuccessful, on the grounds that intervention in the internal affairs of member states was beyond the competence of the parliament. Support for discussion of the conflict was, however, growing. It arose in part out of parliament's desire to extend its role and from its *communautaire* stance and willingness to expand EU competence into areas that states consider their internal affairs. The parliament also saw itself as the moral and political conscience of the EU and it seemed anomalous that it should be able to discuss conflicts elsewhere in the world and not in the EU itself. In addition, since the parliament had limited power, there was little fear of practical consequences following from its debates or resolutions.

The first major debate on the Northern Ireland conflict was held in May 1981 on the hunger strikes and took place despite the attempts of British Conservatives to block it. A motion from two Southern Irish MEPs – Neil Blaney and Paddy Lalor – calling for greater British flexibility on the hunger strikes was rejected in favour of a Conservative-inspired European Democrat amendment which called for measures to ease tensions in Northern Ireland while recognising that the EEC has no competence to make proposals for changes in the Constitution of Northern Ireland. This debate created a precedent and was followed in the subsequent year by a number of other resolutions and debates and the sending of an informal fact-finding mission to Northern Ireland. In autumn 1982, John Hume sought hearings into ways in which the EU could contribute to resolving the crisis in Northern Ireland; in February 1983, against strong unionist and British opposition to such 'interference' in British internal affairs, the Political Affairs Committee was asked to hold an inquiry into the situation in Northern Ireland.

The resulting Haagerup Report, published the following December, favoured a sharing of powers between the two communities and envisaged the establishment of joint British–Irish responsibility in a number of fields. It was adopted by the parliament in March 1984 after a series of (mostly positive) speeches, against unionist opposition and British Conservative abstentions. Since that time, political comments and motions on Northern Ireland have been quite common in the parliament and now touch on all matters relating to the conflict.[38] In

---

[38] See Guelke, *Northern Ireland*, pp. 158–62.

1994, for example, the Social Affairs Committee completed a report on employment discrimination in Northern Ireland which focused on the continuing inequality between the communities and, while recognising the strength of existing legislation, argued that stronger measures were desirable.[39] In addition, debates on general issues of human and minority rights have direct implications for Northern Ireland. In January 1994 the parliament adopted the recommendation that the EU accede to the European Convention on Human Rights – a policy that could further problematise the British derogation from the Convention with respect to Northern Ireland.[40] In February 1994 the Killilea Report on linguistic and cultural minorities in the EU was adopted, with support from unionist MEP Jim Nicholson who hoped that the Ulster-Scots dialect Ullans (not just Irish) would be supported in Northern Ireland.[41]

The parliament's resolutions on the Northern Ireland conflict have taken a distinctive slant, one that is in tune with the EU's guiding values – reform, dialogue, interstate cooperation and compromise and protection of human and minority rights. They have consistently supported power-sharing, opposed terrorism, supported British–Irish cooperation, the Anglo-Irish Agreement and minority cultural rights. The effect, on balance, is that the parliament's resolutions have supported the demands of constitutional nationalists for reform and an institutionalised Irish dimension rather than the unionist demand for a stabilising of existing structures. The resolutions have moral and informational, rather than policy-making, force, but are nonetheless important in influencing European and international opinion.

The parliament has played another role also favourable to the nationalist position. The strong participation of Southern Irish MEPs in debates on Northern Ireland – in which they have been much more prominent than the more numerous British MEPs – has strengthened the impression of an island-wide nationalist consensus in which unionists are a small minority and of Northern Ireland as an Irish, rather than simply or primarily a British, problem. Moreover, Southern MEPs and John Hume have appeared much more in tune with the integrationist, *communautaire* ideology of the EU, with its values of pluralism and shared sovereignty, than the unionist and British MEPs attached to traditional notions of absolute sovereignty.

British and Irish participation in the EU has therefore affected the

---

[39] The Vandemeulebroucke report on employment discrimination in Northern Ireland, a resolution on which was passed by the European Parliament on 22 Apr. 1994.

[40] The recommendation was from a report by the Legal Affairs Subcommittee.

[41] The Killilea Report stemmed from a motion for resolution put by John Hume in December 1989.

power balance between the two communities in Northern Ireland, between nationalism and unionism on the island of Ireland and between the British and Irish states. It has established a greater formal equality between the British and Irish governments, it has created a context in which the British government has been willing to entertain informally, if not formally, derogations from full sovereignty. In doing so it prepared the way for the Anglo-Irish Agreement, the single most important defeat for unionism since the abolition of Stormont. At the same time activities at the level of the European parliament have strengthened the solidarity of Northern and Southern nationalists and have provided them with a platform from which to project a positive – pluralist, conciliatory, 'European' – image at the expense of unionists.

The EU as a context for resolving the conflict

Some commentators have seen in the development of the EU the emergence of a 'new Europe' which could make the terms of the current conflict irrelevant. There are different versions of the argument. One holds that integration will proceed to a point where national boundaries cease to have any meaning and the historic grounds for conflict – the nationalist desire for Irish unity, the unionist fear of it – will simply disappear. A second version believes that as integration proceeds North and South will be drawn more closely together, will learn to work together and will discover that they have more in common economically (and perhaps culturally) than is now apparent; this will in time lay the foundations for Irish reunification by consent. A third version foresees a dissolution of the nation-state within the EU and a new stress on regions; in this new regionalised EU, Northern Ireland will develop its own distinct regional identity and solidarity with which all its citizens will identify.

For the moment there is little evidence of these developments proceeding to a point where they will materially impinge on the conflict. Economic convergence between the member states of the EU – including Britain and the Republic – is very slow and there is little likelihood – still less a guarantee – that it will ever be complete. Ironically the effect of economic integration on Britain and Ireland thus far has been to move the countries farther apart, for example in the breach between sterling and the Irish púnt and the radical decrease in the percentage of Irish exports going to Britain (see chapter 9). Integration has also highlighted the deep structural differences between the economies – the closeness of England to the European core and the remoteness of Ireland, the contrasting importance of agriculture to the two economies which makes Ireland a net beneficiary of EU spending and the UK a net contributor. There has also been little convergence in welfare or social services, tax rates or relative living standards.[42]

Any convergence of economic interests between North and South is further qualified by the different state structures. In currency, taxation, welfare benefits, health provisions, and living standards North and South continue to diverge. The British–Irish Framework Document has proposed cross-border economic institutions, economic harmonisation and procedures for taking the entire island of Ireland as a single unit for EU economic (not political) policies and funding. These will increase economic convergence – to what extent is not yet clear – but economic competition across the border for inward investment and transportation routes is likely to remain.[43] British annual subsidies to Northern Ireland between 1989 and 1993 were about twenty times greater than the funds it received from the EU.[44] Even with the new EU funds, the British contribution will remain much higher. On economic grounds alone, therefore, unionists' interest in retaining the union is not altered by the effects of integration.

On the cultural level, the pace of EU integration is also very slow. Specific programmes of educational and media cooperation are underway and norms of free access to services, of equality of citizenship for men and women, and (less effectively) of minority rights are legislated for and shared. In the Irish context, these modest forms of integration have been important. Irish legislation on women's rights – equality of pay, maternity leave, advertising of jobs, equality in the social welfare code – owes much to European pressure,[45] and is important in bringing the Republic more into line with standards in Northern Ireland and in Britain. However, on other issues of divergence – Irish divorce and abortion laws and the Irish language requirement for teachers in the

[42] John Blackwell, 'The EC Social Charter and the labour market in Ireland', in Anthony Foley and Michael Mulreany, eds., *The Single European Market and the Irish Economy*, Dublin, Institute of Public Administration, 1990; see also Brigid Laffan's discussions of manpower policy, women, industrial relations and consumer law in Keatinge, ed., *Ireland and EC Membership*, chs. 24–8.

[43] James Anderson and Ian Shuttleworth, 'Bordering on the difficult', *Fortnight*, no. 313, 1993, pp. 26–7; Kennedy, 'European Union', p. 171.

[44] Calculation from figures in Kennedy, 'European Union', p. 174; see also Arthur Aughey, 'Community ideals and Northern Ireland', in Arthur Aughey, Paul Hainsworth and Martin J. Trimble, *Northern Ireland in the European Community: An Economic and Political Analysis*, Belfast, Policy Research Institute, 1989; James Anderson and Ian Shuttleworth, 'Bordering on the difficult', *Fortnight*, no. 313, 1993, p. 26.

[45] Laffan, 'Women', in Keatinge, ed., *Ireland and EC Membership*, ch. 26.

Republic, for example – the EU has refrained from interfering.[46] In fact precisely those areas of cultural and religious particularity which are central to the Northern Ireland conflict are expressly excluded from the process of European integration.

Integration and convergence at the level of political culture and identity are also very limited. For the present at least, the EU rests on a base of liberal nationalism rather than post-nationalism and residual national sentiment remains important.[47] Beneath the quasi-federal umbrella of the EU, individual states continue to pursue national projects shaped by tradition, distinctive alignments of social and cultural forces and competition with other European states. Strong *communautaire* attitudes in the Republic are limited to a minority[48] and are even less developed in Northern Ireland where pro-European nationalists and unionists remain as divided in their identity as before. For example, John Hume hopes that EU integration will let the Irish people fulfil their potential and move away from their 'oppressive and obsessive relationship with Britain', while Arthur Green is encouraged that 'nationalist minds no longer rely on pure insularity' and recommends that nationalists 'recognise that they participate in "Europe" from the perspective of the British Isles'.[49]

In such a context the prospects for radical regionalisation are very limited. Pressure has increased for regional representation and consultation but suggestions that important aspects of state power be devolved down to the regions have little effective support, even from the regions themselves.[50] As noted above, there is little inclination among the Commission and Council of Ministers to take responsibility for Northern Ireland; pressure on them to do so would be more likely to arrest than to advance the progress of EU regionalisation. Not only does the legal framework of the EU currently proscribe such intervention

---

[46] The European Court of Justice explicitly rejected the claim that the Republic of Ireland's ban on abortion contravened the Treaty of Rome's guarantee of the right to access to services; on the Irish language requirement for teachers, see Dermot Scott, 'Education', in Keatinge, ed., *Ireland and EC Membership*, ch. 29.

[47] Joseph Ruane, 'Nationalism and European Community integration: the case of the Republic of Ireland', in V. Goddard, J. Llobera and Chris Shore, eds., *Anthropology of Europe: Identity and Boundaries in Conflict*, London, Berg, 1994.

[48] *Ibid.*

[49] John Hume, 'Europe of the regions', in Richard Kearney, ed., *Across the Frontiers: Ireland in the 1990s*, Dublin, Wolfhound, 1988, p. 56; Arthur Green, 'Conservatism meets "cultural traditions"', *Fortnight*, no. 280, 1990, p. 32.

[50] Kennedy, 'European Union', pp. 180–3. The conflicts of interest and different administrative competences of different types of region – strong economically core regions, historic regions, peripheral regions, administrative regions – limit the possibilities of regional devolution.

against the wishes of the state(s) concerned, it might embroil the EU in a conflict which it could not resolve and would create a potentially dangerous precedent for other problem regions in the EU.

There is support in Northern Ireland for a regional approach to the EU on some issues. For example, dissatisfaction with the official United Kingdom representation in Brussels provoked demands from both nationalists and unionists for Northern Irish representation in EU decision-making and a Northern Ireland Centre in Europe was opened in Brussels in October 1991, funded by a range of business and community organisations and local Northern Ireland councils, and supported by the SDLP and UUP.[51] However, convergence on this issue coexists with radically opposed visions of the role of Northern Ireland within the EU; still less does it imply convergence on wider constitutional issues.

The contrasting forms of the British and Irish states thus remain crucial to the conflict in Northern Ireland. Policy-making processes and networks are very different within the two systems. The party systems, electoral practices and role of public representatives have not converged, nor have the constitutional frameworks nor the entrenched habits and expectations of 'statecraft'. The rights guaranteed within each system differ, as do the practices and perceptions of the armed and security forces. Political ideology also differs: the liberal nationalist Irish state elite now conceives of the national interest in a EU context; in Britain national sovereignty remains a core value in the political culture. Divisions between the two communities in Northern Ireland, who identify with the sharply opposed Irish and British perspectives, are thereby reproduced.

Thus far at least, European integration has not removed or even noticeably weakened the conditions of communal conflict in Northern Ireland. Its main effect has been to introduce a new arena for conflict. European elections are fought on local issues and the results interpreted for their local significance. The EU is integrated into party ideology and political debate and even where unionists and nationalists agree on some issue in the EU, they draw different conclusions as to its meaning.[52] For John Hume, North–South cooperation within the EU will soon ensure

---

[51] Bernard Conlon, 'A case for special pleading', *Fortnight*, no. 281, 1990, p. 17.

[52] Paul Hainsworth, 'Direct rule in Northern Ireland: the European Community dimension', *Administration*, vol. 31, 1983; Edward Moxon-Browne, 'The impact of the European Community', in B. Hadfield, ed., *Northern Ireland: Politics and the Constitution*, Buckingham, Open University Press, 1992, pp. 50ff.; Joseph Ruane and Jennifer Todd, 'Ireland – North and South – and European Community integration', in Paul Hainsworth, ed., *Breaking and Preserving the Mould: The Third Direct Elections to the European Parliament (1989) – the Irish Republic and Northern Ireland*, Belfast, Policy Research Institute, 1992.

that 'the Irish Border, like other European borders, will be no more in reality than a county boundary'; for Jim Nicholson, this economic cooperation is of no more political significance than that between Spain and Portugal; for Ian Paisley, John Hume should 'stop blethering about a Europe of the regions and accept that British sovereignty is here to stay'.[53]

The international context and the balance of communal power in Northern Ireland

International opinion has converged on support for the Catholic community in Northern Ireland. This support is in line with past sympathy for Irish nationalism in its struggle with Britain and also draws on the perception of Northern Ireland as a less than fully legitimate political entity.[54] However, it cannot be explained wholly in nationalist terms. There is little active support internationally for traditional Irish nationalism or its concern with reunification. There is no opposition to Irish unity; indeed there would be widespread welcome for it if it could be achieved with the consent of the people of Northern Ireland. But the opposition of the unionist majority is well known, as is the decision of the British government to respect the constitutional preference of the majority. The republican attempt to use violence to override unionist opposition cost Northern Catholics international sympathy and tarnished the image of their community.

Much support for Northern Catholics has come from principles and policies often conceived as antithetical to traditional nationalism: concern with civil and minority rights and a belief that these should be accomodated not by redrawing national boundaries, but by dialogue and, if necessary, cooperation between states in a spirit of pluralism, compromise, tolerance and reconciliation. These principles are among the founding ideals of the European Union. Equality, pluralism, tolerance, compromise and respect for minorities are also entrenched in the political tradition of the US. Constitutional nationalists, aided by the diplomatic resources of the Irish state, have been very effective in articulating their interests and concerns in terms of such principles, and thus in a manner to which international opinion can readily respond. Their success owes much to their refusal to use the language of irredentist nationalism.

---

[53] John Hume, reported *Irish Times*, 17 Nov. 1989; interviews with Jim Nicholson MEP and Rev. Ian Paisley MEP.
[54] Guelke, *Northern Ireland*.

At the same time, the policies of the two states go beyond the normal interpretation of these principles. Liberal unionists have consistently argued that Catholic minority rights can be fully protected within a United Kingdom constitutional framework or by intergovernmental cooperation, which normally involves full recognition of existing frontiers.[55] However, not only is there international acceptance of more radical policies, there has been pressure for them, particularly from the US government. Here international perceptions of Northern Ireland have been important. We have described the category problem Northern Ireland presents to outside observers, the fact that the dualistic nature of the Irish historical experience allows the conflict to be interpreted as an interface–periphery conflict, as colonial, or as a mixture of both. While interpretations vary, there is general recognition that the conflict is not simply one of conflicting nationalisms in an interface–periphery, that it owes something to the legacy of British colonialism in Ireland. As such it points to solutions conceived in more radical terms.

Unionists are increasingly concerned. They have long been aware that nationalists have been more effective in the battle for international sympathy and that, in their own terms, they have 'few friends in the world'. They attribute this not to the fact that Catholics have a better case but to their effectiveness in the propaganda battle and to political bias, particularly among Irish-Americans. They are further convinced that nationalists are using appeals to minority rights and pluralism to advance more traditional nationalist goals. Their primary defence has been to argue against any form of international involvement on the ground that the conflict is internal to the United Kingdom and a matter solely for the British government. International perceptions and British government policies – the increasing British stress on the Irish dimension of the conflict and the intergovernmental level – are making this defence less and less effective.

[55] Kennedy, 'European Union'.

11   An emancipatory approach to the conflict

Partition did not resolve the historic Irish conflict; it defused it temporarily by accommodating the interests of the two communities in direct proportion to their power. Conflict was suppressed for a time but in 1968–9 re-emerged, concentrated in Northern Ireland but involving the South and the British government. In this final chapter, we draw on our analysis to identify the changing structure of the conflict, to explain why it is continuing and to propose an approach to resolving it.

Partition and its consequences

The source of the pre-partition conflict lay in a system of relationships with three levels (chapter 2). The first consisted of a set of analytically distinct but concretely overlapping dimensions of difference in respect to religion, ethnicity, settler-native status, ideologies of progress and backwardness, and nationality. The second level consisted of a structure of dominance, dependence and inequality involving the British state and Protestants and Catholics in Ireland. The third consisted of tendencies toward communal polarisation around the dimensions of difference. These three levels interlocked, fed back on and mutually reinforced each other. But there was also a dynamic for change. It came from the recovery of power by Catholics and their increasing ability to challenge the system which disadvantaged them. Overt conflict occurred when Catholics pressed for reform or more radical change in the face of Protestant and/or British resistance. The Catholic demand for home rule represented a fundamental challenge to the system as a whole, and it led to partition.

The analysis in this book shows that partition did not mark a new beginning. It led to the territorial restructuring of the historic system of relationships, but did not dissolve it or stifle its dynamic tendencies. First, the dimensions of difference survived intact. In the North they underpinned the opposition between Northern Protestant and Northern Catholic communities – Protestant versus Catholic, Ulster-Scots versus

Irish, 'settler' versus 'native', British vs Irish and Protestant attributions of 'modernity' versus 'backwardness'. They also underpinned North–South perceptions. Protestants saw the new state in the South as Catholic, Gaelic, native, backward, Irish; Catholics conceived their national project in terms of removing the British legacy, as modernising but within a neo-traditionalist Gaelic cultural and linguistic idiom. Only the small group of Southern Protestants broke with their past and even then not for several decades and on some dimensions more than others.

Second, partition modified but did not dissolve the traditional structure of dominance, dependence and inequality. The great majority of Catholics on the island were now free of Protestant and British dominance. But Protestant dominance over Catholics continued in Northern Ireland and was resented by Catholics on the island as a whole. Catholic nationalists continued to see the island as a single entity, denied the legitimacy of partition, aspired to reunification and deeply resented the frustration of their national goals. Acutely conscious of their status as a minority on the island, Northern Protestants identified the support of the British government and control in Northern Ireland as the twin conditions of their survival. For their part, the British government supported the Northern state, endorsed Northern Protestants' claim to legitimate authority within it and gave them a free hand. In so doing it secured its own interests in Ireland.

Third, new forms of community – Northern Protestant, Northern Catholic, Southern Protestant, Southern Catholic – emerged but along-side rather than in place of the old. Partition had real consequences but in nationalist eyes – and most Catholics of this period were strongly nationalist – the island remained a single entity. Northern Catholics continued to look to the South and struggled to retain their position as fully-fledged members of the 'Irish nation'. Their interest was less than fully reciprocated in the South but the bonds of solidarity remained strong. Conflict between Southern Catholic and Southern Protestant was overcome and a 26-county Southern imagined community emerged, with Catholics and Protestants as distinct strands within it. In the North, Protestants and Catholics remained bitterly divided.

The system of relationships remained, therefore, broadly intact. Even more striking, the dynamic for change of the earlier period – the tendency for the balance of power on the island to shift towards Catholics – also continued. Over time Northern Catholics evolved from a geographical category ('Catholics in the six counties') to a community ('Northern Catholics') capable of autonomous political action. The political base of the community was strengthened by an expanding middle class and by an increasingly assertive working class. The achievement of an independent sovereign state in the South further increased the power resources of nationalism on the island. Meanwhile the power of Northern Protestants was in decline. Their autonomous economic base was being eroded; their claim on unconditional British support was weakening. Britain itself was a declining power in international terms.

Nationalists and republicans had challenged the Northern state from its foundation but to no avail. By the 1960s the balance of power had shifted sufficiently to make it vulnerable to a different kind of challenge – one focusing on the denial of 'civil rights' to Catholics. Unionists found the form of this challenge very difficult to deal with, and, in opting for repression, revealed the limits of their own strength while exposing their state to outside scrutiny. The British government was forced to intervene. It attempted to reassure Protestants about their position within the United Kingdom but demanded that the Stormont government introduce reform. A reform process began but met with increasing unionist opposition; Catholic protest and rioting continued, provoking unionist pressure for a harder security line. The slowing of the reform process and the harsh security measures alienated even moderate Catholics and provided the climate for republicans to launch a violent campaign for Irish reunification.

The republican campaign and the Unionist and British governments' inability to contain it without further alienating the mass of Catholics finally brought down the Stormont government and opened the way to direct rule. While continuing to reassure Protestants of their position within the United Kingdom, the British government responded to Catholic grievances by institutional reform, and by making power-sharing and a role for the Republic the conditions of any future political settlement. Protestants were unconvinced by British guarantees of their position and determined to yield as little ground as possible. Some resisted Catholic advances through the political process and the security forces, others by paramilitary violence.

The republican campaign failed in its attempt to secure a British withdrawal; its form of violence could not compensate for Catholic demographic, political and economic weakness. But, on balance, the political initiatives and reform programme benefited Catholics and further eroded the Protestant position. It did not produce equality, but it reduced the extent of inequality.

The current conjuncture

What is the situation today? In some respects, Northern Ireland has become more insulated from the rest of the island – more 'a place apart' than it was in 1969. The concentration of conflict and violence in Northern Ireland has differentiated the experiences of Northerners and Southerners; the North is now administratively more integrated into the United Kingdom; contacts between Northern Protestants and the South have reduced significantly; many Northern Catholics are openly hostile to the Republic. But there are also counter-tendencies. There is increasing convergence in nationalist politics North and South; Southern influence in the North is growing; the two governments have proposed further functional integration of the two parts of the island. Most important of all, the system of relationships producing the conflict has remained broadly intact. The two Northern communities continue to divide on the same dimensions of difference and are as polarised as ever; intracommunal conflict has increased but each community maintains its solidarity in opposition to the other. Serious inequality between the communities persists despite the reforms; the Catholic sense of grievance remains strong, even among the new middle class. Northern Protestant perceptions of the South have not fundamentally changed and their fear of abandonment by Britain remains intense.

Northern Catholics are more critical of the South but they also look to it for political and cultural support. Southerners have in the main abandoned traditional nationalism but in favour of liberal nationalism rather than revisionism or post-nationalism.[1] There is greater acknowledgement of unionist rights but also strong support among the public and the political parties for the Northern Catholic demand for parity of esteem with Northern Protestants, and Southerners interpret the phrase in the manner of Northern Catholics, not Northern Protestants. The support for Irish unity expressed in opinion polls remains remarkably high (chapter 9). The launching of the peace process revealed the extent to which an island-wide nationalist community continues to exist and its political importance. Ironically the island-wide consciousness of northern Protestants has also grown over the past twenty-five years, though for negative reasons – an increased fear of the implications of being a minority on a majority Catholic and nationalist island.

Britain also continues in its traditional role, even if now reluctantly. It has few strategic interests in Northern Ireland – except perhaps to protect the union in Britain and to avoid the destabilisation that would follow a precipitate withdrawal. It has obligations to remain, based on past guarantees to the Protestant community and a commitment to respect the wishes of a majority of the citizens of Northern Ireland. But

---

[1] Joseph Ruane, 'Secularization and ideology in the Republic of Ireland', in Paul Brennan, ed., *La sécularisation de l'Irlande*, Caen, forthcoming.

to remain is to underwrite the existence of Northern Ireland and by implication the dominance of Protestants as the majority community. The British government is committed to establishing greater equality between the communities but the problems it faces are immense; these include the still considerable economic and coercive strength of the Protestant community and their capacity to resist reform.

The traditional dynamic – the tendency of the balance of power to shift in the Catholic favour – is also still evident. Catholics have benefited from the pressure for reform coming from the Republic and the United States and their position in the economy, political system and public culture is noticeably stronger than two decades ago. Their demographic position is also stronger. The morale of the Protestant community has suffered as its position has been challenged and its power resources eroded. The influence of the Republic of Ireland over Northern affairs has steadily increased and it acts in favour of Northern nationalists. Unionists have the support of the British government, but only in exchange for their acceptance of continuing reform. Also, while British power will remain dominant in the area, its *relative* decline seems set to continue and the future of the union in Great Britain itself is not assured.

If the historic system of relationships is still intact, some of the changes of the past twenty-five years have introduced more 'play' into it. Ideological reconstruction has opened greater possibilities of dialogue within the North and between unionists and nationalists island-wide. Many Northern Protestants have rethought their political positions and if they remain – in general – unionists, they are so in a more reflective way than in the past. The historic island-wide community is no longer the Catholic nationalist monolith it was in the decades after partition. Its nature and boundaries are now more open to internal contest, and, though Catholicism and nationalism remain central dimensions under-lying the community's constitution, they now coexist in considerable tension. North and South, there are liberal and pluralist tendencies in Catholicism and nationalism that would have been inconceivable even two decades ago. The aspiration to Irish unity remains as an ideal – among Northern Catholics and in the South – but it is not unconditional in either jurisdiction. The reform process in the North has had an impact and many Catholics have abandoned their earlier scepticism about its potential; many Protestants are willing to accept a more equal Northern Ireland. The strong pro-union strands in the British political elite are now, it seems, a minority, and the declaration of the British government that it will withdraw from Northern Ireland if that is the wish of the majority of its people can be accepted.

This combination of continuity and change underlies different approaches to the peace process. For some it is simply a practical accomodation to the current balance of power. The past twenty-five years of political and military struggle have revealed to the different protagonists the extent and limits of their power and the relative stability of the current balance of power. On both sides there has been a change in strategy – a pursuit of traditional goals by other means, at least in the short term. But if this represents no more than a pragmatic, strategic acceptance of the present balance of power, the endorsement of the peace process and of any settlement that follows is good only as long as the present balance of power obtains.

Others – in both communities and in all parties – view the peace process quite differently. They see a real potential to bring the long destructive conflict finally to an end and are genuine in their expressions of moderation and generosity, their desire for reconciliation. For them the peace process is a first step to a permanent resolution of the conflict and an agreed settlement would represent major progress in that direction. There are many in both communities who fluctuate between these two poles in response to events and to their reading of others' attitudes. The actions and policies of the two governments will be a crucial factor in confirming – or disconfirming – that there is now a real potential for resolving the conflict.

The search for a solution: government policies

The current policy directions of the two governments – and their under-lying assumptions about the nature of the conflict – at once embody continuities and contrasts with the past. Initially the British government responded to the conflict as a problem of 'community relations' internal to the United Kingdom; this assumption underpinned the reform process of the period 1969–72 (chapter 5). From the autumn of 1970, a resurgent IRA confronted it with a quite different and much more brutal understanding of the conflict – one in which it was an alien, occupying power. This understanding appeared to be confirmed by the British response to that campaign – internment, interrogation methods perfected in the colonies, and the shooting of unarmed civilians.

The disastrous effect of these policies led the British government to prorogue the Stormont parliament, in the process reopening the 'Irish question' considered closed for half a century. The need for a new settlement of the Irish question which this time took account of Northern Catholics' interests led directly to the institution of a power-sharing executive in Northern Ireland and a Council of Ireland in 1973–4. The loyalist Ulster Workers Council strike brought home to the British government the power of the Protestant community and the limits of its acceptance of Westminster's decisions. The British government entertained the possibility of withdrawal, but instead settled down to manage the conflict as best it could within a United Kingdom context. But the measures it adopted to defeat the IRA served instead to strengthen republicanism, while pressure came from the Republic, the United States and later from the European Union for policies that took more account of Catholic grievances and aspirations.

The British response was to open up a new level in the policy process beyond the influence of the Protestant community – an intergovernmental level of cooperation with the Irish government. Subsequently this became the main motor of policy advance; its value was confirmed by the success (at least in terms of international relations) of the Anglo-Irish Agreement. Much later the full benefits of the 'Irish dimension' became clear when negotiations between the British and Irish governments and the SDLP and Sinn Féin culminated in the republican and loyalist ceasefires. As the Downing Street Declaration and Frameworks Documents make clear (see below), the British government has moved to a view of the conflict as one between two traditions and two communities on the island of Ireland to which it is external. In many ways, of course, this has been the implicit position throughout.

From the outset, the Irish government saw the conflict in the context of the island as a whole and in relation to the conflicts of the past. But it hesitated to press that definition too strongly. Its influence over the British government was very limited; it was gravely worried – not least for its own future – at the ruthlessness and persistence of the republican campaign; it was frightened by the revelation of Protestant communal power in the Ulster Workers Council strike of May 1974. For a time it concentrated its energies on insulating itself from developments in the North, defeating the republican campaign of violence and undermining possible support for republicanism in the South. The policy was but partially successful and carried a price in the further alienation of those in the North who supported the republican campaign.

The dangers of this minimalist approach became clear with the hunger strikes and the rise in electoral support for Sinn Féin. The Irish government now intensified its efforts in support of constitutional nationalism and against republicanism. It gave a new focus to the island dimension of the problem by convening the New Ireland Forum of 1983–4 and negotiating the Anglo-Irish Agreement of 1985. The Agreement strengthened constitutional nationalism but did not defeat republicanism. Ironically only when the Irish government ceased trying to defeat the republican movement and began to offer it opportunities within the political process did it achieve influence over republicans and the long desired ceasefire. The price was the fuller endorsement of the island-wide view of the problem and a commitment to find a solution involving a substantial reintegration of the two parts of the island.

The Joint Declaration of the British and Irish governments at Downing Street on 15 December 1993 (the Downing Street Declaration) and the two Frameworks Documents issued by the two governments on 22 February 1995, represent their current position. The Downing Street Declaration sets out the governments' shared understanding of the nature and origins of the conflict, their goals and the principles they will follow to achieve them. The two Frameworks Documents give practical and institutional expression to the principles of the Declaration. One document presents the British government's proposals for internal devolved structures within Northern Ireland; the other is a joint British–Irish document which sets out the proposals of the two governments for relationships within and between the two islands.

The Downing Street Declaration (DSD) makes clear the emphasis the two governments now place on the Irish context. The conflict is the fruit of a long history that embraces the British Isles as a whole (DSD, Para. 1), but it is not (today at least) a conflict between the people of Britain and Ireland. It is rather between two traditions or communities on the island of Ireland, and in particular within Northern Ireland. The British government is involved, but it has no 'selfish strategic or economic interest' in Ireland. The solution to the conflict lies in achieving agreement on the island of Ireland (DSD, Para. 2) although this requires facilitation from the British government (DSD, Para. 4). The Irish government acknowledges the role of mistrust and suspicion between the two communities/traditions in Ireland in perpetuating conflict. In particular it acknowledges unionist concerns about the Republic and undertakes to remove the causes of unionist concern, though with due regard to the desire to preserve 'inherited values' (DSD, Para. 6).

The solution to the conflict is to be found – indeed can only be found – through dialogue and agreement (DSD, Paras. 2, 7, 8). The right of the 'people of Ireland' or 'the people of the island of Ireland alone' to self-determination is affirmed and formulated in terms of agreement and consent (DSD, Paras. 4, 5). The governments stress the need for dialogue and the growth of trust occurring in the context of new institutions which 'while respecting the diversity of the people of Ireland, would enable them to work together in all areas of common interest' so as to help 'build the trust necessary to end past divisions, leading to an agreed and peaceful future' (DSD, Para. 9).

The Frameworks Documents outline the institutions which are to give expression to these principles. The British government's proposals centre on devolved institutions with legislative and executive responsibility over a wide range of areas, including security – and an elaborate system of checks and balances to protect minority interests – measures to protect basic rights, proportional representation, the requirement of consensus and weighted majorities.

The joint Framework Document (JFD) focuses on North–South and British–Irish relations. It envisages institutions which allow 'agreed, dynamic, new co-operative and constructive relationships' (JFD, Para. 23)between the traditions, North and South. Their purpose is to:

> help heal the divisions among the communities on the island of Ireland; provide a forum for acknowledging the respective identities and requirements of the two major traditions; express and enlarge the mutual acceptance of the validity of those traditions; and promote understanding and agreement among the people and institutions in both parts of the island. (JFD, Para. 38).

The institutions proposed would consist of intergovernmental North–South bodies with administrative backup concerned with issues ranging from the economy to education and culture. They would have executive, harmonising and/or consultative functions, assigned initially by the two governments, later by the Northern and Southern administrations. They would be unboycottable, have a clear institutional identity and purpose (JFD, Para. 25), with no limits placed on their eventual scope (JFD, Para. 28). Decisions by these bodies would be by agreement between North and South (JFD, Para. 35). Institutionalised parliamentary and administrative cooperation is also envisaged (JFD, Paras. 36, 37).

The east–west structures envisaged include a standing Intergovernmental Conference supported by a permanent secretariat staffed by civil servants of the two governments (JFD, Para. 40). Its purpose is to enable the two governments to work together to realise the aims of the Downing Street Declaration – to secure agreement and reconciliation in Ireland and to lay 'the foundations for a peaceful and harmonious future based on mutual trust and understanding between them' (JFD, Para. 41). While some of the responsibilities of the Conference would be transferred to the proposed new devolved government in Northern Ireland (JFD, Para. 45), the British government guarantees to support the new North–South institutions in the event of a breakdown of devolved institutions (JFD, Para. 47). Both governments would ensure the protection of rights in their jurisdictions (JFD, Para. 50) and a charter of such rights is envisaged that could incorporate 'an enduring commitment on behalf of all the people of the island to guarantee and protect the rights, interests, ethos and dignity of the unionist community in any all-Ireland framework that might be developed with consent in the future' (JFD, Para. 52).

The Downing Street Declaration won considerable cross-community support; among the unionist parties only the DUP opposed it; on the nationalist side, the SDLP supported it enthusiastically, Sinn Féin was ambiguous. However the Frameworks Documents, more particularly the joint Framework Document, have polarised the communities, gaining broad nationalist approval and unionist rejection. Unionists were able to accept the understanding of the conflict and the principles enunciated in the Downing Street Declaration, but rejected the way in which the two governments translated these principles into practical proposals. Their objections centre on the North–South bodies and their unease goes deeper than the specific institutions proposed. They reject the basic thrust of policy – the emphasis on the Irish context and the search for a solution through the increasing functional integration of the island of Ireland. For unionists (and for nationalists) this opens the real possibility of future political unity.

The nationalist parties welcomed the Frameworks Documents, though more as a step in the right direction than as a final goal. Even if the institutions proposed were put in place, they would not address all nationalist concerns. North–South relations would be strengthened and – if the bodies were given substantial executive and harmonising powers – the prospect of Irish unity in the middle term would increase. It is less clear that the new institutions would contribute much to reducing economic and cultural inequality in Northern Ireland. The broad parameters of policy would be set down by the Intergovernmental Conference, presumably following the egalitarian and pluralist principles set out in the Forum Report and reiterated since by the two govern-ments.[2] But immediate policy would be the responsibility of the new devolved Northern institutions and, as proposed, these contain so many checks and balances that it is difficult to see them making and enforcing radical change.

At the time of writing, negotiations on these proposals have not yet begun but the prospects for agreement are not good. The two govern-ments are committed to achieving a settlement which can win the agreement of all traditions on the island. They are also committed to a policy which the representatives of the unionist tradition strongly oppose.

[2] Jennifer Todd, 'Equality, plurality and democracy: justifications of proposed constitutional settlements of the Northern Ireland conflict', *Ethnic and Racial Studies*, vol. 18, no. 4, 1995.

A solution to this dilemma may be sought in the process of negotiation, perhaps by diluting the provisions for North–South bodies to satisfy unionists and putting pressure on both communities to accept the new proposals. But there is little room for manoeuvre and in such circumstances it is unlikely that either community would feel secure that its interests were being protected. More important, it would represent a yielding to the politics of power which the peace process has sought to bring to an end. A settlement based on power rather than agreement will last only as long as the current balance of power remains. A temporary settlement is worth striving for, but it must be borne in mind that the collapse of the last one in 1969–72 brought a violent conflict that lasted twenty-five years and led to over 3,000 deaths.

The search for a solution: general paradigms

In the years since the conflict broke out, a number of general paradigms have emerged to guide the search for a solution. Do any of these offer a way out of the current impasse? The three major paradigms are integrationism, regionalism and dualism. Each attempts to transcend or moderate conflict by accomodating the central concerns and interests of each of the communities in Northern Ireland, in particular the Protestant concern about security and the Catholic concern with equality. We assess the extent to which the paradigms meet these opposed sets of interests.

Integrationism

The integrationist paradigm seeks to overcome the conflict by integrating Northern Ireland into a larger political entity which will give full individual political equality while refocussing loyalty from community to state. One version proposes integration into the United Kingdom, the other into the Republic. Despite their differences, the two forms share the perception that full participation in a larger political system based on modern, pluralist, democratic forms of citizenship is the key to overcoming communal polarisation.

Unionist integrationism proposes fuller integration into the United Kingdom.[3] It argues that the separate regional political status and organisation of Northern Ireland is the major factor producing oppo-

---

[3] For integrationist arguments see Arthur Aughey, *Under Siege: Ulster Unionism and the Anglo-Irish Agreement*, Belfast, Blackstaff, 1989, ch. 5; Hugh Roberts, 'Sound stupidity: the British party system and the Northern Ireland question', *Government and Opposition*, vol. 22, no. 3, 1987.

sitional communal politics – it encourages nationalist demands for reunification and intensifies unionist insecurity and Protestant solidarity against Catholic assertion. Full integration into the United Kingdom would settle the constitutional question once and for all and allow normal left–right politics to replace communal politics. Though this is a solution within the union, integrationists argue that it meets most Catholic demands. It ensures full equality of all citizens of the United Kingdom; at the same time Catholics can retain their separate cultural identity since the United Kingdom is a modern, multinational and multiethnic state, pluralist and tolerant, able to accomodate Scottish and Welsh nationalism as well as the ethnic consciousness of small groups.

Unionist integrationism offers an effective critique of the destructiveness of communal zero-sum politics. Its analysis of the conditions of this communal conflict is much weaker.[4] It assumes, first, that Protestants' concerns about their position in Ireland would be fully satisfied by integration and that they would no longer have the incentive to pursue particularist, communal interests in Northern Ireland. Yet the whole of Ireland was once 'irrevocably' integrated into the United Kingdom and this did not prevent either the rise in Catholic power or nationalist mobilisation for home rule. If the shift in the balance of power continues, Protestants are unlikely to relax their vigilance or allow their solidarity to weaken. In fact, the appeal of integration to many Protestants derives not from a desire to get beyond communal politics, but from a belief that integration (by removing the influence of the Irish state) will weaken Catholics and allow Protestants better to secure their own position.[5]

Unionist integrationism assumes, second, that Catholic interests would be met by equal citizenship in the British state. This radically overestimates the neutrality of the British state and the extent to which Catholics in Northern Ireland can achieve equality within it. We have seen (chapter 8) that the ability of the Scots and the Welsh to identify with the British state derives from their different mode of integration into it and their subsequent participation in its development. Irish Catholic integration into the British state meant subordination and marginalisation and their cultural and national identity developed in opposition to

---

[4] Colin Coulter, 'Class, ethnicity and political identity in Northern Ireland', *Irish Journal of Sociology*, vol. 4, 1994.
[5] In opinion polls, the percentage of Protestant favouring integration rises sharply when majority rule devolution is not an option; cf. ch. 3, fig. 3.2, and B. O'Leary, 'Public opinion and Northern Irish futures', *Political Quarterly*, vol. 63, no. 2, 1992, tables 2 and 3.

it. The post-imperial understandings of Britishness which hold an integrative potential for some Northern Catholics are not the understandings of government or state elite (or most unionists), nor have they been sufficient to integrate even the minorities within Great Britain whose demands have been less than those of Northern Catholics (chapter 8). Similarly it is not clear why political integration alone would undo the considerable economic and political inequality which still remains (chapters 5 and 6).

Nationalist integrationism assumes that the historic divisions between Catholic and Protestant, nationalist and unionist, could be overcome in a politically united Ireland in which all would be treated equally. There are different variants of this view. Traditional nationalists see the divisions as artificial and superficial, encouraged by the continued British presence and certain to disappear as soon as the link is broken by political integration of the North into the Southern state. Liberal nationalists believe that the new liberal and pluralist tendencies within nationalism can accomodate all the legitimate interests of Northern Protestants: they foresee a more gradual process of political integration by consent of North and South within a reformed Irish state. Both assume that unity would – at a stroke – address the problem of Northern Catholic cultural and political inequality; economic inequalities might remain at least for a time but they would no longer have the same destructive consequences.

Many Northern Protestants (how many it is impossible to say) believe that if there was a genuine and deep commitment to a reconciliation of 'Protestant, Catholic and Dissenter', a united Ireland, with a radically reconstituted Irish state, could be politically and culturally viable. However, very few believe that such an Ireland is on offer. Their view is well founded. Traditional nationalism has at best a limited understanding of the issues at stake. The new liberal nationalism offers a rhetorical pluralism but its will to challenge the institutions and structures of Southern society to accomodate Protestant interests is not yet proven. Southerners know very little about Northern Protestants and there is a strong underlay of hostility, at best ambivalence, towards them. Moreover, the Republic's ethos and institutions reflect the culture and experiences of the provinces of Munster, Leinster and Connacht rather than Ulster – to a point where Northern Catholics too feel like outsiders. Political integration alone would highlight these problems, not resolve them.

Nor can it be assumed that a politically united Ireland would adequately meet the interests and concerns of Northern Catholics. First, many Northern Catholics now express the same kinds of objections to the South as do Northern Protestants – the weakness of the economy, the dominance of the Catholic church, the illiberality of many of its laws and the strong Southern ethos of the society and state. Second, constitutional equality for Catholics is not simply an abstract concern – it is a means of achieving change in economic, social and cultural life in the immediate localities in which they live. Unity would not necessarily advance change; it might impede it, especially if it was achieved by agreement between Southerners and Northern Protestants seeking to retain their regional power base.

Regionalism

Regionalism looks to dissolve communal and national division into multiple overlapping identities and to offer each of the multiple groups opportunities for equal participation and expression within a devolved, semi-autonomous, regional framework.[6] Like integrationism, but for different reasons, it underestimates the forces making for communal polarisation.

Regionalists seek a resolution of the conflict in the specificity of Northern Ireland conceived as a zone of political and cultural overlap and convergence.[7] They recommend a process of mutual distancing – by the states from their 'client' communities and by the communities from 'their' states – and a common commitment by the people of Northern Ireland to the region they share. A regional commitment would allow the current opposition of national identities and allegiances to be transcended without loss of face by either side. More positively, it would allow the members of each community to express their common regional culture and identity and would remove the pressure to follow oppositional national patterns. Regionalism would protect Protestants from a united Ireland; once their fear of unity was removed, they would more easily accept equality for Catholics within Northern Ireland. Progress towards communal equality would be accompanied by a declining emphasis on communal division.

Regionalism is perceptive on the ideological cross-currents within the

---

[6] This is the thrust of Alliance Party policy; it also informs the Opsahl Commission's proposals, Andy Pollak, ed., *A Citizens' Inquiry, The Opsahl Report on Northern Ireland*, Dublin, Lilliput, 1993.

[7] See the Alliance Party, *Alliance News*, Interparty talks supplement, Nov.–Dec. 1992. Edna Longley's submission to the Opsahl Commission in Pollak, ed., *Citizens' Inquiry*, pp. 339–41; Richard Kearney and Robin Wilson, submission to the Opsahl Commission, published as 'Northern Ireland's future as a European region', *The Irish Review*, no. 15, 1994.

Protestant and Catholic communities and correctly argues that Protestant interests in security and Catholic interests in equality must be met if the conflict is to be resolved. However it overstates the potential of Northern Ireland as a region for this task. In part, this reflects an inaccurate analysis of international trends. Many regionalists have argued that nation-states are in process of dissolution, eroded from above by supranational institutions and from below by a new regional vitality; regionalising Northern Ireland simply brings it into line with a wider European trend.[8] The slowing pace of EU integration and the very diverse nature of European regions raise serious questions about this analysis and suggest that regionalisation will occur only where local conditions are particularly favourable.

Northern Ireland does not offer such conditions. Neither community has a sufficiently strong commitment to the region to outweigh communal interests. Catholics have no positive cultural or political identification with the six-county unit of Northern Ireland which was formed against their will and imposed on them by force. Such an identification is unlikely to emerge while the legacy of Protestant dominance remains so deeply inscribed in the landscape, social structure and culture. Protestants have a strong cultural identification with the region but for most this is with an 'Ulster' conceived as the Protestant people's homeland; they would have to re-imagine Northern Ireland as a region of all its people. Apart from the emotional difficulties this would present, there are important strategic obstacles. A regionalist Northern Ireland would weaken the British link and leave unionists vulnerable if they were to be faced by renewed nationalist pressure. The regionalist proposal seeks to rule out such a nationalist renewal, but this cannot be guaranteed, not least given the difficulties that would be encountered in reconstructing Northern Ireland on more equal and more pluralist lines.

Dualism

Dualists stress the depth and more or less permanent nature of the communal conflict and the need at once to ensure equality and security for both communities. They propose to institutionalise full equality between the communities – usually by means of joint sovereignty or joint or shared authority – while stabilising the power balance between them.

The dualist paradigm views Northern Ireland as a region where two

---

[8] Richard Kearney, 'Introduction: thinking otherwise', in Kearney, ed., *Across the Frontiers: Ireland in the 1990s*, Dublin, Wolfhound, 1988; Kearney and Wilson, 'Northern Ireland's future'.

historic processes of state and nation-building overlapped leaving in their wake two communities with conflicting ethno-national identities and allegiances.[9] The differences between the two communities are profound and cannot be transcended, dissolved or ignored. The goal of policy should be the securing of a fair balance between them.[10] The balance is to be achieved at the constitutional level by dual sovereignty or joint or shared authority with input from the two states and Northern Irish representatives through devolved institutions; it is to be stabilised by constitutional checks on further change.[11] Within Northern Ireland, equality is to be achieved by strong fair employment legislation and practices, reform of the public service and security forces, and recognition of the national symbols of both communities. Equality in all spheres of life will not end the conflict but it will remove the most pressing motives for it.

The dualist approach recognises the central part which inequality and power struggle play in the conflict and the crucial role of the two states. It does not propose to overcome the socio-cultural or ideological conditions of this power struggle or the basic structures of communal organisation and division. Rather, taking these as given, it seeks to address their consequences by equalising the power resources on each side. It proposes to counterbalance the support the British state offers Northern Protestants with an equivalent support for Northern Catholics from the Republic. This will meet Protestant concerns about their future either as a majority or minority community in Northern Ireland and will also create a more favourable climate for addressing Catholic grievances about inequality.[12]

The dualist paradigm views the conflict as symmetrical in form – two historical processes of state- and nation-building, two contemporary states and nations, two communities seeking to be associated with their co-nationals. In fact the two states are vastly different in their paths of historical development and internal structures today. This has one very important consequence: the relationship between the British state and Northern Protestants is not equivalent to that between the Southern state and Northern Catholics. This is most evident in the contrast between

---

[9] B. O'Leary and J. McGarry, *The Politics of Antagonism: Understanding Northern Ireland*, London, Athlone Press, ch. 2.

[10] For dualist approaches, see Frank Wright, *Northern Ireland: A Comparative Analysis*, Dublin, Gill and Macmillan, 1987; O'Leary and McGarry, *Politics of Antagonism*; Brendan O'Leary et al., *Northern Ireland: Sharing Authority*, London, Institute of Public Policy Research, 1993.

[11] O'Leary et al., *Northern Ireland*, pp. 42–6.

[12] *Ibid.*, pp. 61–2 and fn. 24, p. 154 where they say that this is the best solution to the contradiction of interests.

the British state's willingness to withdraw from Northern Ireland and effectively to cut its links with Northern Protestants and the unwillingness or inability of the Irish state to do the same with Northern Catholics. The difference is not simply a matter of current desire or policy, but of fundamental structures of community rooted in two diametrically opposed histories of state-building (chapter 3).

The dualist approach elides these differences in community–state relationships. Northern Protestants, however, do not. On the contrary, they are well aware of the shallowness of the British commitment to Northern Ireland and conscious that the link could be broken. For them, dualist proposals for joint authority are not means of guaranteeing security and equality to both communities; rather they represent a further erosion of their position and the harbinger of worse to come. In contrast to the Protestant perception, the dualist view underestimates the dynamic nature of the processes at work. The fact that a dualist solution can even be considered reflects the increase in Catholic power and the erosion of the Protestant position; joint authority would further improve the position of the Catholic community and open the prospect of further gains.

But the question also arises whether joint or shared authority would adequately address Catholics' immediate concerns about equality. It would deliver greater political equality and would probably accelerate the reform process but inequalities will not easily be eliminated, all the less in a context in which Protestants fear a continued erosion of their position and resist reform. A situation might well develop in which Catholics are using their enhanced power resources to press harder for gains, thus generating further Protestant resistance. The result would be heightened conflict.

In short, none of the dominant paradigms offers the governments a way out of the current impasse; something more will be required. In the last resort, the governments' problem arises from the fact that while they are committed to the principles of agreement and reconciliation, the conditions of conflict – which constitute two communities with radically conflicting interests – make it impossible to achieve such agreement. In our view more favourable conditions can be created, but it will require the dismantling of the historic system of relationships which is causing the conflict.

An emancipatory approach to the conflict

We have argued that the proximate cause of the conflict in Northern Ireland is the existence of two communities there with conflicting economic, political and cultural interests under conditions of an uneven and changing balance of power. Each community feels impelled to struggle to advance or defend its interests. Underlying this communal conflict and producing it is a wider system of relationships that is now centuries old. A resolution of the conflict requires a dismantling of this system of relationships. The fundamental policy question is how this is to be done. In our view it can only be done through an emancipatory process in which all who are part of the system, and who are brought into conflict by it, cooperate in its dismantling. The process would be emancipatory in the sense that it would flow from conscious choice and purposive action designed to bring to an end a mutually destructive power struggle, creating thereby a 'realm of freedom' in which new social and cultural potentials could be realised.

The formal conditions for emancipation can be stated briefly. It would involve a multistranded approach to moderate and differentiate the dimensions of difference, to undo the structure of dominance, dependence and inequality and to weaken the forces producing communal polarisation.

Moderating differences and differentiating dimensions

The conflict rests on sharp and overlapping differences in respect of religion, ethnicity, settler–native status, notions of progressiveness and backwardness, national identity and allegiance. As in any conflict, peace and reconciliation do not demand an end to difference; on the contrary, difference, once accepted and respected, can bring positive riches. But not all differences can be reconciled. Oppositional differences in which each defines the other as its own devalued negation do not permit mutual acceptance or respect. In the current conflict, ethnicity – a sense of Ulster-Scottish versus Gaelic-Irish ancestry – does not divide the communities in Northern Ireland in such an oppositional way, but the other dimensions of difference, or particular strands within them, do.

Calvinist fundamentalism and Roman Catholicism are conceived on radically different and opposed historical, theological and organisational assumptions. The settler–native opposition distinguishes between powerful and powerless, victorious and defeated, possessor and dispossessed. The civility/barbarism and advanced/backward distinctions make fundamental judgements of cultural and moral worth and deny such worth to whole social categories. The distinction between 'British' and 'Irish' is, on the one hand, a claim to a higher status in a wider socio-cultural hierarchy underpinned by power and, on the other, a contestation of the legitimacy of that hierarchy and resistance to it.

Relations between groups constituted by such differences would be difficult even under ideal structural conditions; in the current conflict, oppositional differences exacerbate structurally defined conflicts of interests and encourage communal polarisation. It is not clear how the conflict can be resolved without some moderation of opposition on each dimension. Equally, the overlapping nature of the dimensions ensures that the meanings, oppositions and intensity associated with each dimension transfer to the other dimensions with polarising effects. A greater differentiation of the dimensions is also necessary.

We do not underestimate the difficulties associated with this. The cultural logic and assumptions on which the oppositions are based are deeply internalised, embedded in communal identities and reproduced as much by practical and ritual activity as by conceptual argument (chapter 4). They also serve to maintain group solidarity and to defend vital interests. Each dimension of difference operates in a wider social field whose centre of power lies elsewhere. Roman Catholicism, for example, is a world-wide highly centralised religion presently in a conservative phase – its representatives in Ireland do not have (or at least do not assert) the freedom to evaluate and to innovate to take account of local traditions and circumstances. The discourse of settler versus native refers to a global experience of colonisation and decolonisation. The criteria used to distinguish 'progressive' from 'backward' have their origins in the major international cultural centres and are to a considerable degree imposed by them. Dominant notions of Britishness and Irishness are embedded in British and Irish state structures and the requirements of political legitimation (chapters 8, 9).

Powerful interests are also involved. For example, the Catholic church in the South has benefited from the fusion of religion and national identity; the institutional church and many Catholic fundamentalist groups view any attempt to differentiate them with concern. The unionist parties in Northern Ireland have benefited from the support of the Orange Order and the perception that they defend not simply the union but the Protestant religion; there too there is resistance to change. But more is at stake than institutional interests. The demand to separate these dimensions – Irishness from Catholicism and from a sense of being the true and native people of the island, Britishness from Protestantism and from a self-perception as inherently more progressive – is experienced by many as a threat to their deepest sense of self and communal belonging. Material interests are involved where attributes which previously functioned as cultural capital in the public domain face depreciation.

Without minimising the difficulties involved, there are some hopeful

signs. There is increasing resistance throughout the island of Ireland
to working within the traditional binary oppositions. Ecumenical theo-
logians have sought to understand Calvinism and Catholicism as two
necessary but incomplete (and of themselves distorted) aspects of a fuller
Christianity which has been sundered – even if they have yet to convince
the wider faithful. The binary opposition of British and Irish has been
subjected to conceptual deconstruction, as, more generally, has the
advanced/backward opposition.[13] Historical research has gone some way
to blurring the native–settler distinction by bringing out the historical
complexities of the process of immigration and settlement. On the
communal level, important work has been carried out in the last two
decades by ecumenists, reconciliation groups, womens' groups, in
Cultural Traditions sponsored projects and programmes of 'Education
for Mutual Understanding'.

Disassembling the structure of dominance, dependence and inequality

The conflict is also generated by a distinctive structure of dominance,
dependence and inequality. In the past – in the heyday of European
rivalry and British imperial rule when Ireland as a whole was within the
union – the interests underpinning this were more complex and various
than they are today. Now the immediate source of conflict is the nexus
of Northern Protestant dependence on the British state and dominance
over Northern Catholics. But the other aspects have not quite disappeared. A degree of uncertainty continues regarding British interests
in (or in respect to) Ireland. Southern attitudes to Britain and to
Northern unionists, as well as their identification with and support for
Northern nationalists, show that the past has not been forgotten or –
despite moderation – forgiven.

Disassembling this structure is an essential prerequisite of conflict
resolution. It would require three things. The first is further confirmation
and more positive expression of the British government's declared
position that it has no selfish interests in Ireland, and that it seeks
genuinely to facilitate reconciliation and agreement on the island of
Ireland. Formal statements to this effect are present in the Downing
Street Declaration, but in this as in other areas of politics, principled

---

[13] Seamus Deane, *Civilians and Barbarians*, Field Day pamphlet no. 3, Derry, Field Day,
1983; Declan Kiberd, *Anglo-Irish Attitudes*, Field Day pamphlet no. 6, Derry, Field
Day, 1984; Edna Longley, submission to Opsahl Commission, in Pollak, ed., *Citizens'
Inquiry*, pp. 339–41; Edna Longley, 'From Cathleen to anorexia', in *The Living Stream:
Literature and Revisionism in Ireland*, Newcastle upon Tyne, Bloodaxe Books, 1994.

declarations need to be confirmed by practical action. We have noted the British state's tradition of territorial management using local power-holders and the influence of the changing balance of local power on British policy in Northern Ireland (chapters 5 and 8). Both communities – Catholics for the short term, Protestants for the longer term – will need reassurance that future policies will be shaped more by the goal of reconciliation than the dynamics of local power.

A second prerequisite for disassembling the nexus of dominance and dependence is the construction of an alternative source of security for Northern Protestants on the island of Ireland. At present their mode of defence is partition and the control they exercise as a majority within Northern Ireland. Their demographic, economic, political (including coercive) and cultural resources still give them a decisive power advantage over Catholics in Northern Ireland. Their resources would be less effective in an island context. Protestant numbers as a proportion of the island as a whole have been falling. Their control of the middle levels of the Northern economy is increasingly vulnerable to outside forces, some based in the South of Ireland. Their coercive power depends to a considerable extent on the currently inflated size of the British security forces in Northern Ireland; their political influence owes much to their status as the majority community; much of their cultural power derives from the dominance of British norms and presuppositions in the public sphere. If communal division and power struggle continued in a united Ireland, Northern Protestants would be unlikely to flourish. For the present, they stick to their traditional posture and method of communal defence in part at least because they have no reasonable alternative source of security. But this stance reinforces Catholic inequality, Protestant resistance to reform and generates continuing power struggle. Only when their communal security is guaranteed by other means will Northern Protestants consider a new settlement based on agreement rather than dominance.

Guaranteeing an alternative mode of security for the Northern Protestant community on the island cannot be achieved by a redistribution of power resources – the imbalance on the island is too great. At least three things are required. First, the factors making for communal division on the island – and therefore the salience of power and the implications of unequal power – must be weakened. Second, a new public sphere would have to be created with Northern Protestant participation that would ensure and facilitate the expression of Protestant individual and communal rights and interests throughout the island. Third, insofar as the power imbalance remains relevant, the imbalance would have to be made up by an evident moral and political commitment on the part of the Catholic majority – shown in a range of concrete legal, constitutional and socio-cultural decisions and political negotiations – to the well-being and security of the Protestant community on the island.

A third requirement in disassembling the structure of dominance is the establishment of full economic, political and cultural equality between Northern Catholics and Northern Protestants in whatever future geo-political unit they find themselves. It is difficult to be precise about the content and context of such equality, whether, for example, it would suffice to have full equality of flags and emblems, of economic condition, of policing, of institutional expression of identity within Northern Ireland or whether something quite different would be required. What is certain is that unless Northern Catholics can genuinely feel that the subordination and marginalisation of the past is fully and finally at an end, they will continue their struggle. In that event, the traditional logic of communal conflict would assert itself and the power struggle would go on.

The changes proposed do not rule out a continued British link or a continuation of the union – this would be a matter for negotiation and agreement – but it would make its form qualitatively different. The dependent instrumentalism of the past would go and, for unionists, the link would now be a purer expression of cultural identity and political allegiance. Similarly, the changes do not imply or rule out a united Ireland – that too would be a matter for agreement – but they would require a new and closer relationship between Northern Protestants and the rest of the island. This would be necessary if Protestants are to contribute to the creation of an island-wide public sphere whose norms and values would reflect their interests and concerns. The changes would also imply a relationship between the two historic communities on the island based on contact, cooperation and agreement rather than avoidance, mutual ill-will and conflict.

As before, we do not underestimate the resistance to these changes. The vast majority of Northern Protestants today still cling to the old structure of dominance, placing their hope for the future on the fall in the Catholic birthrate, in the reform process producing divisions in the Catholic community or giving the Catholic middle class a more positive interest in the union, in the South finally abandoning its aspiration to unity, in a revival of British nationalism. That tendency is sometimes attributed to a Protestant 'siege' or 'supremacist' mentality.[14] Such attitudes exist and have political consequences. But for very many

---

[14] For example, J. J. Lee, *Ireland, 1912–1985: Politics and Society*, Cambridge, Cambridge University Press, 1989, pp. 4, 79.

Protestants, the insistence on control arises from reasonable fears for their long-term security and well-being rather than paranoia or cultural supremacism. In a situation where the grounds for those fears were removed, many Protestants would consider new options.

Northern Catholics are unlikely to oppose a process which promises to release them from a condition of economic, political and cultural inequality; their main concern would be to ensure that the promise is delivered. Resistance is more likely in the Republic. The Republic has been an independent state with its own national project and priorities for seventy-five years; Northern Ireland looms large in its public life, but, as the past twenty-five years show, the conflict there can be compartmentalised and its impact on the South contained. The changes we propose would include far-reaching changes in the cultural and political ethos of the South; many would find this both disruptive and psychologically threatening. The financial implications of any proposed changes would also be weighed.

Practical political problems would certainly be encountered in the process of negotiation and reconstruction. The South finds little difficulty in accommodating the concerns of its Protestant minority. But this is a minority of 2–3 per cent which now identifies with the state and its national project. It is quite another matter to accommodate a regionally concentrated 21 per cent minority of whom the South has little direct knowledge and many hostile prejudices, which is culturally 'northern', unionist in politics and has a well-honed rhetoric of contempt for the Southern state and its culture. On the other hand, Southern business and financial interests see advantages in a single island economy; there is widespread popular desire for a settlement that brings peace to the island and growing acceptance that this will require more than token changes in the life of the South. With determined political leadership and all-party consensus, major changes are possible.

Finally, there are reasons to expect a positive British contribution to such a change. Historically the British government created, exploited and manipulated Irish divisions and imbalances of power to meet its own security needs. But for at least a century it has wished to move from such a system of rule to one based on communal harmony and consent. The reconstitution of Protestant dominance in Northern Ireland in 1921 reversed this trend but at the insistence of Ulster unionists rather than as a direct expression of British policy. The cost of that method of rule became clear at the end of the 1960s. Since 1972 the British government has sought a political settlement based on equality, consent and the moderation of division in Northern Ireland. Its policies have not always been consistent with that goal; established traditions of statecraft and party political interests at Westminster have at times taken precedence. But the commitment remains and the British government has a clear interest in resolving a conflict that costs it lives, money and international standing.

Defusing communal polarisation

Conflict is also produced by the tendency towards communal division. Communal polarisation in Northern Ireland means that Catholics and Protestants deal with each other not simply as individuals but as representative members of communities. For many the boundaries of their community define the limits of their capacity for empathy and sense of moral responsibility. Individual and social differences, violence, structural inequality, cultural patterns are all given representative communal meaning and problems are defined and solutions sought in a communal frame of reference. Thus the statistical measure of economic inequality is the relative employment status of Protestants and Catholics, and programmes of fair employment are conceived in communal terms. Communal inequality is real and has to be addressed. But policies designed to advance one community tend to produce resistance from the other with the attendant risk of aggravating the wider problem of communal conflict which the policies seek to address.[15]

Resolving the conflict will, sooner or later, require movement beyond such intense communal consciousness. This process involves, first, greater individualisation – a greater willingness by individuals to explore and give expression to their own needs and desires even if this brings them into conflict with wider communal loyalties and identities. It requires, secondly, the building of cross-community networks based on overlapping interests and concerns. Finally, it involves the forging of new inclusive communities, both in Northern Ireland and on the island as a whole.

Some of these tendencies are already present – we have detailed the extent of individual dissent and internal heterogeneity in both communities and the attempts by bridge-builders to create a more inclusive community in Northern Ireland (chapter 3). At present, the major barrier to more radical individualisation and community restructuring appears to be strategic. Given the interests at stake, most members of

---

[15] This point is made by Wright, *Northern Ireland*, for example p. 18; Arthur Aughey decries an exclusive concentration on communal equality on similar grounds that it detracts attention from individual rights, in 'Ethnic mending', in Damian Smyth, ed., *Conflict and Community*, supplement to *Fortnight*, no. 311, 1992.

each community in Northern Ireland find security in communal membership. They are unwilling to press internal divisions too far or to blur too much communal boundaries, still less to dissolve the community in a larger whole. If, however, there were to be changes at the other levels – a moderation of the extent of socio-cultural and ideological difference and a disassembling of the structure of dominance, dependence and inequality – the strategic and political interests in communal solidarity would weaken and a reconstitution of community would become possible.

The most appropriate new forms of community (and non-community) cannot precisely be anticipated; communities are emergent phenomena and they depend on structures of interest and flows of sentiment that are never fully predictable. But the island-wide context of the conflict means that some form of inclusive island-wide community will be necessary. The mere suggestion of such a community alarms many Protestants; the whole point of partition was to eliminate that possibility. But community can take many forms and the most appropriate one in this instance – undoubtedly one based on civic rather than ethno-cultural criteria – would emerge in the course of negotiation, institutional reform and agreement.

A multilevelled and multistranded approach

We have examined the way in which each level of the system of relationships contributes to conflict. The fact that these levels interlock, act back upon and mutually reinforce each other means that the conflict cannot be resolved by concentrating on one level alone or one level at a time. The approach has to be multilevelled and multistranded. For example, to concentrate simply on moderating differences – by ecumenism, the search for cultural commonalities or a more inclusive sense of national identity – will have little effect without also addressing relations of dominance, dependence and inequality and communal polarisation. Neither community will moderate its sense of difference or deconstruct oppositions if this is likely to weaken its capacity to defend its vital interests. Similarly, the search for an alternative to the current structure of dominance will bear fruit only when the process of moderating difference and easing communal polarisation is under way.

Similar considerations apply within each level. For example, Protestants will (as they already do) resist any attempt to erode their dominance within Northern Ireland unless the question of Catholic dominance at the level of the island is being addressed. Similarly, Northern Catholics will (as they already do) resist any attempt to underwrite the security of Protestants at their expense. Criticising nationalism as backward looking, totalising and irrational while implying that unionism is self-evidently progressive, liberal and rational – as many unionists do – will not moderate or deconstruct the opposition of nationalism and unionism, no more than will a concept of the Irish nation as Gaelic and Catholic allow the dichotomy of settler and native to be transcended. Bridge-building efforts in one community will make little progress unless they meet a positive response in the other. Attempts to satisfy the 'moderates' in each community and to ignore (or repress) the 'extremes' will meet with limited success, given the linkages that exist within each community.

By contrast a multilevelled and multistranded approach would make possible a benevolent cycle of conflict reduction. Moderation of the extent of difference would make it easier to find alternatives to the current structure of dominance, dependence and inequality; this would allow the exploration of new forms of community which would in turn suggest new ways of transcending the traditional differences. In such a process, progress on each strand and at each level would ease progress on the others until a momentum is created which allows the goal of peace and an agreed settlement to be reached.

Conclusion

Emancipation is often viewed as a political ideal rather than a realisable goal of practical politics, a concern of theorists rather than of politicians or governments. We have outlined the difficulties that an emancipatory approach to the Northern Ireland conflict would face. Here too emancipation may seem an impossible ideal from which practically minded politicians will keep their distance. Yet if an emancipatory process is the only hope for a resolution of the conflict, politicians and governments have little choice but to explore its possibilities. This may already be happening. There is the germ of an emancipatory approach in the two major policy statements of the British and Irish governments in recent years – the Downing Street Declaration of 1993 and the Frameworks Documents of 1995.

These documents define the nature of the conflict and the fundamental goals of the governments in emancipatory terms. The stated aims are to work together to remove the causes of conflict, overcome the legacy of history, heal divisions and end a conflict which has been detrimental to all; to achieve peace, stability and reconciliation and to create a new era of trust; to grasp the opportunity for a new beginning and for dialogue that addresses with honesty and integrity the fears of all traditions, to break decisively the cycle of violence (DSD, Paras. 1, 2, 6, 7, 8, 12). It is proposed, in effect, that previously hostile communities and traditions work together to break with the destructive pattern of the past and to build a new future based on cooperation and agreement. This is the essence of an emancipatory approach.

It is not, however, carried forward into the policy proposals of the Frameworks Documents. There the emphasis is on dealing with the conflicting interests and aspirations of the communities and the power imbalances between them through an elaborate system of constitutional and institutional checks and balances. The measures proposed have divided rather than united the communities. Even if agreement were reached the new institutions would not in themselves remove the root causes of division and bring the historical conflict to an end. Rather it is likely that the settlement would last only as long as the current balance of power, to be followed by a further political crisis (above, p. 300). Only measures that break definitively with the logic of power that lies at the heart of the conflict will bring peace, reconciliation and a lasting settlement. The way forward lies, we believe, in a more systematic and determined application of the principle of emancipation.

This book presents one version of an emancipatory approach and the empirical analysis from which it derives. Other versions are possible and indeed necessary to the process of participatory debate from which emancipatory goals emerge. Much more remains to be said about emancipation as political practice, about the role of political actors and groups within civil society, the ideologies that might inform an emancipatory process and the new relationships to follow, the interim constitutional frameworks and institutions that can facilitate the process and pave the way for agreement and reconciliation. Our concern here has been simply to show the necessity and potential of such an approach. That emancipation does not promise a simple or risk-free solution to the conflict is clear. But if the process envisaged seems too radical, too open-ended or too long, we can only affirm that no simpler, quicker, neater solution is possible.

Epilogue

This book went to press at a time – August 1995 – when the peace process faced an impasse over the decommissioning of arms and the proposals of the Frameworks Documents (above, p. 2). Hopes remained high, however, for a positive outcome. As we make the final changes to this epilogue– in June 1996 – these hopes have greatly receded. In early September 1995 the political differences between the two governments became sharper and more public as a planned summit meeting was hastily cancelled. The visit by President Clinton to Belfast in November 1995 led to a temporary improvement. However further differences arose in January 1996 over the British response to the report of the Mitchell Commission on decommissioning and the announcement of elections in Northern Ireland as a precondition to all-party talks. Also, in early September, the Ulster Unionist Party elected a new leader, David Trimble, the most combative and abrasive of the candidates and – at face value – the least likely to entertain a compromise with nationalism.

Throughout the autumn republicans were expressing increasing concern at the slow progress of the peace process, in particular the failure to hold all-party talks, and warning that the process was in serious danger of collapse. On 9 February the IRA ended its ceasefire, exploding a bomb at Canary Wharf in London which killed two people, injured many more and caused £100m of damage. The two governments responded by reinstating the security measures put in abeyance after the ceasefires and curtailing their contacts with Sinn Féin representatives. The relationship between the Irish government and republicans – the cornerstone of the peace process – had been worsening for some time; it now became openly antagonistic. The political representatives of the loyalist paramilitaries reduced their contacts with republicans and warned that, if IRA attacks continued, loyalists too would end their ceasefire.

For some commentators, the peace process was now over. The Northern nationalist parties and the Irish government, however, made clear their continued commitment to it, and the British government

317

brought a new urgency to the political process. It set a date (30 May) for elections to a Northern Ireland forum and for all-party talks (10 June). The parties were deeply divided over these proposals. The nationalist parties said they would boycott the forum since it would be dominated by unionists and could become a reconstituted Northern Ireland assembly. The unionist parties said that at the first meeting of the all-party talks they would raise the issue of the decomisioning of IRA weapons and, failing a satisfactory response, would block progress on other issues. The IRA declared that it would not decommission its weapons in any circumstances short of a final settlement. It also dampened hopes of a new ceasefire and on 24 April failed narrowly in its attempt to blow up Hammersmith Bridge in London.

The May elections and the initiation of the forum and interparty talks provided further evidence of the depth of division. The vote of the middle ground Alliance Party fell to 6.5 per cent. The SDLP remained the largest nationalist party at 21.4 per cent, but lost votes to Sinn Féin which secured its highest ever vote of 15.5 per cent. The UUP remained the largest party overall, with 24.7 per cent of the vote, but lost votes to the DUP (at 18.8 per cent) and to the smaller unionist and loyalist parties. Division also marked the beginning of the forum and interparty talks with wrangling about procedural issues and the role of the chairperson. Sinn Féin was absent from both, refusing to take its seats in the forum and denied admission to the interparty talks in the absence of an IRA ceasefire. On 10 June the IRA killed a garda síochána in an attempted robbery in Adare, County Limerick; on 15 June it exploded a bomb in the centre of Manchester which injured 200 people and caused over £100m of damage.

At the time of writing there is renewed speculation about an IRA ceasefire and about what may, or should, happen if it is not declared. Even if there is a ceasefire, and its terms are acceptable to the other parties, differences remain over decommissioning and, even more serious, about the conditions for a political settlement. Sinn Féin declares its continued commitment to peace but does so on conditions unacceptable to the unionist parties. The success of the peace process is now more than ever in doubt. Yet it represents the single most important effort thus far to resolve the conflict and its achievements to date – if only in the saving of life – have been considerable. For that reason it is important to understand why such serious difficulties have arisen.

The initiative for the peace process came from the nationalist community. Its origins lay in two interrelated developments. One was ideological. The reconstruction of nationalism in the early 1970s placed the achievement of equality between Catholic and Protestant in

Northern Ireland before the traditional goal of Irish unity and took seriously the fears and objections of Northern Protestants about Irish unity. If unity were to occur it would have to be by consent and would first require reconciliation between the two traditions on the island. The second development was structural – the growing political and economic strength of the Catholic community in Northern Ireland since direct rule. Catholics remain the weaker community today but they have a political capacity and self-confidence unknown to earlier generations. They also expect the improvement in their position to continue.

These developments gave rise to three distinct viewpoints within the Catholic community. One believes that the conditions which generated conflict within Northern Ireland and on the island no longer exist and that with sufficient openness, willingness to take radical and imaginative steps and determination to see them through, reconciliation and lasting peace are now possible. A second tendency sees continuing grounds for conflict, but argues that the reforms of the past twenty-five years, and the improvement of the position of Catholics in Northern Ireland, now make it possible to negotiate a 'historic compromise' between the two communities in Northern Ireland and the two traditions on the island. The third tendency believes that the conditions for conflict are still present, but that violence has ceased to be an effective means of nationalist advance. More can now be achieved through an alliance of nationalists throughout the island, led by the Irish government and supported by influential Irish-Americans.

Despite their differences the three strands agree on the use of exclusively peaceful methods and the need for further improvement in the position of Catholics in Northern Ireland. For those who see the conditions of conflict as now over, such improvement would not be at the expense of Protestants, since both communities would gain from peace and reconciliation. For those who seek a historic compromise, Protestants would lose in some respects but gain in others. For those concerned with nationalist advance, Protestants would lose but only because, and to the extent that, the position they now hold and the political arrangements which underpin it are unjust. The new strands of opinion gained ascendance within the Northern Catholic community. They did not, however, convince everyone. Some rejected them outright; others were sceptical; others postponed judgement, waiting to see if the new approach yielded positive results.

Initially unionists were unsure how to respond to the peace process. Its origins in the Catholic community evoked suspicion as to its motives and for some made it unworthy of consideration. Many doubted that the IRA would ever suspend its campaign of violence. When this happened, their immediate fear was that a secret deal had been done with the British government at their expense. When they were assured that this was not the case – that there was no agreement of any kind – different reactions emerged. Traditional loyalists – the Reverend Ian Paisley in particular – were hostile, warning that the process was simply a more duplicitous way of undermining the union. On the other hand, the leaders of the 'new loyalist' parties – the Progressive Unionist Party and the Ulster Democratic Party – accepted it as genuine and responded encouragingly, while making clear that they would not accept any proposal that weakened the union.

Mainstream unionists were divided. Few if any believed that the underlying conditions of conflict in Northern Ireland or on the island had ended. However, some saw the process as a genuine search for a compromise which deserved an imaginative response from unionism. Others saw it as little more than a face-saving acknowledgement by republicans that their twenty-five-year campaign had failed, and an opportunity for unionists to reassert control over political developments. Most were wary, keeping their options open. In particular, they wished to see if the IRA ceasefire would hold and what were British government intentions. The ceasefire lasted, but the IRA was unwilling to declare it permanent, to yield its weapons or to disband its infrastructure. On the political front, unionists found both the tone and content of the Frameworks Documents deeply worrying – in particular the emphasis on the island of Ireland and the proposal to establish North–South bodies with executive power and the potential for growth. For all strands of unionism this was unacceptable and it demanded a vigorous response.

Unionists countered the moral pressure generated by the peace process by focusing on its contradictions and evasions – in particular, the republican claim to be committed to peace while the IRA refused to declare the ceasefire permanent, to decommission its weapons or accept the right of the majority in Northern Ireland to determine its constitutional future. Unionists argued that if the peace process was genuinely about agreement and there was a total commitment to peace, the IRA had no need for weapons, particularly offensive ones, republicans should be willing to accept the principle of consent and the Southern government should end its involvement in Northern Ireland affairs. Failing that, the process would be revealed for what unionists claimed it was – not a genuine search for an agreed settlement but a new offensive against Protestants and the union.

Simultaneously unionists mobilised and strengthened their own power resources. They renewed their traditional stress on unionist cohesion. The UUP elected a young, energetic and combative leader. Leading

UUP politicians established links with the US administration, and to some extent with Irish–American organisations, to counter the support which nationalists had built up over the years. Simultaneously they cultivated support in Britain, particularly within the Conservative Party, linking the union with Northern Ireland with the fate of the union as a whole. Unionist intellectuals published articles and books challenging nationalist assumptions and defending the union. Most important of all, the UUP successfully exploited a quite fortuitous development – the decreasing majority of a divided Conservative Party in the House of Commons.

These strategies were effective. Nationalist influence over political developments was at its height during the first phase of the peace process which culminated in the publication of the Frameworks Documents in March 1995. Thereafter the balance shifted and unionists were increasingly in control of events. By the end of 1995 the Frameworks Documents appeared to have been sidelined and the British and Irish governments were in sharp disagreement about how the process should be advanced.

The unionist recovery reflected changing British government priorities. The British government had entered the peace process in response to nationalist pressure and persuasion. It had done so cautiously, in part because it doubted the willingness of the IRA to declare or to maintain a ceasefire, in part because it was aware that the concessions needed to satisfy nationalists (let alone republicans) would arouse the opposition of unionists. It had no desire for confrontation with unionists and there was to be no repeat of what happened at the time of the Anglo-Irish Agreement. There was little room for manoeuvre. Nevertheless, the possibility of an IRA ceasefire could not be ignored and while the ceasefire was being negotiated the British government leaned towards the nationalist side. Thereafter the balance shifted, and even as the Frameworks Documents were being launched, the British goverment took much care to reassure unionists that they would not be imposed on them.

The shift in British policy reflects the exigencies of different stages in the negotiating process, the balance of communal power in Ireland and the government's growing dependence on unionist votes in the House of Commons. Less clear is the effect of the IRA's refusal to declare its ceasefire 'permanent' or to decommission its arms ahead of all-party talks. The British government made much of both issues, though softening its demands as time went on, accepting that the ceasefire was permanent and demanding the decommissioning of just *some* arms. Its policy on both issues was variously interpreted. Unionists saw the demands as perfectly legitimate to determine whether or not the IRA was genuine in its commitment to peace. Republicans concluded that the British government was deliberately engaged in a delaying tactic. Having failed to defeat the IRA by security measures, it now sought victory by other means – prolonging the ceasefire to the point where the IRA would find it impossible to renew its campaign and begin to disintegrate as an organisation.

The decline in nationalist influence over the direction of the peace process was due also to emerging tensions within the nationalist alliance, centering primarily on the role of the Irish government. The Irish government saw enormous benefits in the peace process for its own citizens and for the island as whole and was the driving force in the process at inter-governmental level. Nevertheless there were problematic aspects to it. The Irish government views itself as the state of a future Irish nation in which all traditions are reconciled on the basis of consent; even now it is committed in principle to the well-being of all on the island. The peace process demanded that it act as the leading representative of the nationalist tradition, which now incorporated republicanism. The contradiction could be resolved only – and then not completely – by the argument that it was necessary to achieve the peace and reconciliation from which all would benefit.

Fianna Fáil under Albert Reynolds was able to resolve what doubts it may have had in that regard. Fine Gael under John Bruton, the main party in government from January 1995, had greater difficulty. This was due in part to the fact that the IRA ceasefire was in place and the priority now was to achieve a settlement with unionists. But Fine Gael had long emphasised the importance of developing the middle ground in Northern Ireland and building bridges with unionism. It was more disposed than Fianna Fáil to accept the legitimacy of Northern Ireland and the democratic claims of its majority, and had greater misgivings on the IRA's refusal to decommission its arms. The new coalition government also included representatives of Democratic Left, a party with roots in the republican tradition but now very hostile to it.

The new government remained committed to its role as representative of nationalism, but less assuredly and assertively than its predecessor at a time when for other reasons the tide was turning against nationalism. The effect was to weaken the cohesion of the nationalist alliance and also – though this is less clear – its capacity to extract concessions from the British government. The extent of that weakness was revealed in January 1996 when the British government gave summary treatment to the report of the Mitchell Commission and adopted a UUP proposal for elections to a new assembly in Northern Ireland as a precondition to all-party talks. The proposal had been strongly opposed by the Northern nationalist parties and the Irish government but to no avail.

This was the context in which the IRA ended its ceasefire on 9 February. Its intentions in doing so are difficult to establish; even the time when the decision was made is uncertain. But the bomb at Canary Wharf was widely seen as a response to the erosion of the nationalist (more particularly, the republican) position over the period of the peace process and intended to remind the British government that the republican capacity and willingness to use violence were undiminished. Nationalist unease at the pace and direction of the peace process at this time can be seen from the reaction to the bombing; while the vast majority of nationalists on the island were shocked, condemned the bombing and attributed moral responsibility for it to the IRA, they attributed political responsibility for what happened to the British government and to unionists.

Initially it was hoped that the Canary Wharf bomb was an isolated incident designed to achieve a specific political objective – to intensify the pace of the peace process and increase nationalist influence over it. It appears to have had this effect. Both governments showed a new urgency about the process and a date was set for all-party talks, the principal republican demand. The balance of British policy also shifted away from the unionists and the Frameworks Documents were again on the agenda for discussion. On the other hand, the two governments demanded a reinstatement of the ceasefire as a condition of Sinn Féin's participation in the talks. Thus far the IRA has refused to do this. Some commentators anticipate a new ceasefire; others do not and call for internment. Even if a new ceasefire is called it is likely to be tactical and conditional, rather than the principled abandonment of violence sought by the two governments.

Each party to the conflict blames the difficulties in the peace process on others while defending its own role. Nationalists criticise the British government for having made unrealistic demands on the IRA (to declare the ceasefire permanent, to decommission its arms); they criticise unionists for failing to appreciate the risks that nationalist leaders took to get the peace process underway, their lack of generosity in response and their exploitation of the Conservative Party's vulnerable position in the House of Commons. Republicans criticise the Irish government for failing to assert itself against the British government; the Irish government criticises republicans for their failure to endorse the principle of unionist consent. Unionists and the British government criticise republicans for refusing to accept the principle of unionist consent and their unwillingness to decommission any of their weapons prior to all-party talks. They criticise other nationalists, including the Irish government, for failing to appreciate the reasonableness of such demands in a modern democracy, especially in view of Northern Protestants' suffering at the hands of the IRA.

Certainly all sides have taken positions which have prevented rapid progress towards a settlement. However this is not a sufficient explanation of the continuing crisis in the peace process. To explain it we have to go beyond events and policies to the structural context and dynamic tendencies of the conflict which set limits to any attempt to find peace. These include deep-rooted historical processes, social and ideological divisions within as well as between the communities, a changing power balance in Northern Ireland across the political, economic and cultural domains that is very difficult to read, the British emphasis on working through the local balance of power, the nature of Southern society, and the changing international context. Together these conditions leave each community in Northern Ireland with the conviction that it has vital interests to defend and that it must defend them with all the resources available to it. In such circumstances power – rather than reconciliation – is the immediate and overriding concern.

The peace process proposed new institutions and constitutional forms as a basis for peace and reconciliation. But the proposals would also change the balance of power. Many nationalists supported them precisely for that reason. Unionists resisted them for that reason. The absence of violence was not sufficient to displace attention from the central question of power; the two communities assigned different meanings to the ceasefire and to the continued holding of arms. Instead they mobilised other forms of power. As the search for reconciliation gave way to a struggle for and about power, hopes for a settlement receded.

The struggle for power undermines the search for a settlement based on agreement. The only approach likely to resolve the conflict in the long term is one which undercuts the logic of power that lies at its heart. The emancipatory process we propose seeks to do this by dismantling the conditions that produce conflict and give power its compelling meaning.

Appendix: Sources of opinion poll material

The main opinion polls used in the figures and text, particularly in chapter 3, are noted below. Jennifer Todd acknowledges the help of John Whyte who gave her access to his collection of opinion poll material.

1967. National Opinion Polls for *Belfast Telegraph*, 8 December.

1968. 'The Loyalty Survey'. Reported in Richard Rose, *Governing Without Consensus*.

1973. May. Carrick James Market Research for Fortnight and the Sunday Times. Reported *Fortnight*, no. 62, 1973.

1974. April. National Opinion Polls for the BBC. *Belfast Telegraph*, 19 April.

1976. National Opinion Polls for BBC and *Belfast Telegraph*, reported *Belfast Telegraph*, 19 March 1976.

1978. Northern Ireland Attitude Survey, reported in Moxon- Browne, *Nation, Class and Creed*.

1982. February. National Opinion Polls conducted for UTV.

1986a. January. Coopers and Lybrand for *Belfast Telegraph*. Reported *Belfast Telegraph* 15 January 1986.

1986b. June. D. J. Smith for SACHR, reported Smith, *Equality and Inequality*, and Smith and Chambers, *Inequality in Northern Ireland*.

1987. May. Coopers and Lybrand for UTV.

1988a. March. Coopers and Lybrand for *Fortnight* and UTV reported in *Fortnight* no. 261, 1988.

1988b. September. Coopers and Lybrand for the *Belfast Telegraph* reported in *Belfast Telegraph*, 4, 5 October 1988.

1990. January. Ulster Marketing Surveys for Belfast Telegraph reported *Irish Political Studies*, vol. 6, 1991.

1991. Rowntree trust, reported O'Leary, 'Public opinion and Northern Irish futures'.

1993. September. Ulster Marketing Surveys for UTV.

December. Ulster Marketing Surveys for UTV.

December. Coopers and Lybrand for the *Irish Times*.

Surveys reported in *Irish Political Studies*, vol. 9, 1994.

Bibliography

Adams, Gerry. *The Politics of Irish Freedom*. Dingle: Brandon, 1986.
A Pathway to Peace. Cork: Mercier, 1988.
Adamson, Ian. *The Identity of Ulster*. Belfast: Pretani, 1982.
Akenson, Donald Harman. *A Mirror to Kathleen's Face: Education in Independent Ireland 1922–1960*. Montreal: McGill-Queens University Press, 1975.
Between Two Revolutions: Islandmagee, Co. Antrim 1798–1920. Dublin: Academy Press, 1979.
God's Peoples: Covenant and Land in South Africa, Israel and Ulster. Ithaca: Cornell University Press, 1992.
Alcock, Anthony. *Understanding Ulster*. Lurgan, Co. Armagh: Ulster Society Publications, 1994.
Allister, James H. *Irish Unification: Anathema. The Reasons why Northern Ireland Rejects Unification with the Republic of Ireland*. Belfast: Crown Publications, n.d.
Allister, Jim. *Alienated but Unbowed: A Unionist Perspective on the Origin, Meaning and Future of the Anglo-Irish Agreement*. Carrickfergus: East Antrim DUP, 1987.
Allister, Jim, Ivan Foster, William McCrea and Peter Robinson. *Northern Ireland: 'A War to be Won'*. Belfast: DUP, 1984.
Amnesty International. *Political Killings in Northern Ireland*. London: Amnesty International British Section, 1994.
Anderson, Benedict. *Imagined Communities: Reflections on the Origin and Spread of Nationalism*. London: Verso, rev. edn, 1991.
Anderson, James and Ian Shuttleworth. 'Bordering on the difficult', *Fortnight*, no. 313, 1993, 26–7.
Arthur, Paul. *Government and Politics of Northern Ireland*. Harlow: Longman, 1980.
'The Mayhew talks 1992', *Irish Political Studies*, 8, 1993, 138–43.
'The Anglo-Irish Joint Declaration: towards a lasting peace?', *Government and Opposition*, 29, 2, 1994, 218–30.
Arthur, Paul and Keith Jeffery. *Northern Ireland since 1968*. Oxford: Basil Blackwell, 1988.
Aughey, Arthur. *Under Siege: Ulster Unionism and the Anglo-Irish Agreement*. Belfast: Blackstaff, 1989.
'Community ideals and Northern Ireland', in Arthur Aughey, Paul Hainsworth, Martin J. Trimble, *Northern Ireland in the European Community:*

An Economic and Political Analysis. Belfast: Policy Research Institute, 1989, 5–27.

'Ethnic mending', in Damian Smyth, ed., *Conflict and Community*, supplement to *Fortnight*, no. 311, 1992, 9–11.

Irish Kulturkampf. Belfast: Ulster Young Unionist Council, 1995.

'The end of history, the end of the union', in A. Aughey, D. Burnside, E. Harris, G. Adams, J. Donaldson, *Selling Unionism, Home and Away*. Belfast: Ulster Young Unionist Council, 1995, 7–14.

Aunger, E. A. 'Religion and occupational class in Northern Ireland', *Economic and Social Review*, 7, 1, 1975, 1–18.

'Religion and class: an analysis of 1971 census data', in R. J. Cormack and R. D. Osborne, eds., *Religion, Education and Employment: Aspects of Equal Opportunity in Northern Ireland*. Belfast: Appletree, 1983, 24–41.

Baker, Sybil E. 'Orange and Green, Belfast 1832–1912', in H. J. Dyos and Michael Wolff, eds., *The Victorian City: A New Earth*, vol. 2. London: Routledge Kegan Paul, 1973, 789–814.

Bardon, Jonathon. *A History of Ulster*. Belfast: Blackstaff, 1992.

Barkley, John M. *Blackmouth and Dissenter*. Belfast: Whiterow, 1991.

Barnard, Toby. 'Planters and policies in Cromwellian Ireland', *Past and Present*, 61, 1973, 31–69.

Barritt, D. P. and Charles F. Carter. *The Northern Ireland Problem: A Study in Group Relations*. Oxford: Oxford University Press, 1962.

Bartlett, Robert. *The Making of Europe: Conquest, Colonization and Cultural Change 950–1350*. London: Penguin, 1994.

Bartlett, Thomas. 'The burden of the present: Theobald Wolfe Tone, republican and separatist', in D. Dickson, Dáire Keogh and Kevin Whelan, eds., *The United Irishmen: Republicanism, Radicalism and Rebellion*. Dublin: The Lilliput Press, 1993, 1–15.

'The origins and progress of the Catholic question in Ireland', in T. P. Power and K. Whelan, eds., *Endurance and Emergence: Catholics in Ireland in the Eighteenth Century*. Dublin: Irish Academic Press, 1990, 1–20.

'From Irish state to British empire: reflections on state-building in Ireland, 1690–1830', *Études Irlandaises*, 20, 1, 1995, 23–37.

Barton, Brian. *Brookeborough: The Making of a Prime Minister*. Belfast: Institute of Irish Studies, 1988.

Beckett, J. C. *The Anglo-Irish Tradition*. London: Faber and Faber, 1976.

Bell, Desmond. 'The community studies tradition and Irish social science', *International Journal of Sociology and Social Policy*, 1, 2, 1981, 22–36.

Acts of Union: Youth Culture and Sectarianism in Northern Ireland. London: Macmillan, 1990.

Benjamin, Walter. 'Theses on the philosophy of history', *Illuminations*, edited H. Arendt. Glasgow: Fontana, 1973, 253–64.

Beresford, David. *Ten Men Dead: The Story of the 1981 Irish Hunger Strike*. London: Grafton, 1987.

Bew, Paul, Peter Gibbon and Henry Patterson. *The State in Northern Ireland 1921–71: Political forces and social classes*. Manchester: Manchester University Press, 1979.

Northern Ireland 1921–1994: Political Forces and Social Classes. London: Serif, 1995.

Bew, Paul and Gordon Gillespie. *Northern Ireland: A Chronology of the Troubles 1968–1993.* Dublin: Gill and Macmillan, 1993.

Bhaskar, Roy. *Scientific Realism and Human Emancipation.* London: Verso, 1986.

Black, Jeremy. *Eighteenth Century Europe 1700–1789.* London: Macmillan, 1990.

Blackwell, John. 'The EC Social Charter and the labour market in Ireland', in Anthony Foley and Michael Mulreany, eds., *The Single European Market and the Irish Economy.* Dublin: Institute of Public Administration, 1990, 350–80.

Bloomfield, Ken. *Stormont in Crisis: A Memoir.* Belfast: Blackstaff, 1994.

Boal, Fred, John A. Campbell and David Livingstone. 'The Protestant mosaic: a majority of minorities', in Patrick J. Roche and Brian Barton, eds., *The Northern Ireland Question: Myth and Reality.* Aldershot: Avebury, 1991, 99–129.

Bolger, Dermot. *A Dublin Quartet.* Harmondsworth/London: Penguin, 1992.

Borooah, Vani. 'Northern Ireland: Typology of a regional economy', in Paul Teague, ed., *The Economy of Northern Ireland: Perspectives for Structural Change.* London: Lawrence and Wishart, 1993, 1–23.

Bossy, John. 'The counter-reformation and the people of Catholic Ireland, 1596–1641', in T. D. Williams, ed., *Historical Studies VIII.* Dublin: Gill and Macmillan, 1971, 155–69.

Bourdieu, Pierre. *Outline of a Theory of Practice,* trans, R. Nice. Cambridge: Cambridge University Press, 1977.

Bowen, Desmond. *The Protestant Crusade in Ireland, 1800–70: A Study of Protestant–Catholic Relations Between the Act of Union and Disestablishment.* Dublin: Gill and Macmillan, 1978.

Bowen, Kurt. *Protestants in a Catholic State: Ireland's Privileged Minority.* Dublin: Gill and Macmillan, 1983.

Boyce, D. G. *Nationalism in Ireland.* London: Croom Helm, 1982.

Ireland 1828–1923: From Ascendancy to Democracy. Oxford: Blackwell, 1992.

Boyce, D. G., R. Eccleshall and V. Geoghegan, eds. *Political Thought in Ireland Since the Seventeenth Century.* London: Routledge, 1993.

Boyle, Kevin. 'The Irish Question and human rights in European perspectives', in Harold Olav Skar and Bjørn Lydersen, *Northern Ireland: A Crucial Test for a Europe of Peaceful Regions.* Norwegian Foreign Policy Studies no. 80, Norwegian Institute of International Affairs, 1993, 87–102.

Boyle, Kevin and Tom Hadden. *Ireland: A Positive Proposal.* Harmondsworth: Penguin, 1985.

Bradshaw, Brendan, Andrew Hadfield and Willy Maley, eds. *Representing Ireland: Literature and the Origins of Conflict, 1534–1660.* Cambridge: Cambridge University Press, 1993.

Brady, Ciaran. 'The decline of the Irish kingdom', in Mark Greengrass, ed., *Conquest and Coalescence: The Shaping of the State in Early Modern Europe.* London: Edward Arnold, 1991, 94–115.

Brady, Ciaran and Raymond Gillespie, eds. *Natives and Newcomers: The Making of Irish Colonial Society 1534–1641.* Dublin: Irish Academic Press, 1986.

Braudel, Fernand. *The Mediterranean and the Mediterranean World in the Age of Philip II.* 2 vols. London: Fontana, 1978.

Breen, Richard, Damian F. Hannan, David B. Rottman and Christopher T. Whelan. *Understanding Contemporary Ireland: State, Class and Development in the Republic of Ireland*. Dublin: Gill and Macmillan, 1990.

Brewer, John D. 'The public and the police', in Peter Stringer and Gillian Robinson, eds., *Social Attitudes in Northern Ireland: The Second Report*. Belfast: Blackstaff, 1992, 52–66.

Brooke, Peter. *Ulster Presbyterianism: The Historical Perspective 1610–1970*. Dublin: Gill and Macmillan, 1987.

Brookeborough, Lord, W. B. Maginnis and G. B. Hanna, *Why the Border Must Be: The Northern Ireland Case in Brief*. Belfast: Government of Northern Ireland publications, 1956.

Brown, Terence. *Ireland: A Social and Cultural History 1922–79*. Glasgow: Fontana, 1981.

The Whole Protestant Community. Field Day pamphlet no. 7. Derry: Field Day, 1985.

'British Ireland', in Edna Longley, ed., *Culture in Ireland: Division or Diversity?*. Belfast: Institute of Irish Studies, 1991, 72–83.

Bruce, Steve. *God Save Ulster: The Religion and Politics of Paisleyism*. Oxford: Clarendon, 1986.

The Edge of the Union: The Ulster Loyalist Political Vision. Oxford: Oxford University Press, 1994.

'The politics of the loyalist paramilitaries', in Brian Barton and Patrick J. Roche, eds., *The Northern Ireland Question: Perspectives and Policies*. Aldershot: Avebury, 1994, 103–20.

Bruce, Steve and Fiona Alderdice. 'Religious belief and behaviour', in Peter Stringer and Gillian Robinson, eds., *Social Attitudes in Northern Ireland: The Third Report*. Belfast: Blackstaff, 1993, 5–20.

Bryson, Lucy and Clem McCartney. *Clashing Symbols*. Belfast: Institute of Irish Studies, 1994.

Buchanan, R. H. 'The planter and the Gael', in F. W. Boal and J. N. H. Douglas, eds., *Integration and Division: Geographical Perspectives on the Northern Ireland Problem*. London: Academic Press, 1982, 49–73.

Buckland, Patrick. *Irish Unionism 1885–1923: A Documentary History*. Belfast: HMSO, 1973.

The Factory of Grievances: Devolved Government in Northern Ireland, 1921–39. Dublin: Gill and Macmillan, 1979.

A History of Northern Ireland. Dublin: Gill and Macmillan, 1981.

Buckley, Anthony D. 'Collecting Ulster's culture: are there *really* two traditions?', in Alan Gailey, ed., *The Use of Tradition: Essays Presented to G. B. Thompson*. Cultra: Ulster Folk and Transport Museum, 1988, 49–60.

Budge, Ian and Cornelius O'Leary. *Belfast: Approach to Crisis: A Study of Belfast Politics 1613–1970*. London: Macmillan, 1973.

Bulpitt, Jim. *Territory and Power in the United Kingdom: An Interpretation*. Manchester: Manchester University Press, 1983.

Butler, David. 'Broadcasting in a divided community', in Martin McLoone, ed., *Culture, Identity and Broadcasting in Ireland*. Belfast: Institute of Irish Studies, 1991, 99–103.

'Ulster unionism and British broadcasting journalism, 1924–1989', in Bill Rolston, ed., *The Media and Northern Ireland: Covering the Troubles*. London; Macmillan, 1991, 99–121.

Cadogan Group. *Northern Limits: Boundaries of the Attainable in Northern Ireland Politics*. Belfast: Cadogan Group, 1992.

Lost Accord: The 1995 Frameworks and the Search for a Settlement in Northern Ireland. Belfast: Cadogan Group, 1995.

Cairns, David and Shaun Richards. *Writing Ireland: Colonialism, Nationalism and Culture*. Manchester: Manchester University Press, 1988.

Cairns, Ed. 'Political violence, social values and the generation gap', in Peter Stringer and Gillian Robinson, eds., *Social Attitudes in Northern Ireland: The Second Report*. Belfast: Blackstaff, 1992, 149–61.

Campbell, Brian, Laurence McKeown and Felim O'Hagan, eds. *Nor Meekly Serve My Time: The H-Block Struggle 1976–1981*. Belfast: Beyond the Pale Publications, 1994.

Campbell, T. J. *Fifty Years of Ulster: 1890–1940*. Belfast: The Irish News, 1941.

Cannadine, David. 'The context, performance and meaning of ritual: The British monarchy and the "Invention of Tradition" c. 1820–1977', in Eric Hobsbawm and Terence Ranger, eds., *The Invention of Tradition*. Cambridge: Cambridge University Press, 1983, 101–64.

Canny, Nicholas. *The Elizabethan Conquest of Ireland: A Pattern Established, 1565–76*. Hassocks, Sussex: Harvester Press, 1976.

From Reformation to Restoration: Ireland 1534–1660. Dublin: Helicon, 1987.

'Conquest and colonisation: the implications of these processes for modern Irish history', in O. MacDonagh and W. F. Mandle, eds., *Irish–Australian Studies: Papers Delivered at the Fifth Irish-Australian Conference*. Canberra: Australian National University, 1989, 42–64.

'Early modern Ireland, c. 1500–1700', in R. F. Foster, ed., *The Oxford Illustrated History of Ireland*. Oxford: Oxford University Press, 1989, 104–60.

'In defence of the constitution? The nature of Irish revolt in the seventeenth century', in Centre de Recherches Historiques, ed., *Culture et Pratiques Politiques en France et en Irlande, XVIe–XVIIIe siècle*. Paris: Centre de Recherches Historiques, 1991, 22–40.

Carmichael, Paul. 'The 1993 local government elections in Northern Ireland', *Irish Political Studies*, 9, 1994, 141–7.

Cathcart, Rex. *The Most Contrary Region: The BBC in Northern Ireland 1924–1984*. Belfast: Blackstaff, 1984.

Chubb, Basil. *The Government and Politics of Ireland*. 3rd edn. London: Longman, 1992.

Clark, Samuel. *Social Origins of the Land War*. Princeton: Princeton University Press, 1979.

Clarke, Liam. *Broadening the Battlefield*. Dublin: Gill and Macmillan, 1987.

Clifford, Brendan. *Parliamentary Despotism*. Belfast: Athol, 1986.

Coates, David. *The Context of British Politics*. London: Hutchinson, 1984.

The Question of UK Decline: The Economy, State and Society. London: Harvester, 1994.

Cochrane, Feargal. 'Any takers? The isolation of Northern Ireland', *Political Studies*, 42, 3, 1994, 378–95.

An Coiste Comhairleach Planála/The Advisory Planning Committee. *The Irish Language in a Changing Society*. Dublin: Bord na Gaeilge, 1986.

Colley, Linda. *Britons: Forging the Nation 1707–1837*. New Haven: Yale University Press, 1992.

Colls, Robert and Philip Dodd, eds. *Englishness: Politics and Culture 1880–1920*. London: Croom Helm, 1987.

Compton, Paul. 'The changing religious demography of Northern Ireland: Some political considerations', *Studies*, 78, 312, 1989, 393–402.
'Employment differentials in Northern Ireland and job discrimination: a critique', in Patrick J. Roche and Brian Barton, eds., *The Northern Ireland Question: Myth and Reality*. Aldershot: Avebury, 1991, 40–76.

Compton, Paul and John Power. 'Migration from Northern Ireland: a survey of New Year travellers as a means of identifying emigrants', *Regional Studies*, 25, 1, 1991, 1–11.

Conlon, Bernard. 'A case for special pleading', *Fortnight*, 281, 1990, 17.

Connolly, James. *Collected Works*, vol. I. Dublin: New Books Publications, 1987.

Connolly, M. E. H. and S. Loughlin. eds. *Public Policy in Northern Ireland: Adoption or Adaptation*. Belfast: Policy Research Institute, 1990.

Connolly, Michael. *Politics and Policy Making in Northern Ireland*. London: Philip Allan, 1990.

Connolly, S. J. *Religion, Law and Power: The Making of Protestant Ireland 1660–1760*. Oxford: Clarendon, 1992.

Conroy, John. *War as a Way of Life: A Belfast Diary*. London: Heinemann, 1988.

Cook, Scott B. 'The Irish Raj: social origins and careers of Irishmen in the Indian civil service 1855–1914', *Journal of Social History*, 20, 3, 1987, 507–29.

Coolahan, John. *Irish Education: Its History and Structure*. Dublin: Institute of Public Administration, 1981.

Coopers and Lybrand. *Poll for Ulster Television/Fortnight Magazine March 1988*. Belfast: Coopers and Lybrand, 1988.

Cormack, R. J. and R. D. Osborne, 'Disadvantage and discrimination in Northern Ireland', in R. J. Cormack and R. D. Osborne, eds., *Discrimination and Public Policy in Northern Ireland*. Oxford: Clarendon, 1991, 5–48.

Cormack, R. J. and R. D. Osborne, eds. *Religion, Education and Employment: Aspects of Equal Opportunity in Northern Ireland*. Belfast: Appletree, 1983.
Discrimination and Public Policy in Northern Ireland. Oxford: Clarendon, 1991.

Cormack, R. J. and E. P. Rooney. 'Religion and employment in Northern Ireland: 1911–1971.' Unpublished paper.

Cormack, R. J., A. M. Gallagher and R. D. Osborne. *Fair Enough? Religion and the 1991 Population Census*. Belfast: Fair Employment Commission, 1993.

Cornford, James. 'Towards a constitutional equation', in Bernard Crick, ed., *National Identities: The Constitution of the United Kingdom*. Oxford: Blackwell, 1991, 157–67.

Coulter, Colin. 'The character of unionism', *Irish Political Studies*, 9, 1994, 1–24.
'Class, ethnicity and political identity in Northern Ireland', *Irish Journal of Sociology*, 4, 1994, 1–26.

Craig, Patricia, ed. *The Rattle of the North: An Anthology of Ulster Prose*. Belfast: Blackstaff, 1992.

Craig, William. Interview with Richard Deutsch, *Études Irlandaises*, 1, December 1976, 159–84.

Crawford, W. H. 'The Ulster Irish in the eighteenth century', *Ulster Folklife*, 28, 1982, 24–32.

Crick, Bernard, ed. *National Identities: The Constitution of the United Kingdom*. Oxford: Blackwell, 1991.

Cronin, Aileen. 'War and Peace: A study of hostility and harmony in Northern Ireland', MA thesis, Politics Department, University College Dublin, 1979.

Crotty, Raymond. *Ireland in Crisis: A Study in Capitalist Colonial Undevelopment*. Dingle: Brandon, 1986.

Crozier, Maurna. 'Good leaders and "decent" men: an Ulster contradiction', in Myrtle Hill and Sarah Barber, eds., *Aspects of Irish Studies*. Belfast: Institute of Irish Studies, 1990, 75–83.

Crozier, Maurna, ed. *Cultural Traditions in Northern Ireland: Varieties of Irishness*. Belfast: Institute of Irish Studies, 1989.

Cultural Traditions in Northern Ireland: Varieties of Britishness. Belfast: Institute of Irish Studies, 1990.

Cultural Traditions in Northern Ireland: All Europeans Now? Belfast: Institute of Irish Studies, 1991.

Crozier, Maurna and Nicholas Sanders, compilers. *A Cultural Traditions Directory for Northern Ireland*. Belfast: Institute of Irish Studies, 1992.

Cullen, Louis. *The Emergence of Modern Ireland 1600–1900*. London: Batsford, 1981,

'Catholic social classes under the Penal Laws', in T. P. Power and K. Whelan, eds., *Endurance and Emergence: Catholics in Ireland in the Eighteenth Century*. Dublin: Irish Academic Press, 1990, 57–84.

Cunningham, Bernadette. 'Seventeenth century interpretations of the past: the case of Geoffrey Keating', *Irish Historical Studies*, 25, 98, 1986, 116–28.

'The culture and ideology of Irish Franciscan historians at Louvain, 1607–1650', in Ciaran Brady, ed., *Ideology and the Historians*. Dublin, Lilliput Press, 1991, 11–30.

Cunningham, Hugh. 'The Conservative party and patriotism', in Robert Colls and Philip Dodd, eds., *Englishness: Politics and Culture 1880–1920*. London: Croom Helm, 1987, 283–307.

Cunningham, Michael J. *British Government Policy in Northern Ireland 1969–89: Its Nature and Execution*. Manchester: Manchester University Press, 1991.

Curran, Frank. *Derry: Countdown to Disaster*. Dublin: Gill and Macmillan, 1986.

Curtice, John and Anthony Gallagher. 'The Northern Ireland dimension', in R. Jowell, S. Witherspoon, L. Brook with B. Taylor, eds., *British Social Attitudes: The 7th Report*. Aldershot: Gower, 1990, 183–216.

Curtis, L. Perry. *Apes and Angels: The Irishman in Victorian Caricature*. Newton Abbot: David and Charles, 1971.

'Moral and physical force: the language of violence in Irish nationalism', *Journal of British Studies*, 27, 2, 1988, 150–89.

Daly, Archbishop Cahal B. *The Price of Peace*. Belfast: Blackstaff, 1991.

Damesick, Peter, 'The evolution of spatial economic policy', in Peter Damesick and Peter Woods, eds., *Regional Problems, Problem Regions and Public Policy in the United Kingdom*. Oxford: Clarendon, 1987, 42–63.

Darby, John. *Dressed to Kill: Cartoonists and the Northern Ireland Conflict*. Belfast: Appletree, 1983.

Darby, John. *Intimidation and the Control of Conflict*. Dublin: Gill and Macmillan, 1986.

Darby, John, ed. *Northern Ireland: The Background to the Conflict*. Belfast: Appletree, 1983.

Darwin, John. *The End of the British Empire: The Historical Debate*. Oxford: Basil Blackwell, 1991.

Davis E. E. and Richard Sinnott. *Attitudes in the Republic of Ireland Relevant to the Northern Ireland Problem*. Dublin: Economic and Social Research Institute, 1979.

Day, Graham and Gareth Rees, eds. *Regions, Nations and European Integration: Remaking the Celtic Periphery*. Cardiff: University of Wales Press, 1991.

Deane, Seamus. *Civilians and Barbarians*. Field Day pamphlet no. 3. Derry: Field Day, 1983.

de Baróid, Ciarán. *Ballymurphy and the Irish War*. Dublin: Aisling, 1989.

Devlin, Paddy. *Yes We Have No Bananas: Outdoor Relief in Belfast 1920–1939*. Belfast: Blackstaff, 1981.

Dewar, M. W. *Why Orangeism*. Belfast: Grand Orange Lodge of Ireland, 1959.

Dickson, Brice. 'Northern Ireland's troubles and the judges', in Brigid Hadfield, ed., *Northern Ireland: Politics and the Constitution*. Buckingham: Open University Press, 1992, 130–47.

Dickson, David. 'Catholics and trade in eighteenth-century Ireland: an old debate revisited', in T. P. Power and K. Whelan, eds., *Endurance and Emergence: Catholics in Ireland in the Eighteenth Century*. Dublin: Irish Academic Press, 1990, 85–100.

New Foundations: Ireland 1660–1800. Dublin: Helicon, 1987.

Diskin, Michael. 'Official or Democratic? The battle for Unionist votes in Northern Ireland', Ph.D. thesis, Centre for the Study of Public Policy, University of Strathclyde, 1985.

Dixon, Paul, ' "The usual English double talk": the British political parties and the Ulster Unionists 1974–1994', *Irish Political Studies*, 1994, 24–40.

Doherty, Paddy. 'A Catholic looks at the Northern state', in John Fairleigh et al., *Sectarianism: Roads to Reconciliation*. Dublin: Three Candles, 1975, 36–42.

Donnan, Hastings and Graham MacFarlane. 'Informal social organisation', in John Darby, ed., *Northern Ireland: The Background to the Conflict*. Belfast: Appletree, 1983, 110–35.

Doyle, John. 'Workers and Outlaws: unionism and fair employment in Northern Ireland', MA thesis, Politics Department, University College Dublin, 1992.

'Workers and outlaws: unionism and fair employment in Northern Ireland', *Irish Political Studies*, 9, 1994, 41–60.

Drucker, Henry, Patrick Dunleavy, Andrew Gamble, and Gillian Peele, eds. *Developments in British Politics 2*. Houndsmills: Macmillan, 1988.

Duffy, Eamonn. '"Englishmen in Vaine": Roman Catholic allegiance to George I', in Stuart Mews, ed., *Religion and National Identity*. Oxford: Basil Blackwell, 1982, 345–65.

Dunleavy, Patrick. 'Topics in British politics', in Henry Drucker, Patrick Dunleavy, Andrew Gamble and Gillian Peele, eds., *Developments in British Politics 2*. Houndsmills: Macmillan, 1988, 329–72.

Dunlop, John. *A Precarious Belonging: Presbyterians and the Conflict in Ireland*. Belfast: Blackstaff, 1995.

Dunn, Seamus, ed. *Facets of the Conflict in Northern Ireland*. London: Macmillan, 1995.

Dunn, Seamus and Valerie Morgan. *Protestant Alienation in Northern Ireland: A Preliminary Survey*. Coleraine: Centre for the Study of Conflict, 1994.

Eames, Robin. *Chains to be Broken: A Personal Reflection on Northern Ireland and its People*. London: Weidenfeld and Nicolson, 1992.

Eccleshall, Robert. *British Liberalism: Liberal Thought from the 1640s to the 1980s*. London: Longman, 1986.

'Anglican political thought in the century after the Revolution of 1688', in D. G. Boyce, R. Eccleshall and V. Geoghegan, eds., *Political Thought in Ireland since the Seventeenth Century*. London: Routledge, 1993, 36–72.

Edwards, Owen Dudley. 'Wales, Scotland and Ireland', in John Osmond, ed., *The National Question Again: Welsh Political Identity in the 1980s*. Llandysul: Gomer, 1985, 32–57.

Edwards, Ruth Dudley. *An Atlas of Irish History*. London: Methuen, 1973

Elliott, Sydney. 'Voting systems and political parties in Northern Ireland', in Brigid Hadfield, ed., *Northern Ireland: Politics and the Constitution*. Buckingham: Open University Press, 1992, 76–93.

Empey, Reg. 'Climate of submission'. Ulster Unionist Information Institute, Issue no. 10, Feb. 1993.

Eversley, David. *Religion and Employment in Northern Ireland*. London: Sage, 1989.

Religion and Employment in Northern Ireland: Additional Tables. Belfast: Fair Employment Agency, 1989.

Fair Employment Agency. *Industrial and Occupational Profile of the Two Sections of the Population in Northern Ireland: An Analysis of the 1971 Census*. Belfast: Fair Employment Agency, 1978.

Investigation into the Northern Ireland Electricity Service. Belfast: Fair Employment Agency, 1982.

Investigation into the Non-Industrial Northern Ireland Civil Service. Belfast: Fair Employment Agency, 1983.

Investigation into the Fire Authority for Northern Ireland. Belfast: Fair Employment Agency, 1984.

Progress Report on the Third Monitoring Exercise in Short Brothers PLC. Belfast: Fair Employment Agency, 1985.

Investigation into the Ulster Museum. Belfast: Fair Employment Agency, 1986.

Fair Employment Commission. *Annual Review 1992–3*. n.d.

A Profile of the Northern Ireland Workforce. Summary of the 1993 Monitoring Returns. Monitoring Report no. 4. Belfast: Fair Employment Commission, 1994.

A Profile of the Northern Ireland Workforce. Summary of the 1994 Monitoring Returns. Monitoring Report no. 5. Belfast: Fair Employment Commission, 1995.

Fanning, Ronan. *The Irish Department of Finance 1922–58.* Dublin: Institute of Public Administration, 1978.

Farrell, Michael. *Northern Ireland: The Orange State.* London: Pluto, 1980.

Arming the Protestants: The Formation of the Ulster Special Constabulary and the Royal Ulster Constabulary, 1920–27. London: Pluto, 1983.

Farrell, Michael. ed. *Twenty Years On.* Dingle: Brandon, 1988.

Faul, Denis and Raymond Murray. 'Christ and the prisoner', *The Furrow*, 31, 3, 1980, 171–4.

'H-Block and its background', *Doctrine and Life*, 30, 11, 1980, 482–9.

'Christian humanism in prison', *The Furrow*, 32, 3, 1981, 160–62.

'The alienation of Northern Ireland Catholics', *Doctrine and Life*, 34, 2, 1984, 63–72.

Faulkner, Brian. 'Ireland today', *Aquarius*, 1971; reprinted in David Bleakley, *Faulkner: Conflict and Consent in Irish Politics.* London: Mowbrays, 1974, 154–62.

Fay, Brian. *Critical Social Science.* Cambridge: Polity, 1987.

Feldman, Allen. *Formations of Violence: The Narrative of the Body and Political Terror in Northern Ireland.* London: University of Chicago Press, 1991.

Fennell, Desmond. *The Northern Catholic: An Inquiry.* An extended version of a series of articles published in the *Irish Times*, 5–10 May 1958. Dublin: Mount Salus Press, n.d.

The State of the Nation: Ireland since the Sixties. Swords: Ward River Press, 1983.

Fieldhouse, D. K. *The Colonial Empires: A Comparative Study from the Eighteenth Century.* London: Macmillan, 1982.

Fitzgerald, Garret. *All in a Life.* Dublin: Gill and Macmillan, 1991.

Fitzpatrick, Brendan, *Seventeenth-Century Ireland: The Wars of Religions.* Dublin: Gill and Macmillan, 1988.

Fogarty, Michael, Liam Ryan and Joseph Lee. *Irish Values and Attitudes: The Irish Report of the European Value Systems Study.* Dublin: Dominican Publications, 1984.

Foley, Anthony and Michael Mulreany, eds. *The Single European Market and the Irish Economy.* Dublin: Institute of Public Administration, 1990.

Follis, Bryan A. *A State under Siege: The Establishment of Northern Ireland 1920–1925.* Oxford: Clarendon Press, 1995.

Ford, Alan, 'The Protestant reformation in Ireland', in C. Brady, and R. Gillespie, eds., *Natives and Newcomers: The Making of Irish Colonial Society 1534–1641.* Dublin: Irish Academic Press, 1986, 50–74.

Foster, John Wilson. 'Who are the Irish?', *Studies*, 77, 308, 1988, 403–17.

Foster, R. F. *Modern Ireland 1600–1972.* Allen Lane: Penguin Press, 1988.

Foucault, Michel. *Power/Knowledge*, ed. C. Gordon. Brighton: Harvester, 1980.

Fulton, John, *The Tragedy of Belief: Division, Politics and Religion in Ireland.* Oxford: Clarendon, 1991.

Gallagher, A. M. *Employment, Unemployment and Religion in Northern Ireland. The Majority Minority Review, No 2.* Coleraine, University of Ulster: Centre for the Study of Conflict, 1991.

'Civil liberties and the state', in Peter Stringer and Gillian Robinson, eds., *Social Attitudes in Northern Ireland: The Second Report.* Belfast: Blackstaff, 1992, 81–101.

'Community relations', in Peter Stringer and Gillian Robinson, eds., *Social Attitudes in Northern Ireland: The Third Report.* Belfast: Blackstaff, 1993, 33–48.

'The approach of government: community relations and equity', in S. Dunn, ed., *Facets of the Conflict.* London: Macmillan, 1995, 27–42.

Gallagher A. M. and S. Dunn. 'Community relations in Northern Ireland: attitudes to contact and integration', in Peter Stringer and Gillian Robinson, eds., *Social Attitudes in Northern Ireland.* Belfast: Blackstaff, 1991, 7–22.

Gallagher, A. M., R. D. Osborne, and R. J. Cormack. *Fair Shares? Employment, Unemployment and Economic Status.* Belfast: Fair Employment Commission, 1994, reprinted March 1995.

Gallagher, Eric and Stanley Worrall. *Christians in Ulster, 1968–1980.* Oxford: Oxford University Press, 1982.

Gallagher, Frank. *The Indivisible Island.* London: Victor Gollanz, 1957.

Gallagher, Michael. 'Do Ulster unionists have a right to self-determination?', *Irish Political Studies*, 5, 1990, 11–30.

'How many nations are there in Ireland?', *Ethnic and Racial Studies*, 18, 4, 1995, 715–39.

Gamble, Andrew. *Britain in Decline: Economic Policy, Political Strategy and the British State*, 3rd edn. London: Macmillan, 1990.

Garvin, Tom. *The Evolution of Irish Nationalist Politics.* Dublin: Gill and Macmillan, 1981.

Nationalist Revolutionaries in Ireland 1858–1928. Oxford: Clarendon, 1987.

Gellner, Ernest. *Nations and Nationalism.* Oxford: Basil Blackwell, 1983.

Gibbon, Peter. *The Origins of Ulster Unionism: The Formation of Popular Protestant Politics and Ideology in Nineteenth Century Ireland.* Manchester: Manchester University Press, 1975.

Gillespie, Raymond. *Colonial Ulster: The Settlement of East Ulster 1600–1641.* Cork: Cork University Press, 1985.

Gillmor, Desmond A. *Economic Activities in the Republic of Ireland: A Geographical Perspective.* Dublin: Gill and Macmillan, 1985.

Girvin, Brian. *Between Two Worlds: Politics and Economy in Independent Ireland.* Dublin: Gill and Macmillan, 1989.

Goldring, Maurice. *Faith of our Fathers: The Formation of Irish Nationalist Ideology.* Dublin: Repsol, 1982.

Belfast: From Loyalty to Rebellion. London: Lawrence and Wishart, 1991.

Goldthorpe, John. H. and Whelan, Christopher T., eds. *The Development of Industrial Society in Ireland.* Proceedings of the British Academy, 79. Oxford: Oxford University Press, 1992.

Goulbourne, Harry. *Ethnicity and Nationalism in Post-Imperial Britain.* Cambridge: Cambridge University Press, 1991.

Graham, Charles with John McGarry. 'Codetermination', in John McGarry and Brendan O'Leary, eds., *The Future of Northern Ireland*. Oxford: Clarendon, 1990, 162–81.

Grainger, J. H. *Patriotisms: Britain 1900–1939*. London: Routledge and Kegan Paul, 1986.

Gray, John. *City in Revolt: James Larkin and the Belfast Dock Strike of 1907*. Belfast: Blackstaff, 1985.

Green, Arthur. 'Conservatism meets "cultural traditions"'. *Fortnight*, 280, 1990, 31–2.

Greene, Jack P. *Peripheries and Center: Constitutional Development in the Extended Polities of the British Empire and the United States 1607–1788*. London: Norton, 1990.

Greenwood, Liah. *Nationalism: Five Roads to Modernity*. Cambridge, Mass.: Harvard University Press, 1992.

Griffin, Brian. 'Religion and opportunity in the Irish police forces, 1836–1914', in R. V. Comerford, Mary Cullen, Jacqueline Hill and Colm Lennon, eds., *Religion, Conflict and Coexistence in Ireland*. Dublin: Gill and Macmillan, 1990, 219–34.

Guelke, Adrian. *Northern Ireland: The International Perspective*. Dublin: Gill and Macmillan, 1988.

'The United States and the Northern Ireland question', in Brian Barton and Patrick J. Roche, eds., *The Northern Ireland Question: Perspectives and Policies*. Aldershot: Avebury, 1994, 189–212.

Hadden, Tom. 'The census: not just a sectarian headcount', *Fortnight*, 195, 1983, 9.

Hadden, T., K. Boyle and C. Campbell, 'Emergency law in Northern Ireland: the context', in A. Jennings, ed., *Justice Under Fire: The Abuse of Civil Liberties in Northern Ireland*. London: Pluto, 1988, 1–26.

Hadfield, Andrew, and John McVeagh, eds. *Strangers to that Land: British Perceptions of Ireland from the Reformation to the Famine*. Gerrards Cross: Colin Smythe, 1994.

Hadfield, Brigid, 'The Northern Ireland Constitution', in Brigid Hadfield, ed., *Northern Ireland: Politics and the Constitution*. Buckingham: Open University Press, 1992, 1–12.

Hainsworth, Paul. 'Direct rule in Northern Ireland: the European Community dimension 1972–1979', *Administration*, 31, 1, 1983, 53–69.

Hamill, Desmond. *Pig in the Middle: The Army in Northern Ireland 1969–1985*. London: Methuen, 1985

Hamill, Felim. 'Belfast: the Irish language', *Éire-Ireland*, 21, 4, 1986, 146–50.

Hamilton, Andrew, Clem McCartney, Tony Anderson and Ann Finn. *Violence in the Communities: The Impact of Political Violence in Northern Ireland on Intra-community, Inter-community and Community–State Relationships*. Coleraine: Centre for the Study of Conflict, 1990.

Harbison, Robert. *No Surrender*. London: Faber and Faber, 1966.

Harkness, David. *Northern Ireland since 1920*. Dublin: Helicon, 1983.

Harris, Mary. *The Catholic Church and the Foundation of the Northern Irish State*. Cork: Cork University Press, 1993.

Harris, R. I. D., C. W. Jefferson and J. E. Spencer, eds. *The Northern Ireland Economy: A Comparative Study in the Economic Development of a Peripheral Region*. London: Longman, 1990.

Harris, Rosemary. *Prejudice and Tolerance in Ulster: A Study of Neighbours and 'Strangers' in a Border Community*. Manchester: Manchester University Press, 1972.

Hayley, Barbara. 'A reading and a thinking nation: periodicals as the voice of nineteenth-century Ireland', in B. Hayley and E. McKay, eds., *Three Hundred Years of Irish Periodicals*. Mullingar: Lilliput Press, 1987, 29–48.

Hayton, D. 'From barbarian to burlesque: English images of the Irish *c*. 1660–1750', *Irish Economic and Social History*, 15, 1988, 5–31.

Healy, Cahir. *The Mutilation of a Nation*. Derry: Derry Journal, 1945.

Hempton, David and Myrtle Hill. *Evangelical Protestantism in Ulster Society, 1740–1890*. London: Routledge, 1992.

Hennessey, Thomas. 'Ulster unionist territorial and national identities 1886–1893: province, island, kingdom and empire', *Irish Political Studies*, 8, 1993, 21–36.

Hepburn, A. C. 'Catholics in the north of Ireland, 1850–1921: the urbanization of a minority', in A. C. Hepburn, ed., *Minorities in History*. London: Edward Arnold, 1978, 84–101.

The Conflict of Nationality in Modern Ireland. London: Edward Arnold, 1980.

'Employment and religion in Belfast, 1901–1951', in R. J. Cormack and R. D. Osborne, eds., *Religion, Education and Employment: Aspects of Equal Opportunity in Northern Ireland*. Belfast: Appletree, 1983, 42–63.

'Work, class and religion in Belfast, 1871–1911', *Irish Economic and Social History*, 10, 1983, 33–50.

Hewitt, Christopher. 'Catholic grievances, Catholic nationalism and violence in Northern Ireland during the civil rights period: a reconsideration', *British Journal of Sociology*, 32, 3, 1981, 362–80.

'The roots of violence: Catholic grievances and Irish nationalism during the civil rights period', in Patrick J. Roche and Brian Barton, eds., *The Northern Ireland Question: Myth and Reality*. Aldershot: Avebury, 1991, 17–39.

Hezlet, Sir Arthur. *The 'B' Specials*. London: Tom Stacey, 1972.

Hill, Christopher. *Reformation to Industrial Revolution*. Harmondsworth: Penguin, 1969.

Hillyard, Paddy and Janie Percy Smith. *The Coercive State: The Decline of Democracy in Britain*. London: Fontana, 1988.

Hobsbawm, Eric and Terence Ranger, eds. *The Invention of Tradition*. Cambridge: Cambridge University Press, 1983.

Holland, Jack. *The American Connection*. Dublin: Poolbeg, 1989.

Holmes, Finlay. *Our Irish Presbyterian Heritage*. Belfast: Publications Committee of the Presbyterian Church in Ireland, 1985.

Holmes, Michael. 'Symbols of national identity and sport: the case of the Irish football team', *Irish Political Studies*, 9, 1994, 81–98.

Hoppen, K. Theodore. *Ireland since 1800: Conflict and Conformity*. London: Longman, 1989.

Hornsby-Smith, Michael P. 'Social and religious transformation in Ireland: a case of secularisation?', in J. H. Goldthorpe and C. T. Whelan, eds., *The Development of Industrial Society in Ireland*. Proceedings of the British Academy 79. Oxford: Oxford University Press, 1992, 265–90.

Hughes, Eamonn, ed. *Culture and Politics in Northern Ireland*. Milton Keynes: Open University Press, 1991.

Hume, John. 'Europe of the regions', in Richard Kearney, ed., *Across the Frontiers: Ireland in the 1990s*. Dublin: Wolfhound, 1988, 45–57.

Hutchinson, John. *The Dynamics of Cultural Nationalism: The Gaelic Revival and the Creation of the Irish Nation State*. London: Allen and Unwin, 1987.

Hyde, H. M. *Carson: A Biography*. London: Heinemann, 1953.

Inglis, Tom. *Moral Monopoly: The Catholic Church in Modern Irish Society*. Dublin: Gill and Macmillan, 1987.

Irish Commission for Justice and Peace. 'Statement on H-Block', issued 13 Oct. 1980, reprinted in *The Furrow*, 31, 12, 1980, 814–16.

Jackson, Alvin. *The Ulster Party: Irish Unionists in the House of Commons 1884–1911*. Oxford: Clarendon, 1989.

Jay, Richard and Rick Wilford. 'Fair employment in Northern Ireland: a new initiative', *Irish Political Studies*, 6, 1991, 15–36.

Jefferson, Clifford W. 'The labour market', in R. I. D. Harris, C. W. Jefferson and T. E. Spencer, eds., *The Northern Ireland Economy: A Comparative Study in the Economic Development of a Peripheral Region*. London: Longman, 1990, 148–77.

Johnson, D. S. and L. Kennedy. 'The two economies of Ireland in the twentieth century', in T. W. Moody, F. X. Martin, F. J. Byrne and W. E. Vaughan, eds., *A New History of Ireland*, vol VII, Oxford: Oxford University Press. (forthcoming)

Kearney, Hugh. *The British Isles: A History of Four Nations*. Cambridge: Cambridge University Press, 1989.

Kearney, Richard, ed. *Across the Frontiers: Ireland in the 1990s*. Dublin: Wolfhound, 1988.

Kearney, Richard and Robin Wilson, 'Northern Ireland's future as a European region', *The Irish Review*, 15, 1994, 51–69.

Keatinge, Patrick. *A Place among the Nations: Issues of Irish Foreign Policy*. Dublin: Institute of Public Administration, 1978.

   'Foreign policy', in Patrick Keatinge, ed. *Ireland and EC Membership Evaluated*. London: Pinter, 1991.

Keenan, Desmond. *The Catholic Church in Nineteenth-Century Ireland: A Sociological Survey*. Dublin: Gill and Macmillan, 1983.

Keenan, Joe. *An Argument on Behalf of the Catholics of Northern Ireland*. Belfast: Athol, 1987.

Kellas, James G. 'The social origins of nationalism in Great Britain: the case of Scotland', in John Coakley, ed., *The Social Origins of Nationalist Movements: The Contemporary West European Experience*. London: Sage, 1992, 165–86.

Kennedy, David. 'Whither Northern nationalism?', *Christus Rex*, 13, 4, 1959, 269–83.

Kennedy, Dennis. *The Widening Gulf: Northern Attitudes to the Independent Irish State 1919–1949*. Belfast: Blackstaff, 1988.

'The European Union and the Northern Ireland question', in Brian Barton and Patrick J. Roche, eds., *The Northern Ireland Question: Perspectives and Policies*. Aldershot: Avebury, 1994, 166–88.

Kennedy, Kieran 'The context of economic development', in J. H. Goldthorpe and C. T. Whelan, eds., *The Development of Industrial Society in Ireland*. Proceedings of the British Academy 79. Oxford: Oxford University Press, 1992, 5–29.

Kennedy, Kieran, Thomas Giblin and Deirdre McHugh. *The Economic Development of Ireland in the Twentieth Century*. London: Routledge, 1988.

Kennedy, Liam and Philip Ollerenshaw, eds. *An Economic History of Ulster 1820–1939*. Manchester: Manchester University Press, 1985.

Kenny, Colum. 'The exclusion of Catholics from the legal profession in Ireland, 1537–1829', *Irish Historical Studies*. 25, 100, 1987, 337–57.

Kerr-Smiley, P. *The Peril of Home Rule*. London: Cassell and Co Ltd, 1911.

Kiberd, Declan. *Anglo-Irish Attitudes*. Field Day pamphlet no. 6. Derry: Field Day, 1984.

'The elephant of revolutionary forgetfulness', in Máirín Ní Dhonnchadha and Theo Dorgan, eds., *Revising the Rising*. Derry: Field Day, 1991, 1–20.

Killen, John. *John Bull's Famous Circus: Ulster History Through the Postcard*. Dublin: O'Brien Press, 1985.

Kilroy, Phil. 'Protestantism in Ulster, 1610–1641', in Brian MacCuarta SJ, ed., *Ulster 1641: Aspects of the Rising*. Belfast: Institute of Irish Studies, 1993, 25–36.

Koenigsberger, H. G. 'Composite states, representative institutions and the American revolution', *Historical Research*, 62, 148, 1989, 135–53.

Kureishi, Hanif, 1989. 'London and Karachi', in Raphael Samuel, ed., *Patriotism: The Making and Unmaking of British National Identity*, vol. II. London: Routledge, 1989, 270–87.

Laffan, Brigid. 'Women', in Patrick Keatinge, ed., *Ireland and EC Membership Evaluated*. London: Pinter, 1991, 244–51.

Larsen, S. S. 'The Glorious Twelfth: the politics of legitimation in Kilbroney', in Anthony P. Cohen, ed., *Belonging: Identity and Social Organization in British Rural Cultures*. Manchester: Manchester University Press, 1982, 278–91.

Lebow, Ned. 'British images of poverty in pre-Famine Ireland', in Daniel J. Casey and Robert E. Rhodes, eds., *Views of the Irish Peasantry 1800–1916*. Connecticut: Archon Books, 1977, 57–85.

Lee, J. J. *Ireland 1912–1985: Politics and Society*. Cambridge: Cambridge University Press, 1989.

Leersen, Joseph Th. *Mere Irish and Fíor-Ghael: Studies in the Idea of Irish Nationality, its Development and Literary Expression Prior to the Nineteenth Century*. Amsterdam: John Benjamins, 1986.

Leighton, C. D. A. *Catholicism in a Protestant Kingdom: A Study of the Irish Ancien Régime*. Dublin: Gill and Macmillan, 1994.

Lennon, Colm. *Sixteenth-Century Ireland: The Incomplete Conquest*. Dublin: Gill and Macmillan, 1994.

Lewis, Jim and Alan Townshend, eds. *The North–South Divide: Regional Change in Britain in the 1980s*. London: Paul Chapman, 1989.

Longley, Edna. 'From Cathleen to Anorexia: the breakdown of Irelands', in Edna Longley, *The Living Stream: Literature and Revisionism in Ireland*. Newcastle upon Tyne: Bloodaxe Books, 1994, 173–95.

Loughlin, John P. 'The Anglo-Irish Agreement: federal arrangement or affirmation of the nation-state?', paper presented at the World Congress of International Association of Federal Centres, College of Europe, Bruges, 1989.

Lustick, Ian S. *Unsettled States, Disputed Lands: Britain and Ireland, France and Algeria, Israel and the West Bank–Gaza*. Ithaca: Cornell University Press, 1993.

Lydon, James. 'The middle nation', in James Lydon, ed., *The English in Medieval Ireland*. Dublin: Royal Irish Academy, 1984, 1–26.

Lyons, F. S. L. 'The minority problem in the 26 counties', in Francis MacManus, ed., *The Years of the Great Test*. Cork: Mercier, 1967, 92–103.

MacDonald, Michael. *Children of Wrath: Political Violence in Northern Ireland*. Cambridge: Polity, 1986.

Mac Gréil, Micheál. *Irish Political Attitudes and Opinions*. Maynooth: Survey and Research Unit, St Patrick's College, 1992.

MacIntyre, Alasdair. 'Causality and history', in Juha Manninen and Raimo Tuomela, eds., *Essays on Explanation and Understanding*. Dordrecht: D. Reidel, 1976, 137–58.

MacKnight, T. *Ulster as it is, or Twenty Eight Years Experience as an Irish Editor*. London: Macmillan, 2 vols., 1896.

Maguire, Martin. 'A socio-economic analysis of the Dublin Protestant working class, 1870–1926', *Irish Economic and Social History*, 20, 1993, 35–61.

McAllister, Ian. 'Political opposition in Northern Ireland: the National Democratic Party, 1965–1970', *Economic and Social Review*, 6, 3, 1975, 353–66.

McAughtry, Sam. *Down in the Free State*. Dublin: Gill and Macmillan, 1987.

McAuley, James W. *The Politics of Identity: A loyalist community in Belfast*. Aldershot: Avebury, 1994.

McBride, Ian. 'Presbyterians in the penal era', *Bullán*, 1, 2, 1994, 73–86.

McBride, Lawrence. *The Greening of Dublin Castle: The Transformation of Bureaucratic and Judicial Personnel in Ireland 1892–1922*. Washington: Catholic University of America Press, 1991.

McCann, Eamonn. *War in an Irish Town*. 2nd edn, London: Pluto, 1980.

McCarthy, Thomas. *The Critical Theory of Jürgen Habermas*. Cambridge, Mass.: MIT Press, 1981.

McCartney, R. L. *Liberty and Authority in Ireland*. Field Day pamphlet no. 9. Derry: Field Day, 1985.

McCaughey, Terence. *Memory and Redemption: Church, Politics and Prophetic Theology in Ireland*. Dublin: Gill and Macmillan, 1993.

McCreadie, Robert. 'Scottish identity and the constitution', in Bernard Crick, *National Identities: The Constitution of the United Kingdom*. Oxford: Blackwell, 1991, 38–56.

McCrudden, Christopher. 'The evolution of the Fair Employment (Northern Ireland) Act 1989 in parliament', in R. J. Cormack and R. D. Osborne, eds., *Discrimination and Public Policy in Northern Ireland*. Oxford: Clarendon, 1991, 244–64.

McElroy, Gerald. *The Catholic Church and the Northern Ireland Crisis 1968–86*. Dublin: Gill and Macmillan, 1991.

McFarlane, Graham. ' "Its not as simple as that." The expression of the Catholic and Protestant boundary in Northern Irish rural communities', in Anthony P. Cohen, ed., *Symbolising Boundaries: Identity and Diversity in British Cultures*. Manchester: Manchester University Press, 1986, 88–103

McGarry, John and Brendan O'Leary. *Explaining Northern Ireland: Broken Images*. Oxford: Basil Blackwell, 1995.

McGarry, John and Brendan O'Leary, eds. *The Future of Northern Ireland*. Oxford: Clarendon, 1990.

The Politics of Ethnic Conflict Regulation. London: Routledge, 1993.

McKeown, Ciaran. *The Passion of Peace*. Belfast: Blackstaff, 1984.

McKeown, Michael. *The Greening of a Nationalist*. Lucan, Co. Dublin: Murlough Press, 1986.

McLoone, Martin, ed. *Culture, Identity and Broadcasting in Ireland: Local Issues, Global Perspectives*. Belfast: Institute of Irish Studies, 1991.

McMinn, J. R. B., ed. *Against the Tide: J. B. Armour, Irish Presbyterian Minister and Home Ruler 1869–1914*. Belfast: PRONI, 1985.

McNeill, R. *Ulster's Stand for Union*, London, John Murray, 1922.

Mair, Peter. 'Breaking the nationalist mould: the Irish Republic and the Anglo-Irish Agreement', in Paul Teague, ed., *Beyond the Rhetoric: Politics, the Economy and Social Policy in Northern Ireland*. London: Lawrence and Wishart, 1987, 81–110.

Mandeville, Anne. 'La professionnalisation d'une unité de maintien de l'ordre, étape de la secularisation du système politique nord-irlandais? Le cas de l'Ulster Defence Regiment', paper presented to conference, 'L'Irlande: vers une société laïque', Centre Universitaire d'Études Irlandaises, Paris, 22–3 May 1992, forthcoming in Paul Brennan, ed., *La sécularisation de l'Irlande*, Caen.

Mandle, W. F. 'The Gaelic Athletic Association and popular culture, 1884–1924', in O. MacDonagh, W. F. Mandle and P. Travers, eds., *Irish Culture and Nationalism, 1750–1950*. London: Macmillan, 1983, 104–21.

Mansergh, Nicholas. *The Unresolved Question: The Anglo-Irish Settlement and its Undoing 1912–1972*. London: Yale University Press, 1991.

Martin, F. X. 'The image of the Irish – medieval and modern – continuity and change', in Richard Wall, ed., *Medieval and Modern Ireland*. Totowa: Barnes and Noble, 1988, 1–18.

Marx, Karl. 'The Eighteenth Brumaire of Louis Bonaparte', in David McLellan, ed., *Karl Marx: Selected Writings*. Oxford: Oxford University Press, 1977, 300–25..

Massey, Doreen. 'What's happening to UK manufacturing?', in John Allen and Doreen Massey, eds., *The Economy in Question*. Milton Keynes: Open University, 1988, 45–90.

Meenan, James. *The Irish Economy since 1922*. Liverpool: Liverpool University Press, 1970.

Mews, Stuart, ed. *Religion and National Identity*. Oxford: Basil Blackwell, 1982.

Miller, David. *Queen's Rebels: Ulster Loyalism in Historical Perspective*. Dublin: Gill and Macmillan, 1978.

Miller, R. L. *Attitudes to Work in Northern Ireland*. Belfast: Fair Employment Agency, 1978.

Miller, R. L. and R. D. Osborne, 1983. 'Religion and unemployment: evidence from a cohort survey', in R. J. Cormack and R. D. Osborne, eds., *Religion, Education and Employment: Aspects of Equal Opportunity in Northern Ireland*. Belfast: Appletree, 1983, 78–99.

Mjøset, Lars. *The Irish Economy in a Comparative Institutional Perspective*. Dublin: National Economic and Social Council, 1992.

Moloney, Ed and Andy Pollak. *Paisley*. Swords, Co. Dublin: Poolbeg Press, 1986.

Morgan, Valerie. 'Bridging the divide: women and political and community issues', in Peter Stringer and Gillian Robinson, eds., *Social Attitudes in Northern Ireland: The Second Report*. Belfast: Blackstaff, 1992, 135–48.

Morris, Jonathan, Philip Cooke, Goio Etxebarria and Arantxa Rodrigues. 'The political economy of regional industrial regeneration: the Welsh and Basque "models"', in Graham Day and Gareth Rees, eds., *Regions, Nations and European Integration: Remaking the Celtic Periphery*. Cardiff: University of Wales Press, 1991, 177–91.

Morrow, Duncan. *The Churches and Inter-community Relationships*. Coleraine: Centre for the Study of Conflict, 1991.

'Warranted interference? The Republic of Ireland in the politics of Northern Ireland', *Études Irlandaises*, 20, 1, 1995, 125–47.

Moxon-Browne, Edward. *Nation, Class and Creed in Northern Ireland*. Aldershot: Gower, 1983.

'Alienation: the case of Catholics in Northern Ireland', *Journal of Political Science*, 14, 1–2, 1986, 74–88.

'National identity in Northern Ireland', in Peter Stringer and Gillian Robinson, eds., *Social Attitudes in Northern Ireland*. Belfast: Blackstaff, 1991, 23–30.

'The impact of the European Community', in Brigid Hadfield, ed., *Northern Ireland: Politics and the Constitution*. Buckingham: Open University Press, 1992, 47–59.

Moxon-Browne, Edward and Cynthia Irvine. 'Not many floating voters here', *Fortnight*, 273, 1989, 7–9.

Munck, Ronnie and Bill Rolston. *Belfast in the Thirties: An Oral History*. Belfast: Blackstaff, 1987.

Murphy, Anthony with David Armstrong. *A Picture of the Catholic and Protestant Male Unemployed*. Employment Equality Review Research Report no. 2. Belfast: Central Community Relations Unit, 1994.

Murray, Dominic. *Worlds Apart: Segregated Schools in Northern Ireland*. Belfast: Appletree, 1985.

Murray, Dominic and John Darby. *The Vocational Aspirations and Expectations of School-leavers in Londonderry and Strabane*. Belfast: Fair Employment Agency, 1980.

Murray, R. C. and R. D. Osborne. 'Educational qualifications and religious affiliation', in R. J. Cormack and R. D. Osborne, eds., *Religion, Education and Employment: Aspects of Equal Opportunity in Northern Ireland*. Belfast: Appletree, 1983, 118–45.

Nairn, Tom. *The Break-up of Britain*. London: Verso, 1977.

The Enchanted Glass: Britain and its Monarchy. London: Hutchinson Radius, 1988.

Nelson, Sarah. *Ulster's Uncertain Defenders: Loyalists and the Northern Ireland Conflict*. Belfast: Appletree, 1984.

New Ulster Movement. *The Reform of Stormont*. Belfast: New Ulster Movement, 1971.

Two Irelands or One?. Belfast: New Ulster Movement, 1972.

Tribalism or Christianity in Ireland?. Belfast: New Ulster Movement, 1973.

New Ulster Political Research Group. *Beyond the Religious Divide*. Belfast, 1979.

Newe, G. B. 'The Catholic in the Northern Ireland community', *Christus Rex*, 18, 1, 1964, 22–36.

Newsinger, John. 'Connolly and his biographers', *Irish Political Studies*, 5, 1990, 1–9.

Northern Ireland Census 1971. Religion Tables. Belfast: HMSO, 1975.

1991. Religion Report. Belfast: HMSO, 1993.

Norton, Philip. 'The Glorious Revolution of 1688: its continuing relevance', *Parliamentary Affairs*, 42, 2, 1989, 135–47.

'The Constitution: Approaches to reform', *Politics*, September, 1993, 2–5.

O'Brien, Conor Cruise. *Writers and Politics*. London: Chatto and Windus, 1965.

Ancestral Voices: Religion and Nationalism in Ireland. Dublin: Poolbeg Press. 1994.

Ó Buachalla, Breandán. 'James our true king: the ideology of Irish royalism in the seventeenth century', in D. George Boyce, Robert Eccleshall and Vincent Geoghegan, eds., *Political Thought in Ireland since the Seventeenth Century*. London: Routledge, 1993, 7–35.

O'Connor, Fionnuala. *In Search of a State: Catholics in Northern Ireland*. Belfast: Blackstaff, 1993.

O'Donnell, Rory. 'Regional policy', in Patrick Keatinge, ed., *Ireland and EC Membership Evaluated*. London: Pinter, 1991, 60–75.

O'Dowd, Liam. 'New introduction', in Albert Memmi, *The Colonizer and the Colonized*. London: Earthscan, 1990, 29–66.

'Intellectuals and the national question in Ireland', in Graham Day and Gareth Rees, eds., *Regions, Nations and European Integration: Remaking the Celtic Periphery*. Cardiff: University of Wales Press, 1991, 125–39.

'Development or dependency? State, economy and society in Northern Ireland', in P. Clancy, S. Drudy, K. Lynch and L. O'Dowd, eds., *Irish Society: Sociological Perspectives*. Dublin: Institute of Public Administration , 1995, 132–77.

O'Dowd, Liam, Bill Rolston and Mike Tomlinson. *Northern Ireland: Between Civil Rights and Civil War*. London: CSE Books, 1980.

Offe, Claus. *Contradictions of the Welfare State*. London: Hutchinson, 1984.

Ó Gráda, Cormac. *A New Economic History of Ireland*. Oxford: Clarendon Press, 1994.

O'Halloran, Clare. *Partition and the Limits of Irish Nationalism: An Ideology Under Stress.* Dublin: Gill and Macmillan, 1987.

O'Hearn, Denis. 'Catholic grievances, Catholic nationalism: a comment', *British Journal of Sociology*, 34, 3, 1983, 438–45.

O'Leary, Brendan. 'Public opinion and Northern Irish futures', *The Political Quarterly*, 63, 2, 1992, 143–70.

O'Leary, Brendan and John McGarry. *The Politics of Antagonism: Understanding Northern Ireland.* London: Athlone Press, 1993.

O'Leary, Brendan, Tom Lyne, Jim Marshall and Bob Rowthorn. *Northern Ireland: Sharing Authority.* London: Institute of Public Policy Research, 1993.

Oliver, Dawn. 'Citizenship in the 1990s', *Politics*, September, 1993, 25–8.

Oliver, John A. 'The Stormont administration', in Patrick J. Roche and Brian Barton, eds., *The Northern Ireland Question: Myth and Reality.* Aldershot: Avebury, 1991, 77–98.

O'Malley, Padraig. *The Uncivil Wars: Ireland Today.* Belfast: Blackstaff, 1983.

Biting at the Grave: The Irish Hunger Strikes and the Politics of Despair. Belfast: Blackstaff, 1990.

Ó Murchadha, Ciarán. *Land and Society in Seventeenth-Century Clare.* Ph.D. Thesis, Department of History, University College Galway, 1982.

Opsahl, Torkel. 'Some comments on Kevin Boyle's contribution', in Harald Olav Skar and Bjørn Lydersen, *Northern Ireland: A Crucial Test for a Europe of Peaceful Regions.* Norwegian Foreign Policy Studies no. 80, Norwegian Institute of International Affairs, 1993, 103–8.

Orr, Philip. *The Road to the Somme: Men of the Ulster Division Tell their Story.* Belfast: Blackstaff, 1987.

Osborne, R. D. 'Discrimination and fair employment', in Peter Stringer and Gillian Robinson, eds., *Social Attitudes in Northern Ireland.* Belfast: Blackstaff, 1991, 31–38.

Osborne, R. D. and R. J. Cormack. 'Unemployment and religion in Northern Ireland', *Economic and Social Review*, 17, 3, 1986, 215–25.

Religion, Occupations and Employment: 1971–1981. Belfast: Fair Employment Agency, 1987.

'Religion and the labour market: patterns and profiles', in R. J. Cormack and R. D. Osborne, eds., *Discrimination and Public Policy in Northern Ireland.* Oxford: Clarendon, 1991, 49–71.

Osborne, R. D., R. J. Cormack, N. G. Reid, and A. P. Williamson. 'Political arithmetic, higher education and religion in Northern Ireland', in R. J. Cormack and R. D. Osborne, eds., *Religion, Education and Employment: Aspects of Equal Opportunity in Northern Ireland.* Belfast: Appletree, 1983, 177–200.

Osborne, R. D., R. J. Cormack and A. M. Gallagher. 'Educational qualifications and the labour market', in R. J. Cormack and R. D. Osborne, eds., *Discrimination and Public Policy in Northern Ireland.* Oxford: Clarendon, 1991, 93–119.

Osmond John, 'Coping with dual identity', in John Osmond, ed., *The National Question Again: Welsh Political Identity in the 1980s.* Llandysul: Gomer, 1985, xix–xlvi.

The Divided Kingdom. London: Constable, 1988.

Patterson, Henry. *Class Conflict and Sectarianism: The Protestant Working Class and the Belfast Labour Movement 1868–1920.* Belfast: Blackstaff, 1980.

The Politics of Illusion: Republicanism and Socialism in Modern Ireland. London: Hutchinson, 1989.

Phoenix, Eamon. *Northern Nationalism: Nationalist Politics, Partition and the Catholic Minority in Northern Ireland 1890–1940.* Belfast: Ulster Historical Foundation, 1994.

Pieterse, Jan Nederveen. 'Emancipations, modern and postmodern', *Development and Change,* 23, 3, 1992, 5–41.

Pocock, J. G. A. 'British history: a plea for a new subject', *Journal of Modern History,* 47, 4, 1975, 601–28.

'Conservative enlightenment and democratic revolutions: The American and French cases in British perspective', *Government and Opposition,* 24, 1, 1989, 81–105.

The Political Vetting of Community Work Working Group. *The Political Vetting of Community Work in Northern Ireland.* Belfast: Northern Ireland Council for Voluntary Action, 1990.

Pollak, Andy. 'The civil service investigation: the FEA's last chance?', *Fortnight,* 188, 1982, 8–11.

Pollak, Andy, ed. *A Citizens' Inquiry: The Opsahl Report on Northern Ireland.* Dublin: Lilliput, 1993.

Poulantzas, Nicos. *State, Power, Socialism.* London: Verso, 1978.

Prager, J. *Building Democracy in Ireland: Political Order and Cultural Integration in a Newly Independent State.* Cambridge: Cambridge University Press, 1986.

Pringle, Dennis. *One Ireland, Two Nations: A Political Geographical Analysis of the National Conflict in Ireland.* Letchworth: Research Studies Press, 1985.

Purdie, Bob. ' "The Friends of Ireland": British Labour and Irish nationalism 1945–49', in Tom Gallagher and James O'Connell, eds., *Contemporary Irish Studies.* Manchester: Manchester University Press, 1983, 81–94.

'The Irish Anti-partition League, South Armagh and abstentionism', *Irish Political Studies,* 1, 1986, 67–77.

Politics in the Streets: The Origins of the Civil Rights Movement in Northern Ireland. Belfast: Blackstaff, 1990.

Quinn, D. B. *The Elizabethans and the Irish.* Ithaca: Cornell University Press, 1966.

Rabb, Theodore. *The Struggle for Stability in Early Modern Europe.* New York: Oxford University Press, 1975.

Rees, Gareth and Kevin Morgan. 'Industrial restructuring, innovation systems and the regional state: South Wales in the 1990s', in Graham Day and Gareth Rees, eds., *Regions, Nations and European Integration: Remaking the Celtic Periphery.* Cardiff: University of Wales Press, 1991, 155–76.

Rees, Merlyn. *Northern Ireland: A Personal Perspective.* London: Methuen, 1985.

Ridley, F. F. 'There is no British constitution: a dangerous case of the emperor's clothes', *Parliamentary Affairs,* 41, 3, 1988, 340–61.

Robbins, Keith, 'Religion and identity in modern British history', in Stuart Mews, ed., *Religion and National Identity.* Oxford: Basil Blackwell, 1982, 465–87.

The Eclipse of a Great Power: Modern Britain 1870–1975. London: Longman, 1983.

Nineteenth Century Britain: England, Scotland and Wales. The Making of a Nation. Oxford: Oxford University Press, 1989.

Roberts, Hugh. 'Sound stupidity: the British party system and the Northern Ireland question', *Government and Opposition*, 22, 3, 1987, 315–35.

Robinson, Philip. *The Plantation of Ulster: British Settlement in an Irish Landscape.* Dublin: Gill and Macmillan, 1984.

Roebuck, Peter, ed. *Plantation to Partition: Essays in Ulster History in honour of J. L. McCracken.* Belfast: Blackstaff, 1981.

Rokkan, Stein. 'Territories, centres and peripheries: toward a geoethnic-geoeconomic-geopolitical model of differentiation within western Europe', in Jean Gottman, ed., *Centre and Periphery: Spatial Variation in Politics.* London: Sage, 1980, 163–204.

Rokkan, Stein and Derek W. Urwin. *Economy, Territory, Identity: Politics of West European Peripheries.* London: Sage, 1983.

Rolston, Bill, 1989. *Politics and Painting: Murals and Conflict in Northern Ireland.* London and Toronto: Associated University Presses, 1989.

Rolston, Bill, ed. *The Media and Northern Ireland: Covering the Troubles.* London: Macmillan, 1991.

Rose, Richard. *Governing without Consensus: An Irish Perspective.* London: Faber and Faber, 1971.

Understanding the United Kingdom: The Territorial Dimension in Government. London: Longman, 1982.

Rose, Richard, Ian McAllister and Peter Mair. *Is There a Concurring Majority About Northern Ireland?* Glasgow: Centre for the Study of Public Policy, University of Strathclyde, paper no. 22, 1978.

Rosenbaum, S., ed. *Against Home Rule: The Case for the Union.* London: Frederick Warne, 1912.

Rowthorn, Bob and Naomi Wayne. *Northern Ireland: The Political Economy of Conflict.* Cambridge: Polity, 1988.

Ruane, Joseph. 'Colonialism and the interpretation of Irish historical development', in M. Silverman and P. Gulliver, eds., *Approaching the Past: Historical Anthropology Through Irish Case Studies.* Columbia: Columbia University Press, 1992, 293–323.

'Ireland, European integration and the dialectic of nationalism and post-nationalism', *Études Irlandaises*, 19, 1, 1994, 183–93.

'Nationalism and European Community integration: the case of the Republic of Ireland', in V. Goddard, J. Llobera, and Chris Shore, eds., *Anthropology of Europe: Identity and Boundaries in Conflict.* London: Berg, 1994, 125–41.

'Colonial legacies and cultural reflexivities', *Études Irlandaises* (Numéro hors série), 1994, 107–20.

'Secularization and ideology in the Republic of Ireland', in Paul Brennan, ed., *La sécularisation de l'Irlande.* Caen: Université de Caen, forthcoming.

Ruane, Joseph and Jennifer Todd. ' "Why can't you get along with each other?" Culture, structure and the Northern Ireland conflict', in Eamonn Hughes, ed., *Culture and Politics in Northern Ireland.* Milton Keynes: Open University Press, 1991, 27–43.

'The social origins of nationalism in a contested region: the case of Northern Ireland', in John Coakley, ed., *The Social Origins of Nationalist Movements: The Contemporary West European Experience*. London: Sage, 1992, 187–211.

'Ireland – North and South – and European Community integration', in Paul Hainsworth, ed., *Breaking and Preserving the Mould: The Third Direct Elections to the European Parliament (1989) – the Irish Republic and Northern Ireland*. Belfast: Policy Research Institute, 1992.

'Division, diversity and the middle ground in Northern Ireland', *Irish Political Studies*, 7, 1992, 73–98.

Said, Edward. *Orientalism*. Harmondsworth: Peregrine, 1985.

Samuel, Raphael, ed. *Patriotism: The Making and Unmaking of British National Identity*, 3 vols. London: Routledge, 1989.

Scammell, G. V. *The World Encompassed: The First European Maritime Empires c. 800–1650*. London: Methuen, 1981.

Schwarz, Bill. 'Conservatism, nationalism and imperialism', in James Donald and Stuart Hall, eds., *Politics and Ideology: A Reader*. Milton Keynes: Open University Press, 1986, 154–86.

Scott, Dermot. 'Education', in P. Keatinge, ed., *Ireland and EC Membership Evaluated*. London: Pinter, 260–69.

Sharp, Paul. *Irish Foreign Policy and the European Community: A Study of the Impact of Interdependence on the Foreign Policy of a Small State*. Aldershot: Dartmouth, 1990.

Sharpe, L. J. 'Devolution and Celtic nationalism in the UK', *West European Politics*, 8, 3, 1989, 82–100.

Shea, Patrick. *Voices and the Sound of Drums: An Irish Autobiography*. Belfast: Blackstaff, 1981.

Sims-Williams, Patrick. 'The visionary Celt: the construction of an ethnic preconception', *Cambridge Medieval Celtic Studies*, 2, 1986. 71–96.

Sinclair, T. 'The position of Ulster', in S. Rosenbaum, ed., *Against Home Rule: The Case for the Union*. London: Frederick Warne, 1912, 170–81.

Sinn Féin/SDLP. *Sinn Féin/SDLP Talks*. Belfast: Sinn Féin, 1988.

Sinnott, Richard. 'Interpretations of the Irish party system', *European Journal of Political Research*, 12, 3, 1984, 289–307.

'The North: party images and party approaches in the Republic', *Irish Political Studies*, 1, 1986, 15–31.

Skar, Harald Olav and Bjørn Lydersen. *Northern Ireland: A Crucial Test for a Europe of Peaceful Regions*. Norwegian Institute of International Affairs, Norwegian Foreign Policy Studies no. 80, 1993.

Smith, David J. *Equality and Inequality in Northern Ireland*. Parts 1–3. London: Policy Studies Institute, 1987.

Smith, David J. and Gerald Chambers. *Inequality in Northern Ireland*. Oxford: Clarendon, 1991.

Smith, Dennis. 'Englishness and the liberal inheritance after 1886', in Robert Colls and Philip Dodd, eds., *Englishness: Politics and Culture 1880–1920*. London: Croom Helm, 1987, 254–82.

Smyth, Clifford. *Ian Paisley: Voice of Protestant Ulster*. Edinburgh: Scottish Academic Press Ltd, 1987.

Smyth, Michael. 'The public sector and the economy', in Paul Teague, ed., *The Economy of Northern Ireland: Perspectives for Structural Change*. London: Lawrence and Wishart, 1993, 121–40.

Smyth, W. Martin. 'A Protestant looks at the Republic', in John Fairleigh, et al., *Sectarianism: Roads to Reconciliation*. Dublin: Three Candles, 1975, 25–35.

Standing Advisory Commission on Human Rights (SACHR). *Religious and Political Discrimination and Equality of Opportunity in Northern Ireland: Report on Fair Employment*. London: HMSO, 1987.

Stewart, A. T. Q. *The Narrow Ground: Aspects of Ulster 1609–1969*. London: Faber and Faber, 1977.

Stringer, Peter and Gillian Robinson, eds. *Social Attitudes in Northern Ireland*. Belfast: Blackstaff, 1991.

Social Attitudes in Northern Ireland: The Second Report. Belfast: Blackstaff, 1992.

Social Attitudes in Northern Ireland: The Third Report. Belfast: Blackstaff, 1993.

Task Force Report. *An End to Drift*, abridged version. Belfast, 1987.

Taylor, Peter J. 'The English and their Englishness: "A curiously mysterious, elusive and little understood people"', *Scottish Geographical Magazine*, 107, 3, 1991, 146–61.

Teague, Paul, ed. *Beyond the Rhetoric: Politics, the Economy and Social Policy in Northern Ireland*. London: Lawrence and Wishart, 1987.

The Economy of Northern Ireland: Perspectives for Structural Change. London: Lawrence and Wishart, 1993.

Thatcher, Margaret. *The Downing Street Years*. London: Harper Collins, 1993.

Tilly, Charles. *Coercion, Capital, and European States*. Oxford: Basil Blackwell, 1990.

Todd, Jennifer. 'Two traditions in unionist political culture', *Irish Political Studies*, 2, 1987, 1–26.

'Northern Irish nationalist political culture', *Irish Political Studies*, 5, 1990, 31–44.

'Unionist political thought 1920–1970', in D. G. Boyce, R. Eccleshall, and V. Geoghegan, eds., *Political Thought in Ireland since the Seventeenth Century*. London: Routledge, 1993, 190–211.

'Beyond the community conflict: historic compromise or emancipatory process?', *Irish Political Studies*, 10, 1995, 161–78.

'Equality, plurality and democracy: justifications of proposed constitutional settlements of the Northern Ireland conflict', *Ethnic and Racial Studies*, 18, 4, 1995, 818–36.

Townshend, Charles. *Political Violence in Ireland: Government and Resistance Since 1984*. Oxford: Clarendon Press, 1983.

Townshend, Charles, ed. *Consensus in Ireland*. Oxford: Clarendon, 1983.

Trench, Brian. 'In search of hope: coverage of the Northern conflict in the Dublin daily papers', in Bill Rolston, ed., *The Media and Northern Ireland: Covering the Troubles*. London: Macmillan, 1991, 136–51.

Ulster Society. *Ulster, an Ethnic Nation?* Lurgan: Ulster Society, 1986.

Ulster Political Research Group. *Common Sense*. Belfast, 1987.

Ultach. 'The real case against partition', *The Capuchin Annual*, 1943, 283–312.

Van Voris, W. H. *Violence in Ulster: An Oral Documentary*. Amherst: University of Massachusetts Press, 1975.

Walker, B. M. *Ulster Politics: The Formative Years 1868–1886*. Belfast: Ulster Historical Foundation and Institute of Irish Studies, 1989.

Walker, B. M., ed. *Parliamentary Election Results in Ireland, 1918–1992*. Belfast: Institute of Irish Studies, 1992.

Wallace, William. 'Foreign policy and national identity in the United Kingdom', *International Affairs*, 67, 1, 1991, 65–80.

Wallerstein, Immanuel. *The Modern World System: Capitalist Agriculture and the Origins of the European World-economy in the Sixteenth Century*. New York: Academic Press, 1974.

The Modern World System II: Mercantilism and the Consolidation of the European World-economy, 1600–1750. New York: Academic Press, 1980.

The Modern World System III: The Second Era of Great Expansion of the Capitalist World-economy, 1730–1840s. New York: Academic Press, 1988.

Waters, John. *A Race of Angels: Ireland and the Genesis of U2*. Belfast: Blackstaff Press, 1994.

Whelan, Kevin. 'Catholic mobilisation, 1750–1850', in Centre de Recherches Historiques, ed., *Culture et Pratiques Politiques en France et en Irlande, XVIe–XVIIIe Siècle*. Paris: Centre de Recherches Historiques, 1991, 235–58.

'The United Irishmen, the enlightenment and popular culture', in David Dickson, Dáire Keogh and Kevin Whelan, eds., *The United Irishmen: Republicanism, Radicalism and Rebellion*. Dublin: The Lilliput Press, 1993, 269–96.

Whitelaw, William. *Whitelaw Memoirs*. London: Aurum, 1989.

Whyte, J. H. *Church and State in Modern Ireland 1923–1970*. Dublin: Gill and Macmillan, 1971.

'How much discrimination was there under the Unionist regime?', in Tom Gallagher and James O'Connell, eds., *Contemporary Irish Studies*. Manchester: Manchester University Press, 1983, 1–35.

Interpreting Northern Ireland. Oxford: Clarendon, 1990.

Williams, Gwyn. *When Was Wales? A History of the Welsh*. Harmondsworth: Penguin, 1985,

Williamson, Arthur H. *Scottish National Consciousness in the Age of James VI: The Apocalypse, the Union and the Shaping of Scotland's Public Culture*. Edinburgh: John Donald, 1979.

Wilson, Des. *An End to Silence*. Cork: Royal Carbery, 1985.

Wilson, Thomas. 'Introduction' to R. I. D. Harris, C. W. Jefferson and J. E. Spencer, eds., *The Northern Ireland Economy: A Comparative Study in the Economic Development of a Peripheral Region*. London: Longman, 1990, 1–20.

Wilson, Tom. *Ulster: Conflict and Consent*. Oxford: Basil Blackwell, 1989.

Wolf, Eric. *Europe and the People Without History*. Berkeley: University of California Press, 1982.

Wright, Frank. *Northern Ireland: A Comparative Analysis*. Dublin: Gill and Macmillan, 1987.

Wright, Patrick. *On Living in an Old Country: The National Past in Contemporary Britain*. London: Verso, 1985.

Index of names

Index of subjects